I0831729

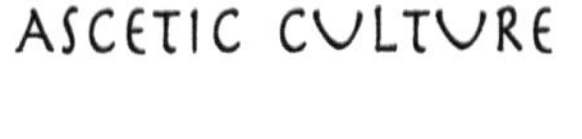
ASCETIC CULTURE

PHILIP ROUSSEAU

Photo credit: Ed Pfueller/The Catholic University of America

ASCETIC CULTURE

Essays in Honor of Philip Rousseau

edited by

BLAKE LEYERLE

and

ROBIN DARLING YOUNG

University of Notre Dame Press

Notre Dame, Indiana

Notre Dame, Indiana 46556
www.undpress.nd.edu

Published in the United States of America

Library of Congress Cataloging-in-Publication Data

Ascetic culture : essays in honor of Philip Rousseau /
edited by Blake Leyerle and Robin Darling Young.
pages cm
Includes bibliographical references and index.
ISBN-13: 978-0-268-03388-0 (cloth : alk. paper)
ISBN-10: 0-268-03388-9 (cloth : alk. paper)
1. Asceticism—History—Early church, ca. 30–600.
I. Rousseau, Philip. II. Leyerle, Blake, 1960–editor of compilation.
BV5023.A74 2013
248.4'709—dc23

2013023354

∞ *The paper in this book meets the guidelines for permanence and durability of the Committee on Production Guidelines for Book Longevity of the Council on Library Resources for*

PHILIP

Contents

Abbreviations

BIBLE

Follow NRSV abbreviations.

PAPYRI AND OSTRACA

Papyri and ostraca (signaled by "P." or "O.") are abbreviated according to the American Society of Papyrologists' *Checklist of Greek, Latin, Demotic and Coptic Papyri, Ostraca and Tablets*, compiled by J.F. Oates et al. Latest version (January 2013) at http://scriptorium.lib.duke.edu/papyrus/texts/clist.html.

MODERN WORKS

BDAG	*A Greek-English Lexicon of the New Testament and Other Early Christian Literature*, edited by W. Bauer, F.W. Danker, W.F. Arndt, and F.W. Gingrich, 3rd ed. Chicago: University of Chicago Press, 2000.
CCAG	*Catalogus codicum astrologorum graecorum*. 12 vols. Brussels: Lamertin, 1898–1940.
Lampe	*Patristic Greek Lexicon.*

New Pauly	*Brill's New Pauly Encyclopaedia of the Ancient World.* Ed. Hubert Cancik and Helmuth Schneider. English ed. Christine F. Salazar (Leiden: Brill, 2008).
R-E	Pauly, August Friedrich, von, and Georg Wissowa, eds. *Paulys Real-Encyclopädie der classischen Altertumswissenschaft.* Stuttgart: Metzler, 1894–1967.

SERIES

ACW	Ancient Christian Writers
AW	Athanasius Werke
CCSL	Corpus Christianorum–Series Latina
CS	Cistercian Studies
CSCO	Corpus scriptorum Christianorum Orientalium
CSEL	Corpus scriptorum Ecclesiasticorum Latinorum
DOPM	Dakhleh Oasis Project Monographs
GCS	Die Griechischen Christlichen Schriftsteller
FC	Fathers of the Church
LCL	Loeb Classical Library
NPNF	Nicene and Post-Nicene Fathers of the Christian Church
PG	Patrologia Graeca
PO	Patrologia Orientalis
PTS	Patristische Texte und Studien
SC	Sources chrètiennes
TCH	Transformation of the Classical Heritage
TU	Texte und Untersuchungen

JOURNALS

CH	*Church History*
HTR	*Harvard Theological Review*
JECS	*Journal of Early Christian Studies*
JTS	*Journal of Theological Studies*
REG	*Revue des études grecques*
SM	*Studia monastica*
SP	*Studia patristica*
TP	*Theologie und Philosophie*
VC	*Vigiliae Christianae*

Introduction

Like the children of Israel, Philip Rousseau has spent forty years in the desert. During that time, the monks of early Christianity have been both his companions and his subjects, and they have accompanied him from Oxford to New Zealand and to the United States.

From the date of his completion of the doctoral thesis at Wolfson College, Oxford, in 1972, to his present occupancy of the Mellon Chair of Early Christian Studies at the Catholic University of America, he has forged a new path in the scholarship of early Christian monasticism — a path that has allowed him, and his readers, to spy out the social world of these odd new inhabitants of the empire, a world that shaped and qualified their theological ideas and their spiritual ambitions. As Rousseau himself has noted, he did not intend to inhabit that land, the marginal and imagined territory where monastics dwelt, and in his daily life he is just as much a man of the city as the subject of his splendid biography, Basil, bishop of ancient Caesarea, and beyond that, a paterfamilias.

The desert Rousseau has made his own is, of course, the wilderness exurbs of the fourth and early fifth centuries, where the single men and women — deliberately segregating themselves from the obligations of marriage and the household — imagined and created new institutions among the Christian assemblies in the late ancient Mediterranean world. Beginning with *Ascetics, Authority and the Church in the Age of Jerome and Cassian,* he belonged to, and help shape, a new movement in scholarship. The study of ancient asceticism has not flagged since he started to write.

Philip Rousseau was born on November 3, 1939, the son of a British naval officer and his wife; he has vivid memories of the family's posting to Washington, D.C., during World War II. Later, as beneficiary of the Jesuits' mighty *ratio studiorum*, he gained his first postsecondary degree in 1962, at Heythrop College in Oxfordshire. Thus, when Rousseau came to Wolfson College, Oxford, for his master's and doctoral degrees, he was already familiar with the neighborhood of the university. He had earned his licentiate in philosophy, had lived for a time in Maria Laach, a Benedictine monastery in Germany, and had taught in Africa. It was in Africa that Philip met another teacher, an extraordinary young woman named Thérèse, who would become his life's companion.

At Wolfson, Rousseau joined a circle of scholars from whom he learned the craft of the historian, and was by his own account charmed by the company of Isaiah Berlin, then president of Wolfson College. As his companions, he names John Matthews, Timothy Barnes, and Peter Brown — all scholars who, then young men, by now have shaped the study of late antiquity for the past four decades and have trained their own students. The eminences Arnaldo Momigliano, Richard Southern, and Ronald Syme were present in Oxford, along with Geoffrey de Sainte Croix, Michael Wallace Hadrill, and Karl Leyser. As he himself attests, he was both part of, and simultaneously on the edge of, a historiographical movement that produced two new generations of scholars who continue to pursue the study both of late antiquity and of monasticism and asceticism in the period.

In 1972, after the completion of his thesis, Rousseau joined the faculty of the University of Auckland in New Zealand. In 1978 his thesis had appeared as *Ascetics, Authority, and the Church*, and in 1985 he published *Pachomius*, a study of the first monastic legislator. In an essay that serves as his *retractationes*, Rousseau avers that the shortcoming of the first book was its relative neglect of Pachomius and that the mistake of the second was its acceptance of the term *desert* as a literal, instead of a textualized — that is to say, ideal — space.[1] But Rousseau was moving in the direction of studying the episcopal office as it emerged in the fourth century, and the result was *Basil of Caesarea*, published in 1994.

During these years, Rousseau continued to teach at Auckland; but he also migrated among the research centers of the academic world, as a Senior Fellow at Dumbarton Oaks (1981–82); as a Visiting Professor at the University of California, Berkeley (1985); as an Honorary Research Fellow at the University of Exeter, England (1990); as a Member of the Institute for Advanced Study, Princeton (1990); as a Visiting Scholar at his alma mater, Wolfson College, Oxford (1995); and as a Bye Fellow at Robinson College, Cambridge (1996).

In 1998, Rousseau decided to leave New Zealand for the United States and a position as the Andrew W. Mellon Distinguished Professor in the Program of Early Christian Studies at the Catholic University of America, in Washington, D.C. The three daughters he had raised with Thérèse were now back in England, and the Rousseaus took up residence in the city of Washington. For Philip, the position at Catholic meant the directorship of a strong program in the study of early Christianity, distributed among several departments. For the first time, he was able to direct master's and doctoral students himself, and he turned the program into a thriving Center for Early Christian Studies that not only trained students but also provided scholars in the field with a place for discussion and study.

Since coming to Catholic, Rousseau has continued to converse eagerly with other scholars, both in Washington, D.C., and nearby cities, and farther afield, as Distinguished Scholar in the Senter for Høyere Studier, Norwegian Academy of Science and Letters (2003); and as Visiting Scholar at the Center for Medieval and Renaissance Studies, University of California, Los Angeles (2010).

At Catholic, Rousseau has continued to develop his thinking on both asceticism and early Christianity. In 2002, he broadened his scope as he published *The Early Christian Centuries*, a thematic treatment of movements and important personages in the various constellations of Christian groups from the first through the fifth centuries. In 2009, *A Companion to Late Antiquity* appeared under his sole editorship; he coedited a Festschrift for Peter Brown and a collection on studies on Gregory Nazianzus. He is currently working on a book he will call *The Social Identity of the Ascetic*

Master in Late Roman Christianity. He will also publish a collection of his essays as *Essays on Jerome and Some Contemporaries*.

To list Rousseau's books and monographs is not, of course, to exhaust the list of his publications. Each year has seen reviews and articles that prepare the way for the monographs. In addition, he has lectured annually, as Mellon Professor, on more recent construals of early Christianity and the social setting of the scholars who constructed those interpretations.

As all know who have had the good fortune to converse with Philip Rousseau, his curiosity is insatiable and his industry steady. The diverse essays collected in this volume necessarily engage his rich and wide-ranging scholarship. They reassess the self-presentation and legacy of prominent monastic figures, explore the impact of the rules, consider the role of ancient educational and literary models, investigate the relationship between ascetic master and disciple, and trace the evolving legacy of scholarship.

The first group of essays discusses Egyptian monastic reading programs and the circulation of texts. Joel Kalvesmaki explores the significance of Pachomius's use of letter symbolism. It functioned, he argues, as a means of converting prognostication and other theurgic activities into a Christian form, and of prodding readers to higher spiritual reflection. Janet Timbie's essay reexamines the use of scripture in early Egyptian monasticism. Although scripture is not used in the early rules of the *Koinonia* or of the White Monastery, these rules are themselves written to sound like scripture. In later legislation (the *Rule of Horsiesius* and the *Canons* of Shenoute), Timbie finds not only allusions but actual quotations of scripture to reinforce or defend monastic practice.

The essays of both Malcolm Choat and Samuel Rubenson focus on the *Life of Antony*. Malcolm Choat investigates the popularity of the *Life of Antony* in its Egyptian context. He finds that, by the second half of the fourth century, the *Life of Antony* was not widely known in Pachomian circles; Athanasius's prescriptions on the behavior of virgins, as well as Anthony's own *Letters,* exerted more influence. Samuel Rubenson's essay draws attention to the overlooked but sustained contrast between Anthony and Pythagoras and argues that an apologetic agenda drives the *Life of Antony*. Prompting this rivalry, Rubenson argues, is the figure of Porphyry, whose attack on Christianity gained renewed currency in the late fourth century with the ascension of Emperor Julian.

Rounding out this section, Georgia Frank's essay explores Athanasius's treatment of the Psalter in his *Letter to Marcellinus*. Noting the unusual completeness of Athanasius's treatment, his careful deployment of the canons of classical rhetoric, and the fragmentation of the Psalter into various thematic lists, she argues that the letter was designed to guide Marcellinus in his memorization and subsequent recollection of the psalms as a strategy for the formation and knowledge of the self.

The second group of essays engages the topic of disciplinary culture in a variety of ascetic contexts. The first two essays focus on institutional discipline: its modalities and ends. Daniel Caner's essay explores the emergence of penance and mourning as dominant goals in early Byzantine monasticism by focusing on John Climacus's arresting description of "the Prison," a penitential monastery outside Alexandria for monks who had "stumbled into sin." While the spectacular nature of these public penances did not pass without criticism, abbots increasingly incorporated such displays within monasteries as a means of stimulating and sustaining a spirit of contrition. The goal, Caner argues, was to sharpen the monks' awareness of their participation in the drama of heavenly judgment and redemption, to create, in effect, what Heussi calls a *Sonderwelt*.

Catherine Chin reexamines the categories of the individual and the collective in Cassian's *Institutes* by drawing on the idea of "distributed cognition." Cassian's starting point, Chin argues, is the person embedded in a specific material system that extends outside the boundaries of the body. Through the common life, the ascetic person is reconfigured in terms that evoke the Origenist doctrine of the *apokatastasis*. The aim of the group, in which reunification happens, is the production not of perfected individuals but of Christ, understood as "a person produced by an interlocking network of ascetic contributors who serve as his 'interior.'"

The following two essays turn to the household and the city as disciplinary spaces. Virginia Burrus's essay sets Macrina's household within the evolving history and practice of education, sexuality, and the family. A close reading of Gregory's *Life of Macrina*, she argues, reveals an erotically charged "feminine community of pedagogical formation," over which Macrina presides and into which she allows Gregory to enter.

Susanna Elm reexamines the common portrait of Gregory Nazianzen "as a self-centered recluse" by focusing on Gregory's turbulent relationship with Maximus the Philosopher in the period between Theodosius's proclamation of *cunctos populos* in 380 and the emperor's arrival in Constantinople in November of that same year. While *Oration* 25 eulogizes and *Oration* 26 vilifies Maximus, both forcefully present the characteristics of the ideal ascetic and ecclesiastical leader — characteristics that Gregory himself abundantly displays — and represent an astute bid on the part of Gregory "to regain and solidify his control."

The third cluster of essays engages the topic of imaginary landscapes and ascetic self-fashioning. The essay by James Goehring examines the cultural myth of the desert as the product of selective and purposeful memory. When Athanasius came to write the *Life of Antony,* for example, he "forgot" the urban ascetics, who had been so instrumental in protecting him, and tied ascetic renunciation firmly to the physical practice of withdrawal. The stature of these desert dwellers, already enhanced by their rugged surroundings, was further bolstered by a narrative process that redrew these heroes in the powerful but simplified likeness of biblical figures and erased the complex confessional diversity of early monasticism. The myth of the desert was thus "both a product of the emerging Christian culture of orthodoxy and an important player in its success."

Robin Darling Young's essay explores the theme of *xeniteia* in the writings of the great monastic theoretician Evagrius. Arguing that it should be translated as "exile," rather than "wandering," Young suggests that it provided a way for Evagrius to imagine himself and his ascetic readers. Deeply informing his presentation of the monastic life is the figure of Odysseus, besieged with temptations and beset with difficulties on his journey home.

Patricia Cox Miller analyzes the relationship of Adam to the "cascade of animals" that accompanies him on an ivory diptych dating from the turn of the fifth century. Instead of seeing this image as an expression of Adam's dominance over irrational beasts, Cox Miller reads these animal bodies as signs of carnality and desire. As such, they provided a means of self-discernment, or, what Foucault has called a technique of the self. Because humans shared "not only the body but also behavior" with animals, animal stories could be used, as they were in Basil's *Hexaemeron*, "to craft an ascetic self."

The ascetic impact of John Chrysostom's use of nature imagery is the focus of Blake Leyerle's essay. The countryside emerges from his writings as a place of healthful and pleasurable simplicity as well as orderly bounty; and nature teaches observers about the majesty and providence of God as well as the necessity of restraint. While much of this picture is derived from classical traditions of bucolic poetry and the Golden Age, the typical inhabitants are no longer farmers but rather monks and martyrs. Chrysostom even presents himself as either a noble farmer or a piping shepherd. This bucolic imagery, Leyerle argues, was designed to mitigate the growing divide between ascetic and nonascetic Christians.

The final group of essays examines how the culture of nineteenth-century scholarship, first in Germany and then in North America, shaped the emerging picture of early Christianity. Claudia Rapp shows how Adolf Harnack rehabilitated Christianity — its history, theology, and material culture — as a scholarly discipline within academic circles in the late nineteenth century. Influenced by contemporary science, especially recent discoveries in geology and biology, and by his friendship with Edwin Hatch of Oxford, Harnack developed a periodization of Christianity. His own interest lay in what he termed the "palaeontological layer" of church history, the period from the mid-second through the third century, when Christianity forged a synthesis with Hellenism that led to a consolidation of identity through doctrinal development, ritual stabilization, and ecclesiastical organization. For Harnack, it was thus "not the external political circumstances created by the Emperor Constantine that determined the triumph of Christianity but the religion's own inner forces."

Tracing the emergence of church history as a discipline in America, Elizabeth Clark focuses on the divergent assessments of Eastern and Western asceticism. Influenced by German historiography, their own religious formation, and their conviction that western lands — and America in particular — represented progress, nineteenth-century scholars viewed Eastern asceticism as degenerate and fanatical. In their eyes, Symeon Stylites stood as the epitome of "insane devotion," whereas Western monasticism was to be lauded for its service and industry and proto-Protestant concentration on "inward spirituality."

Taken together, these essays bear witness to the vitality of ascetic culture in late antiquity. *Culture* seems an especially apt term for this defining phenomenon. Lexically rooted in the world of agriculture, its meaning was indissociably tied to the reality of bodily labor consistently expended over time. In this sense *ascetic culture* verges on the redundant, as asceticism is defined by a series of sustained bodily practices.

Already in Augustine, we find the self figured as a field that must be worked (*Conf.* 10.16). Later, *culture* came to designate the ideals of high literary and aesthetic sensibilities, the possession of which served, in turn, to mark the elite. This more rarified meaning captures the prestige of ascetic lifestyles in the philosophical and religious climate of late antiquity and the elevated social status of asceticism's most prominent practitioners. In our own day, of course, *culture* is used more often to refer to an inclusive set of social characteristics, institutions, and beliefs that, when taken together, define a group. This broad definition points to the crucial contribution both of the context in which early Christianity took shape and of asceticism in defining Christian identity.

To talk of culture is, finally, also to return to the honoree of this volume. Philip Rousseau is a man of culture in the broadest sense of this generous term: a scholar of wide erudition, whose deep knowledge of late antiquity is the product of intense labor sustained over many years and pursued on almost every continent; whose keen aesthetic appreciation for literature, music, and art informs his many books and numerous articles; and whose gift for nurturing friendship has enriched our separate lives, created contexts for shared conversation, and helped define the community of scholars of late antiquity. It is thus to Philip that we offer these essays in admiration and gratitude for the many ways in which his distinctive scholarly vision has shaped our field and his exemplary, generous friendship has supported our common life.

NOTES

The editors would like to acknowledge the support of the University of Notre Dame Press. Thanks go especially to Barbara Hanrahan, who embraced the idea of this project with such enthusiasm, and to Charles Van Hof and Rebecca DeBoer, who shepherded the manuscript to print. A great debt is owed to Albertus Horsting, a PhD candidate in the Department of Theology, who helped format the initial essays and created the bibliography, and to Elisabeth Magnus, a copy editor for the Press, who imposed order and consistency on a very challenging manuscript. Wendy McMillen designed the lovely cover.

1. Rousseau, "Introduction to the Second Edition," in *Ascetics, Authority,* ix–xxvii.

PART I

Books as Guides

Chapter One

Pachomius and the Mystery of the Letters

JOEL KALVESMAKI

The only writings left behind by Pachomius, father of cenobitic monasticism, are thirteen brief epistles — all terse, all puzzling. The puzzle lies in Pachomius's cryptic use of the letters of the alphabet, the result of a spiritual language an angel was said to have taught him. This alphabet recurs time and again in Pachomius's epistles, rendering many of them unintelligible to all but the recipients, who were said also to know and use this language. For instance, to one of his monastic leaders, Cornelius, Pachomius writes: "Do the work of the ι, which was called ο in the old days. Place δ also before your eyes, so that it might be good for your soul. ϱ has stretched out his hand to reach you; this is ι, which is the sepulcher, your resting place. Sing to the ω, lest the ω sing to you. Let the shameless age rejoice with you so that you do not rejoice with the shameless age" (example 1).[1] In this passage, a mix of admonition and teaching, each Greek letter acts as a noun or nominal phrase. Cornelius is expected to do something about whatever these letters symbolize, but exactly what is unclear. In some epistles even the grammatical or semantic function of the letters is a mystery. Consider this example (2): "*Honor God and you will be strong* (Prov 7:1). Remember the groanings of the saints σφ."[2] Are the sigma and phi initials for specific saints? Do they represent a sentence? If so, is the pair of letters an admonition, doctrinal instruction, question, statement, or something else? Sometimes contextual clues attenuate into wisps. For example (3), to the abbots Sourous and John he writes, "We should not fear ruin in the place of our pilgrimage; but we must fight to be able to have peace with those who keep the commandments of God. η. *What will be your gain if you win the whole world* (Mt 16:26; Mk 8:36; Lk 9:25) and have enmity with God?"[3] If the eta represents a noun, like the eta used in the first example, or any other single part of speech, how does it — indeed, how could it — connect with the sentences that precede and follow?

Even if one could tease out what a letter means in one epistle, that same letter used in other epistles can seem incoherent. At one place Pachomius writes (example 4), "Write ν above η and θ; write ζ above χ, μ, λ and ι, when you have finished reading these characters."[4] These seem to be instructions in scribal habits. He is not asking his readers to believe something, or to live their life a certain way (although such overtones may be present). He explains that he is writing "so that you might understand the mysteries of the characters,"[5] but what mystery is there about how a letter is situated on the page? We find ourselves simultaneously contemplating two very different things, the mosaic of meaning and the rituals of writing. In passages such as example 4, are we to think of symbols and the symbolized, or tools and goals? Are we to peer in, to detect meaning and mystery behind the letters, or to gaze out, to think of the design on the page and how the pen affects the world? In that same epistle a sequence of coded letters symbolizes Pachomius's named identity. He writes (example 5), "Therefore I wrote to you σφθμ, lest perhaps some one might say that my name is not written σφθμ. . . . Now, therefore, σφθμλουυουυλιλ."[6] It is not apparent what he means, particularly since he does not explain "name," and we do not have enough context to discern whether these letters were to be understood orally, visually, or, more likely, both.[7] Perhaps in the autograph, now lost, the letters were written in a certain shape, like the eight-by-eight block of letters associated with epistles 9a and 9b.[8] And if this is his name, how does it explain another epistle where Pachomius adapts the cipher: "*The Lord takes pleasure in those who fear him* (Ps 147 [146]: 11) σφθμλ"?[9]

Two of Pachomius's epistles, addressed to no one specifically, follow a peculiar alphabetic pattern quite different from all the above examples. Each epistle consists of twelve lines, each starting with a pair of Greek letters, and each letter matched with its mirror opposite in the alphabet, like a Hebrew atbash cipher (in which aleph is substituted for tav, beth for shin, etc.). The alpha-omega pair appears in line 1; beta-psi marks the second line; and so on, down to the mu-nu pair that marks the last line. Each mysterious letter pair is answered at the end of the sentence by a single letter, treated as its predicate (example 6):

αω: The generations have effervesced with evil, which is δ;
βψ: The fruit has been accomplished on the lips, which is τ;
[γ]χ: God caused me to forget the poverty in my house, from the beginning of the mountains to their summit, which is ϱ;[10]

Even though we have in theory a grammatical context for the final alphabetic letter, we have no semantic one. And we have neither for the opening pair. What did Pachomius want the reader to do with these strange letters?

Perhaps no one but the original recipients will ever know what to do with these letter ciphers. The material is so opaque that most scholars discussing Pachomius and his monasteries pass over the epistles with little comment. This is a pity, since the epistles are the only extant texts attributed to Pachomius. Recognizing the potential to recover his otherwise lost teachings, a few scholars from the early twentieth century attempted to unlock the meaning, but with mixed results. The only scholar to publish anything recently is Christoph Joest, who has, in several articles, suggested a comprehensive solution to the ciphers.[11]

By sifting carefully through each of the thirteen epistles Joest has assembled a key to the meaning behind the various letters. Working on the assumption that the same letter means the same thing from one epistle to the next, Joest has located for each letter a word cluster (*Wortfeld*) that has at its root a Greek or Coptic word that begins with that letter. Alpha means new beginning or redemption (ἀρχή); beta stands for kingship (βασιλεία); gamma is earth (γῆ); and so on.[12] With this key in hand, he deciphers the spiritual messages Pachomius intended for his followers.

Intriguing as such an approach may be, it leads, in my opinion, to insoluble problems. For example, it seems incorrect to assume that from one epistle to the next each letter signifies the same word cluster. Can the iota in example 1 above, which Joest says means "Jesus," really symbolize the same thing as the iota in example 4? Or what would it mean to translate the beginning of example 5: "Therefore I wrote to you Savior Light Death Small"?[13] Pachomius's letter symbols vary in meaning from one epistle to the next. In one the omega is to be spurned; in another, to be embraced. In one the sigma is interpreted for its numerical value; in other places such an interpretation would be forced.[14] To expect consistency from the epistles is to reduce to principles of human grammar what Pachomius considered angelic.

Other inconsistencies affect Joest's analysis. He looks for solutions almost exclusively from the Greek alphabet, even though uniquely Coptic letters also feature in the epistles.[15] The Coptic alphabet enters only when an answer does not easily present itself.[16] The various grammatical and syntactic differences from one epistle to the next, noted in the few examples above, are not deeply considered. Some passages that do not fit the key are passed over, and some passages are forced to conform to the key.[17] At many places Joest's solutions seem correct, but the resultant readings merely iterate what Pachomius states elsewhere, or what Christians of the time always taught. For example, to take Joest's solution to the first clause in example 1, it was no secret that one should do the work of Jesus. Why would Pachomius bother to encode the obvious?

Just because the epistles are difficult to interpret convincingly, they are not useless to historians. Although we may not know *what* they mean, we may learn quite a bit about Pachomius and his monasteries by asking *how* they mean, and *why* they mean. How did alphabetic ciphers function in an ascetic context? Why did Pachomius present himself in an alphabet that he knew would be obscure to anyone but the recipients? How did he expect his readers to interact with the epistles? Answers to these questions would illuminate how Pachomius crafted spiritual instruction, how he interacted with his community, and how he wanted to be seen by the church at large.

Other texts from the period can provide instructive parallels. Our first inclination might be to consider various gnosticizing texts, treatises of astrology or magic, or Jewish hekhalot literature. Similarities are there, indeed, but the comparison can be more confusing than illuminating. The authors of these texts were not abbots, and their readers were not monks. These texts were not written to help readers in their ascetic struggles. And they circulated in communities quite different from the Pachomian monasteries, which were integrated into local Egyptian church life and were orthodox in doctrine and temperament. So to understand how cryptic letters functioned in an orthodox ascetic context, we should first consider parallels from ancient texts that more closely mirror the author-reader relationship found in Pachomius's epistles.

At first blush, this may seem impossible. Other ascetic writers from late antiquity do not use the alphabet the way Pachomius does. Although we have abundant evidence for cryptography in the scribal and monastic tradition — it was popular equally with monks and magicians — surviving examples are not quite analogous. Unlike Pachomius's epistles, these ciphers, consisting of letter-for-letter substitutions, are rather easy to crack.[18] Pachomius's epistles only hint at cryptography proper; they rely more firmly upon other unusual aspects that recur in ancient ascetic literature. Take, for example, Pachomius's tendency to find a cryptic symbol — be it a letter, a biblical character, or something else — and spiritualize it nearly to obscurity. He does this even absent his angelic alphabet: "The stewards have committed a crime in their basket. So they had the sword of their destruction under their breast, which is the garden, and at the doors of hell they pursued the abundance of the earth, or the goods that God has given to men."[19] Plain words, clotted meaning. This practice recurs throughout the mystical tradition of fourth-century ascetic literature. Take, for example, the abstruse symbols found in the writings of the monastic theologian Evagrius of Pontus. He explains those symbols to deepen, not clarify, the mystery.[20] This practice can be found in the writings of numerous early ascetics, even those of Antony the Great.[21] Each author compels readers to ponder his words, to sink deeper into the symbol.

Within the later Pachomian tradition is a prophetic text by a certain Apa Charour, a text that consists of cryptic sayings peppered with recondite (perhaps nonsense) words, each saying usually followed by an explanation that interprets it for the Pachomian community. For example,

"We made *emese*-wood staffs, we made onion-skin textiles, we threw the fennel-wood *aš* on the riverbank: that is: we rolled around in sleep, we put in place headmen with crooked hearts, we put in *deuterarioi* who were despondent in their thoughts." Charour's jabberwocky — to adopt, with Leslie MacCoull, Lewis Carroll's term — resembles the obfuscating formulas found in Pachomius's epistles.[22]

But the best parallel has only recently come fully to light: *On the Mystery of the Letters* (Περὶ τοῦ μυστηρίου τῶν γραμμάτων). This unusual treatise is important here because it mixes vision, commentary, and polemic to explain how the alphabet demonstrates the truth of Christianity. An edition of an early Coptic translation was published in 1902 by Adolphe Hebbelynck, to near obscurity. Yet not long ago the Greek original was identified by Cordula Bandt, who in 2007 published an edition and a German translation.[23]

On the Mystery of the Letters, which is roughly the length of one of the four Gospels, presents itself as a revelation given by an angel to an anchorite, a certain "Apa Seba," according to the Coptic. Clues in the text point to a setting in sixth-century Palestine, so perhaps *On the Mystery* originates from circles around St. Sabas, the famous Palestinian ascetic and monastic leader. In this revelation the monk — let's call him Seba — learns that the two alphabets in the world, the Greek and the Semitic, are etched with the plan of divine salvation. The letters of the alphabets were given a specific shape and sequence to embody the stages in the creation of the world and to foretell the incarnation of Jesus Christ. Both alphabets consist of twenty-two letters. (Although the Greek alphabet we know has twenty-four letters, *On the Mystery* claims that it started out with twenty-two: the godless Greek philosophers later introduced the xi and psi.) The shapes of the first fourteen letters of the Greek alphabet depict the stages of Creation, from the looped alpha ⲁ, representing the spirit of God hovering over the waters, down to the omicron (o), symbolizing in its circle the entire creation. The remaining eight letters are signs of Christ and of the salvation of the world. The crossbar of the pi represents Christ as the bridge connecting the Jews and the Gentiles, who are signified by the legs. And the pattern of interpretation continues through rho and sigma, and down to omega, whose two intersecting loops represent the end of this age and the beginning of the age to come. The treatise plays with letter forms, interspersing labels and calligraphy to drive home the alphabet symbolism. For example, Christ as the pi is illustrated in the manuscripts as shown in the following figure. "The Christ" hovers over the crossbar. "People of the Jews" and "people from [the] nations" label the left and right legs.

λαὸς	∴ ὁ XC	
ιου	Π	λαὸς
δαί		εξ ε
ων		θνῶν

Although this interpretation of the history and meaning of the Greek alphabet is designed to rebuke Greek intellectuals, Seba wants also to correct the Jews, who he says have forgotten the meaning of their alphabet. But in his explanation of the "Syrian" alphabet — for him Hebrew, Aramaic, and Syriac all use a single alphabet he calls Syrian — Seba focuses upon the meaning of the letters' names, not their design. Following in a long Christian tradition of using Hebrew onomastics, Seba sets out to show that the names of the letters of the Syrian alphabet reveal the mysteries of Creation and of the Incarnation.

On the Mystery of the Letters provides a lengthy voyage through both alphabets, opening to the reader unexpected conceptual territory. If the alphabet was mundane and unreflectively familiar to the Christian before he or she started to read the text, it became at the end a new Christian terrain, a cohesive linguistic map of the world and the history of salvation. Although a summary of the main features of Seba's alphabetical topography would take too long and might well distract us from Pachomius's epistles, even a brief consideration of the preface can open a unique window into the realm of letter symbolism and into how and why it worked in an ascetic context.

After the necessary preliminaries — invocation of the Trinity, title, and so forth — the author puts in the mouth of Seba these words:

> It came to me once, he said, as I persistently devoted myself in prayer to God in the desert. Now one day I took in my hand the book of Revelation, which St. John the Theologian saw on Patmos. And I read in it

> until I came to the passage where Christ said to John: "I [am] Alpha and Ω" [Rev. 1:8, 21:6, 22:13], and then again he said for a second and third time, "I am the Alpha and Ω." And as I heard this, I considered suddenly in my heart a certain other saying in the Gospel of the Lord, who said: "Not a single iota or a single stroke shall pass away until all these things come to pass" [Mt. 5.18].
>
> Immediately I thought, there exists a mystery of God in the letters of the alphabet, and that it has not been revealed to us. And so I believed with all my heart on Christ, who said, "Ask and it will be given to you, seek and you will find, knock and the door will be opened. For whoever asks will receive, and he who seeks will find, and he who knocks it will be opened to him" [Mt. 7.7–8].
>
> And so I steadfastly prayed for his goodness, that he would illumine my understanding concerning this mystery, which is hidden in the letters of the alphabet. And his great and ineffable goodness always comes to the worthy and unworthy alike.[24]

Abba Seba then says that God answered his prayer by sending to him the same angel that gave words to Balaam's donkey. This angel led the ascetic by a light: "And at night, as if coming into an ecstasy, I saw myself standing on Mount Sinai, where the divine law and the revelation of the genesis of the world was revealed by God to the great Moses, from the treatise of Genesis. I saw a despotic power worshipped by a multitude of people in fear. From this I heard and learned about the letters. So there the untaught teacher taught me the eternally concealed mystery of that alphabet."[25] In these quotations we find a vivid description of how the ascetic encountered the mysteries of the alphabet. The revelation begins with Seba's passionate thirst for prayer, which leads him to ponder the scriptures, to locate a problem, and to seek the answer. Taking Christ up on his promise to the persistent knocker, Seba prays even harder and finds himself in the angelic realm, and then transported to Mount Sinai. He stands in the place of Moses and learns the mystery, while the people at the base of Mount Sinai worship a despotic power. At the pinnacle of the imagery combined from Exodus and Revelation stands the alphabet.

Now, Pachomius and Seba differ in many ways. *On the Mystery of the Letters*, like the contemporary writings of Barsanuphius and John, involves no secret language or code.[26] Rather, it proposes to explain, perhaps even to mystify, the ordinary use of the alphabet. Seba and Pachomius are separated by two centuries and come from distinct cultures. Nevertheless, *On the Mystery of the Letters* provides a window into Pachomius's world. *On the Mystery* is written by an ascetic master for adepts. It reveals the dynamics of a Christian holy man entering into alphabet symbolism. It hints at how he wanted to be seen by those who read the treatise. It shows that the alphabet could be an ascetic's testing ground and the apex of vision. There are parallels in several details. Pachomius and Seba are each led by an angel. Each man learns a new mystery and becomes a divine spectacle. Each one discovers, uses, and understands his innovative insight only through diligent ascetic practice, and each is completely indebted to the grace of God, who cannot be manipulated. Each man declares (Seba directly and Pachomius indirectly) that intellectual prowess is an obstacle to such revelation. And in both cases the readers are treated as outsiders given a special dispensation to consider the mystery being revealed: although Seba recorded the vision, it is set within a treatise written by his disciples; and Pachomius writes ostensibly for members of his inner circle, but it is reasonable to think that he knew many others would be gazing over their shoulder.

As I have already suggested, the use of alphabet symbolism was not uniquely Christian. In late antiquity Jews, Platonists, Pythagoreans, astrologers, and heretics set out their own forms of letter symbolism, drawing from and contributing to the larger tradition.

The alphabet was treated intrinsically as an object of contemplation and a device to shape the world. Sentences using all the letters of the Greek alphabet without repetition — pangrams, such as "Quartz jock vends BMW glyph-fix"— were used in antiquity both as grammatical exercises and as religious or mystical formulas. These formulas were taken seriously by late antique thinkers such as Clement of Alexandria and the Neoplatonist philosopher Porphyry.[27] In the *Sefer Yetsira*, a Jewish mystical text from late antiquity, the universe is built upon thirty-two building blocks: the ten numbers and the twenty-two letters of the alphabet. Out of the alphabet comes three basic elements, and from these, creation: "Three primary letters — Alef, Mem, Shin — in the universe: air, and water and fire. Heaven was created first from fire, and earth was created from water, and air was created from the Spirit, holding the balance between them."[28] From these same letters the human is formed: from the shin comes the head, from the mem comes the belly, and from the alef the chest.[29] Out of the triad of letters comes a heptad of letters, then a dodecad. The author weaves these numbers and letters into the fabric of creation, paying special attention to labeling the stars and the human body with the alphabet. Early gnosticizing Mandaean texts are similar. They include diagrams of humans, the various body parts labeled by letter combinations. Such diagrams accompany Creation narratives where the alphabet gives shape to the cosmos.[30] The letter-cosmos connection complements diagrams found in astrological treatises, where pairs of letters are assigned to each of the twelve houses of the zodiac.[31]

This practice of attaching pairs of letters to the stars may date back to the second century CE, when the word *alphabet* (ἀλφάβητος) was coined. The earliest datable use of the word occurs in Irenaeus's account of the teachings and revelations of the Valentinian Marcus (pejoratively called the Magus). Marcus recorded a revelation where the supercelestial being Truth came to him as a naked woman. Each of her twelve body parts was marked by two Greek letters: alpha and omega were assigned to the head, beta and psi to her neck, and so on, down to her feet, mu and nu.[32]

Pachomius's atbash pairing of letters (epistles 9a and 9b; example 6 above) is strikingly similar to that of the above examples. The broad range of backgrounds to the texts that mystically use the alphabet show that symbolic atbash was a part of the culture and therefore familiar to Pachomius's audience. But the mere similarity would not have compelled readers to think that Pachomius was advocating astrology or Valentinian heresy. Given the context of the thirteen epistles — their constant call to a life of ascetic purity and their circulation and use within the *koinonia*— ancient readers would have known that Pachomius was here utilizing familiar tools for new ends, ends that themselves rendered the tools less familiar. The letters (and the epistles that used them) were intended to serve two functions.

First, the letters served as a guide for ascetics seeking spiritual knowledge. In a few of the epistles that feature letter symbolism Pachomius indicates this purpose: "We were at your place but because we were in too much of a hurry, we could not have a spiritual talk with you; therefore we talk to you now in a letter." "I have written to you with images and parables so that you would search them with wisdom, following the footsteps of the saints, and that instructed in the words of God you will not fall under his judgement. . . . I wrote you all these things so that, laboring now, you may have rest in the future." "I wrote to you so that you might understand the mysteries of the characters." "The smell of your [Souros's and John's] wisdom has reached us and has compelled us to write you these things." "Place δ before your eyes that it may be good for your soul."[33]

Pachomius's letter symbolism was also a tool of conversion. This is not stated explicitly in any of his epistles. But Seba's use of the alphabet, which was partly intended to make Jews and pagans think about and use the alphabet differently, shows that this was within the realm of possibility. Another clue that this might be the case comes from the successors of Pachomius, who, as Philip Rousseau has shown, were ideally situated in temperament and outlook to adapt for their own use the esoteric texts found at Nag Hammadi.[34] Traces of this competitive element are evident in epistles 9a and 9b, which are, according to their titles and internal structure, devices to discern what will happen in the future. Comparable devices, such as those of Marcus Magus and the astrological texts, link the prognosticating letters of the alphabet through representations of physical objects, such as the human body or the zodiac. But Pachomius's letters transport the user through spiritual meditations or scripture. In epistles 9a and 9b a reader would have consulted the letter or letters on one end of a given line to get to the letter or letters on the other (see example 6). But on the way the reader had to go through, and so somehow process, a line of scripture or a spiritual saying. One may reasonably question how distinct Pachomius's goal was from the pagans' (why did he write a tool to predict the future?) but the tool he furnished reroutes prognostic activity along a Christian path.[35]

Such an attempt to reshape culture can be seen in other examples. Take the battology found in magical texts from antiquity; they contain instructions to draw strange letters and to write the familiar ones, especially vowels, in specific shapes or diagrams. One text tells the practitioner to "write with pure myrrh ink these names . . .

ioerbeth	iopakerbeth
ioerbe	opakerbeth
ioerb	pakerbeth
ioer	akerbeth
ioe	erbeth
io	rbeth
i	eth
	th"[36]

The emphasis here and in other winglike formations is the position of the letters on the page. The shapes of the letters, individually and collectively, were of paramount importance, both to force a person into submission and to cajole spiritual powers into acting on one's behalf. On occasion the given alphabet was not enough, and a god would reveal a new alphabet of contorted letters, frequently with loops, whorls, and tiny circles at the ends of the strokes.[37]

The careful visual manipulation of the alphabet found in astrological and magical texts resembles the practices of both Pachomius (examples 4 and 5) and Abba Seba (who argued his points on the basis of specific letter shapes). But once again, the similarities are merely apparent; the differences show that Christian letter symbolism was competitive. In the magical texts the unusual characters were meant to contribute to the efficacy of a spell, to engage supramundane forces to change the material or social world of the user, usually beyond or against human will or agency. And the magical texts are individualistic: community is neither assumed nor enjoined. In contrast, the instructions Pachomius gives for how to write and arrange certain letters beckon Sourous and John to plumb spiritual mysteries and to deepen their already-close bonds of spiritual and social fellowship. Epistles 4 and 6 are written conversationally, the letter patterns functioning as the corporate spiritual exercises of elite ecclesiastics. The alphabet was used by the ascetics to lead one another to higher spiritual knowledge. This intent is paralleled by the teachings of the *Mysteries* on the nature of allographs. For Abba Seba, the letters are to be written in certain shapes and orders, not to curse an enemy or make a love potion, but to be an icon of Creation and redemption. Seba's alpha must be written so as to depict the power of the Spirit at Creation. Its placement at the top of a vertical row of four letters is key to a theological insight Seba has on the sequence and direction of Creation. Unlike Pachomius, Seba intended to make that insight known to all his readers, not just an elite. But the goal was the same: to induce a community to ascend to pure spiritual knowledge, a knowledge wrapped in every symbol, even those of the alphabet. He was prescient: the tradition of illuminated initial letters, one of the most colorful conventions of medieval manuscripts, began to flourish shortly after the *Mysteries* was written. This is not to say that Seba invented the scribal and painterly practice of animating and decorating the first letter of a treatise, but he certainly contributed to the culture that produced that habit.[38]

Christian ascetics like Pachomius and Seba, committed to orthodox sensibilities and comity, created through the same symbols used by those they considered pagans and heretics a unique conceptual bridge for their communities. On the one hand the ascetic vied for terrain associated with Platonists, astrologers, and heretics and offered the Christian reader a godly way to walk that terrain. He set his reader squarely in the orthodox Christian culture of the *koinonia.* He contributed to the wider ascetic effort to Christianize metaphysical philosophy and noumenal speculation — that is, paraphrasing Philip Rousseau, to invade the chief components of late Roman culture.[39]

But on the other hand, Pachomius and Seba stretched the conceptual horizons of their inner circles, and through them the church as a whole. Pachomius's secret language should be seen as an integral component of his emphasis on education and literacy, of his requirement that his monks be taught to write "letters, syllables, nouns, and verbs."[40] The secret alphabet was one of several revelations Pachomius customarily received, either directly from God or through an angel.[41] And it placed over the requirement for mastery of conventional literacy a new, divine level. According to the first Greek *vita*, he wrote to the leaders of his monastery in the secret spiritual language so that they could govern and so that these leaders, being holy, could reply in the same language.[42] When he organized his monasteries, Pachomius associated the letters of the alphabet with spiritual qualities, then assigned letters to companies of monks. He would ask about his monks' welfare through their assigned letter, the meaning of which only the spiritual understood.[43] That small circle of spiritual leaders included Cornelius, Sourous, and John, all mentioned in the epigraphs to the epistles.

These glimpses into Pachomius's habits clarify not what the alphabetic code meant but how it meant. The code conveyed spiritual meaning and insight, and it allowed Christians to contend in a special site of struggle. It also prompted Pachomius's followers to find in the alphabet at least a part of their self-identity, and it provided a benchmark to separate the most spiritually accomplished from everyone else. To know the alphabet was to reside with the angels, to participate in the charism of the leaders, who were fluent in the new language, and it invited awed devotion. Pachomius integrated his alphabetic code into his persona as holy man, and he used that code to inspire his followers to participate in the re-creation of society. The obfuscating letters were as much for the incognizant as for the cognoscenti, to delimit and lionize the spiritual elite.

I suspect Pachomius knew that the public would read his epistles, because he used the code in texts that have no specific addressee.[44] Whether or not he anticipated their popularity, his ciphers took on a new life among admirers outside his inner circle, both those who knew the Pachomian monasteries and those who had only read of them. Pachomius's monks asked for a book of his mystery letters so they could continue to be spiritually trained by him.[45] The epigraph to *Epistle* 1, a comment perhaps by the translator from Coptic into Greek, states that the writer has heard the angelic language but has not been able to understand it.[46] Gennadius and Palladius, in their accounts, report Pachomius's spiritual language with comparable wonder. And Shenoute of Atripe approvingly quotes from Pachomius's letter, taking a phrase from example 1 to mean "Sing to the world, lest the world sing to you."[47] Jerome, in his preface to his translation of Pachomius's writings, finds it necessary to say something about the epistles, and he explains why he did not convert the alphabet to Latin: "If we have imitated the simplicity of the Egyptian speech, we have done so out of fidelity to the text, lest rhetorical speech should alter what has been said by apostolic men filled with spiritual grace."[48] So Jerome treats the code as a conduit to the saints and thus further hallows the saint and his mysterious, bordering on magical, alphabet for his audience. In the manuscript tradition we imperfectly glimpse the wonder of the average anonymous reader, the kind of reader Jerome was hoping to reach. Although the epistles survive only fragmentarily in Coptic and Greek, at least thirteen Latin manuscripts are extant, indicating how the *Pachomiana* stirred

Western readers' imagination. Many of these Latin manuscripts are filled with obvious errors in the alphabetic code, but they were nevertheless read and copied, mistakes and all.

So the further Pachomius recedes in time and culture, the greater the wonder of the reader. The phenomenon resembles that of pilgrimage in late antiquity, where the only written accounts we have come from Latin pilgrims, not Greek, even though virtually all pilgrimage took place in the Levant and Egypt. Jerome and the Latin copyists treat Pachomius's epistles like pilgrim's contact relics. This attitude is exhibited best by their concern to preserve the strange, now-garbled alphabet. In that act of preservation, the distance in time and culture could be bridged, to keep Pachomius close to his readers, and to build among the later readers of the *Pachomiana* a sense of solidarity, even *koinonia.* Perhaps this is also why Abba Seba's *On the Mystery of the Greek Letters* was preserved, circulated, and translated. The mystery of the letters was not to be forcibly unlocked but to be received and adored with imperfect understanding.

NOTES

Under Philip Rousseau I learned, in his many seminars, to go beyond (but not abandon) the whats of a text, to discover its whys and hows. I am grateful to him for showing me the range of questions that can and should be brought to a subject. I also thank those who gave me early feedback on this article, Cordula Bandt, James Goehring, Aaron Johnson, and Janet Timbie in particular.

1. Pachomius, *Ep.* 1.2. Editions of the letters in Coptic and Greek translation (both fragmentary) are in Pachomius, *Briefe Pachoms,* ed. Quecke. Jerome's Latin translation, which preserves all the letters, is in Boon, *Pachomiana Latina*, 77–101. All English translations of Pachomius's letters are from Veilleux, *Pachomian Koinonia*, 3:51–83.
2. Pachomius, *Ep.* 3.1.
3. *Ep.* 4.4.
4. *Ep.* 6.1.
5. *Ep.* 6.2.
6. *Ep.* 6.4–5.
7. Although all texts were read aloud in antiquity, there was a strong theoretical difference between oral (στοιχεῖα) and written (γράμματα) letters. See *Scholia in Dionysius Thrax Artem grammaticam* 32.16–20; 192.24–193.7;

196.16–20; 197.15–23; 323.28–324.7, ed. Hilgard, *Grammatici Graeci,* 1:3. See also Förster, *Marcus Magus,* 198–99.

8. See the blocks of characters in Veilleux, *Pachomian Koinonia*, 3:76, and Quecke's appendix to *Briefe Pachoms*, 116.

9. *Ep.* 11a.

10. *Ep.* 9a.

11. For earlier attempts, see Quecke's intro. to *Briefe Pachoms*, 18–40 (with references to older literature), and Opelt, "Lingua ab angelo tradita." Joest's endeavors include "Anliegen des Pachomius," "Geheimschrift Pachoms," "Pachomianische Geheimschrift," "Buchstabenquadrat im Pachomianischen Briefcorpus," and "Pachom-Briefe 1 und 2."

12. For the complete key, see Joest, "Pachom-Briefe 1 und 2," 62–63.

13. An adaptation of Joest's key because at ibid., 50, he seems to misread two phi's in *Ep.* 11a as psi's.

14. Omega: *Ep.* 1.2 vs. 3.2. Sigma: *Ep.* 11b vs. 1.3 and 2.1.

15. Pachomius, *Ep.* 1.3, 6.9. See Pachomius, *Briefe Pachoms,* ed. Quecke, intro., 78–79, note to line 17 (99), and app. crit.; and Boon, *Pachomiana Latina,* note to lines 8–9 (94) and app. crit.

16. Concerning rho, Joest ("Pachom-Briefe 1 und 2," 53) suggests the Coptic *r ahe* because he is unable to find a Greek word for "life," his desired solution. Joest also appeals to psephic formulas that add to 100, but without regard for how psephy was used and treated in the period, and without any apparent connection to the concept "life."

17. For example, Joest argues (ibid., 37) from four pairs of letters in *Ep.* 2 that are identical to the letter pairs in *Ep.* 9a and 9b, that the latter unlock the code in the former. But he ignores the five pairs of letters in *Ep.* 2 that contradict the pairing of *Ep.* 9a and 9b. Taking the eta to mean Pascha and the Resurrection, Joest (40) bypasses *Ep.* 4.4 and 6.1–3, where eta is used cryptically. His resolution (59) of HΘAM at *Ep.* 11a.8 ("The patience of the poor is a pledge ηθαμ") permits contradictory meanings for the theta and renders the mu, taken to mean "small" and therefore "the poor," redundant. He takes omicron to mean "heavens" (50–51), so at *Ep.* 1.2 (reproduced above as my example 1) one would expect this to mean that Jesus was called "heaven" in the old days. Against the standard use of relative pronouns in the epistle, Joest takes "heaven" to refer to "work" and connects it with the Lord's Prayer (yet leaves "in the old days" unexplained in this context). Other examples could be adduced.

18. On ancient and Byzantine cryptography, see Wisse, "Language Mysticism." The practice occurs in numerous Byzantine manuscripts. See, e.g., Constantinides and Browning, *Dated Greek Manuscripts*, 238, 244–45, 255, 257. On the earlier, pagan tradition of cryptography, see Dieleman, *Priests, Tongues, and Rites*, 84–87.

19. *Ep.* 10.1.

20. For one example of many, see Evagrius's use and explanation of the symbols "times" and "hours" in his *Ep. fidei* 7.24–25.

21. E.g., the symbols of the house in his fifth and sixth epistles.

22. MacCoull, "Prophecy of Charour," 50; ed. Lefort, *Oeuvres,* CSCO 159.100–104 (text), 160.100–108 (French translation). MacCoull's dating the prophecy to the late sixth to early seventh century does not, in my opinion, disallow parts of it — the "jabberwocky" — from deriving from the fifth century or earlier. Carroll's term has been used often by scholars studying similar ancient texts; see P. Miller, "In Praise of Nonsense," 487.

23. Bandt is preparing an English translation. The earliest edition (in Coptic) is Hebbelynck's *Mystères des lettres grecques*. The critical edition is Bandt, *Traktat.* I have identified only a handful of studies in the twentieth century that even refer to this text.

24. *On the Mystery of the Letters,* Prologue, 102.11–104.5, ed. Bandt, *Traktat,* my translation.

25. Ibid., 104.1bis–7bis.

26. Barsanuphius and John, *Ep.* 132–37b, reflect two different approaches to ascetic letter symbolism in mid-sixth-century Palestine: that of an anonymous monk who has a penchant for obscure letter symbols (not unlike Seba's) and that of the "Great Old Man," who counsels the monk to avoid such enigmas, preferring instead a letter symbolism that points away from the alphabet (*Ep.* 137b). Cf. Bitton-Ashkelony, "Counseling through Enigmas."

27. Callanan, "Rediscovered Text of Porphyry," esp. 223–25.

28. *Sefer Yetsira* 28, ed. and trans. Hayman, *Sefer Yesira*, 117.

29. *Sefer Yetsira* 30.

30. Cohn-Sherbok, "Alphabet."

31. Dornseiff, *Alphabet,* 84–89. Manuscripts: *CCAG,* 4:146–49 (dated 1162), 7:61 (fifteenth century), 7:161 (sixteenth century), 11.2:134 (fifteenth century). The first of these is attributed to Vettius Valens (fl. 2nd c. CE), whose astrology shows how easily the letters of the alphabet could fit the zodiac. See, e.g., the chart in his *Anthology* 5.6. Cf. also *Papyri Graecae magicae* 7.810–21, ed. Preisendanz and Henrichs, and examples in P. Miller, "In Praise of Nonsense," 497–99.

32. Irenaeus, *Against Heresies* 1.14.3. The word ἀλφάβητος appears in the titles of Herennius Philo and Cyranides (fl. late first or early second century) but these titles were almost certainly added well after the compositions.

33. *Ep.* 4.1, 4.6, 6.2, 6.11, 11b (= 1.2).

34. Philip Rousseau, "Successors of Pachomius," esp. 157.

35. Our temptation to equate all forms of divination might also be hasty. We do not know for what kinds of future events Pachomius's device was intended.

36. Trans. Hock, in Betz, *Greek Magical Papyri*, 143 (scores more examples passim).

37. On forcing into submission and cajoling, see, e.g., *Papyri Graecae magicae* 7.940–68, ed. Preisendanz and Henrichs. On new alphabets, see, e.g., 36 and 49 (diagrams reproduced in Betz, *Greek Magical Papyri*, 270, 273, 274, 283) and *CCAG* 10:87–96.

38. On the origin of illuminated initial letters, see Fanar, *Byzantine Illuminated Initial Letters*.

39. Rousseau, "Monasticism," ch. 25 in Cameron, Ward-Perkins, and Whitby, *Cambridge Ancient History,* 14.745.

40. Pachomius, *Precept* 139, ed. Lefort, *Oeuvres,* CSCO 159 (my translation). See also Bandt's introduction to *Traktat,* 85–87.

41. Ammon, *Letter of Ammon* 9.

42. *Vita Prima Graeca Pachomii* 99. See also the epigraphs to Pachomius's epistles.

43. Palladius, *Historia Lausiaca* 32.4–5.

44. See *Ep.* 9a, 9b, 11a, 11b. Cf. the general audience assumed in the epigraphs to *Ep.* 5, 7, 8, and 10.

45. *Vita Prima Graeca Pachomii* 99. If such a book was compiled, I doubt it was the collection of epistles we have today: numerous epistles don't have the code, and in length and content the collection can scarcely be described as a book.

46. Interestingly, he describes it as an aural, not written, phenomenon, so Pachomius's alphabet had utility in both spheres. See above, note 7.

47. Pachomius, *Briefe Pachoms,* Quecke's intro. (48) and appendix (111).

48. Jerome, *Pachomiana* praef. 9, trans. Veilleux, *Pachomian Koinonia*.

Chapter Two

Writing Rules and Quoting Scripture in Early Coptic Monastic Texts

JANET A. TIMBIE

In his book on Pachomius, Philip Rousseau remarked: "It is surprising in the face of such general allusions that there is so little quotation from scripture in the *Rules*."[1] Occasionally, in the Coptic texts of the Pachomian *Rules*, there are statements such as "Everything contrary to the standard of the scriptures, all these, the steward (ⲟⲓⲕⲟⲛⲟⲙⲟⲥ) shall judge."[2] The Pachomian *Rules*, as they survive in both Coptic and Latin, do not include explicit quotations from scripture in the rule itself, which is usually brief and specific:[3] "No man shall take shoes or anything else to oil [them], except the housemasters [ⲛ̄ⲣⲙ̄ⲛ̄ⲏⲓ] only."[4] Most of the surviving rules of the Pachomian communities are found in lists of specific orders, which can be stated either positively or negatively ("he shall" [ⲉϥⲉ] versus "he shall not" [ⲛ̄ⲛⲉϥ]). The Pachomian rules are preserved in manuscripts that were part of the White Monastery library, and none of these manuscripts were produced earlier than the eighth century, so it is likely that they were copied and recopied in the central monastery of the White Monastery Federation. The White Monastery, founded by Pcol and led for many years by Shenoute (leader from 385 to 465), preserved written rules in a different form and in the Pachomian form, but with the same lack of explicit scriptural quotation.[5] The *Canon* texts collected and written by Shenoute include many rules in this form: "Cursed be any, whether male or female, who undertake to sit near their neighbor, with a filthy desire in their heart."[6] Others are close to the Pachomian form: "No person [ⲣⲱⲙⲉ] who enters these congregations [ⲥⲩⲛⲁⲅⲱⲅⲏ] at any time to become a monk shall say, 'The work that I did in my home, I am going to do it here.'"[7] A little after this, Shenoute states, "The work for which each one came here [i.e., to the monastery], the scriptures and the books written for us tell us about it."[8] There is a "general allusion" to scripture here but no quotation in the rule.

Why is there no scriptural quotation in the Pachomian rules or in those of the White Monastery Federation? Where is the scriptural foundation of the rules presented in detail if it is not actually in the rules? I will begin with an examination of some texts from the Pachomians and Shenoute that bring explicit quotation of scripture into proximity with rules, thereby answering the second question just posed. Comparison of these texts suggests contact of some sort between the Pachomian *Koinonia* and the White Monastery Federation, which agrees with other evidence.[9] Yet just as the Pachomians labeled their enterprise a *koinonia* and Shenoute usually referred to the monastic *synagoge*, the characteristic form of their rules is different.[10] "No one shall" is found in both Pachomian and Shenoutean works, while "Cursed be" occurs only in White Monastery rules.[11] Some exploration of these contrasting biblical formulas may suggest a speculative "answer" to the first question: Why is there no quotation in the rules?

The *Rule of Horsiesius* is a Pachomian text that weaves together rules, arguments in favor of the rules, and quotations from scripture that support the arguments.[12] Johannes Leipoldt included this text in his publication of the works of Shenoute, but later work by L.-Th. Lefort and Armand Veilleux showed that it is a Pachomian text.[13] Vocabulary such as *Apa* without a name following and *koinonia* is Pachomian, but there is no support for attributing the text to Horsiesius (the third leader after Pachomius). The text, which is about seventeen pages long in the Lefort edition, is partially preserved in one White Monastery codex, with short excerpts or citations preserved in three other codices.[14]

In the *Rule of Horsiesius*, rules for behavior during typical monastic activities — prayer, food preparation, and farming — are followed by exhortation from the author and allusions to or quotations from scripture. The statement of a rule can be just as brief as in the Pachomian *Precepts*, but it is often embedded in a minisermon. For example, instructions on how to make the sign of the cross at the beginning of prayers are justified by an allusion to Ezekiel: "We must seal ourselves at the beginning of prayers with the seal of baptism; we must make the sign of the cross on our forehead [ⲧⲉϩⲛⲉ] as on the day we were baptized and as it is written in Ezekiel; we must not bring our hand down to our mouth or to our beard first and then take it up to our forehead."[15] This alludes to Ezekiel 9:4: "Make a sign on the forehead [Bohairic ⲧⲉϩⲛⲓ] of all the men who cry out and grieve over all the lawlessness."[16] The rule about precisely how to make the sign of the cross is supported by pointing to scripture that contains the key word *forehead* (ⲧⲉϩⲛⲉ in Sahidic), but the text is not quoted. In the same way, rules about rising in the night to recite scripture (ⲙⲉⲗⲉⲧⲁ) are supported with simple references to "the curse that the scriptures pronounce upon the sluggard."[17] The key word is *sluggard* (ⲡⲣⲉϥϫⲛⲁⲁⲩ), and several scriptural passages have the word. Proverbs 6:9 connects this word with lying in bed: "How long are you lying down, O sluggard [ⲣⲉϥϫⲛⲁⲁⲩ]? Are you going to rise from sleep now?" Sirach 22:2 condemns him by likening him to a disgusting object: "The sluggard [ⲣⲉϥϫⲛⲁⲁⲩ] is like filthy dung." Only Matthew 25:26–30 has something like a curse: "O evil and slothful [ⲣⲉϥϫⲛⲁⲁⲩ] servant. . . . Whoever has not, even what he has will be taken from him. Throw the useless servant into the outer darkness."[18]

But other sections weave together rules, exhortation, and explicit quotation. One section of the *Rule of Horsiesius* begins with a rule about the need for permission from the leader: "It is right not to sell or buy or do anything, from large to small, without the [permission] of the head of the monastery and . . . [text breaks off]."[19] It continues with rules about other things, "from small to large," about which care must be taken. And if all the leaders act properly, "no one is careless about anything so that it is ruined, since he understands that it [represents] the work of others or his work. . . . For nothing is hidden from God, up to the 2 coins of a widow and a cup of cold water. And one so great as Abraham said, ‘from a string to a shoe strap’ [Gen 14:23].”[20] The rule is supported by brief allusions and one explicit quotation referring to small things, though the message of the biblical story of Abraham seems different.[21] Abraham refuses to accept anything from the king of Sodom, “lest you say, ‘I made Abram rich.’” The key words—*coins* (ⲗⲉⲡⲧⲟⲛ), *cup* (ϫⲱ), *string* (ϩⲱⲥ), *strap* (ⲙⲟⲩⲥ)—are all sorts of small things that are the models for how to deal with the small and large concerns of the monastery.

A quotation from Ecclesiastes 10:19 governs behavior in the bakery: “Everyone who sits at the board, but also all of us involved in the work in the kneading room shall do everything, each one in the way it is assigned in obedience and without a lot of talking and calling out. And no one shall dare to laugh, so that the reproach of the scriptures does not apply to us, ‘It is for laughter that they make bread’ [Eccl 10:19].”[22] The rule and the scriptural passage both have the words *bread* (ⲟⲉⲓⲕ) and *laughter* (ⲥⲱⲃⲉ). Again, the surface meaning of the passage from Ecclesiastes seems different, since it suggests that bread, wine, and oil are prepared so that the living can enjoy (ⲉⲩⲫⲣⲁⲛⲉ) them.

In a more complicated passage, rules for meals are supported by three different quotations that stress equal treatment or only minor concessions in certain cases. “There must be no different meals for anyone who works in the kneading room . . . as the father of the *Koinonia*, *Apa*, ruled from the beginning. . . . Even though other fathers who came after him made rules allowing a different meal for the bakers, they did it just as Moses did it. As we hear in the gospel, ‘Because of your hardheartedness, Moses gave the means for you to cast off your wives . . .’ [Mt 19:8].”[23] The text continues and sets out a rule by which some who work a little harder (ⲟⲩⲕⲟⲩⲓ̄ ⲛ̄ϩⲓⲥⲉ ⲛ̄ϩⲟⲩⲟ) may have a different meal, but the brothers who are assigned to other tasks in the monastery are not allowed to eat with them. The meal should be an occasion for unity: “For the unity of the *Koinonia*, there is a single standard for everyone in accordance with the practice of the saints.”[24] The practice of David in sharing spoils among all the Israelites is then cited: “He did not obey those who were bad [ⲡⲟⲛⲏⲣⲉⲩⲉ] [and said], ‘We will not give to them’ [1 Sam 30:22].”[25] Next, a gospel parable (Mt 20:15, the laborers in the vineyard) is quoted, perhaps because it has a noun form (ⲡⲟⲛⲏⲣⲟⲥ) of the key word.[26] The *Rule of Horsiesius* material is organized around discussion of who gets special meals (ϭⲓⲛⲟⲩⲱⲙ), the importance of not being different (ϣⲓⲃⲉ) from other brothers, and the freedom of the leaders to make adjustments. The scriptural quotations reinforce these points.

The end of this section on meals, before the text turns to agriculture, contains an exhortation to do everything for the glory of God: whether meals (ϭⲓⲛⲟⲩⲱⲙ) or activities in the field (ⲥⲱϣⲉ) or the synaxis (ⲥⲟⲟⲩϩⲥ̄) or contacts with nonmonastics (ⲛ̄ⲕⲟⲥⲙⲓⲕⲟⲥ).[27] There is a Pauline allusion (1 Cor 10:31) in the phrase "simply, every deed and every word for (the) glory of God" and in other places in this section, but the explicit, marked quotations in this section are from the Pentateuch and from Old Testament historical books, connected by means of key words: *glory, blessing, bread, field.* "We know that the written word is true, 'Whoever glorifies me, I glorify him' [1 Sam 2:30]." Later, "he will bless our bread and our water, as it is written, 'If you keep the commands [ⲉⲛⲧⲟⲗⲏ] of the Lord your God, you will be blessed in the city and the field [ⲥⲱϣⲉ]' [Deut 28:1–3]." This quotation does not follow the scripture word for word, but it is marked as a direct quote, "as it is written," unlike the Pauline allusion.[28] The section concludes with another quotation: "If Christ dwells inside . . . then we will hear God with our ears, [He] who appeared saying, 'What you did not ask for, I gave you, glory and great wealth' [1 Kgs 3:13]."[29] This section on food preparation and consumption ends, and a heading ("the rules of farming") marks a new topic, which then proceeds with the same alternation of specific rules and general principles, though the text is fragmentary here and ends after a few pages.

The other major source of monastic rules in Coptic is the writings of Shenoute. From the time of his earliest known work, the so-called *Letter* 1, written before he became the leader of the community, up to the time when he can say, "More than a hundred years I have been in the desert," Shenoute combines fairly short rules, explanations of why the rules are necessary, and scriptural allusion and quotation in defense of the rules.[30] No completely unadorned list of rules — comparable to the Pachomian *Precepts*— survives that represents the White Monastery practice that began with Pcol in the mid-fourth century.[31] Pachomian texts were in the library of the White Monastery at some point, and Shenoute certainly spent years reading and studying in the monastery before becoming its leader. It is possible that Pachomian texts were already available in the White Monastery library during that period of study. Born around 348–49, and in the monastery by 371–72, Shenoute became the father of the monastery in 385.[32] Yet his earliest work, the first letter, cites some rules of the community in the distinctive, non-Pachomian, "Cursed is" form, suggesting that the form was the work of earlier leaders in the White Monastery lineage.[33] As Shenoute continues to write and preach to his community, he quotes rules with various verbal patterns, sometimes in the same form in which they appear in Pachomian texts. But as in the *Rule of Horsiesius*, the rules that Shenoute quotes lack scripture, while the sermonizing that follows the rule citation is based on scripture, either by allusion or by quotation.

Consider an example from Shenoute's earliest surviving work, which is letter 1. Stephen Emmel analyzed it to reconstruct the early career of Shenoute and thereby understand the transition from Pcol to Ebonh to Shenoute as leaders of the White Monastery.[34] However, it can also be studied as an example of the way Shenoute combines rules and scripture in an early attempt at original Coptic composition for the purpose of monastic instruction. The beginning of the text is lost, but two pages of material survive near the beginning that include fourteen rules, sometimes termed the Rule of Pcol.[35] A four-page gap follows, and then the letter continues with warnings and accusations in biblical language. As Emmel notes, most of the rules mentioned prohibit sexual contact, either implicitly or explicitly: "Cursed is any male who will lie upon a male as on a bed," compared to the less explicit "Cursed is any novice who shaves any novice without being assigned or in a place apart."[36] All fourteen rules have the "Cursed is" (ϥⲥϩⲟⲩⲟⲣⲧ̄) form. Two of these rules have the same content as the Pachomian rules against removing thorns from the foot of another monk and shaving another monk, but the form is different. Pachomian *Precepts* 96 and 97 limit thorn removal and shaving but are expressed in the form "No one shall" (ⲛ̄ⲛⲉⲗⲁⲁⲩ).[37] These fourteen early White Monastery rules lack any scriptural allusion or quotation in the rule itself. Shenoute quotes these rules because he claims direct knowledge that they have been broken, thereby putting the whole community at risk.

After a four-page gap, Shenoute alternates encouragement and warning as he applies scripture to the troubles in the monastery. If behavior changes, "God will 'save their soul from the sword' [Ps 21:20 LXX] of the enemy. He will save them from 'the hand of the dogs' [Ps 21:20]—meaning the demons. He will save their 'lowliness from the horn of the unicorn' [Ps 21:21]—meaning the devil."[38] Quotes from scripture are not signaled by "as it is written," or some other formula, but exact phrases from Psalm 21 are woven into the passage with slight alterations in number, mainly from singular to plural.[39]

When Shenoute turns to warning the community, the procedure is the same. Words and phrases from various Old Testament texts (and one Pauline passage) are woven together. "The Destroyer [1 Cor 10:10, alluding to Num 14:2–37, 16:1–35] came to you. The Destroyer [ⲣⲉϥⲧⲁⲕⲟ] ruled a part of you and he took it captive to a distant land. He tore down the wall of the enclosure of your community [ⲥⲩⲛⲁⲅⲱⲅⲏ]. He destroyed its choice bunches from the grape vine [Hos 2:12] and stripped its shoots [Isa 18:5]. He destroyed the fig trees, he destroyed the pomegranate trees and the apple trees and the olive trees [all trees mentioned in Joel 1:12]."[40] And so on to lambs and rams. This vocabulary appears in various prophetic texts, and, as noted in parentheses, some of the biblical texts have the exact word or combination of words that is found in Shenoute.[41] *The Destroyer* is a term that Paul uses, and he connects it to the fate of some Israelites—as described in Numbers 14 and 16 (where the group is labeled ⲥⲩⲛⲁⲅⲱⲅⲏ)—who complained and were destroyed: "Do not grumble as some of them grumbled and perished due to the destroyer [ⲡⲉϣⲁϥⲧⲁⲕⲟ] [1 Cor 10:10]."[42] At the end of this section, Shenoute paraphrases Isaiah 1:9 and states: "For unless a remnant [ϣⲱϫⲡ] is among us due to the Lord, we will become like Sodom and resemble Gomorra." In Sahidic manuscripts of Isaiah, the prophet states: "Unless the Lord Sabaoth left [ϣⲱϫⲡ] a seed for us, we became like Sodom and resembled Gomorrah."[43] The verb *leave* in Isaiah becomes the noun form *remnant* in Shenoute, and the past tense *became* is future *will become.* This is how Shenoute applies scripture to specific conditions in his community, and it is a very early example of a technique that he uses in all his later writing: changing the number, gender, tense, and part of speech to adapt the scripture to the context.[44] He goes on to adapt Jeremiah 6:11: "I increased my wrath [and] I restrained it, says the Lord."[45] Shenoute then paraphrases and pulls out bits and pieces of Jeremiah 6:11–12 in the next two pages of his letter.[46] All of this eventually leads back to the rules that were quoted near the beginning of the letter: speaking in the voice of a prophet, on behalf of the Lord, "I will pour out my wrath and my anger on all males who sleep with each other as in the lawlessness of Sodom."[47] Shenoute begins this letter by quoting rules, including some about "sins of Sodom," then moves to quote a prophetic warning about Sodom (Isa 1:9) and details about the wrath of punishment (Jer 6:11) before condemning specific sexual sins being committed in the monastery in violation of the rules. His exegesis of Jeremiah 6:11–12 is meant to counter the exegesis of others in the community who only noted that the Lord said, "I restrained my wrath" and so felt safe to continue their activities.[48] At this point in the history of the White Monastery, Shenoute's message must have resonated with other monks, because he became the third leader not long after this letter was written.[49]

In mid- and late-career works, Shenoute continues the same practice of quoting rules, quoting scripture and showing how the scripture applies to the practice of the monastery.[50] He often quotes — and ridicules — the arguments of monks who disagree with him about both rules and scripture. In *You, God the Eternal*, from book 5 of the *Canons,* Shenoute states the rule against name-calling: "If any man is found among us, or a woman, calling their brothers, in laughter or mockery, blind or deaf or liar or stuck-up . . . or any other name like this at all, they shall be punished. . . . [People in] our way of life restrain their lips, knowing that those who restrain their mouth and their tongue 'guard their soul' [Prov 13:3]. But 'the lips of the fool will bring him evils; his harsh mouth summons death. The mouth of the fool is destruction for him, and his lips are a trap for his soul' [Prov 18:6–7]."[51] He supports the rule with explicit quotes from Proverbs. The gospel warning against name-calling (Mt 5:22, "Whoever says 'fool' is liable to the Gehenna of fire") is not mentioned.

Later in this text, a long series of rules regulating visits by monks or nuns to the sick or dying (either inside or outside the monasteries) is quoted. For example, "No woman among you shall go at any time to ask about those to whom she is related by blood, whether they are sick or dying."[52] This is followed by many rules for conduct at burials. Some complain about the rules ("Who wrote this?"), but Shenoute responds with relevant scriptural texts that mention actions undertaken with or without permission: "You will find it written in [the papyrus sheets] that the Word of God condemns those 'who run without being sent' [Jer 23:23] and blesses 'those who preach the good' [Rom 10:15] when the Lord sends them."[53] "Papyrus sheets" (ⲭⲁⲣⲧⲏⲥ) seems to refer to written records containing rules that guide the monastery. Shenoute continually defends the monastery's practices against complaints that such rules are not scriptural or not part of monastic tradition. Opponents say, "Where does what is written speak in these words or about these practices?"[54]

In *God Who Alone Is True*, book 9 of the *Canons*, written later in life, Shenoute states rules for eating, using the "No one shall" pattern.[55] "No person among us [ⲛ̄ⲛⲉⲣⲱⲙⲉ ϩⲣⲁⲓ ⲛ̄ϩⲏⲧⲛ̄] shall scorn anything he is going to eat or [that] his stomach does not want [to eat], though all the brothers eat it."[56] This is a rule against complaining about the food while others are eating it without complaint. Only the sick are allowed to refuse food. Others claim to be sick but still eat their fill with continual complaints. Other rules in this text are formulated as conditional sentences: "If some people [ⲉⲩϣⲁⲛ] in these communities say at any time, 'We shall not comply with the rules that are set down for us,' whether it is a man or a woman, they shall be cast out [ⲉⲩⲛⲁⲛⲟϫⲟⲩ] from among us."[57] Shenoute goes on to say that leaders who neglect to have new monks swear to accept the rule are even worse than those who refuse to comply. Such leaders should not keep their office, since "they are even blinder, though they are leading the blind."[58] The Gospel passage about the blind leading the blind (Mt 15:14) is adapted to provide rhetorical support, but scripture is not offered as the reason for the rule.

In another passage from the same *Canon* text, a rule is connected to scripture with a key word: *ask* or *seek* (ϣⲓⲛⲉ). The point of the rule is that it is necessary to ask permission or get authorization first from monastic authorities. "If someone is found asking those who work at a craft for something, either to take something or [that they] make it [for them], they shall be punished, . . . [since] they did not ask [ϣⲓⲛⲉ] first, according to the rules set down for us, to ask [ϣⲓⲛⲉ] about every matter like this. . . . For from the fathers of our fathers, and from the beginning of the age until now, every benefit and every advantage and every correction is in asking, according to the scriptures."[59] Shenoute does not spell out which scriptural advice about asking he has in mind. The key word *ask* (ϣⲓⲛⲉ) is found in Gospel statements ("Ask and it shall be given to you,"

Lk 11:9, Mt 7:7) and in texts such as Psalm 118:100 LXX ("Since I asked about your rules [ⲉⲛⲧⲟⲗⲏ] I learned more than elders") and Proverbs 18:15 ("The ears of the wise ask for a reminder").[60] The same conditional form (ⲉⲣϣⲁⲛ, ⲉⲩϣⲁⲛ) is found in sections of the *Rule of Horsiesius* related to asking: "If the need arises for someone to ask his neighbor a question, it is fitting that he ask him quietly, without calling out."[61]

The key words *desire/wish* (ⲟⲩⲱϣ) and *empty/vain* (ϣⲟⲩⲉⲓⲧ) connect another rule to scripture in *God Who Alone Is True*. "If someone who governs these communities at any time moves a man from place to place or from job to job because of [the man's] wish [ⲟⲩⲱϣ] for it, or even his hate for it, it is a sin for him. . . . His action will be examined, since the wish of the man is vain [ϣⲟⲩⲉⲓⲧ], just as his plans [ⲙⲟⲕⲙⲉⲕ] are also, according to the scriptures."[62] Shenoute may have several passages from Psalms and Ecclesiastes in mind, all linked by the key words. The theme of vanity or emptiness recurs in Ecclesiastes: "My heart saw everything. . . . Behold even this is a [mere] wish [ⲟⲩⲱϣ] of spirit. [Eccl 1:17]. . . . Behold even this is empty [ϣⲟⲩⲉⲓⲧ] [Eccl 2:1]." The key words *wish/desire* (ⲟⲩⲱϣ) and *empty/vain* (ϣⲟⲩⲉⲓⲧ) are combined in Ecclesiastes 2:11: "Behold, all is empty and a [mere] wish of spirit." Psalm 93:11 connects the key terms *plans* (ⲙⲟⲕⲙⲉⲕ) and *empty* (ϣⲟⲩⲉⲓⲧ): "The Lord knows the plans [ⲙⲟⲕⲙⲉⲕ] of men; they are empty [ϣⲟⲩⲉⲓⲧ]."[63] The rule that forbids monastic leaders from catering to the whims of monks when assigning them to residences or jobs is supported by reference to a repeated message of scripture — human plans and wishes are worthless — rather than by explicit quotation of a single passage.

An untitled work, A22 in book 3 of the *Canons*, is certainly from the latest period of Shenoute's career.[64] The surviving material from A22 begins with his account of how he prays and confesses his sins, and then he continues with an expression of gratitude: "I believe that He is merciful to me through your prayers, brothers."[65] He then adds a warning to those belonging to another group of monks, who are disobedient: "It is those that He will burn in unquenchable fire."[66] In light of this looming threat to some monks, Shenoute announces a change in his daily life: "I told you, 'I want to remain in my house repenting for all the days of my life.' But now, I tell you that I want to remain among my brothers . . . so we can benefit each other, since this is the will of God and this is the will of my fathers, [for] more than a hundred years [that] I am living in the desert."[67] Shenoute may be writing at a time when he stopped living in a hermit's cell on the border of the Federation and returned to the main monastery, late in his life.[68] It was always "the will of God" that he and other monks assist each other, but now Shenoute states that he will work for this from the main house. He continues with words of encouragement to those who are "working out their salvation" and warnings to those "disobedient in everything."[69] Encouragement alternates with warning; each type of behavior is summed up as an example of circumcision or uncircumcision. "Those always . . . in disobedience . . . it is they who are uncircumcised in their heart and their ears, according to the scriptures."[70] He may be alluding to Acts 7:51 (uncircumcised in heart and ears), as well as Leviticus 26:41 (uncircumcised heart) and Jeremiah 6:10 (uncircumcised ears). At this point, A22 shifts to quotation of specific rules in the "Cursed is" form: "Cursed is a man or woman among us who will wash their feet wrongly due to [a feeling of] lust, or wash secretly in water, or anoint them secretly in oil, without asking the Eldest first for us [men], or without asking the Eldest Woman for you [women]."[71] Rules are individually labeled as "canon" (ⲕⲁⲛⲱⲛ) in one manuscript of book 3 of the *Canons* (which includes text A22), and each occurrence of the "Cursed is" (ϥⲥϩⲟⲩⲟⲣⲧ) formula is numbered in the margin of the same manuscript.[72] Since this formula appeared in the earliest works of Shenoute, written before he became the leader, it seems that it is an inherited pattern that continued in use while Shenoute was leader. But it is likely that the content of the rules grew and changed over the very long period of his leadership, from 385 to 465.

After several pages of rules in A22 in the form "Cursed is the man or woman who," the pattern changes to "Whoever shall do . . . he shall be cursed." For example, "Whoever will shave himself or those who will shave a person among us, either male or female, without being ordered, shall be cursed since they transgressed the rules that our fathers appointed for us."[73] The rule against shaving another person was quoted by Shenoute in *Letter* 1 — the earliest text — in the shorter "Cursed is" form.[74] So it is a clear example of a rule "that our fathers appointed for us," now being stated in A22. In the midst of the series of curse rules, general scriptural allusions are offered to support or explain the rule. If a time comes when "sin is in power over those who dwell in this place [i.e., the monastery]," the monk may flee and go to some other place in the desert, "in the place the Lord God chose for him, according to the scriptures," without being subject to the curses.[75] Shenoute adapts the phrase that is often repeated in Deuteronomy, "the place which the Lord your God shall choose," in directions to the people of Israel.[76] Monks who join the community and do not give up all their possessions "shall be cursed" since they did not "take up their cross," using the Gospel formula (Mt 10:38, 16:24, etc.). Similarly, those who join and give up their possessions, then change their minds and want to regain their possessions, "shall be cursed," since they are like Ananias and Sapphira, Cain, and others, "with whom the Lord was not pleased."[77] Both Old Testament and New Testament stories are cited to support the monastic rule, but in a shorthand fashion, without extended, explicit quotation.

Later in text A22, Shenoute quotes a few more rules in the "Cursed is" form: for example, "Cursed is the one who says, creating a disturbance, 'I saw in a dream that so-and-so and so-and-so were destroying themselves in every evil deed,' whether [it is] a man or woman."[78] Such behavior will lead God to become angry and turn "his face away angrily."[79] God is compared to a "just man who turned to leave some people because of their evil deeds. According to the prophet, 'Who will give me a distant dwelling in the desert, so that I can leave this people behind and separate from them?' [Jer 9:2]."[80] In this passage, Jeremiah is quoted by Shenoute and reinterpreted to provide a warning against the consequences of sin in the monastery. God will "turn to leave."[81] Shenoute then turns from citing rules to explaining important biblical sayings that seem to be in conflict, ending with advice on problems posed by individuals in the women's community and with a warning: "I sent the Eldest to you," presumably to deal with the disciplinary problem on orders from Shenoute.[82] As Emmel notes, text A22 should probably be divided into more than one work, but there is no manuscript evidence to indicate how this might be done.[83] However, it is clear that A22—a very late work of Shenoute—contains rules in the "Cursed is" form known from his earliest works, as well as some in the longer "If someone does such-and-such, he shall be cursed" pattern. Scripture is introduced to support the rules by means of allusion to basic principles (e.g., "take up their cross"), but there is only a small amount of explicit scriptural quotation. Also, as in the early works, passages from the prophets are an important part of this limited set of quotations.[84]

In both the Pachomian *Koinonia* and the White Monastery Federation, the monastic rules are fairly short and concise. The *Rule of Horsiesius* contains some of the same rules as the surviving Coptic texts of the Pachomian *Precepts*, but the rule is sometimes supported by a brief word of exhortation and quotes from scripture in the *Rule of Horsiesius*. Pachomian *Precept* 116 states, "No man shall speak while kneading in the evening, nor [shall] those at the baking or at the board in the morning. Rather they shall recite together until they finish. If they need anything, they shall not speak but they shall knock for a signal."[85] While some of the Pachomian *Precepts* and *Precepts and Institutes* are considerably longer, they have the same "do this" structure and lack of rhetorical and scriptural support.[86] In the *Rule of Horsiesius*, on the other hand, a paragraph sets out the general principles for communal bread making: all work at this task, while reciting scripture (ⲉⲛⲙⲉⲗⲉⲧⲁ ⲙ̄ⲡϣⲁϫⲉ ⲙ̄ⲡⲛⲟⲩⲧⲉ); everyone does his appointed task without many words or calling out (ⲭⲱⲣⲓⲥ ⲣ̄ϩⲁϩ ⲛ̄ϣⲁϫⲉ ϩⲓⲱϣ ⲉⲃⲟⲗ); no one dares to laugh during this work so that the reproach of the scriptures will not apply to them, "They make bread while laughing" (Eccl 10:19).[87] The *Rule of Horsiesius* grounds the practice of the *Koinonia* in scripture.

At the White Monastery, bare lists of rules are lacking, since nearly all evidence comes from the *Canons* of Shenoute, in which he combines orders about specific problems with more general words of warning and encouragement. But Shenoute's earliest writings, which predate his term as leader, quote the existing rules in a short form: "Cursed is a novice who will take a thorn from the foot of another novice without being assigned."[88] His later works combine similar rule quotation with sermon-like discussion that includes scripture quotes, as in the section of book 5 of the *Canons* (*You, God the Eternal*) discussed above, in which rules for burial of monks are supported by quotes from Jeremiah and Romans.[89] Perhaps Shenoute's predecessors as head of the White Monastery Federation compiled lists of rules along the lines of the Pachomian *Precepts*, and then Shenoute made them the basis for *Canon* texts that are closer in style to the *Rule of Horsiesius*.

As noted above, the Coptic Pachomian texts, including rules, were preserved in White Monastery manuscripts. There is other evidence that monks in the White Monastery read Pachomian rules in a form close to that of the later manuscript copies of Pachomian material. In book 8 of the *Canons*, in a work titled *So Listen*, Shenoute argues with monks who object to one of the monastic rules. Book 8 contains works written in Shenoute's later life, when he lived in an isolated cell and was ill for long periods of time.[90] In *So Listen*, Shenoute argues with opponents in the monastery who try to undermine a rule with heavy sarcasm: "You laugh at the saying that our fathers — of whom you are not worthy — spoke, [by saying] 'Do not speak in the dark. Surely they also said, "Do not speak in the light"?' . . . O scornful man who despises those with whom God made a covenant, [such as] Pachomius the Great, the father of myriads of disciples!"[91] These opponents know the rule against nighttime conversation in the cell and have also learned that it was traced back to Pachomius. In the *Precepts* it is stated as "None shall speak together in the dark."[92] While the Pachomian text has the usual "no one shall" (ⲛ̄ⲛ̄ⲉⲗⲁⲁⲩ), the White Monastery monks quote this as a negative imperative, "do not" (ⲙⲡ̄ⲣ̄).

Therefore, there is evidence in the works of Shenoute for both direct literary influence and general awareness of continuity in the cenobitic enterprise between the Pachomian *Koinonia* and the White Monastery Federation. Another work, which is not part of the written *corpus* of Shenoute and is known as the *Encomium on Pcol*, praises an early, unnamed leader (not Pcol) of the White Monastery and identifies him as an heir to the monastic tradition of Pachomius.[93] This unnamed leader strengthens the monastic community by building workshops and planting trees.[94] Eventually the community reaches thirty or more members, and the leader has them accept a written document (ϩⲟⲙⲟⲗⲟⲅⲓⲁ) containing the rules of "Apa Pcol and those after him."[95] This covenant (ⲇⲓⲁⲑⲏⲕⲏ) "exists today in the papyrus documents [ⲭⲁⲣⲧⲏⲥ]."[96] After the oath ceremony, the leader addresses the monks and refers to "this perfect man, on whose holy foundation we form ourselves today, namely, our father Pcol."[97] Pcol did not promote different rules but simply put more rules "beside" (ⲡⲁⲣⲁ) those that the founding fathers, "namely, Pachom and those after him," wrote.[98] Pcol did not reject earlier practice but added good elements to it; and in the same way, "Moses built an ark for the Lord and a tent in the desert made of skins . . . but Solomon . . ."[99] The text breaks off here, but the point is likely that Solomon added precious decorations to the ark and built the temple, just as Pcol added to monastic tradition. The *Encomium* quotes the leader's praise of earlier monks "who began a new work, namely the communal life [ⲡⲃⲓⲟⲥ ⲛ̄ⲕⲟⲓⲛⲱⲛⲓⲁ], since there were not yet many monks in the land of Egypt."[100] But the leader does not label his group as a *koinonia*, in the Pachomian manner; rather, the text refers to the leader's *synagoge*, as in the White Monastery works of Shenoute.[101] The *Encomium* shows the same preference for Old Testament imagery and vocabulary in another incident. At the beginning of the fragmentary text, the leader is encouraging the monks and so their numbers are increasing. "Who is it who saw them in their rank [ⲧⲁⲝⲓⲥ] without crying out, 'This is the encampment [ⲡⲁⲣⲉⲙⲃⲟⲗⲏ] of God' [Gen 32:1]!"[102] The *Encomium* is important evidence that is separate from the Shenoutean *corpus* but also points to influence and continuity between the Pachomian *Koinonia* and the White Monastery Federation.

In the earliest work of Shenoute, the first letter, a rule is quoted that has exactly the same content as a Pachomian precept: compare "Cursed [ϥⲥϩⲟⲩⲟⲣⲧ̄] is any novice who shaves any novice without being assigned" (in the first letter) to "No man shall [ⲛ̄ⲛⲉⲣⲱⲙⲉ] shave a man unless he is ordered" (*Precepts* 96).[103] The content — and thus the behavior being controlled, close contact between males in the monastery — is the same, but the verbal construction is different. The phrase "cursed is" uses a Coptic stative form, while "no one shall" or the positive "he shall" uses an optative construction.[104] The same constructions are found in Coptic versions of the Septuagint, translating the curses of Deuteronomy and the Ten Commandments in Exodus. "Cursed is he who sleeps with the wife of his father" (ϥⲥϩⲟⲩⲟⲣⲧ̄ ⲛϫⲉⲫⲏⲉⲧⲛⲁⲉⲛⲕⲟⲧ ⲛⲉⲙⲧⲥϩⲓⲙⲓ ⲙ̄ⲡⲉϥⲓⲱⲧ [Deut 27:20]).[105] Deuteronomy 27:15–26 has a series of curses in this stative verbal pattern, all followed by an affirmation in the optative, "All the people shall say, 'So be it.'"[106] Exodus 20:4 states, "You shall not make for yourself any idol or image" (ⲙ̄ⲛⲉⲕⲑⲁⲙⲓⲟ ⲛⲁⲕ ⲛ̄ⲟⲩⲓⲇⲱⲗⲟⲛ ⲟⲩⲇⲉ ⲥⲙⲟⲧ ⲛⲓⲃⲉⲛ) in a negative optative construction.[107] Both types of rules use the language of the Coptic translation of the Bible and use constructions that are prominent in the Pentateuch (and also used occasionally in the Gospels and Paul when scriptural precedents are cited).[108] Therefore, while there is no scripture in the rules, the rules from both the

Koinonia and the White Monastery sound like scripture and can be read as additions to the commandments, blessings, and curses in the Coptic version of the Pentateuch. This is a possible answer to the first question posed in this essay: Why is there no scripture in the rules? Perhaps the rules are a "bible" for a monastic community that understands itself as carrying on the task of the people of Israel in the wilderness.[109]

The preference in the rules for language that imitates the Pentateuch fits with the preference in the *Rule of Horsiesius* and the *Canons* of Shenoute for Old Testament citations and allusions when rules are explained and promoted. The major difference between *Koinonia* and White Monastery terminology and catechesis is the presence of "curse" rules in the White Monastery texts.[110] And these are found in the earliest work of Shenoute and thus are traceable to those who led the White Monastery before him. The more that connections of literary and personal influence between the Pachomians and the White Monastery become clear, the more it is possible to focus on new elements introduced by Pcol or his successors, including Shenoute. Perhaps Pcol created the curse rule form to supplement material inherited from the *Koinonia* [and thereby to strengthen his concept of the new White Monastery organization: "This is the encampment [ⲡⲁⲣⲉⲙⲃⲟⲗⲏ] of God!"[111]

NOTES

1. Rousseau, *Pachomius,* 101 n. 70.

2. *Precepts and Institutes* 10, ed. Lefort, *Oeuvres,* CSCO 159.34; see also the positive side of this, "Stay within the measure of the scriptures" (CSCO 159.33; ⲛⲉⲛⲧⲁⲩⲁϩⲉⲣⲁⲧⲟⲩ ϩⲙ̄ⲡϣⲓ ⲛ̄ⲛⲉⲅⲣⲁⲫⲏ).

3. Boon, *Pachomiana Latina*. Adalbert de Vogüé can point to only one possible scriptural allusion in Jerome's Latin text of the Pachomian rules in "Deux réminiscences scripturaires."

4. *Precepts* 104, ed. Lefort, *Oeuvres,* CSCO 159.32.

5. B. Layton, "Rules, Patterns." Layton reviews the chronology of Shenoute as well as the manuscript evidence for White Monastery rules. See also B. Layton, "Ancient Rules."

6. Translation is slightly altered from that of B. Layton, "Rules, Patterns," 62 n. 96. Layton also states (46) that the surviving 1,300 pages of the *Canons* contain five hundred rules, probably representing a larger original number. The

Coptic text is in *Canons*, bk. 3, YA 316, ed. Leipoldt, *Sinuthii archimandritae vita,* CSCO 73.124. Subsequent citations of the *Canons* are by manuscript, manuscript page, and published edition's volume and page numbers; see Emmel, *Shenoute's Literary Corpus*, 1:111–234, for a description of the *Canon* volumes and the manuscript terminology. Translations are my own.

7. *Canons,* FM 188, ed. Leipoldt, *Sinuthii archimandritae vita,* CSCO 73.163. See also B. Layton, "Rules, Patterns," 56 n. 69, for a slightly different translation.

8. *Canons,* FM 188, ed. Leipoldt, *Sinuthii archimandritae vita,* CSCO 73.163.

9. See Emmel, *Shenoute's Literary Corpus*, CSCO 599.6–13, on the history of the White Monastery, and also Stephen Emmel, "Shenoute the Monk."

10. B. Layton, "Social Structure," 28 n. 20, notes passages in the *Canons* where Shenoute refers to the community as a *koinonia*.

11. Keil, "Zur Form der Regel," offers a brief analysis of the rule forms in Shenoute's work. B. Layton, "Rules, Patterns," 60–63, discusses the process of entry into the monastery with illustrations from curse rules and in his "Ancient Rules," 78–79, reviews all the basic rule language used in Shenoute.

12. *Rule of Horsiesius*, ed. Lefort, *Oeuvres,* CSCO 159.82–99 (Coptic text), CSCO 160.81–99 (French translation). English translation appears in Veilleux, *Pachomian Koinonia*, CS 46.197–220.

13. Published by Leipoldt in *Sinuthii archimandritae vita,* CSCO 73.129–53, then discussed by Lefort in *Oeuvres*, CSCO 159.xxii–xxx, and by Veilleux in *Pachomian Koinonia,* CS 46.11–13.

14. See Lefort's intro. to *Oeuvres*, CSCO 159.xxii–xxx, for these details.

15. *Rule of Horsiesius,* ed. Lefort, *Oeuvres,* CSCO 159.84, trans. Veilleux, *Pachomian Koinonia*, CS 46.199].

16. This passage in Ezekiel in not preserved in Sahidic. For a guide to major published Bohairic biblical texts, see bibliography in Shisha-Halevy, *Coptic Encyclopedia*, s.v. "Bohairic."

17. *Rule of Horsiesius*, ed. Lefort, *Oeuvres,* CSCO 159.86–87.

18. For Prov 6:9 and Sir 22:2 in Sahidic, see Horner, *Coptic Version . . . Southern Dialect;* for Mt 25:26–30, see Thompson, *Coptic (Sahidic) Version*.

19. *Rule of Horsiesius*, ed. Lefort, *Oeuvres,* CSCO 159.90; head of the monastery (ⲡⲣⲱⲙⲉ ⲛ̄ⲧⲥⲟⲟⲩϩⲥ̄) refers to the leader of one of the affiliated monasteries (such as Tabennesi) in the *Koinonia*.

20. Ibid., with allusions to Lk 21:12 and Mt 10:42 and quotation of Gen 14:23.

21. The same passage (Gen 14:23) is used in *Testament of Horsiesius* 21 (see Veilleux, *Pachomian Koinonia,* CS 47.186) and Pachomius, *Catechesis* 1.53 (see Veilleux, *Pachomian Koinonia,* CS 47.37), to support another message: the monk should not crave possessions.

22. *Rule of Horsiesius,* ed. Lefort, *Oeuvres,* CSCO 159.92. See Eccl 10:19 in Sahidic in Ciasca, *Sacrorum Bibliorum Fragmenta,* 2:211, "Men prepare bread for laughter, and wine and oil so that the living should rejoice."

23. *Rule of Horsiesius*, ed. Lefort, *Oeuvres,* CSCO 159.95.

24. Ibid., CSCO 159.95.

25. Ibid., CSCO 159.95–96.

26. Ibid., CSCO 159.96.

27. Ibid., CSCO 159.97; the summary continues on 98.

28. Ibid., CSCO 159.97.

29. Ibid., CSCO 159.98.

30. YA 295, ed. Leipoldt, *Sinuthii archimandritae vita,* CSCO 73.115. The chronology of Shenoute is reviewed in Emmel, *Literary Corpus*, CSCO 599.6–14, and in Emmel's article, "Shenoute the Monk." B. Layton, "Ancient Rules," 77–78, briefly summarizes the occasions in the White Monastery when rules would be expounded.

31. Emmel, "Shenoute the Monk," 157.

32. Termed "the Father of These Congregations"; see Layton, "Rules, Patterns," 54.

33. See discussion in Emmel, "Shenoute the Monk," 164. B. Layton, "Rules, Patterns," 67, also states that Shenoute was not the author of all the rules preserved in the *Canons*, and in "Ancient Rules," 79, suggests that Shenoute had access to an earlier rule book written in the curse form.

34. Emmel, "Shenoute the Monk," 155–58.

35. XC 7–8, unpublished manuscript described in Emmel, *Literary Corpus*, CSCO 599.456. The label "rule of Pcol" is convenient as long as we remember that it is shorthand for White Monastery rules that predated Shenoute's leadership. Thus far, they cannot be tied to the period of Pcol's leadership. See also Keil, "Zur Form der Regel."

36. Coptic text in Emmel, "Shenoute the Monk," 164–65 nn. 38, 40; my translation.

37. Emmel, "Shenoute the Monk," 164.

38. XC 13, ed. Leipoldt, *Sinuthii archimandritae vita,* CSCO 42.195.

39. This is standard practice in Shenoute; see Timbie, "Non-canonical Scriptural Citation."

40. XC 13–14, ed. Leipoldt, *Sinuthii archimandritae vita,* CSCO 42.195–96.

41. For the location of Sahidic versions of biblical texts, see Schüssler, *Biblia Coptica*. Other dialects preserve biblical texts also, and for these a helpful guide is Atiya, *Coptic Encyclopedia*.

42. Horner, *Coptic Version . . . Southern Dialect*, 1 Cor 10:10; note the use of substantivized relative here, compared to the noun ⲡⲣⲉϥⲧⲁⲕⲟ in Shenoute. Bohairic NT (Horner, *Coptic Version . . . Northern Dialect*) has ⲡⲓⲣⲉϥⲧⲁⲕⲟ, and several Greek manuscripts of the NT have a noun for *destroyer.*

43. XC 14, ed. Leipoldt, *Sinuthii archimandritae vita,* CSCO 42.196. Compare "ⲛⲥⲁⲃⲏⲗ ⲅⲁⲣ ϫⲉϥϣⲟⲟⲡ ⲛϩⲏⲧⲛ ⲛϭⲓⲟⲩϣⲱϫⲡ ⲉⲃⲟⲗ ϩⲓⲧⲙⲡϫⲟⲉⲓⲥ, ⲛⲉⲛⲛⲁϣⲱⲡⲉ ⲛⲑⲉ ⲛⲥⲟⲗⲟⲙⲁ ⲁⲩⲱ ⲛⲧⲛⲉⲓⲛⲉ ⲛⲅⲟⲙⲟⲣⲣⲁ" in Shenoute to a Sahidic text of Isa 1:9, "ⲁⲩⲱ ⲛ̄ⲥⲁⲃⲏⲗ ϫⲉ ⲁⲡϫⲟⲉⲓⲥ ⲥⲁⲃⲁⲱⲑ ϣⲱϫⲡ̄ ⲛⲁⲛ ⲛ̄ⲟⲩⲥⲡⲉⲣⲙⲁ ⲉϣϫⲉ ⲁⲛϣⲱⲡⲉ ⲛ̄ⲑⲉ ⲛ̄ⲥⲟⲗⲟⲙⲁ ⲁⲩⲱ ⲁⲛⲉⲓⲛⲉ ⲛ̄ⲅⲟⲙⲟⲣⲣⲁ." See Ciasca, *Sacrorum bibliorum fragmenta*, 2:219, for text. Emmel, "Shenoute the Monk," 166, believes that this is Shenoute's own translation from the Greek. Since it is a paraphrase, it seems just as likely to be based on the Coptic Bible.

44. Timbie, "Non-canonical Scriptural Citation," 632.

45. XC 15, ed. Leipoldt, *Sinuthii archimandritae vita,* CSCO 42.196. No Sahidic version of this part of Jeremiah survives, but the Bohairic is structurally similar to the language of Shenoute while using distinctive Bohairic vocabulary.

46. XC 14–16, ed. Leipoldt, *Sinuthii archimandritae vita,* CSCO 42.196–97. The words and phrases (*pour out, wrath, children, assembly,* etc.) are repeated and put in different contexts, with many rhetorical questions and references to the "prophet" and "our father, Jeremiah."

47. XC 16, ed. Leipoldt, *Sinuthii archimandritae vita*, CSCO 42.198.

48. XC 14, ed. Leipoldt, *Sinuthii archimandritae vita,* CSCO 42.196.

49. See Schroeder, *Monastic Bodies*, 30–53, on the events that resulted in Shenoute's becoming leader.

50. See Emmel, *Literary Corpus,* CSCO 600.553–58, on chronological order of the nine books of the *Canons*, and 794–95 on the role of Shenoute in assembling the *Canons.*

51. XS 351–52, ed. Leipoldt, *Sinuthii archimandritae vita,* CSCO 73.59. Shenoute follows the Sahidic text of Proverbs quite closely.

52. XS 354, ed. Leipoldt, *Sinuthii archimandritae vita*, CSCO 73.61.

53. XS 360, ed. Leipoldt, *Sinuthii archimandritae vita,* CSCO 73.64.

54. Ibid.

55. See Emmel, *Literary Corpus*, CSCO 599.217–33, 600.600–601, for brief descriptions of this text and of the surviving manuscripts of bk. 9 of the *Canons*. It can be placed fairly late in Shenoute's life by an apparent reference to his trip to the Council of Ephesus in 431.

56. DF 49, ed. Leipoldt, *Sinuthii archimandritae vita,* CSCO 73.85.

57. DF 181, ed. Leipoldt, *Sinuthii archimandritae vita*, CSCO 73.101. Many rules in the *Rule of Horsiesius* begin with the same conditional construction; see Lefort, *Oeuvres,* CSCO 159.84–85, for several examples.

58. DF 181, ed. Leipoldt, *Sinuthii archimandritae vita,* CSCO 73.101.

59. FM 191, ed. Leipoldt, *Sinuthii archimandritae vita*, CSCO 73.165.

60. See also Ps 104:4 and Prov 8:17, 15:14, in Sahidic; see Schüssler, *Biblia Coptica,* for references.

61. *Rule of Horsiesius*, ed. Lefort, *Oeuvres,* CSCO 159.93, has several examples.

62. FM 190, ed. Leipoldt, *Sinuthii archimandritae vita,* CSCO 73.164.

63. Sahidic text reference in Schüssler, *Biblia Coptica*.

64. Emmel, *Literary Corpus*, CSCO 600.556, 572.

65. YA 293, ed. Leipoldt, *Sinuthii archimandritae vita,* CSCO 73.114.

66. YA 295, ed. Leipoldt, *Sinuthii archimandritae vita*, CSCO 73.115.

67. Ibid.

68. See biographical summary in Emmel, *Literary Corpus*, CSCO 599.6–14.

69. YA 296, ed. Leipoldt, *Sinuthii archimandritae vita,* CSCO 73.116.

70. YA 300, ed. Leipoldt, *Sinuthii archimandritae vita*, CSCO 73.118.

71. YA 303, ed. Leipoldt, *Sinuthii archimandritae vita*, CSCO 73.118–19.

72. Emmel, *Literary Corpus*, CSCO 600.571; B. Layton, "Ancient Rules," 79.

73. YA 314, ed. Leipoldt, *Sinuthii archimandritae vita,* CSCO 73.123.

74. Since this rule is also found in the Pachomian *Precepts* 97, ed. Lefort, *Oeuvres,* CSCO 159.31, in the "no one shall" form, Shenoute may have many monastic "fathers" in mind.

75. YA 312, ed. Leipoldt, *Sinuthii archimandritae vita,* CSCO 73.121–22.

76. Deut 12:5, 11, 14, and elsewhere.

77. YA 313, ed. Leipoldt, *Sinuthii archimandritae vita*, CSCO 73.122. B. Layton, "Rules, Patterns," 60, sees this renunciation of property as a key step in entering the monastery and forging a new identity.

78. YA 422, ed. Leipoldt, *Sinuthii archimandritae vita*, CSCO 73.125. See Emmel, *Literary Corpus*, CSCO 600.711–18, for sequence of surviving pages of A22 in *Canon* 3.

79. YA 422, ed. Leipoldt, *Sinuthii archimandritae vita,* CSCO 73:125.

80. Ibid.

81. Ibid.

82. YA 517, in Shenoute, *Oeuvres*, ed. Amélineau, 1:17. For an analysis of Shenoute's method of directing the women's community through letters and personal representatives, see Krawiec, *Shenoute.*

83. Emmel, *Literary Corpus*, CSCO 600.570–71.

84. For example, Jer 9:2, in YA 422, ed. Leipoldt, *Sinuthii archimandritae vita*, CSCO 73.125; see also Isa 1:25, in ZC 304, ed. Leipoldt, *Sinuthii archimandritae vita*, CSCO 73.206.

85. *Precepts* 116, ed. Lefort, *Oeuvres,* CSCO 159.32.

86. See for example *Precepts and Institutes* 5, ed. Lefort, *Oeuvres,* CSCO 159.34, on not wasting anything in the various workshops.

87. *Rule of Horsiesius*, ed. Lefort, *Oeuvres,* CSCO 159:92.

88. Emmel, "Shenoute the Monk," 64, translates ϣηρε ϣημ, which is literally "young boy," as "novice," meaning newcomer to the monastery.

89. Burial was highly regulated in both the *Koinonia* and the White Monastery. See *Precepts* 127–29, ed. Lefort, *Oeuvres,* CSCO 159.33.

90. Emmel, *Literary Corpus*, CSCO 600.593–94; Schroeder also discusses Shenoute's long illness and connects it with his concept of purity in *Monastic Bodies*, 85–86.

91. Coptic text XO 35, in Shenoute, *Oeuvres,* ed. Amélineau, 1:461. For analysis of the way Shenoute argues with opponents in the *Canons*, see Behlmer, "Do Not Believe."

92. *Precepts* 94, ed. Lefort, *Oeuvres,* CSCO 159.31.

93. Published by Amélineau, in *Monuments* [1895], pt. 1, 229–36, as *Encomium on Pcol*, but Ladeuze, *Étude sur le cénobitisme*, 148–49, demonstrated that it is written in praise of a successor of Pcol. Emmel, *Literary Corpus,* CSCO 600.896, lists this text among spurious attributions to Shenoute.

94. *Encomium*, ed. Amélineau, *Monuments,* [1895] pt. 1, 231–32.

95. Ibid., 234.

96. Ibid.

97. Ibid., 235.

98. Ibid.

99. Ibid., 236.

100. Ibid., 235.

101. Ibid., 234. See the numerous entries for ⲥⲩⲛⲁⲅⲱⲅⲏ in the index of Lefort's edition, *Sinuthii archimandritae vita*, CSCO 73.229–30.

102. *Encomium*, ed. Amélineau, *Monuments* [1895], pt. 1, 231. The term ⲡⲁⲣⲉⲙⲃⲟⲗⲏ is also common in Exodus, Leviticus, and Numbers in reference to the camp of the Israelites in the desert.

103. Emmel, "Shenoute the Monk," 162, versus *Precepts* 96, ed. Lefort, *Oeuvres,* CSCO 159.31.

104. B. Layton, *Coptic Grammar*, 236–37, 263–64.

105. For Bohairic text, see Lagarde, *Pentateuch koptisch*; this passage is not preserved in Sahidic.

106. Ibid., Deut 27:16, ⲟⲩⲟϩ ⲉⲩⲉϫⲟⲥ ⲛϫⲉⲡⲓⲗⲁⲟⲥ ⲧⲏⲣϥ ⲉⲥⲉϣⲱⲡⲓ.

107. Ibid., Exod 20:4. Positive commandments in Exodus (at least in Bohairic) use imperative rather than optative: "Honor your father and your mother" (Exod 20:12; ⲙⲁⲧⲁⲓⲉⲡⲉⲕⲓⲱⲧ ⲛⲉⲙ ⲧⲉⲕⲙⲁⲩ).

108. See, for example, Gal 3:10, 13, "It is written, 'Cursed is everyone . . . ,'" alluding to Deut 27:26, 21:23. See Mt 19:17–19 for a restatement of some of the commandments.

109. Rapp, "Desert, City, and Countryside," discusses the ways in which Egyptian monks saw themselves "as the successors to ancient Israel" (99).

110. Already noted by Keil, "Zur Form der Regel," 44.

111. *Encomium*, ed. Amélineau, *Monuments* [1895], pt. 1, 231.

Chapter Three

The *Life of Antony* in Egypt

MALCOLM CHOAT

In the famous Greek and Latin monastic texts, written mostly by visitors to Egypt for foreign audiences, the influence of the *Life of Antony* looms large.[1] It is *the* model, both for monastic life and in particular for monastic *Lives*. Its influence on the conception of monastic life and the tradition of narrating monks' lives can be traced in the Greco-Roman world from soon after its appearance and its quick translation into Latin. The success of the monastic agenda explicitly outlined in the *Life*—that for which it was apparently designed—is plain: the "monks in foreign parts" to whom the work is addressed seem to have wholeheartedly accepted the message.[2] This contribution investigates the legacy of the *Life* in its Egyptian context, seeking to trace, and perhaps qualify, its influence on the successors of the monks within Egypt who provided, along with Antony, the model for emulation.

Debate over the authorship of the *Life*—and by extension over its original language—which has been sustained at some length over the last two decades, seems now to have died down.[3] A fresh and full study of the Syriac *Life* has shown that it shares with other early Syriac translations a tendency to paraphrase and expand on its Greek source and thus need not depend on a different Greek *Life* from that which we now possess.[4] Most scholars have likewise reaffirmed Athanasius as the author of the *Life*.[5] Insofar as I engage this question at all, the results of this study bear on the question of the *Life*'s intended audience, raised by Barnes and more recently by Rousseau.[6] Given how quickly Athanasius's authorship was accepted within Egypt and abroad, that question is largely moot from the point of view of this investigation.[7] The purpose of the *Life*— to establish orderly hierarchies leading toward ecclesiastical authority — speaks strongly against its having been a production internal to early monasticism;[8] nor are there coherent linguistic reasons for positing an original composition in Coptic.[9] It is much easier to believe this is a Greek work, written in (or under the influence of) Alexandria.

Rather than engaging in this question or further expounding the program or agenda developed in the work, I wish to ask here how popular the *Life* was within monastic circles in Egypt in the centuries after its publication. This may seem an obtuse question, as the enduring influence of Antony can be read not only in texts but in the walls of the monastery of St. Antony, which still stands near the "inner mountain" to which he withdrew; in his image staring out from frescos and icons from as early as the sixth century, and in the collective memory of the living monastic tradition in Egypt.[10] Here I wish to position this consensus against two soundings, one taken among early monastic literature from Egypt, the other among monastic library holdings as they are recorded in the papyri.

The time is long past when one could assume that a Coptic translation of a work was necessary for it to have been influential among Egyptian monastic communities. The participation of most monastic communities in both Greek and Egyptian languages and cultures, expressed most prominently in a bilingual milieu, has been demonstrated with reference to both literary sources and the papyri. Nevertheless, communities such as that of Pachomius and Shenoute clearly articulated themselves most prominently in Egyptian (i.e., Coptic), and it is thus of interest to ask how long before our ninth-century manuscripts the *Life of Antony* was translated into Coptic, and how influential the *Life* was within predominantly Egyptian-speaking monastic circles.

The Coptic *Life*, as often noted, is a very literal translation;[11] the implication — although this is not usually stated — is that little can be learnt from it that cannot be learnt from the original.[12] The nature of the translation itself does little to narrow its date: the translator's excellent command of Greek (surpassing on occasions that of the Latin translators) does not prevent it from having been made as late as the seventh — or perhaps even eighth — century.[13]

A number of interesting variations between the Greek and Coptic versions could be noted,[14] but I will restrict myself to noting one that serves as a springboard to examining Antony in the Egyptian tradition. In the closing discussion of Antony's fame (*Vit. Ant.* 93), the Greek notes that "Antony was not known through writings [ἐκ συγγραμμάτων]"; the Coptic records that "Antony was not known through books that he wrote filled with pronouncements" (ⲉⲧⲃⲉϩⲉⲛϫⲱⲱⲙⲉ ⲉⲁϥⲥⲁϩⲟⲩ ⲉⲩⲙⲉϩ ⲛⲥⲩⲛⲧⲁⲅⲙⲁ). We will find this hint from the translator that Antony did leave writings, but not voluminous books, reflected in the early monastic memory of Antony in Egypt.[15]

THE *LIFE OF ANTONY* AMONG EGYPTIAN MONASTIC AUTHORS

While explicit mentions of the *Life of Antony* are easily located in authors from outside Egypt, including those such as Palladius who spent time in Egypt, they are not as easy to explicitly trace in the early Egyptian record.[16] The influence of the *Life of Antony* is most easily detected in the texts produced first in Greek in Lower Egypt: while there is only one explicit mention of the *Life* in the *Apophthegmata patrum*, many sayings echo, borrow directly from, or are perhaps in some cases sources for the *Life*.[17] Evagrius knows an *Apophthegm* of Antony,[18] but he does not mention the *Life*.[19] A letter attributed to Athanasius's contemporary Serapion of Thmuis, but more probably written in the fifth century, refers to the *Life* without naming its author.[20] Authors writing in Coptic in the sixth and seventh centuries, however, clearly have access to the *Life of Antony*, and probably in a Coptic version. The anonymous *Life of Athanasius,* which survives in several recensions, certainly shows a familiarity with the *Life of Antony*, even if it draws on other sources for its account of the interaction between Athanasius and Antony.[21] John of Schmun, who lived in the second half of the sixth or early seventh century, draws much more directly on the *Life* in his *Encomium on Antony*,[22] and he probably used the *Life* in Coptic, even though it is likely that he had before him a different Coptic version from the one that survives next to the *Encomium* in the Pierpont Morgan manuscript that transmits the text of both.[23]

The Pachomians, Antony, and Athanasius

To trace the tradition earlier, I turn first to the Pachomian texts. Athanasius's interactions with the Pachomian monks are well known and require no further discussion here.[24] Here I will focus rather on the reception of the *Life of Antony* in the various recensions of the *Life of Pachomius*. The first Greek *Life* makes specific reference to the *Life of Antony* as an actual text and as authored by Athanasius: "The life [βίος] of our most ascetic and truly virtuous father Antony was like that of the great Elijah, of Elisha, and of John the Baptist, as the most holy archbishop Athanasius attested, writing about him [ἐγγράφως μαρτυρεῖ περί αὐτοῦ] after his death, revealing at the same time the same conduct of our holy father Amoun, chief monk of the brothers on the mountain of Nitria, and of Theodore, his companion."[25] The parallel section in the Bohairic *Life* has a different emphasis: "[For such was the life distinguished] in virtues of our holy father Apa Antony; in like manner also was the life [ⲃⲓⲟⲥ] of the great Elijah, of Elisha, and of John the Baptist. We have been told [ⲉⲩⲧⲁⲙⲟⲛ] that this was also the way of life [ϫⲓⲛⲱⲛϩ] of our holy father Apa Amoun, father of the brothers living on the mountain of Pernouč, and of Theodore his faithful disciple."[26] Arabic *Lives* that seem to translate a Coptic *Life* earlier than the common source of *SBo* and G[1] reflect the emphasis of the surviving Coptic text: "C'est vraiment ainsi que le conduite du dévot Antoine, le dévot, le fort, rassembla à la vie du prophète Élie, d'Élisée et de Jean le Baptiste. Le saint anba Amoun, le pere des frères qui habitant la montagne de Pernoudj suivit le meme chemin."[27] The Bohairic and Arabic versions, then, note only that the lives with a small "l," that is, the lived deeds, of Antony and Amoun provide a virtuous example for the monastic life. The references to Amoun and Theodore in *Vit. Ant.* 60 allow the discussion of the general context not to be disrupted by the insertion of details over the *Life*'s authorship. The reference to Theodore of Enaton is also found in the Coptic,[28] but it need not derive from the *Life of Antony*, as stories about Amoun and Theodore circulated in the *koinonia*.[29] The Arabic *Life*, which I suggest here represents the earliest form of this passage, does not mention Theodore. At the outset of the work, then, the Greek *Life of Pachomius*, unlike the Coptic, explicitly places itself within the narrative and biographical tradition of the *Life of Antony* as written by Athanasius.

Similarly, the redactor of the first Greek *Life* shows further awareness of the *Life of Antony*'s authorship and original character when describing the agenda and program of recording Pachomius and Theodore's lives. "This text we have just written, we have not written for the sake of writing but as a memorial, as is the case with the letters that holy bishops and fathers have written for edification, as with the Life of the Blessed Antony sent to the monks and brothers in foreign parts [ὁ βίος τοῦ μακαρίου Ἀντωνίου πρὸς τοὺς ἐν τῇ ξένῃ μοναχοὺς ἐπεστάλη] who had asked the most holy father Athanasius for it. In fact, it was after consulting well-informed monks that he wrote accurately about him."[30] The Bohairic *Life* lacks this section, although it does refer to the reception and translation into Coptic in the Pachomian community of Athanasius's well-known festal letter for 367 defining the canon, as well as giving the text of two letters sent by Athanasius to Horsiesios.[31]

The influence of the *Life of Antony* is also much more apparent in the Greek *Life* when Pachomius faces demons, as all great monks must.[32] The Greek *Life* makes an explicit comparison with Antony,[33] and the chapters that lead up to this in the Greek *Life* tell of Pachomius's struggles in terms that show clear affinities with the *Life of Antony* (esp. *Vit. Ant.* 17–18).[34] The Bohairic *Life* includes the demon stories but does not mention Antony;[35] although the influence of the narrative of demonic conflict in the *Life of Antony* can be detected, the Coptic *Life* does not seem to have been elaborated in the light of the *Life of Antony* to the extent that the Greek Pachomian tradition has.

One section of the Coptic *Lives* does show the clear influence of the *Life of Antony*. A Sahidic *Life* (Lefort's S⁵) likely to be close to the *vorlage* of the Bohairic text (which is itself lost at this point) records (as does G[1]) the meeting between Antony and the Pachomians.[36] When the anchorite tells them of his early career, the relationship with the *Life of Antony* is clear.

Vit. Pach. SBo 127

ⲕⲁⲓ ⲅⲁⲣ ϩⲙ̄ⲡⲉⲩⲟⲉⲓϣ ⲛ̄ⲧⲁⲓ̈ⲣ̄ⲙⲟⲛⲟⲭⲟⲥ
ⲛⲉⲙⲛ̄ⲗⲁⲁⲩ ⲛ̄ⲕⲟⲓⲛⲱⲛⲓⲁ ϩⲓϫⲙ̄ⲡⲕⲁϩ
ⲉⲧⲣⲁϣⲱⲡⲉ ϩⲱ ϩⲛⲟⲩⲕⲟⲓⲛⲱⲛⲓⲁ ⲁⲗⲗⲁ
ϩⲉⲛⲟⲩⲁ ⲟⲩⲁ ⲛⲉⲧⲉϣⲁⲩⲣ̄ⲡⲃⲟⲗ
ⲙ̄ⲡⲉⲩϯⲙⲉ ⲛ̄ⲟⲩⲕⲟⲩⲓ̈ ⲛ̄ⲥⲉⲉⲥϭⲣⲁϩⲧ
ⲉⲣⲟⲟⲩ[37]

Life of Antony, Coptic Version, 3

ⲉⲛⲉⲙⲡⲁⲧⲟⲩϣⲱⲡⲉ ⲅⲁⲣ ϩⲛⲕⲏⲙⲉ
ⲉⲡⲧⲏⲣϥ ⲛϭⲓ ⲙⲙⲟⲛⲁⲥⲧⲏⲣⲓⲟⲛ ⲉⲧⲟϣ
ⲁⲩⲱ ⲉⲛⲉⲙⲡⲁⲧⲉⲙⲙⲟⲛⲟⲭⲟⲥ ⲥⲟⲩⲛ̄ⲡ-
ϫⲁⲉⲓⲉ ⲉⲧⲟⲩⲏⲩ ⲁⲗⲗⲁ ⲉϣⲁⲣⲉⲡⲟⲩⲁ
ⲡⲟⲩⲁ ⲛⲛⲉⲧⲟⲩⲱϣ ϫⲓϩⲣⲁϥ ⲉⲣⲟϥ
ⲉⲣ̄ⲡⲃⲟⲗ ⲙⲡⲉϥϯⲙⲉ ⲛⲛⲟⲩⲕⲟⲩⲓ
ⲛϥ̄ϣⲱⲡⲉ ϩⲛⲧⲁⲥⲕⲏⲥⲓⲥ ⲙⲁⲩⲁⲁϥ

For at the time when I became a monk, there was no *koinonia* in the land that I might myself dwell in a *koinonia*. Rather some few people would withdraw a little way outside their village and live alone.

For in all Egypt monasteries were not yet numerous, and no monk knew the distant desert; But each who wished to give heed to himself went out from his village a little and practiced *ascesis* alone.

Vit. Pach. G[1] 120

κατὰ τὴν ἀρχήν, ὅτε μοναχὸς
γέγονα, οὐκ ἦν κοινόβιον
θρέψαι ἄλλας ψυχάς· ἀλλ'
ἕκαστος τῶν ἀρχαίων μοναχῶν
μετὰ τὸν διωγμὸν κατὰ μόνας
ἠσκεῖτο.

Life of Antony 3.2

Οὔπω γὰρ ἦν οὕτως ἐν Αἰγύπτῳ
συνεχῆ μοναστήρια, οὐδ' ὅλως
ᾔδει μοναχὸς τὴν μακρὰν
ἔρημον, ἕκαστος δὲ τῶν
βουλομένων ἑαυτῷ προσέχειν
οὐ μακρὰν τῆς ἰδίας κώμης
καταμόνας ἠσκεῖτο.

In the beginning, when I became a monk, there was no community to nurture other souls; but each of the ancient monks after the persecution practiced *ascesis* in solitude.[38]

For there were not yet many monasteries in Egypt and no monk knew at all the great desert; but each one who wished to give attention to himself practiced *ascesis* in solitude not far from their own village.

The syntax has been altered to allow Antony to acknowledge the achievement of Pachomius, but the dependence on the *Life of Antony* is clear. Both the Greek and the Coptic freely rework the text, although in the final sentence the Greek approaches the original much more closely, while the Coptic *Life of Pachomius* eschews mention of *ascesis* altogether at this point. Compositional factors required the syntactic recasting, but the lexical differences (in which both the Greek and Coptic depart from the *Life of Antony* in different ways) might also allow the suggestion that the redactors of the original form of the narrative had learnt the story about Antony in an oral context.[39]

It may be significant that this validating section of the *Life*, in which the Pachomians meet Antony, comes in material covering the period after Pachomius's death that forms an appendix to the *Life* and that may or may not have been part of the *Life* as originally conceived.[40] This appendix does not seem to have been in the common source of *SBo* and G^1 and is not found in the most reliable Arabic *Life*.[41] The long section shows the importance of Antony to the compilers of the Pachomian tradition but also reveals multiple sources for this influence. Beyond whatever direct historical contacts lie behind the stories (and it is not necessary to assume they are completely invented), a Sahidic *Life* quotes a letter from Antony to the Pachomians, which may well be authentic.[42] The *Epistula Ammonis* also preserves (in Greek) a letter sent by Antony to Theodore, which may also be genuine.[43] Another mention of Antony raises other possibilities: when Pachomius praises both Athanasius and Antony (as well as his own *koinonia*) as the three things flourishing with the favor of God in man in Egypt at the time (*SBo* 134, *G^1* 136), it should be noted not only that (the much more pro-Athanasian) Theodore is remembering the words of the founder but also that they seem to be a reworking of an apophthegm that is elsewhere attributed to Antony himself.[44] Epistolary and oral traditions may thus have been more primary mediating forces between Antony and the Pachomians than was the *Life of Antony*.

I make no claim here to an impact on the discussion on the early Pachomian textual tradition. Yet the contrast in the Greek and Coptic material as regards Antony and his biography requires explanation. Neither the Bohairic *Life* nor the first Greek *Life* is now considered to represent the "original" state of the tradition: both modify a common source (or set of sources) in different ways. I suggest that among the ways the Greek tradition altered this source was the addition of references, and a more explicit literary debt, to the *Life of Antony*. The first Greek *Life of Pachomius* shows textual signs of redaction after Athanasius's death and also omits matters that might confuse or offend an international audience, most notably removing terms such as *apotaktikos*.[45] It would have been at this stage that the explicit references to the *Life of Antony* as a text and to its authorship were added.[46] This would make sense if the redactor of G^1 was, as has been suggested, an Alexandrian cleric, but this is not the only possibility.[47]

The Coptic sections we have been discussing come either from the Bohairic *Life* or from Sahidic recensions that belong to the same "family" of *Lives*. These are secondary to the earlier Sahidic versions, which are now largely lost. It is difficult, however, to see why details about Antony and his *Life* would have been excised from earlier Coptic versions, and I submit that they were in fact never there. Given the important (if slightly more confrontational) role reserved for Antony in the Bohairic *Life*, the omission of the mentions of the *Life of Antony* is not likely to be part of a hostile agenda. The Coptic texts may in this regard look back to the first stage of the collection of the memories of the founder, which started before the *Life of Antony* was written.[48] It also might be argued, in light of the more competitive tone regarding Antony and anchoretic monasticism that the Coptic *Lives* adopt at points, that the compilers of the early Pachomian traditions did not feel the need to place their work in the explicit tradition of the *Life of Antony*.[49] I would suggest, however, the omission indicates rather that in the second half of the fourth century not only was the *Life of Antony* not widely known in Pachomian circles, but it had probably not yet been translated into Coptic.[50]

Shenoute, Besa, Athanasius, and Antony

More explicitly than the *Life of Pachomius*, the *Life of Shenoute* acknowledges the primacy of Antony among Egyptian monks: "Even if all the monks of this time came together in a single place," Shenoute tells some visiting ascetics, "they would not make a single Antony";[51] it is Antony, along with Pachomius and Pshoi, whom Shenoute calls to lead his soul to heaven.[52] These are the only mentions of Antony in the Bohairic *Life of Shenoute* as we have it, but there seems no obvious reason for an excision from the Sahidic traditions from which the Bohairic *Life* was drawn.[53]

We better access Shenoute's world, however, through his own writings.[54] In "Scripture Has Said," Shenoute mentions the *Life of Antony*: ⲛⲉⲧϯⲥⲃⲱ ⲇⲉ ⲛⲧⲟⲟⲩ ⲕⲁⲗⲱⲥ ⲛⲑⲉ ϩⲱⲱϥ ⲙⲡⲉⲛⲉⲓⲱⲧ ⲁⲛⲧⲱⲛⲓⲟⲥ ⲡⲛⲟϭ ⲛⲁⲛⲁⲭⲱⲣⲓⲧⲏⲥ ⲛⲧⲁ ⲡⲛⲟⲩⲧⲉ ⲁⲁϥ ⲛⲥⲟⲉⲓⲧ ϩⲙ ⲡⲕⲁϩ ⲧⲏⲣϥ ⲛⲑⲉ ⲉⲧⲥⲏϩ ϩⲙ ⲡⲉϥⲃⲓⲟⲥ ⲙⲡⲟⲩϫⲉ ϣⲁϫⲉ ⲛⲧⲉⲓⲙⲓⲛⲉ ϫⲉ ⲟⲩⲛ ⲇⲓⲕⲁⲓⲟⲥ ϩⲛ ⲁⲙⲛⲧⲉ[55] (And those who are taught well — like our father Antony the great anchorite, whom God made famous throughout the whole land, as is written in his *Life* — they did not say anything like "There is a just man in Hades"). The reference is something of a tangential observation in the discussion about how the saints do not claim that there are righteous people in hell. ⲛⲑⲉ ⲉⲧⲥⲏϩ ϩⲙ ⲡⲉϥⲃⲓⲟⲥ (as is written in his *Life*) leaves no doubt that Shenoute knows the written *Life of Antony*. He may be merely gesturing toward the fact that the *Life* has made Antony well known, but we might also consider this an echo of passages such as *Vit. Ant.* 94.1.[56] Whether or not this is an actual quotation, this awareness of the *Life* does not seem to translate into a high profile for the work elsewhere in the Shenoutean corpus. In "God Says through Those Who Are His," Shenoute mentions the visit of the God-loving count Chossaroas, who is made to tell Shenoute that "you have made the desert a city."[57] Yet this most famous of sentences from the *Life of Antony* need not indicate any literary dependence, for it could easily have become a "saying" by this stage.[58]

However, we gain further insight into how the monks of the White Monastery knew of Antony by reading further in "Scripture Has Said." The mention of Antony serves to introduce a quotation from one of Antony's letters where the subject of the just in hell is discussed.[59] This is *Letter* 18, which survives under the name of Antony only in the Arabic tradition;[60] in Greek and Syriac it is found among the letters of Antony's disciple Ammonas.[61] The quotation by Shenoute, however, shows that the attribution to Antony is of great antiquity. Immediately after quoting *Letter* 18, Shenoute quotes from a different work of Antony that cannot be identified, introducing the quotation by noting the profit for all those who hear or read Antony's words.[62] In an excerpt from an otherwise lost work from *Canon* 3 contained in the so-called Florilegium of Shenoute's Canons found in White Monastery codex XL, Shenoute also mentions the *Letters of Antony*, introducing a discussion of righteousness with "according to what he said in his *Letters*, namely our father the elder Antonios."[63] What immediately follows is a scriptural reminiscence, but an unrecognized quotation of a letter of the great monk probably lurks somewhere on the page.[64] Shenoute's successor Besa also cites the sixth letter of Antony in two of his own letters.[65]

Thus both Shenoute and Besa show more knowledge, and make more use, of the letters of Antony than they do of the *Life of Antony*. Both know and cite works by Athanasius that deal with asceticism, but these are overwhelmingly letters and other works in which Athanasius directed himself against other models of virginity than that of which he approved. This was as important a part of Athanasius's ascetic agenda as was the *Life of Antony*, but the setting of the debate over "virginity and ecclesiastical politics," as David Brakke has it, is not monasticism as Shenoute and his monks lived it, but rather the urban world where the virgins over which Athanasius struggled to assert his control dwelt.[66]

In an acephalous discourse on virginity, Shenoute cites Athanasius's "First Letter to the Virgins"— which itself survives in Coptic in a codex from the White Monastery library — in which a number of cardinal virtues of virginity are praised.[67] Shenoute also cites Athanasius in support of virgins not keeping night vigils and quotes a condemnation by Athanasius of virgins who break their vows and marry.[68] Neither work has survived independently. He also knows the *Festal Letters* of Athanasius, although primarily *Letter* 39's attacks on heresy.[69]

The White Monastery library contained, at this early stage, other pastoral letters of Athanasius; this is shown by Besa's citation of an acephalous work of Athanasius, (generally referred to as "On the Moral Life") in a letter to his fellow monks.[70] Again, the text is not only cited by Besa but also found in a White Monastery codex.[71] This text certainly deals with asceticism, but far more broadly than just with monasticism; the homily speaks to ascetics and lay Christians; and the citation supports Besa's argument about the need for unity, "Do not let anyone see you behaving unseemly." Finally, Shenoute cites the letters of Athanasius as the source of unfavorable opinions about the Manichaeans, although the themes he dwells on are in fact closely related to the *Acta Archelai*, a common source of anti-Manichaean propaganda, which Shenoute clearly knew.[72]

Thus the early White Monastery abbots seem to have a range of Athanasian texts at their disposal. Yet in the currently published Shenouteiana (and I stress "currently," given how much remains unedited), Shenoute does not seem to build on the *Life of Antony* to any great degree. He knows of it, and the White Monastery is thus likely to have possessed a copy. It is important to remember, however, that Shenoute, contrary to the previously popular picture of his monolingualism, would have been able to have read the work in Greek, and his mention of the *Life* in "Scripture Has Said" need not imply the existence of a Coptic translation by this point in time.[73] What we see more clearly is the influence of Antony's own letters and of Athanasius's prescriptions on the behavior of virgins.

MANUSCRIPTS AND LIBRARIES

A much wider range of monastic literature from Egypt could of course be surveyed. As a final aspect of this assessment, however, I will turn to the remains, and catalogues, of later monastic libraries in Egypt.[74] In the first place we have of course the Coptic manuscripts of the *Life of Antony* itself.[75] The most complete, and oldest, was donated to the library of the monastery of St. Michael the Archangel at Phanntoou, near modern Hamouli in the Fayum, in 822/823 CE.[76] It is part of a codex that also contains the encomium of Antony by John of Schmun, and two encomia of Athanasius by Constantine of Assiut, as well as other hagiographical texts.[77] Parts of the *Life* are also preserved in the remains of three further codices dating from the ninth to the twelfth century that were once in the library of White Monastery.[78]

The fact that the two major (somewhat) intact libraries from early medieval Coptic monasteries that survive today both owned copies of the *Life of Antony* suggests it may not have been an uncommon possession during the "golden age" of Coptic manuscript production from which these codices survive.[79] Tracing the record earlier, we find that other monastic libraries that have survived from Egypt exist in a rather more fragmentary state, usually as papyrus assemblages recovered during excavation (scientific or amateur) or purchased on the antiquities market. The larger assemblages, such as those from the monasteries of Apa Thomas at Wadi Sarga, Apa Apollo at Bala'izah, or Epiphanius at Thebes, yield no trace of the *Life of Antony*, although the latter two do contain works by (or attributed to) Athanasius.[80] The Monastery of Epiphanius also contained what the Western tradition knows as Athanasius's second letter to the monks, painted on the wall of the abandoned tomb of Daga, from which the monastery grew.[81] Frange, a well-known monastic correspondent in Theban texts from the late seventh / early eighth centuries, compares the holiness of two of his correspondents to that of Antony, "the pillar of light."[82] This epithet is given to Antony by Hilarion in the *Apophthegmata patrum*;[83] when Frange compares his love for his addressees to that of Paphnoute the confessor for Antony, however, he echoes a tradition found first in the *Life of Antony* (58.3), albeit much amplified thereafter.[84]

Papyrus assemblages always survive in a fragmentary and disorganized state and provide no certainty about what was not contained in a library. We might look to actual library catalogues for a better indication of what was held. That of the White Monastery survived until the early twentieth century.[85] The text was inscribed, probably around the twelfth century, on the walls of the "secret chamber" that housed the ancient library when it was rediscovered in the nineteenth century.[86] Two of the inscriptions are devoted to "the Lives of the Saints" (ⲚⲂⲒⲞⲤ ⲚⲚⲈⲦⲞⲨⲀⲂ).[87] Here we find *Lives* of Pachomius, Shenoute, Besa, Severus, Pisthentius, and Pamin, as well as a considerable number of other lesser-known monks. Nowhere is the *Life of Antony* mentioned. However, since this inscription is long lost and cannot be checked, since it was copied by someone who on his own admission did not know Coptic, and since lacunae were recorded even when it was visible, we cannot be sure that the *Life of Antony* was not listed. Moreover, we know — seeing as parts of them still survive — that around this time codices containing the *Life* were contained in the monastery's library.

Other catalogues of books, however, mirror that of the White Monastery in not mentioning the *Life of Antony*. The best preserved is that of the monastery of Apa Elias of the Rock, from the Theban region, whose book catalogue was written on a piece of limestone in the seventh or eighth century.[88] The many books the monastery owned included copies of six works by Athanasius, as well as an encomium on him.[89] The library also contained the *Life of Pachomius* and works of Pachomius and Shenoute, as well as *Apophthegmata*, a number of martyrdoms, *Lives* of Macarius and Macrina, and *History of the Church*. The *Life of Antony* is conspicuous by its absence. Many other lists of books in Greek or Coptic on ostracon or papyrus have survived in various states of preservation from sixth–eighth century Egypt.[90] Most are dominated by scripture, but some contain references to hagiographical or "patristic" texts.[91] Among the many references to books among letters between monks we also sometimes find some references to monastic literature.[92] The *Life of Antony*, however, is notably absent from them all. Much more would have to be said to constitute a full survey of the books that circulated in late antique and early Islamic Egypt, and many of the lists cited here are fragmentary, preventing certainty on what they once contained.[93] That we cannot find a secure reference to the *Life of Antony* is nevertheless surprising and suggests a more restricted diffusion among monasteries than we might have expected.

On the basis of these soundings, we are entitled to position what we have learnt here against several well-supported conceptions about the *Life of Antony*. The evidence seems sufficient to suggest that the circulation of the *Life of Antony* among predominantly Egyptian-speaking monastic circles may not have been as wide as has been supposed. There is no good evidence that it was translated into Coptic before the sixth century; early monastic literature composed in Coptic seems detached from the *Life of Antony*; and the records of monastic libraries indicate that its circulation may not have been as prolific in Egypt as in the West. It is possible that the importance of the *Life* in late antique Egypt may have been overemphasized precisely because of its importance in the early medieval world beyond Egypt, especially in the West.

We thus have cause to reconsider how the Athanasian agenda that has been detected in the *Life* was promulgated throughout Egyptian monasticism. The history of Athanasius's dealings with monasticism in Egypt is usually written through the *Life of Antony*, making it the programmatic centerpiece of his ascetic agenda, embodying the direction monasticism should (and, in the fullness of time, largely was to) take in the future. The narrative as laid out by Brakke on Athanasius's relationship with monasticism, for example, seems to require that the *Life of Antony* had a wide dissemination among Egyptian monks; it is the "climactic" or "ultimate" weapon against "monastic sympathy for the Arian cause."[94] The *Life* is explicitly part of Athanasius's agenda to win the monks to his cause. In the reception of the *Life* among Egyptian monastic communities, then, we may have a hint that if the work did aim at unity between monasticism and the church in Egypt, it may not have been as successful as the author may have hoped.[95] If this did happen over time, it may have been more dependent on factors other than the *Life*. We may need to place more stress on Athanasius's personal contacts with the monastic milieu and to note that among the ascetic works of Athanasius, his epistles and sermons on virginity are more widely cited in early Coptic literature then the *Life of Antony*.

What we have seen also validates Antony's own role in the construction of his legacy. In the early period, Antony's own letters, sent to the Pachomians and kept in the White Monastery's library, seem more influential than his *Life*. Antony's *own* role in the formation of the early Egyptian monastic tradition, in his own words, not as mediated by a *Life* written by someone else, should be emphasized. Even if we now consider some of the documents that are cited as Antonian to be inauthentic, their circulation under his name shows the propagation of a monastic theology largely independent of the *Life* under his name.

We lose sight of parallel models of ascetic authority such as this if we focus only on the picture given in the *Life*. And we have some trouble detecting the *Life*'s influence among the very monks it was, apparently, intended to convince. For Brakke, soon after the death of Antony, the "historical Antony" was superseded by the "Athanasian Antony."[96] Internationally, this process was almost instantaneous.[97] But in Egypt itself, where independent traditions continued to circulate, and the *Life* was not swiftly translated into Coptic, different emphases remained for much longer, fading only under the weight of dogmatic disputes, ecclesiastical politics, and a thoroughgoing program of Coptic translation in the sixth and following centuries.

NOTES

It is the greatest pleasure to include this essay in a volume honoring Philip Rousseau, to whom I will always — and happily so — be in debt for his assistance and advice. An earlier version of this essay was presented in the Coptic Studies Lecture Series convened by Assoc. Prof. Jacco Dielemann at UCLA in November 2006; I am grateful to the audience on that occasion for valuable feedback. The following abbreviations are used: *Vit. Ant.* = *Life of Antony*; *Vit. Pach.* = *Life of Pachomius*; *SBo* = the recension of the Coptic *Life of Pachomius* represented by the Bohairic and several Sahidic *Lives*, ed. Lefort, *S. Pachomii Vita Bohairice Scripta* and *S. Pachomii Vitae Sahidice*, trans. Veilleux, *Pachomian Koinonia*; *G1* = the first Greek *Life of Pachomius*, ed. Halkin, *S. Pachomii Vitae Graecae*; *Apophth. patr.* = *Apophthegmata patrum*, Alphabetical Collection, PG 65.72–440; *Ep. Am.* = *Epistula Ammonis*, ed. Goehring, *Letter of Ammon*; CMCL = *Corpus dei Manoscritti Copti Letterari* (http://cmcl.let.uniroma1.it/); Coptic codices from the White Monastery (MONB) and other collections (e.g. MICH) are referred to according to the codicological scheme found in the CMCL. Papyri and ostraca (signaled by *P.* or *O.*) are abbreviated according to Oates et al., *Checklist of Editions*.

1. Throughout I refer to the following editions and translations of the *Life*: *Vie d'Antoine,* ed. Bartelink; *S. Antonii vitae,* ed. Garitte; *Coptic Life of Antony,* trans. Vivian.

2. The manuscript titles that make this explicit are of course later additions, but that this was the audience envisaged is strongly indicated by the preface of *Life*. The *Life* in its original form is usually considered to have opened with an epistolary address; Bartelink chooses a title from among the many attested in the Greek tradition (see Bartelink's intro. to *Vie d'Antoine*, 124) that describes the work as an *epistole*; no trace of an epistolary introduction (if there ever was one) remains in the Greek text, though see the opening to the Latin translation of Evagrius: *Athanasius episcopus ad peregrinos fratres*. Other Greek manuscripts describe Athanasius's enterprise as a *sungrapheia*, or a *bios*, but the *Life* itself shows that Athanasius conceived of his enterprise as a *diegesis* (see Rapp, "Storytelling as Spiritual Communication," 436–37). The Coptic preface combines the designation *bios* and the observation that it was "a letter which he sent to the brothers in foreign parts" with the description that Athanasius narrated (ⲉⲁϥϩⲓⲥⲧⲟⲣⲓⲍⲉ) the *Life*.

3. This debate was begun by Draguet in his edition of the Syriac Life (*Vie primitive*), whose thesis was developed and popularized by Barnes, "Angel of Light"; Barnes summarizes the course of the modern debate in *Early Christian Hagiography*, 160–70. See also Tetz, "Athanasius."

4. See Takeda, "Syriac Version" and "Monastic Theology."

5. Louth, "St. Athanasius"; Abramowski, "Vertritt die syrische Fassung"; Lorenz, "Griechische *Vita Antonii*"; Rubenson, *Letters of St. Antony*, 126–32; Barrett-Lennard, *Christian Healing*, 345–51; Brakke, "Greek and Syriac Versions" and *Athanasius*, 15 n. 31 and ch. 4; Bartelink's intro. to *Vie d'Antoine*, 27–35. The honorand of the present volume is a notable exception; see Rousseau, "Antony as Teacher," esp. 100–104. See also Barnard, "Did Athanasius Know Antony?" and Barnes, *Early Christian Hagiography*, 165–70. Against the idea that the author's source was Serapion, see Fitschen, *Serapion von Thmuis*, 106–16.

6. Barnes, "Angel of Light"; Rousseau, "Antony as Teacher," 103–4.

7. For acceptance of Athanasius's authorship in Egypt, see especially *Vit. Pach.* G1 2, 99. As for recognition of it abroad, Gregory of Nazianzus, Jerome, Rufinus, and Ephraim all cite Athanasius as the author; see Bartelink, intro. to *Vie d'Antoine*, 37–42.

8. See especially Brakke, *Athanasius.* Rousseau argues that some of the language of submission is more neutral than has been commonly conceived; see "Antony as Teacher," 99–100.

9. As argued by Barnes, "Angel of Light" (though see now his *Early Christian Hagiography*, 164); see especially Brakke, "Greek and Syriac Versions."

10. On the monastery of St. Antony, see Bolman, *Monastic Visions*, 10–16; R.-G. Coquin et al., "Dayr Anba Antuniyus." Regarding images, Antony is presumably the Apa Antonius who stands between Athanasius and Apa Pamoun on the walls of Chapel LVI in the monastery of Bawit, painted in the sixth to seventh century (see Clédat, *Monastère et la nécropole,* 161–62, plates 136, 137; cf. 156–57); for the early thirteenth-century wall painting of "Apa Antonios, father of the monks," and Paul of Thebes side by side in the nave of the old church in the monastery of St. Antony, see Bolman, *Monastic Visions*, xiii (fig. 7), xi (fig. 5); cf. the icons from other monasteries illustrated at 9 and 17. For Antony's influence on the living monastic tradition in Egypt, see Meinardus, *Monks and Monasteries*, 1–4.

11. See, e.g., Brakke, review of *The Life of Antony,* Vivian and Athanassakis's parallel translations of the Greek and Coptic *Lives,* 248; Garitte, "Texte grec," 7.

12. See Browne, "Coptico-Graeca." I have the impression that the translation would repay additional study with further insights.

13. Ibid.

14. For extensive observations, see Vivian's introduction and footnotes to Athanasius, *Coptic Life of Antony*. The following points are worthy of note: Antony emerges from his isolation in *Vit. Ant.* 14 neither as a "mystical initiate" (Greek) nor as an "angel of Light" (Syriac), but in the Coptic simply "with God";

in the same chapter the most famous phrase in the *Life* has been altered so that the desert is not made a city by monks but is rather simply "filled with monks." The traditional Greek vocabulary of holiness that the Greek *Life* uses to contextualize Antony's early ascetic journey (e.g., "shrines" [12]; "divine mysteries" [14]) is also largely expunged; see *Coptic Life of Antony*, trans. Vivian, 6–7.

15. By ⲥⲩⲛⲧⲁⲅⲙⲁ, did the translator have in mind a monastic Rule? Yet these are more commonly given the title ⲕⲁⲛⲱⲛ.

16. I mean here a reference to the *Life* itself or clear echo or citation. What follows is by no means a comprehensive survey, although one would be instructive.

17. These are particularly in the *Sayings* of Antony, esp. *Apophth. patr.* Antony 10 (compare *Vit. Ant.* 85), 30 (*Vit. Ant.* 59–60), 31 (*Vit. Ant.* 81); cf. Rubenson, *Letters of St. Antony*, 153 n. 3. Elsewhere see, e.g., *Apophth. patr.* Sisoes 25. The question of priority in the Antonian sayings is of course vexed. The one explicit mention of the *Life* in the *Apophthegmata patrum* is *Apophth. patr.* Peter of Dios 1.

18. *Praktikos* 92; cf. *Vitae Patrum* (PL 73.108c), as well as *Vit. Ant.* 72–80; cf. Rubenson, "Evagrios Pontikos," 395. On the reassessment of the relationship between the thought of Evagrius and Antony in light of Rubenson's arguments for the authenticity of the letters of Antony, see Rubenson, "Evagrios Pontikos," 394 ff.; O'Laughlin, "Closing the Gap."

19. At least in his works that survive in Greek; I have not checked those preserved only in Syriac.

20. Serapion, *Epistula ad monachos*, PG 40.940: "From you (the renowned) Abba Antonios arose on account of his supreme life; of whom the written *Life* is kept (up till now) with you" [ἐξ ὑμῶν ἀββᾶ Ἀντόνιος (ὁ περιώνυμος) δι' ἀκρότατον βίον γενόμενος· οὗ καὶ ὁ βίος ἔγγραπτος παρ' ὑμῖν (μέχρι καὶ νῦν) διασώζεται]; the text in parentheses represents variants found in another manuscript. On this passage, which goes on to mention Amoun, John (Kolobos?), and Macarius (the Egyptian?), and which on its own is sufficient to consign the author to a period later than the fourth century, see Fitschen, *Serapion von Thmuis*, 80–81. On the letter's pseudonymity and nonepistolary character despite its title, see Fitschen, *Serapion von Thmuis*, 79–84.

21. For an instance in the *Life of Athanasius* showing familiarity with the *Life of Antony,* see Orlandi, *Testi Copti*, esp. 110 (so too the Bodleian fragment of the *Life* edited by P. Kahle as *P.Bal.* 1.35), where the narrator of the *Life* (not seemingly Athanasius, who is described throughout in the third person) states that on the basis of reports from Antony's disciples (ⲙⲁⲑⲏⲧⲏⲥ, see *P.Bal.* 1.35) about his life (*bios*) "we wrote it in a book [so the Bodleian text: 'another book' in the Turin MS primarily used by Orlandi] by itself alone." For where the *Life of Athanasius* draws on other sources, see especially the episode in Orlandi, *Testi Copti*, 108–9, where Athanasius meets Antony.

22. On John of Schmun (i.e., Ashmunein/Hermopolis), who lived in the second half of the sixth or early seventh century, see Orlandi, "John of Shmun." The *Encomium* is edited by Garitte, "Panégyrique de Saint Antoine"; there are parallels in *P.Lond.Copt*. 1.184. Cf. the translation of Vivian in Athanasius, *Life of Antony*, trans, Vivian and Athanassakis, 9–35.

23. See Garitte, "Panégyrique de Saint Antoine," 107–8, adding *Encomium* 34 (compare *Vit. Ant.* Pr. 3) to the list of places identified by Garitte where the text given by John differs from that in the Coptic *Vit. Ant.* It remains possible, of course, that John made his own translation of the Greek.

24. See Brakke, *Athanasius,* 111–29; Barnard, "Athanasius and the Pachomians."

25. *G*1 2 (trans. Vielleux, *Pachomian Koinonia,* 1:298, adjusted). The second Greek *Life* and the closely related Latin translation of Dionysius Exiguus acknowledge Athanasius more even elaborately; see *Vit. Pach.* Latin 1 = *G*2 4, in Cranenburgh, *Vie latine de Saint Pachôme*, 86–87.

26. Lefort, *S. Pachomii vita Bohairice scripta*, CSCO 89.1. The first two pages of the text are missing in the MSS; the opening of the sentence is translated here in accordance with the restoration of Lefort (see his translation, CSCO 107.1); it is likely to have been similar to the Arabic translation quoted above. Cf. the translation by Vielleux, *SBo* 3 (*Pachomian Koinonia,* 1:24), on which the translation offered here is based.

27. The oldest *Life* of this Arabic group, Göttingen MS 116, is unpublished but is similar in large part to that published by Amélineau, *Monuments* [1889], 337–711; I quote Amélineau's translation of the relevant passage on 339; cf. Lefort, *Vies coptes*, 79 n. 1. On the Arabic *Lives*, see Veilleux, *Liturgie dans le cénobitisme*, 49–68 (on the various Arabic *Lives*) and 69–82 (comparing the principal Arabic, Greek, and Coptic recensions); Lefort, *Vies coptes*, xv–xviii; and see now Grossmann, "Some Observations."

28. See elsewhere *Apophth. patr.* Theodore of Enaton 1–3; he also features in several texts that repeat the story found in *Vit. Ant.* 60; see *Letter of Ammon*, ed. Goehring, 281 (note to 153.4–5).

29. See *Ep. Am.* 30, where Theodore (of Tabennese) tells Ammon about various monks dwelling in Nitria, including "Theodore, who was with the holy Amoun."

30. G1 99; trans. Vielleux, *Pachomian Koinonia*, 1:366, adjusted.

31. The reference to the reception and translation of the festal letter is in *SBo* 189; cf. Camplani, *Lettere festali di Atanasio,* 49–50. The text of the two letters from Athanasius to Horsiesios is in *SBo* 204 (resolving conflict between Horsiesios and Theodore), where the Greek gives the circumstances but not the text of the letter at G1 143–44, and in G1 150 = *SBo* 210 (after hearing of Theodore's death), where the Greek must be the original; on these Athanasian

interventions, see Brakke, *Athanasius*, 120–28. Note that the introductory formula of the letters has been altered in the Coptic to conform to the Egyptian style of letter writing; see further Choat, "Epistolary Formulae."

32. In G1 22; see Brakke, *Demons.*

33. "Wrestling with demons as an athlete of the truth, like the most holy Antony," G1 22 (trans. Vielleux, *Pachomian Koinonia*, 1:311); compare especially *Vit. Ant.* 5–6; cf. Brakke, *Demons,* 21–47.

34. On demons in the Pachomian tradition, see Brakke, *Demons,* 78–96; on the relationship with the *Life of Antony,* see esp. 80, 84.

35. *SBo* 21 (Lefort, *S. Pachomii Vita Bohairice Scripta*, 21).

36. Lefort, *S. Pachomii Vitae Sahidice Scriptae*, CSCO 99.131–203.

37. Lefort, *S. Pachomii Vitae Sahidice Scriptae*, CSCO 99.178.7–10; the parallel text S6 breaks off just before this section.

38. Trans. Vielleux, *Pachomian Koinonia,* 1:382–83, adjusted.

39. Lefort, *Vies coptes*, 269, leaves open the possibility that literary dependence is not involved.

40. Lefort, *Vies coptes*, lxxviii–lxxxii; Veilleux, *Pachomian Koinonia,* 1:2.

41. Göttingen MS 116; see Grossmann, "Some Observations," 51 with nn. 48–50; cf. 56 n. 75.

42. S5.17 (Lefort, *S. Pachomii Vitae Sahidice Scriptae*, CSCO 99.183–84 = *SBo* 133); G1 120 has incorporated some of the content of the letter into Antony's dialogue (alternately, but less likely in my opinion, the letter is invented from the dialogue). Note Antony's firm suggestion that the Pachomians refer to Horsiesius as an Israelite, a term that is repeatedly used in the letters attributed (probably authentically) to Antony; see Rubenson, *Letters of St. Antony*, 168–69.

43. *Ep. Am.* 29. It may be genuine even if the episode that frames the letter does not reflect Pachomian theology as evident elsewhere and may have been created around the letter; see Goehring's commentary in Ammon, *Letter of Ammon*, 275–78; Rubenson, *Letters of St. Antony*, 170–72.

44. Amélineau, *Monuments* [1894], 27–28, where Antony remarks that the spirit of God has come upon three men, Athanasius, Macarius, and Pambo. Rubenson, *Letters of St. Antony*, 166–67, tentatively supports the priority of the *Apophthegm*. See also the (later) Coptic *Historia ecclesiastica*, where the four pillars supporting the fourth-century church are said to be "Athanasius in Alexandria, Antony and Pachomius in the southern country (i.e. Upper Egypt), and Basil in Cappadocia" (ed. Orlandi, *Storia della Chiesa*, 2:38.10–15).

45. For a textual sign of redaction, see *G*1 94, "not only the most holy Athanasius who was then sitting on the archbishop's throne but whoever sat on it" (trans. Veilleux, *Pachomian Koinonia*, 1:361). *Apotaktikos* is a term for a monk that is used as a self-designation by Pachomian monks in Coptic recensions of the *Life of Pachomius* but is largely excised in the Greek and Latin

translations; see Goehring, "Through a Glass Darkly," 69; M. Choat, "Development and Use," 12–17. Note also the preservation of the account of the Synod of Lycopolis (*G*1 112), which the Coptic tradition attempted to excise from the *koinonia*'s history.

46. Bousset, *Apophthegmata*, 231–36, remarks on how the Greek *Lives* make relations with Athanasius closer; cf. Veilleux, *Liturgie dans le cénobitisme*, 192–93.

47. The suggestion is in Peeters, "À propos de la Vie sahidique."

48. On the circumstances, see Rousseau, *Pachomius*, 45–48.

49. Regarding the competitive tone of the *Lives,* see, in addition to the encounter with Antony (on which cf. Rousseau, *Pachomius*, 72–73), Pachomius's reflections on the superiority of the coenobitic over the anachoretic life at *SBo* 105; cf. Bacht, "Antonius und Pachomius," esp. 100–107.

50. The failure of the Coptic *Lives* of Pachomius to mention the *Life of Antony* also speaks strongly against the suggestion of Barnes, "Angel of Light," 357, that the *Life of Antony* "was originally composed in Coptic . . . for the benefit of the Pachomian communities in the Thebaid"; there is briefly stated opposition also in Abramowski, "Vertritt die syrische Fassung," 56; see also Brakke, "Greek and Syriac Versions," 50. Rousseau, "Antony as Teacher," 103–4, is however inclined to consider an Egyptian audience.

51. Leipoldt, *Sinuthii Archimandritae vita*, CSCO 41.68–69 (trans. Bell, *Life of Shenoute*, 61–62).

52. Leipoldt, *Sinuthii Archimandritae vita*, CSCO 41.185 (trans. Bell, *Life of Shenoute*, 91). For parallel references in the Sahidic and Arabic *vita* traditions, see Leipoldt, *Shenute von Atripe*, 106 n. 2.

53. On these, see now Lubomierski, *Vita Sinuthii*.

54. It remains premature, of course, to say anything definitive on the contents of Shenoute's work before their full publication; I offer here such insights as I have been able to glean from the currently published texts, with recognition of their inadequacies (especially those of Amélineau's edition) and in the full expectation that more can be said on this in the future.

55. Shenoute, "Scripture Has Said," ed. Amélineau, *Oeuvres de Schenoudi*, 1:192. On this work, part of the *Discourses* of Shenoute, see Emmel, *Shenoute's Literary Corpus*, 2:666–67.

56. Where it is remarked that reading the *Life* will teach monks that the Lord will make monks famous (φανεροὺς καὶ διαβοήτους ποιεῖ / ⲛ̄ϥⲁⲁⲩ ⲛ̄ⲥⲟⲉⲓⲧ) for their virtue and good deeds. Leipoldt, *Shenute von Atripe*, 78, may have believed this, for he characterizes the passage as a "ein Zitat aus der vita Antonii"; cf. 86. See also *Vit. Ant.* 93.3 ("Antony was famous in every place" [τὸ πανταχοῦ δὲ τοῦτον διαβεβοῆσθαι / ⲉϥⲟ ⲛⲥⲟⲉⲓⲧ ϩⲙ̄ⲙⲁ ⲛⲓⲙ]) and *Vit. Ant.* 10.3.

57. See Emmel, *Shenoute's Literary Corpus*, 2:638–41. Quotation and translation at 2:640.

58. See the comment of Krueger, *Writing and Holiness*, 13: "That an author knows the story of Antony does not mean that he has a copy of Athanasius's *Life of Antony* before him."

59. Shenoute, "Scripture Has Said," ed. Amélineau, *Oeuvres de Schenoudi*, 1:192–93. On the letters, see now Rubenson, *Letters of St. Antony*; reaction to his careful study asserting the authenticity of the letters has been largely positive; for references to work critical of Rubenson's arguments, see Bumaznov, "Evil Angels," 501 n. 9 and 502 n. 10. Bumaznov himself approves of the nuancing of the question by Rowen Williams cited in the latter note, emphasizing the possibility of later "Origenizing" of the letters.

60. There is a Latin translation of the Arabic in PG 40.1047b; cf. Garitte, "À propos des lettres," 20–22.

61. Ammonas, *Ep.* 12, *Ammonii Erimitae Epistolae,* ed. Kmosko; Ammonas, *Ep.* 1, ed. Nau, *Ammonas, successeur*.

62. Shenoute, "Scripture Has Said," ed. Amélineau, *Oeuvres de Schenoudi*, 1:193: "ⲡⲉϫⲁϥ ⲟⲛ ⲛϭⲓ ⲡϩⲗⲗⲟ ⲉⲧⲛⲁⲛⲟⲩϥ ⲡⲁ ⲡⲥⲟⲟⲩⲛ ⲉⲧⲙⲉϩ ⲛϩⲏⲩ ⲛⲓⲙ ⲙⲯⲩⲭⲏ ⲛⲓⲙ ⲛⲛⲉⲧⲥⲱⲧⲙ ⲉⲛⲉϥϣⲁϫⲉ ⲁⲩⲱ ⲉⲧⲱϣ ⲙⲙⲟⲟⲩ" (He also says, the good elder, the one with the knowledge which is full of every profit for every soul who hears his words and reads them).

63. ⲕⲁⲧⲁⲑⲉ ⲉⲛⲧⲁϥϫⲟⲟⲥ ϩⲛ̄ⲛⲉϥⲉⲡⲓⲥⲧⲟⲗⲏ ⲛ̄ϭⲓⲡⲉⲛⲉⲓⲱⲧ ⲛ̄ϩⲗ̄ⲗⲟ ⲁⲛⲧⲟⲛⲓⲟⲥ. For the text of XL 41–42, see Bellet, "Nou Testimoni," 255 (ⲙⲁ [41], lines 7–11). On the lost work from *Canon* 3, see Emmel, *Shenoute's Literary Corpus*, 1:111–25; the section that relates to *Canon* 3 is listed at 122; on *Canon* 3, cf. Emmel, *Shenoute's Literary Corpus*, 2:570–72.

64. Emmel says, "In XL 41, Shenoute refers to Anthony's letters without giving any direct quotation" (*Shenoute's Literary Corpus*, 2:667 n. 605), but I am inclined to agree with Bellet (who, however, thought the author was Besa, not Shenoute), who believed there is a free, rather than literal, citation of a letter of Antony somewhere on XL 41 ("Nou Testimoni," 252).

65. Besa, *Ep.* 29, to Antinoë, ed. Kuhn, *Letters and Sermons*, 97; Besa, *Ep*. 30, to Herai, ed. Kuhn, *Letters and Sermons,* 99–100, 100–101; cf. Garitte, "À propos des lettres," 22–28; Rubenson, *Letters of St. Antony*, 16.

66. Brakke, *Athanasius,* 17–79.

67. Shenoute's discourse on virginity is acephalous work A17 in the numeration of Emmel, *Shenoute's Literary Corpus*, 2:688; part of this text was edited by Leipoldt, *Sinuthii Archimandritae vita,* CSCO 42, no. 35 ("*De virginitate*"); cf. Brakke, "Authenticity," 21. For Athanasius's "First Letter to the Virgins," see Leipoldt, *Sinuthii Archimandritae vita,* CSCO 42.108.19–27; the Athanasian citation is given in full by Lefort in Athanasius, *Lettres festales*,

CSCO 150.106.22–108.3; cf. Lefort, "Athanase, Ambroise et Chenoute." For the full text, see Athanasius, *Lettres festales,* ed. Lefort, CSCO 150.73–99 (trans. Brakke, *Athanasius,* 274–91); with the Shenoute citation, cf. 95–98. Shenoute's citation allows the restoration of at least a page at the beginning of a lacuna in the MS of the Athanasian text. The text of Athanasius's letter is in White Monastery codex AN, which dates to the fifth or sixth century according to Lefort's intro. to Athanasius, *Lettres festales,* xviii–xxii. The codex also contained a Pseudo-Clementine epistle on virginity *falsely* attributed to Athanasius; see Brakke, "Authenticity," 20 n. 8. Shenoute does omit the elaborations in Athanasius's text, which may not have stood in his copy and are perhaps not original in any case (see Brakke, "Authenticity," 21, and *Athanasius,* 289 n. 3).

68. On night vigils, see Shenoute's "Since It Behooves Christians" (Emmel, *Shenoute's Literary Corpus*, 2:668, 858); the text, from MONB.HD 208–209, is in Shenoute, *Oeuvres de Schenoudi*, ed. Amélineau, 1:204–5, and Athanasius, *Lettres festales,* ed. Lefort, CSCO 150.108.6–18. On virgins who break their vows and marry, see his "I Have Been Reading the Holy Gospels" (Emmel, *Shenoute's Literary Corpus*, 2:651–52, 836); text from MONB.GP 66–67 in Athanasius, *Lettres festales,* ed. Lefort, CSCO 150.108.20–109.4.

69. In a version different from that later copied at his monastery, and probably in the original Greek, in his work "I Am Amazed" (see Emmel, *Shenoute's Literary Corpus*, 2:646–48); see Shenoute, *Shenute contra Origenistas,* ed. and trans. Orlandi, 24 (319); cf. Camplani, *Lettere festali*, 49; see 192 on the translation into Coptic of the letter, probably made after Shenoute's death. Other echoes of the *Festal Letters* are at Shenoute, *Oeuvres de Schenoudi*, ed. Amélineau, 1:212–20, see Camplani, *Lettere festali*, 274.

70. Besa, "*Letters and Sermons,* ed. Kuhn, CSCO 157.82.13 ff. (no. 27, pp. 78–91), "Besa the most humble it is who writes to his beloved brothers in the Lord," which Kuhn calls "To the Brethren on Maintaining Unity"; cf. the translation in CSCO 158.79.

71. In a codex (MONB.CP) dating from the twelfth century (according to Lefort, *Lettres festales*, xxix, xxxi; tenth to twelfth according to Crum, *P.Ryl.Copt.*, 241) which Besa's quotation follows exactly; presumably Besa had this manuscript's archetype before his eyes seven centuries earlier. Another (which differs and clearly represents a different translation) is preserved in BL Or. 6007 = *P.Lond.Copt.* 1.990 (dated VII/VIII by Lefort). The text is edited by Lefort (Athanasius, *Lettres festales,* CSCO 150.121–29); on the MSS, cf. xxxi–xxxiii.

72. For Shenoute's citation of Athanasius's letters on the Manichaeans, see "Who Speaks through the Prophet" = "The Lord Is Long-Suffering" (Emmel, *Shenoute's Literary Corpus*, 1:356–57, 2:682; W. Bang and Gabain, "Türkische Turfan-Texte," 429–30). Another work, which Leipoldt titles *De Actis Archelai* (in *Sinuthii Archimandritae vita*, CSCO 42, no. 36) and Emmel titles "And It Is

Also Good for Us to Say to You" (in *Shenoute's Literary Corpus*, 2:660), demonstrates more clearly Shenoute's knowledge of the *Acta*, perhaps through Epiphanius's *Panarion*.

73. As supposed by Garitte, "Texte grec," 7: "Chenoute fait allusion à une Vie d'Antoine qui ne peut avoir été que copte." On Shenoute's literacy in Greek, see, e.g., Emmel, "From the Other Side," 99. He may also have delivered sermons and composed in Greek; see Lucchesi, "Chenoute a-t-il ecrit en grec?," 201–10, with Depuydt, "In Sinuthiam Graecum." The quotation from Aristophanes' *Frogs* and explicit citation of *The Birds* in "The Lord Thundered" suggests contact with high Hellenic culture (see Emmel, *Shenoute's Literary Corpus*, 2:618–19, cf. 614–15; text in Shenoute, *Oeuvres de Schenoudi,* ed. Amélineau, 1:386; cf. Erman, "Schenute und Aristophanes"; Treu, "Aristophanes bei Shenoute").

74. See in general Scholten, "Nag-Hammadi-Texte," 153–57; Kotsifou, "Books and Book Production."

75. On the circa 165 Greek MSS of the *Life*, none of which come from Egypt, see Bartelink's intro. to Athanasius, *Vie d'Antoine*, 77–95; Garitte, "Texte grec," 1–4.

76. It was presumably copied during this year or shortly before.

77. Pierpont Morgan Library M 579 (= MICH.BL), see Depuydt, *Catalogue of Coptic Manuscripts,* no. 162 (pp. 317–21); cf. Garitte's intro. to Athanasius, *S. Antonii Vitae Versio Sahidica*, i–ii. On the library, see Emmel, "Library of the Monastery."

78. See Garitte's intro. to Athanasius, *S. Antonii Vitae Versio Sahidica*, ii–iv (which requires updating in light of more recent codicological observations); the codices (none of which preserve more than a few folia of the *Life*) are MONB.AH (= Garitte Codex A), MONB.AI (= Garitte Codex B+C), MONB.LY (= Garitte Codex D, a miscellany of mainly hagiographical works, including an extract from the end of the *Life* (*Vit. Ant.* 91–93), beginning "The same [i.e., Apa Athanasius the archbishop of Alexandria], on the death of the great Antonios the anchorite"); the CMCL does not treat the folia Bibliothèque nationale de France 131.5.063 and 131.5.113, which Garitte lists under his Codex C, as part of that codex, but lists them separately. Cf. Garitte, "Texte grec," 7–8.

79. It is not, however, found among the many codices of the ninth and following centuries recovered from the Church of St. John in Tin (Thinis) now in Turin (CMCL GIOV. AA–AS; cf. Orlandi, "Papyrus coptes"; the Library of the Monastery of St. Macarius in Wadi Natrun (Sketis; CMCL MACA. AA–EI; cf. Zanetti, *Manuscrits de Dair Abû Maqâr*); or the Library of the Monastery of St. Mercurius at Tbo (Edfu; CMCL MERC. AA–BD).

80. The assemblages from Wadi Sarga, Apa Apollo, and Epiphanius are collected in Crum and Bell, *Wadi Sarga,* Kahle, *Bala'izah,* and Winlock, Crum, and Evelyn-White, *Monastery of Epiphanius,* respectively. The texts from Apa

Apollo include *P.Bal.* 1.35, a *Life of Athanasius,* and *P.Bal.* 1.44, "A Sermon of Our God-Bearing Father and Great Apostle the Holy Athanasius the Archbishop of Alexandria When He Returned from the First Exile." The texts from Epiphanius include a discourse of Athanasius, "Against Drunkenness," copied on limestone (*P.Mon. Epiph.* 51), and an extract of a sermon "On the Cross" (*P.Mon. Epiph.* 49) in a papyrus codex also containing hymns.

81. *P.Mon.Epiph.* 585, with extensive prior bibliography, to which few critical additions are now possible, as the inscription was lost by 1883. The nineteenth-century assertion that the inscription dates from the fourth century, based on as little as the fact that Athanasius himself lived in that century, is still repeated (e.g., Brakke, *Athanasius,* 134 n. 240 ("a 4th century Greek inscription"); cf. Lefebvre, *Recueil des inscriptions*, no. 380 (pp. 70–71); *SB* V 8698. However, the monastery was founded and flourished in the sixth and seventh centuries, so the inscription must date to that period (cf. Haelst, *Catalogue des papyrus*, no. 625; Bagnall, *Egypt in Late Antiquity*, 305).

82. *P.Mon.Epiph.* 247, to Isaac and Elias; the same phrase is used in another letter probably also written by Frange; see Boud'hors and Heurtel, *Ostraca coptes*, no. 61. In a note on *P.Mon.Epiph.* 247, Crum cites an unpublished Berlin ostracon in which the addressee is described as being "filled with all virtues [ἀρεταί] like Antony."

83. *Apophth. patr.* Hilarion 1 (PG 65.241).

84. *P.Mon.Epiph.* 247.17–19. On the various traditions involving the confessor Paphnoute, see A. Martin, *Athanase d'Alexandrie*, 43–49.

85. Crum, "Inscriptions from Shenoute's Monastery"; see now Orlandi, "Library of the Monastery," 213–15.

86. See Orlandi, "Library of the Monastery," and Takla, "Library of the Monastery," both of whom question whether this room was in fact the monastery's library in antiquity.

87. B.22 and B. 23 in Crum's enumeration, "Inscriptions from Shenoute's Monastery," 565–67; Orlandi, "Library of the Monastery," 214–15.

88. Coquin, "Catalogue de la bibliothèque."

89. "Exodus, with the Canons [*kanon*] of Apa Atha[nasius]" (recto a.9–10); "A Small Book of Exegesis of Apa Athanasius" (recto b.41–42); "A Book of Precepts [*entole*] of the Apa Athan[asius]" (verso 7); "The *keregmata* [i.e., Festal Letters] of Apa Athanasius" (verso 8); "A Dialogue [*logos*] of Apa Athanasius Which He Spoke with a Philosopher" (verso 25); "Apa Athanasius Concerning the Priests and Monks" (ⲉⲧⲃⲉ ⲛ̄ⲟⲩⲏⲏⲃ ⲙⲛ̄ ⲙ̄ⲙⲟⲛⲟⲭ") (verso 34–35); and "Apa Peter with the Encomia of Apa Athanasius with Some Others" (recto b.47–49).

90. See *P.Mon. Epiph.* 554–57; *O.Crum.* 457–59, Ad. 23; *O.Vind.Copt.* 147; *O.CrumST* 162, 165–66; *P.Fay.Copt.* 44; *P.Prag.* 1.87; *P.Vindob.Gr.* 26015; *P.Leid.Inst.* 13. Most are certainly or probably from monastic contexts, but others

(e.g., *P.Leid.Inst.* 13) may relate to church libraries. On Greek lists of books, see Otranto, *Antiche liste di libri*, especially "*Alia tempora, alii libri:* Notizie ed elenchi di libri cristiani su papiro," 123–44; Minnen's intro. to *P.Leid.Inst.* 13, 45–46.

91. E.g., *P.Leid.Inst.* 13, which includes *Lives* of Macrina and Placidia, the writings of Serapion of Thmuis, various martyrdoms, and works by Basil, John Chrysostom, and Gregory Nazianzus as well as encomia on Constantine, Basil, and Athanasius. In *P.Prag.* 1.87, note particularly τὸ (βιβλίον) τῶν γερώντων, presumably the *Apophthegmata patrum*. The list of articles in *O.Crum* 459 includes "a *kathegesis* of Apa Shenoute," and the *Life* of Apa Chrysaphius the Ethiopian.

92. See especially *O.Crum* 250, a letter asking for the "*Paradise of Shihet*" (Sketis), the "*Paradise of Phosm*" (Nitria), and an *asketikion* (for the *Paradise* cf. *O.Crum* 252); *P.Mon.Epiph.* 375, mentioning "(the *Life* of) my father Hilarion" (i.e., by Jerome); *O.Crum* 252 and *P.Mon.Epiph.* 393, which both mention the *logismoi* of Evagrius (i.e., "On the Eight Thoughts"; see Evagrius of Pontus, *Greek Ascetic Corpus,* ed. Sinkewicz, 66–90).

93. Especially *P.Leid.Inst.* 13, in which two lines (8 and 40) list *bioi* where the name of the saint is lost; the lacuna at line 8 seems too short for Ἀντωνίου, and the editor reads]ο̣.[in the middle of the lost words at line 40. There are, however, many lines on the papyrus (as on others) in which the title of the book is completely lost.

94. Brakke, *Athanasius,* 135–41 and esp. ch. 4, quotes on 135, 137.

95. Regarding the hypothesized aim of achieving unity between monasticism and the church in Egypt, see the question posed by Rousseau, "Antony as Teacher," 104. More speculatively, I wonder if we may be able to suggest that despite the *Life's* stated audience, it was aimed as much at telling people how to relate to monks as how monks should behave.

96. Brakke, *Athanasius,* 265.

97. Indeed, it may be argued that outside Egypt the "historical Antony" never existed.

Chapter Four

Apologetics of Asceticism

The *Life of Antony* and Its Political Context

SAMUEL RUBENSON

Why was the *Life of Antony* written? Was it to promote Antonian tradition or to rectify its influence in Egyptian monasticism? Was it part of a campaign against Arianism in Egypt, or rather propaganda for Egyptian monasticism in the West? Is the text part and parcel of the propaganda and ecclesial struggle of Athanasius of Alexandria, or does it represent the monastic tradition of Antony? And, more basically, is the text, as transmitted in Greek, one literary unit consciously composed by an author or a compilation made from a variety of sources?

Although the issues of authorship, literary unity and character, model, and purpose of the text have been discussed extensively since the early and mid-twentieth century, no agreement has yet been reached.[1] In the early twentieth century a lively discussion on the literary character was begun by Mertel and Holl and continued by List, Cavallin, and Priessnig, but it yielded little consensus and has had almost no impact on recent debate.[2] The early doubts about the literary unity of the text voiced by Reitzenstein were soon silenced, and the more recent suggestion that Bishop Serapion was a coauthor have received little attention.[3] To most scholars the unity and integrity of the text is a given. Questions about purpose and literary character have thus become intimately linked to the issue of authorship, and to most scholars the question is why Athanasius wrote or could have written the text.[4] Traditionally the reply has been to regard the *Vita* as part of Athanasius's promotion of the monastic tradition in general or of a specific version of it.[5] More recent interpretations detect wider polemical purposes and argue that the *Life* was part of Athanasius's anti-Arian campaign directed against Arian monastic sympathizers, or an attempt to redefine Antony and his story in order to integrate his monastic followers into the theological framework or simply the ecclesiastical authority of the Alexandrian bishop, or even a refutation of Greek *paideia* directed against earlier depictions of an accommodation between Greek philosophy and Christian faith.[6]

There is here an obvious development from early attempts to interpret the *Vita* in relation to biographical traditions in late antiquity in general or monastic and hagiographical literature in particular, without much attention to the author, generally assumed to be Athanasius, to later interpretations reading the *Vita* in relation to internal affairs within the church in Egypt, and more specifically to emerging Egyptian monasticism and its relationship to the bishopric of Alexandria.[7] The issue of purpose has thus been made dependent less on a literary analysis of the text itself and more on external evidence or speculations on how the relations between Athanasius and the early Egyptian monks represented by Antony are understood, and how the *Life* can be related to Athanasius's anti-Arian struggle and his ecclesiastical politics. Doubts about an Athanasian authorship are, moreover, founded on problems of how to relate the text to Athanasius's other writings and his preoccupation with the Trinitarian conflict and imperial policies.[8]

But the purpose of the text is not the only issue that has been made dependent on the interpretation of evidence outside the text. Even the specific question of whether Athanasius wrote the text has been answered primarily on the basis of attributions in the manuscript tradition and the early attestations by Gregory of Nazianzus, Jerome, and the Pachomian histories.[9] If we look closely at the text itself, it reveals little about the identity of the author. Instead, as I will argue here, the text tells us more about the objectives of the author than has often been recognized.

In the preface to the *Life of Antony* the author is vague about his own identity and connection to Antony. There is nothing to reveal his position, and while on the one hand he gives the impression of being a close relation to the monk, on the other he states that he needed to collect information. He says both that he met Antony "often" (πολλάκις), which could, of course, mean anything from several times to regularly, and that his problem was that he had no time to interview the monks who really knew him and thus had to resort to a single disciple of Antony's.[10] The only mention of Athanasius in the *Vita* itself tells us about how Antony at his death donates his only belongings to the two bishops Athanasius and Serapion, but there is nothing that indicates that the text here refers to its author.[11] The only first-person eyewitness reference is also vague, implying simply that the author was part of the group of Alexandrians who escorted Antony out of the city after his anti-Arian visit to the city.[12] Moreover, in the index to the festal letters of Athanasius the visit is dated as taking place in July/August AD 337, several months before Athanasius returned from his first exile on November 23, 337. This date fits well with the reference in the *Life of Antony* to the invitation being issued "by the bishops" in plural, that is, not by Athanasius, but also with the fact that the imminent return of Athanasius was made known to the Christians in Alexandria in a letter from the emperor in late July.[13]

Further, if Athanasius really was well acquainted with Antony and authored the *Vita,* it is strange that Antony appears only once in Athanasius's corpus. The passage in which he is mentioned is, moreover, problematic. In the *Historia arianorum* Athanasius tells the story of how a military commander, Balacius, died from an accident as a result of his disdainful treatment of one of Antony's letters.[14] The same story appears, albeit with significant differences, in the *Life of Antony.* In the *Historia arianorum* Antony is writing to Bishop George, the Arian replacement of Athanasius during his second exile, and only accidentally is the letter shown to Balacius, who, on the instigation of the bishop, spits on it. In the *Life of Antony* Antony writes to the commander himself to stop him from persecuting Christians, especially monks, whereupon Balacius laughs, spits on the letter, mistreats the emissaries, and threatens Antony. The two versions are evidently based on the same story interpreting the death of Balacius in 345, a date when Athanasius was in either Rome or Trier. But the objectives are quite different. In the *Historia arianorum* the story is used to denigrate Bishop George by referring to his trust in secular power, whereas in the *Life of Antony* the story makes Balacius into a persecutor of the Christians and Antony into a courageous martyr. There are good reasons to regard the version in the *Historia arianorum* as both earlier and more trustworthy.[15] It is certainly much more likely that Antony wrote to the bishop of Alexandria than to the *dux*; and the influence of the imagery and the vocabulary from martyr literature upon the *Life of Antony* version is manifest.[16] The totally different way the story is told in the *Life of Antony* does not speak for its having being penned by the same author, and certainly not within a very short time.

Had it not been for the very strong external attestation in manuscripts, as well as in early testimonies, scholars would, no doubt, in spite of some internal arguments linking the *Vita* to Athanasian themes and texts, long ago have decided against an Athanasian authorship.[17] Adding to the external evidence the desire for a known author has, however, meant that even suggestions that Athanasius revised an earlier version have met with little approval. Neither Martin Tetz's suggestion that our Athanasian version is a revision of a text originally written by Bishop Serapion nor René Draguet's more bold suggestion that the Greek text is a revision of a primitive Coptic text represented by the Syriac version has been accepted.[18] Although scholars are ready to admit that the author could have used earlier sources for several passages, in particular material paralleled in the letters of Antony and thus considered to have originated directly from Antony's circle, the text is generally treated as representing Athanasius's own views.[19]

Following some leads of Philip Rousseau in his analysis of Antony as a teacher, my own analysis of the structure of the text and its models, and recently Arthur Urbano in his discussion of the text, my purpose here is to leave the issue of authorship aside and return to the interpretations of the early twentieth century, suggesting a somewhat different setting for the text from the one usually assumed.[20] As Rousseau pointed out, the *Vita* presents Antony not only as a model to imitate but also as "one who taught, in ways familiar to 'philosophical' or neo-Pythagorean pedagogues of the age."[21] Antony in the *Vita* is the teacher and founder of "a new culture, a new pattern of learning."[22] An ascetic society forms around him, "drawn together by his words."[23] Through his teaching the desert becomes a city.[24] In Urbano's analysis Antony is not only a teacher but also a philosopher serving in Athanasius's apologetic against pagan philosophical claims as well as against Christian accommodation to these. To him the *Vita* must be read as part of a "competition" in which "an alternative Christian *paideia* was proposed, one founded on Christian texts, doctrines and authorities, in which the Church and its leaders, most notably bishops and monks, preserved and transmitted an education of real value."[25]

I will go a step further and argue that the basis for the apology for Christianity in the form of a monastic biography lies in the fact that the monastic tradition grew out of and in relation to the neo-Pythagorean philosophical revival. Here I disagree with Urbano, who claims that the *Life of Antony* portrays Antony as the cultural opposite of the Greek philosophers as well as of Alexandrian "academic" theology.[26] Antony is not superior to Pythagoras, or to an Arian theologian, by being radically different but by not being led astray. His rural and Coptic identity is not a sign of a rejection of urban and Greek culture but proof that Christianity is conquering the world.

ANTONY AND PYTHAGORAS

In a penetrating article published in 1914 and since then often cited but apparently less frequently read and reflected upon, Richard Reitzenstein proved that a passage in the *Vita Antonii* was borrowed almost word for word from a *Life* of Pythagoras.[27] By comparing the two extant *Lives* of Pythagoras, one by Porphyry, the other by Iamblichus, Reitzenstein could prove that the author of the *Vita Antonii* had used a source common to the Pythagorean *Lives*. In the description in chapter 14 of the *Vita Antonii* we are told about how Antony emerged from his seclusion in a fortified well where he had lived for twenty years. Here the author copies

Porphyry, *Vita Pythagorae* 35

τὸ σῶμα ὥσπερ ἐπι στάθμῃ **τὴν αὐτὴν ἕξιν** διεφύλαττεν, οὐ ποτὲ μὲν ὑγιαῖνον ποτὲ δὲ νοσοῦν, **οὐδ᾽ αὖ ποτὲ μὲν πιαινόμενον** καὶ αὐξανόμενον ποτὲ δὲ λεπτυνόμενον καὶ **ἰσχναινόμενον**, **ἥ τε ψυχὴ** τό ὅμοιον **ἦθος** ἀεὶ διὰ τῆς ὄψεως παρεδήλου. **Οὔτε γὰρ ὑφ᾽ ἡδονῆς** διεχεῖτο πλέον οὔθ᾽ **ὑπ᾽ ἀνίας συνεστέλλετο**, οὐδ᾽ ἐπίδηλος ἦν χαρᾷ ἢ λύπῃ **κάτοχος, ἀλλ᾽ οὐδὲ γελάσαντα** ἢ **κλαύσαντά** τίς ποτ᾽ ἐκεῖνον ἐθεάσατο.

kept his body always in the same condition, as if in a scale. He was not sometimes healthy and sometimes sick, nor again sometimes **getting fatter** and increasing in girth, sometimes **losing weight and thinning down**. **His soul, too,** always revealed through his appearance **the same disposition**, **for he was not** much **relaxed by pleasure nor constricted by grief**, nor did he ever seem to be in the grip of joy or sadness; indeed, no one ever saw him **either laughing** or **weeping**.

Vita Antonii 14

τό τε σῶμα τὴν αὐτὴν ἕξιν ἔχον, **καὶ μήτε πιανθὲν** ὡς ἀγύμναστον, μήτε **ἰσχνωθὲν** ὡς ἀπὸ νηστειῶν καὶ μάχης δαιμόνων, τοιοῦτον δὲ οἷον καὶ πρὸ τῆς ἀναχωρήσεως ᾔδεισαν αὐτόν. **Τῆς δὲ ψυχῆς** πάλιν καθαρὸν **τὸ ἦθος**. **Οὔτε γὰρ ὡς ὑπὸ ἀνίας συνεσταλμένη ἦν, οὔτε ὑφ᾽ ἡδονῆς διακεχυμένη οὔτε ὑπὸ γέλωτος** ἢ κατηφείας **συνεχομένη**.

his body had kept its former condition, **neither fat** from lack of exercise, **nor thin** from fasting and combat with demons, but was just as they had known him prior to his withdrawal. **The state** of **his soul** was one of purity, for it was **not constricted by grief**, **nor relaxed by pleasure**, nor affected by either **laughter** or **sorrow**.

almost verbatim a description found in Porphyry's biography on Pythagoras in chapter 35.[28] In addition to the almost word-for-word agreement between these two passages, Reitzenstein pointed out several other passages where the *Life of Antony* follows the description of Pythagoras.[29]

Comparing Porphyry's text with the *Life of Antony*, as well as with Iamblichus's description of Pythagoras, Reitzenstein came to the conclusion that Athanasius had used and plundered a lost *Life of Pythagoras (Vit. Pyth.)* for the bulk of the first part of his biography.[30] A parallel reading of the two stories confirms this. Both Antony and Pythagoras are said to have lost their fathers when they were still young. Both renounce their possessions and flee the world at the age of eighteen, and both are said to have struggled through studies, piety, and ascetic practice to gain freedom from care. Both search out and learn from previous spiritual masters and afterwards retreat into solitude, undisturbed and undeterred. Antony goes into the desert and enters a deserted well, where he stays for twenty years, whereas Pythagoras goes to Egypt, where he is initiated into divine mysteries in the shrines over a period of twenty-two years.[31] For Antony's stay in the underground shrine Reitzenstein also adduces a passage from Lucian where the teacher of Arignotus, the Pythagorean, is described as "remarkably wise," as "a holy man, intelligent, but not fluent in Greek," and as having "lived twenty-three years in underground shrines" and afterwards being able to swim with crocodiles — this last detail is perhaps echoed in the *Life of Antony,* which in the chapter after Antony's emergence from seclusion tells how he unharmed crossed a canal full of crocodiles.[32]

Just as essential as these similarities, according to Reitzenstein, are the parallels in the recurrent descriptions of the two heroes.[33] In these descriptions Reitzenstein finds evidence for a neo-Pythagorean ideal as the background for Athanasius's vision of the ideal monastic life. In contrast to an emphasis on ascetic exploits, miracles, and superhuman qualities, which according to him represents the real monastic tradition, Reitzenstein points toward the philosophical ideals that recur throughout the *Life of Antony*: purity of soul, harmony, and accord with nature. For these he finds parallels in Iamblichus and in Diogenes Laertius, as well as in Athanasius's *Contra gentes.*[34] To these more general ideals can be added some direct parallels between Antony and Pythagoras in vocabulary as well as examples of virtues. Pythagoras is said to be revered as a "child of God," and Antony as a "friend of God."[35] They are both said to have been "loved by all." Both are described as having a noble character and elegant manners, as well as sharp eyes and remarkable discernment.[36] Both Pythagoras and Antony settle in caves, where followers visit them, and both have to flee because of their popularity. Both gain control of irrational animals that are admonished not to attack humans or destroy the crops, and both heal diseases and restore harmony.[37] Both are said to have established cities where the people who come to them settle down in a kind of communal life governed by the teaching of the masters.[38] And although differently, both teach at length and in partly quoted sermons.[39]

To Reitzenstein the discovery of the parallels between the *Life of Antony* and the Pythagorean biographies had two main implications. First, the *Life of Antony* must be regarded, not as a simple literary unit, but as a composite actually put together somewhat clumsily from different sources. To create his biography Athanasius used as a literary model a *Life of Pythagoras,* from which he also drew many of the characterizations of his hero. To this he added two long speeches created by himself (chapters 16–43 and 72–80), a long passage of traditional monastic stories about miracles (chapters 48, 51–66), a series of chapters in which Antony is described in close association with the Pythagorean tradition (67–71), and finally a section closely linked to Athanasius's own anti-Arian struggle (81–88). Second, Reitzenstein saw in the *Life of Antony* a conscious criticism of the prevalent monastic tradition (characterized by radical ascetic ideals and superhuman miracles), a criticism based on "the philosophical-mystical" tradition of the neo-Pythagoreans adapted by Athanasius to his Christian views.[40]

Overwhelmed by the parallels he found, and caught by his dichotomy between a philosophical-mystical tradition represented by the neo-Pythagoreans and what he regarded as the superstition of the monks, Reitzenstein seems not to have reflected upon, or even to have observed, the pointed contrasts between Pythagoras and Antony in the *Life of Antony.* But as important as the adduced parallels are the passages where Antony is described as the exact opposite of Pythagoras. Already in the first chapter Antony is said to have refused to go to school, whereas the *Lives* of Pythagoras from the outset stress the fact that he received a broad education.[41] Directly after the revealing passage found by Reitzenstein and quoted above, Pythagoras after his initiations leaves Egypt and travels all over the world to study, while Antony in the long sermon after his initiation ridicules the Greeks who cross the sea to obtain wisdom, when it is actually to be found within oneself.[42]

Porphyry, *Vita Pythagorae* 12	*Vita Antonii* 20
ἐκ γὰρ τῆς περὶ ταῦτα τὰ ἔθνη πλάνης ὁ Πυθαγόρας τὸ πλεῖστον τῆς σοφίας ἐνεπορεύσατο	Ἕλληνες μὲν οὖν ἀποδημοῦσι καὶ θάλασσαν περῶσιν, ἵνα γράμματα μάθωσιν, ἡμεῖς δὲ οὐ χρεῖαν ἔχομεν οὔτε ἀποδημίας διὰ τὴν βασιλεῖαν τῶν οὐρανῶν οὔτε περᾶσαι θάλατταν διὰ τὴν ἀρετήν
It was from his travels among these peoples that Pythagoras gained his wisdom.	The Greeks go abroad and cross the sea to study, but we have no need to go abroad for the kingdom of heaven or to cross the sea for virtue.

This very pointed difference is underlined by the subsequent argument in Antony's sermon that since what is essential is to live according to nature, κατὰ φύσιν, to which the Pythagoreans would agree, the only necessary thing for man is to remain as he was created. The extensive travels depicted in the lives of Pythagoras are thus of no avail.

Reitzenstein's lack of awareness of the polemical nature of the text is also evident in his difficulties in interpreting the many encounters with the demons, which he dismisses as representing ancient and crude popular imagination.[43] But as David Brakke has shown, the encounters with the demons are best interpreted as part of a polemic with Graeco-Roman religion that borrows its imagery from the stories about how the martyrs defeated their pagan persecutors.[44] The story of Antony's presence in Alexandria during the persecutions, marking the transition from the first to the second part of the *Vita*, establishes the purpose of his way of life, a daily martyrdom facing the evil powers of daily persecution in the shape of the demons. These demons are presented as taking the shape of pagan deities and taking up their role of giving oracles and prophetic utterances.[45] They are alarmed at the presence of a Christian and are in vain trying to prevent the spread of Christianity and the entrance of Antony and his monastic disciples into their own realm, the desert. When Antony is attacked, his reply is essentially the same as the martyr's in front of his persecutors, a stubborn reference to Christ, the sign of the cross, and the use of scriptural quotations.[46] Antony the martyr becomes also Antony the holy man, the one who ousts and replaces the gods/demons as the medium of divine aid to people. As Christ's slave, Antony clears the desert of its lord and his troops for the Christian monks, who can practice their discipline secure in the knowledge that the devil and his demons are powerless to thwart them.[47]

The polemical character of the work is, however, most manifest in the specific antithesis between the literate and weak pagan Greek philosopher and the uneducated but powerful Christian monk developed in the three stories about Antony's encounters with Greek philosophers, stories bypassed by Reitzenstein but discussed by Rousseau and Urbano.[48] Placed at the end of the *Vita*, after Antony's victories over the demons, his miracles, and his attack on heretics, and followed by his protest against the persecutions of the *dux* and his advice to the emperors, the encounters with the philosophers are clearly intended to celebrate the victory of Christianity over paganism. When Antony is questioned by his pagan interlocutors his reply is essentially the same and echoes his reply to the demons and to the persecuting Roman *dux*: "I am a Christian."[49] It is as a Christian that he is questioned and later ridiculed, and it is as a Christian that he defends himself.

In three consecutive scenes, the essential differences between Antony and the philosophers are spelled out. In the first debate Antony proves himself to be wise and sophisticated in spite of being unlettered, and to be civilized and polite in spite of living in the mountain. Thus the main argument of the philosophers, that the Christian is simpleminded and rustic, is totally destroyed. In the second debate the philosophers concentrate on Antony's lack of education and are again defeated by Antony's emphasis on the priority of the sound mind in relation to studies. Again it is clear that the kind of argument that the *Life of Antony* replies to is the accusation by pagan intellectuals that Christianity was a religion for fools. The third encounter, developed into an extensive attack on pagan beliefs, also begins with the issue of wisdom and knowledge. But here the authorial voice parenthetically states that those who came "were among those who by the Greeks are considered wise" and that Antony first "pitied them for their ignorance."[50] Common to all three encounters is that the philosophers who come to Antony want to ridicule his faith and firmly believe they can outwit him since he has no education and has lived his entire life in the desert. They think, wrongly, that he is a fool, an ἰδιώτης, a μῶρον, the opposite of what they are, civilized, πολιτικοί.

In the third encounter Antony's superior sagacity is then manifested in a long defense of the Christian faith's intellectual superiority to pagan tradition. The philosophers ridicule Christian belief and especially the teachings about the Incarnation and the Crucifixion. To this Antony replies with an attack on pagan myth as being even more ridiculous and senseless. He accuses the pagan philosophers of not having read the Christian texts properly and of inventing numerous allegories to defend their own. He then argues that belief, πίστις, is prior to demonstration, proving at the end that Christian faith works miracles, whereas the demonstrations of the pagan philosophers are to no avail. The central issue in the debate is the question of change and decline and what this implies for the relations between God, Mind, and Soul. A closer look at Antony's arguments reveal that his replies to the philosophers who come to him are directed against some major ideas in the teachings of Pythagoras as reported by Porphyry. Although both agree that the soul is immortal, Pythagoras's teaching about the transmigration of the soul and especially its migration into animals is ridiculed, and where Pythagoras claims that everything recurs, Antony states the opposite.[51]

CHRISTIANS AND NEO-PYTHAGOREANS

Although the fact of a literary borrowing from a *Life of Pythagoras* in the *Life of Antony* has been accepted, Reitzenstein's views have made little impact, and the question of why a *Life of Pythagoras* was used seems never to have been asked earnestly.[52] Reitzenstein's reason seems mainly to have been that Athanasius needed a good model and shared the cultural background of the neo-Pythagoreans. To Bartelink, who later edited the *Life of Antony*, the relationship of the *Life of Antony* to classical literature was of little interest, since the *Life of Antony* had to be treated as the first writing of a new specifically Christian genre, for which the Bible and its biographical material constituted the model.[53] The quotation from Pythagoras was just a single borrowing of a famous passage to show that

Antony surpassed even Pythagoras. Thus even though Reitzenstein and Bartelink had totally different views on the *Life of Antony,* both agreed that there was no real connection between the worlds of Antony the monk and Pythagoras the philosopher.

With more recent views on early monasticism and Antony as representing a tradition of ascetic teachers dependent on the philosophical traditions of Alexandria, the time is ripe for a fresh analysis of the evidence once presented by Reitzenstein, as well as the evidence neglected by him. We have to ask ourselves what the neo-Pythagorean background visible throughout the *Life of Antony* indicates. What does it actually imply that Pythagorean tradition is alluded to in order to prove that Antony was superior to Pythagoras? What does it tell us about the intended readers and their understanding of the relation between the lives of neo-Pythagorean philosophers and the monks? What could the author achieve by his hidden references to Pythagoras? How do we account for such a strong, but hidden, reception of the works of a neo-Pythagorean author in a Christian text written around 360? And why do we find them in a text on monastic life? In searching for answers, we have to look for a plausible setting in which a rivalry between Antony and Pythagoras makes sense, a setting in which the stories about and the teachings attributed to Pythagoras as well as the biblical stories are well known and appreciated.

For a better understanding of the *Life of Antony* and its objective, it is thus essential to look at the biographies of Pythagoras and their reception in the mid-fourth century. The authors of the two preserved biographies of Pythagoras, Porphyry and Iamblichus, were both well known to Christian intellectuals at the time. Porphyry (232–ca. 305), who is primarily known to us as Plotinus's disciple and the editor of the *Enneads*, was a prolific writer in his own right; some sixty works of his are known, although few survive.[54] His *Life of Pythagoras* is part of his history of classical philosophy, in which he makes Pythagoras the founder of true philosophy and the teacher of all humanity. Among Christian intellectuals in the fourth century Porphyry was, however, not only a famous philosopher but primarily the feared author of probably the most learned and dangerous attacks on Christianity. The best known of these, a work with the title *Contra Christianos*, is extant only in scattered quotations.[55]

Together with another work of his, *Philosophy from Oracles*, it has been regarded as a major influence on the circles behind the great persecution under Diocletian.[56] His potential for creating hatred against Christians is manifest from Constantine's mention of him in a letter quoted by Socrates Scholasticus.[57]

Porphyry knew the Bible and Christian teaching quite well, even to the extent that some thought he had been raised a Christian. He was aquainted with Origen, and his refutations of Christianity are deeply indebted to Origen's treatment of problems in the biblical text.[58] Porphyry especially ridicules the Christians for their incredulity and lack of education, their belief in strange tales and unsophisticated texts. He argues that the Christians have abandoned the worship of the supreme God by worshipping Jesus, a man. Instead of worshipping what is changeless, they have been led astray.[59]

In spite of, or perhaps because of, Constantine's prohibitions, the works of Porphyry remained a concern of educated Christians throughout the century. John Chrysostom mentions copies of his anti-Christian writings still extant in his time, and as late as 448 Theodosius ordered that all remaining copies be burnt.[60] Their impact on Christians is clearly visible in the fact that in the fourth century Christian authors, beginning with Eusebius and Methodius and ending with Jerome and Augustine, repeatedly refuted them. In the same period as the *Life of Antony* was composed, Apollinarius is reported to have written thirty books against Porphyry; and Didymus, who knew both Athanasius and Antony, discussed Porphyry's allegorical method in ways reminiscent of Antony's attack on the allegorizations of the classical myths.[61] As is clear from the writings of Eusebius, Porphyry's history of the philosophers, of which the *Life of Pythagoras* was a part, was also known in Christian circles at the time. No doubt anyone who, like Athanasius, had been educated in Alexandria in the first decades of the fourth century and who was familiar with the discussions in the city throughout the larger part of the century knew the writings of Porphyry and his severe refutation of the Christians.

Iamblichus, who was born around 250 and died in 326, had probably studied with Porphyry in his youth and was the head of an important school of neo-Pythagorean thought in Syria in the days of Athanasius's youth.[62] His biographical work on Pythagoras is an introduction to a long and detailed work on the Pythagorean life, the ideal life promoted by the disciples of Porphyry and ultimately his teacher Plotinus. Of central concern to Iamblichus was the question of the efficacy of religion and in particular of prayer, and the granting of visions, questions of central importance in the *Life of Antony.*[63]

The influence of Iamblichus on Julian, through Aedesius, and Julian's attachment to the neo-Pythagorean teacher Maximus must have been well known to Christian intellectuals long before Julian became emperor. With Julian's growing power in the late 350s and his support of pagan philosophy and religion, there are good reasons to think that the Christians were increasingly worried. With Julian, neo-Pythagoreanism became a real political, social, and intellectual force exactly at the time when the biography of Antony, the desert philosopher, was published. To Christians in Athanasius's days, Pythagoras was thus not a sage of old; he was a living ideal, the hero of radical groups of intellectuals with influence in the highest level of society. As the ascension of Julian in 361 showed, Christians could not be confident that their philosophy would win the day. It is easy to forget that Christians at this time were still a minority in the empire, and undoubtedly so among the elite.

Neo-Pythagorean ideals were not confined to small philosophical circles and the imperial court. Alexandria had a strong neo-Pythagorean tradition evidenced by both Clement and Origen,[64] and there are good reasons to suppose that the ascension of Julian was part of a general revival of Greek philosophical tradition as a reaction to Christian triumphalism.[65] Cyril's vehement refutation of Julian's works in the 420s, and Zacharias Scholasticus's account of conflicts between Christians and neo-Pythagoreans in Alexandria in the 480s, point to a strong tradition in the city long after Julian's death.[66] Any Christian bishop of Alexandria thus had every reason to find ways to counteract the influence of Porphyry and Iamblichus and show that the true philosopher was not the pagan ascetic but the Christian.

The link to the philosophical schools at the time becomes even more intriguing if we look at the main arguments against Christianity encountered by Athanasius and his contemporaries. In his analysis of the anti-Christian writings of Porphyry and Julian, Anthony Meredith concludes that the most persisting feature of their attacks was their concern to present Christians as men of no culture and education. They had their faith and their Bible and should stick to these and not try to use "alien wisdom" in support of their superstition.[67] To a large extent scholars have traditionally accepted this kind of characterization of Christians and especially monks. But perhaps we should see the attacks on Christians as uncultured and lacking education rather as a sign of the opposite, that Christians were actually becoming a problem because of their growing influence in the schools and among intellectuals.

When Reitzenstein made his discovery of the use of a *Life of Pythagoras* in the *Life of Antony*, he had no intention whatsoever of suggesting that there was any real similarity between Antony and Pythagoras, or even between early monastics and the contemporary followers of Plotinus's most prominent disciples, Porphyry and Iamblichus. But with a new understanding of the rise of monasticism in general and a new interpretation of the intellectual culture of Antony, the parallels become much more interesting. The sharp dichotomy between the pagan philosophical schools of the third and fourth centuries and the early monastic tradition is no longer possible to uphold. Not only is the monastic life in our early sources constantly and self-consciously referred to as a philosophical life, but the early monastic literature itself indicates a strong emphasis on education in philosophy, as the term was understood at the time.[68] The early monastic letters, the stories by Palladius and the anonymous author of the *Historia monachorum in Aegypto*, and the *Apophthegmata patrum* and the Pachomian literature all attest an emphasis on education, books and teaching, as well as close links to Alexandria and its intellectual traditions.[69]

Instead of presupposing a contrast between the real Antony and the Pythagorean ideal Antony of the *Life of Antony*, we need to ask if there are indications of neo-Pythagorean traditions within the emerging monastic traditions of Egypt. Recent scholarship on early Egyptian monasticism has shown that we have to think of a quite diversified movement, with ascetic teachers of various philosophical lifestyles claiming a variety of ancestry and authoritative texts.[70] As I have argued elsewhere, there are good reasons to think that the monastic teachers of the generation of Antony and his immediate successors were living in a context where the borders between pagan philosophy, heterodoxy, and orthodoxy were fluid and that for many young intellectuals seeking a teacher to follow the first question was perhaps not whether he was a Christian or not but whether his teaching was effective and convincing. The debates between monks and philosophers reported not only in the *Life of Antony* but also in the *Life of Pachomius* and other sources were part of an ongoing struggle to gain adherents and disciples, a struggle within a shared culture. The Pythagorean emphasis on primordial and divine unity and on "the one as a sort of essence" links not only Origen but also Antony's letters to Pythagorean thought.[71] The shared culture of many of the Nag Hammadi texts with Pythagorean traditions on the one hand and the monastic tradition on the other is an important area that is still underresearched. In such a setting, the image of the ultimate teacher, whether Antony or Pythagoras, was of prime interest, and biographies were an important weapon in the battle for adherents. To be effective these needed to invoke similarity as much as difference.

The argument in this essay is that the problem of purpose and setting for the *Life of Antony*, which has been a matter of debate for more than one hundred years, and which is fundamental to the issue of authorship and literary unity of the text, can be solved only if the presupposed ideals and the arguments in the text are taken into account and reconciled with one another. It is necessary to find a plausible setting that explains not only the extensive use of Pythagoras as a model but also the debate with the specific philosophical views articulated. For this the recent revisions of the traditional views on early Egyptian monasticism are quite helpful. If neo-Pythagorean and other non-Christian ascetic traditions were possible alternatives competing with Christian traditions among the monks, and the monks were, moreover, regarded as part of philosophical school traditions, we may find a solution that takes into account both the pagan model and the antipagan apologetic character of the *Life of Antony* and makes it possible to see the *Life of Antony* as addressed to an intellectual milieu that was common to a variety of Christian monks and philosophical teachers.

In the *Life of Antony* the Christian monk is a philosopher not lacking in any of the characteristics of the most famous philosophers. He is a teacher of an ideal society, living in harmony with nature. He is cultured and civilized and is able to argue his case. His philosophy is simple, rational, and stable, in contrast to that of believers in deities that are arbitrary and unstable. Pagan philosophers have had to travel to learn, but Antony has a superior source of knowledge, since he has a power that helps him to defeat the onslaught of demons, the violence of persecutors, and ridicule of competing philosophers. He is similar, but different. The difference is, moreover, focused on his rejection of pagan philosophers' sources of formation, their studies, and their texts. The emphasis is not on Antony's lack of education but on his alternative education, on the superiority of his educational program and his texts, and thus of his superiority as a teacher.[72]

The superiority of his teaching is, however, not only argued for but also proved by its efficacy. Through his prayers and his quotations of his holy texts Antony is able to defeat the representatives of pagan religion, whether demons, persecutors, or competing philosophers. The emphasis on efficacy and divine intervention including visions is not something that sets Antony apart as a Christian but something he shares with the neo-Pythagorean tradition of his day. Both Iamblichus and Julian would have recognized and accepted the arguments of the *Life of Antony* as valid.

The above analysis of the *Life of Antony* does not depend on a decision about authorship but places the text in the shared intellectual culture of emerging monasticism, neo-Pythagorean revival, and Alexandrian theological and philosophical tradition. The *Life of Antony*, no doubt, shares many of the ideas and arguments of Athanasius's apologetic works, but this does not prove that Athanasius wrote the text. In view of the apparent difficulties in harmonizing a number of passages in the *Life of Antony* and the lack of any firm internal evidence, one should be cautious in grounding the purpose of the text on an analysis of Athanasius's policies. Instead, there are good reasons to return to the attempts of Reitzenstein and Tetz and to search for possible sources and revisions in the text as it is preserved. Not only the Syriac version of the *Life of Antony* but also the textual history of works such as the *Historia monachorum* and the *Historia Lausiaca,* not to mention the *Apophthegmata patrum*, reveals the extent to which early monastic texts were already being revised and augmented in their early circulation.

NOTES

1. For previous research on *Vita Antonii* (*Vit. Ant.*), see Rubenson, *Letters of St. Antony,* 126–32, Brakke, *Athanasius,* 201–65, and Bartelink, intro. to Athanasius, *Vie d'Antoine*, 27–67; and for a succinct summary of the debate on authorship, see Urbano, "Read It Also," 893–94 n. 53.

2. For the discussions of the text by Mertel, *Biographischen Formen*; Holl, "Schriftstellerische Form"; Reitzenstein, *Athanasius Werk*; Priessnig, *Biographischen Formen*; List, *Antoniusleben des Hl. Athanasius*; and Cavallin, *Literarhistorische und textkritische Studien*, see Bartelink, "Literarische Gattung der *Vita Antonii*"; Bartelink's intro. to Athanasius, *Vie d'Antoine,* 62–67; Hägg, "Life of St. Antony," 17–34; and more generally P. Miller, *Biography in Late Antiquity,* 45–65.

3. See Tetz, "Athanasius," refuted by Fitschen, *Serapion von Thmuis*, 106–16.

4. For an unusual attempt to "start with the text rather than with the author," see Rousseau "Antony as Teacher," 102, an article to which I am greatly indebted.

5. The emphasis on monastic formation is found in the prologue of the *Vit. Ant.* itself and recurs in most commentaries beginning with Reitzenstein, *Athanasius Werk*, 5, and manifest in Bartelink's edition of *Vie d'Antoine*. For the *Vit. Ant.* as a revision of other forms of monasticism, see Dörries, *Vita Antonii als Geschichtsquelle,* and M. Williams, "*Life of Antony*."

6. On the *Life* as part of an anti-Arian campaign, see in particular Gregg and Groh, *Early Arianism*, 131–59, and Brakke, *Athanasius,* 135–38. On the *Vita* as representing both a specific Athanasian spirituality and a specific ecclesiastical agenda promoting his "political goal of a Church united under the Alexandrian episcopate," see Brakke, *Athanasius,* 202–3 and 264: "The *Life of Antony* served Athanasius primarily as a tool for achieving political unity within the Egyptian Church." On the work as a refutation of Greek *paideia,* see Urbano, "Read It Also," with a special emphasis on a contrast between *Vit. Ant.* and Eusebius's account of Origen.

7. But as Rousseau rightly points out, it is hard to explain "how a work written for ascetics elsewhere could have been designed chiefly as a means of achieving unity within Egypt itself." Rousseau, "Antony as Teacher," 104.

8. For doubts, see Barnes, "Angel of Light," echoed in Barnes, *Athanasius and Constantius*, 240.

9. See Bartelink's intro. to Athanasius, *Vie d'Antoine,* 28, and his list of MSS, 77–95. For the attestations, see 37–42.

10. *Vit. Ant.* Prologue. References to the text of *Vit. Ant.* are to Athanasius, *Vie d'Antoine,* ed. Bartelink. The version printed by Migne implies that this dis-

ciple was the author himself, giving rise to the idea that Athanasius in his youth had been Antony's disciple. The better reading used in Bartelink's edition has given rise to speculations about this disciple and an identification with Bishop Serapion of Thmuis. See Tetz, "Athanasius," 6–11.

11. *Vit. Ant.* 91: καὶ Ἀθανασίῳ μὲν τῳ ἐπισκόπῳ δότε τὴν μίαν μηλωτὴν καὶ τὸ ὑπεστρωννυόμην ἱμάτιον ("Give my *melotê* and my cloak on which I have slept, to Athanasius, the bishop"). The recipient is again referred to in the third person in the next chapter.

12. *Vit. Ant.* 69–71.

13. On the invitation's issuing from the bishops, see *Vit. Ant.* 69. The index to the festal letters of Athanasius states quite ambiguously that Antony's visit happened in July and that Athanasius returned in November the same year, leaving it open which happened first depending on what calendar is used. The account has been discussed at length (see Lorenz, "Griechische *Vita Antonii*," 3–6; Brakke, *Athanasius,* 204–6; and Rousseau, "Antony as Teacher," 102), but no attempt to interpret the reference so that Athanasius returns before the visit of Antony is convincing, although this is generally taken for granted. On the letter from the emperor on Athanasius's return, see Barnes, *Athanasius and Constantius*, 34.

14. Athanasius, *Hist. ar.* 14. As noted by Rousseau, "Antony as Teacher," 102 n. 37, the differences cannot be brushed aside as has most often been done. *Vit. Ant.* 86.

15. Although the date of the *Hist. ar.* is debated, it must have been written late in 357 or early in 358. See Barnes, *Athanasius and Constantius*, 126–32. Barnard's arguments, in "Date of S. Athanasius' *Vita Antonii*," 169–75, for the *Vit. Ant.* being written before the *Hist. ar.* are convincingly disproved by Brennan, "Dating Athanasius' *Vita Antonii*," 52–54. It is, moreover, not self-evident that the entire text of the *Vit. Ant.* is to be dated to the same year.

16. See Gemeinhardt, "*Vita Antonii*," 79–114.

17. The links are almost exclusively between *Vit. Ant.* and *Contra gentes / De incarnatione.* For a list, see Bartelink's intro. to Athanasius, *Vie d'Antoine,* 36–37. More detailed discussions on *Vit. Ant.* in relation to Athanasius's other writings and his theology are found in Roldanus, *Christ et l'homme,* and "*Vita Antonii* als Spiegel"; Gregg and Groh, *Early Arianism*, 131–53; Brakke, *Athanasius,* 201–65; Anatolios, *Athanasius*, 164–203; and Urbano, "Read It Also." Although, as Rousseau points out ("Antony as Teacher," 101), it is possible to interpret the parallels as a common Alexandrian tradition, the arguments for an Athanasian imprint on the discourses of Antony in the *Vit. Ant.* as outlined in Urbano ("Read It Also," 899–902) are rather persuasive.

18. See Tetz, "Athanasius," and for a refutation, Fitschen, *Serapion von Thmuis*, 106–16. See also Draguet, intro. to Athanasius, *Vie primitive de S. Antoine,* and for references to the critics, Urbano, "Read It Also," 893–94. But al-

though Draguet's linguistic arguments have lost their value, some of the arguments raised by Timothy Barnes in his favorable comment to Draguet have not been sufficiently answered. See Barnes, "Angel of Light," 353–68.

19. For the letters of Antony, see Rubenson, *Letters of St. Antony,* 132–44; for the relation between the letters and the *Vit. Ant.,* see Brottier, "Antoine l'ermite," and Bartelink's intro. to Athanasius, *Vie d'Antoine,* 71–73.

20. See Rousseau, "Antony as Teacher"; Rubenson, "Anthony and Pythagoras"; Urbano, "Read It Also."

21. Rousseau, "Antony as Teacher," 89.

22. Ibid., 92.

23. *Vit. Ant.* 15; cf. Rousseau, "Antony as Teacher," 95.

24. *Vit. Ant.* 14.

25. Urbano, "Read It Also," 895.

26. Ibid., 913.

27. Reitzenstein, *Athanasius Werk,* 14–18.

28. Porphyry, *Vit. Pyth.* 35, trans. Hadas, 118–19; Athanasius, *Vita Antonii* 14, translation my own.

29. The most prominent of these are in the same chapter in the *Vita.* After his appearance, Antony heals and comforts those who have come, echoing almost exactly Porphyry's desciption of Pythagoras healing and comforting his friends (*Vit. Pyth.* 33). Athanasius then describes how they settle in the desert, using the verb πολίζειν precisely as Porphyry and Iamblichus describe how those who heard Pythagoras's first speech settled into a community governed by his laws (*Vit. Pyth.* 20; Iamblichus, *De vita Pyth.* 30). The term κενόβιον, used in Pythagoras's case, however, is replaced by μοναστήριον. For texts and details, see Reitzenstein, *Athanasius Werk*, 16; for the use in *Vit. Ant.,* see Rousseau, "Anthony as Teacher," 92.

30. Reitzenstein, *Athanasius Werk*, 18.

31. *Vit. Ant.* 1–3; Porphyry, *Vit. Pyth.* 1–12; Iamblichus, *Vita Pythagorica* 3–18. For a discussion, see Reitzenstein, *Athanasius Werk*, 17. Parallels can also be found in Philostratus's *Vita Apollonii*. Apollonius of Tyana received a broad education, "learning from all, but especially from Pythagoras" (1.7); he lost his parents at the age of twenty (1.13), turned the temple into a school, divested himself of his property, and decided to live a celibate life.

32. Lucian, *Philopseudes* 34; cf. *Vit. Ant.* 15.

33. Reitzenstein, *Athanasius Werk*, 31–36.

34. Ibid., 34–35.

35. *Vit. Ant.* 4; Iamblichus, *Vit. Pyth.* 10.

36. Noble character and elegant manners: *Vit. Ant.* 73; Porphyry, *Vit. Pyth.* 18 (cf. *Vita Plotinii* 13). Sharp eyes and remarkable discernment: *Vit. Ant.* 87–88; Porphyry, *Vit. Pyth.* 13, 30–31; Iamblichus, *Vit. Pyth.* 34. Cf. Porphyry, *Vita Plotini* 11.

37. Control over animals: *Vit. Ant.* 50; Porphyry, *Vit. Pyth.* 23–24; Iamblichus, *Vit. Pyth.* 60–62. Healing of diseases and restoration of harmony: *Vit. Ant.* 54–64; Porphyry, *Vit. Pyth.* 30–33; Iamblichus, *Vit. Pyth.* 34.

38. *Vit. Ant.* 14; Porphyry, *Vit. Pyth.* 20–22; Iamblichus, *Vit. Pyth.* 27–30.

39. *Vit. Ant.* 16–43, 55; Porphyry, *Vit. Pyth.* 37–53; Iamblichus, *Vit. Pyth.* 37–59.

40. Reitzenstein, *Athanasius Werk*, 18–26.

41. *Vit. Ant.* 1: γράμματα μὲν μαθεῖν οὐκ ἠνέσχετο. Cf. Porphyry, *Vit. Pyth.* 1–8; Iamblichus, *Vit. Pyth.* 9, 12–13, 18.

42. *Vit. Ant.* 20; Porphyry, *Vit. Pyth.* 2. See also Iamblichus, *Vit. Pyth.* 19.

43. Reitzenstein, *Athanasius Werk*, 12, 36.

44. Brakke, *Demons,* 23–47.

45. Ibid., 42–45.

46. *Vit. Ant.* 6, 52.

47. "In this way Athanasius sums up Antony's earlier combats with the demons as the triumph of Christianity itself over traditional religions" (Brakke, *Demons,* 36). See esp. *Vit. Ant.* 52 and 53, where there is a clear reference to pagan imagery and where a demon, i.e., a pagan god, is killed.

48. Reitzenstein, *Athanasius Werk*, 9, refers to the encounters as the λόγος πρὸς Ἕλληνας but does not discuss the purpose of the apology and its relation to the rest of the *Vit. Ant.* The apologetic character of the three encounters is recognized and analyzed by Rousseau, "Antony as Teacher," 96–98, and Urbano, "Read It Also," 906–12.

49. *Vit. Ant.* 72, cf. ch. 8, 46.

50. τῶν παρ' Ἕλλησι δοκούντων εἶναι σοφῶν (*Vit. Ant.* 74.1); οἰκτείρας αὐτοὺς ἐπὶ τῇ ἀγνωσίᾳ (*Vit. Ant.* 74.2).

51. See Porphyry, *Vit. Pyth.* 19, for a summary of precisely what Antony contradicts in *Vit. Ant.* 74.

52. An exception is Festugière, "Sur une nouvelle edition," who points out that the use is accompanied by marked contrasts.

53. Bartelink, "Literarische Gattung," 52.

54. For Porphyry as a critic of Christianity, see Wilken, *Christians,* 126–63.

55. For a discussion, see Barnes, "Angel of Light," and Meredith, "Porphyry and Julian," 1126–37.

56. See Wilken, *Christians,* 134–35, 156–59, and Barnes, "Scholarship or Propaganda," an article in which Barnes argues that *Contra Christianos* may even have been composed in direct relation to the persecutions under Diocletian.

57. Socrates Scholasticus, *Historia ecclesiastica* 1.9.30.

58. See Eusebius, *Historia ecclesiastica* 6.19.4–8. The debate between Porphyry and Eusebius about the common background of Origen and Plotinus is well described in Urbano, "Read It Also," 885 and n. 31.

59. Wilken, *Christians,* 151–54, quoting Augustine's discussion of Porphyry in *De civitate Dei* 23.

60. Wilken, *Christians*, 126.

61. See Sellew, "Achilles or Christ?" 79–100.

62. On Iamblichus, see the commentary in *Jamblich. Pythagoras,* ed. Albrecht.

63. Wilken, *Christians,* 67, quoting Iamblichus, *De mysteriis* 2.11.

64. For a discussion, see Bostock, "Origen and the Pythagoreanism," 465–78; and Runia, "Why Does Clement," 1–22.

65. For the emergence of a new type of Platonism in the third and fourth centuries, the importance of Pythagorean traditions in it, and Christian involvement, see Urbano, "Read It Also," 883–86, with references to George Boys-Stones and Edward Watts. For an analysis of this as a reaction to Christian triumphalism, see Meredith, "Porphyry and Julian," 1147–48.

66. See Zachyriah of Mitylene, *Life of Severus*. See also Haas, *Alexandria in Late Antiquity*, 187–88, 278–330.

67. Meredith, "Porphyry and Julian," 1147.

68. Rubenson, "Monasticism."

69. Ibid.

70. Goehring, "Monastic Diversity."A close study of the description of the ascetics in the writings of Porphyry, Iamblichus, and others may well reveal numerous parallels with descriptions in early monastic texts.

71. For Pythagorean emphasis on unity and the quotation from Aristotle, see Bostock, "Origen and the Pythagoreanism," 467.

72. Here I have problems with the views articulated by Edward Watts and echoed by Arthur Urbano, that there was a radical break with earlier Alexandrian tradition of a close interaction between school and church in the fourth century, and that Christian intellectuals, like Athanasius, were "isolated from the social and intellectual networks of Alexandrian Greeks." See Urbano, "Read It Also," 899, with reference to Watts, *City and School,* 175–77.

Chapter Five

The Memory Palace of Marcellinus

Athanasius and the Mirror of the Psalms

GEORGIA FRANK

In 2002, a new product hit the Bible market. The "Survival Bible" consisted of a viewing panel into which users could insert one of several "scripture scrolls." Each scroll was devoted to a specific topic (e.g., faith, love, healing) and contained about a dozen biblical quotations on that specific topic. The variety of scrolls ensured that whatever situation one faced, an apt scroll would be at hand. Available in a home edition with a handsome three-drawer wooden cabinet or a six-inch traveler's version, the "Survival Bible" promised that "the word of God will reveal the way in and the out of every situation."[1]

The Survival Bible stands in a long line of devices that fragment and reorder the Bible. In antiquity, physical devices, such as the codex, altered how Christians encountered the Bible.[2] The *Diatessaron* (ca. 170 CE), Tatian's harmony of the four canonical Gospels into a single narrative, soon became one of the most popular editions of the Gospels. It also served very practical purposes: its compactness made it easier to transport and less costly to produce.[3] And its unified narrative allowed greater ease in locating a Gospel episode. Some complete Bible codices included various tables and other tools to transform the reader into a navigator. Eusebius of Caesarea, for instance, devised a system of nine tables to facilitate locating similar Gospel texts. Whereas he left the Gospels themselves complete, his canon tables cross-referenced passages found in all four Gospels or in specific combinations of Gospels. Evagrius of Pontus's *Antirhêtikos*, or "Talking Back," assembled 498 biblical passages, each one preceded by the type of thought or situation for which it was best suited.[4] Over time, more devices were introduced to organize the Bible for specific purposes: lectionaries listed scripture lessons for particular divine services; "chains," or *catenae*, linked biblical verses appeared with excerpts from patristic commentaries.[5] Such *instrumenta* allowed codices not only to be put to different uses, say, as reference works, but also to organize information for easier retrieval and retention.[6] All these devices both fragmented and reordered the Bible to transform readers into navigators. In addition to constructing these formal devices, Christian commentators were known to advise audiences on when, where, and how to read scripture in their private devotions.[7] Guides for interpretation, then, also involved guides for use.

Viewed against this biblical toolbox, Athanasius of Alexandria's *Letter to Marcellinus* can be understood as one such user's device. Probably written in the early 360s, the *Letter* lays out a regimen of psalm reading for the ailing Marcellinus.[8] Within a century of its composition, the *Letter to Marcellinus* already served as a biblical device. It prefaced the psalms in the oldest complete Bible, the fifth-century *Codex Alexandrinus,* along with prologue and summary pages. This accretion of study tools for the psalms suggests that readers depended on these devices to navigate the Psalter.[9]

Athanasius's advice consists of stirring praises of the depths and joys of psalmody along with several lists pairing a given circumstance with the requisite psalm number. Why the barrage of lists? Can the lauds and the lists be reconciled? By calling attention to the lists, this essay aims to understand the formation of a self in Athanasius's lists of psalm references. I explore how ancient conventions of memory training shaped Athanasius's advice to Marcellinus. By asking how memory worked in antiquity, one is in a better position to understand the function and purpose of the lists of psalm numbers in the *Letter to Marcellinus.* Thus I explore parallels between Athanasius's advice and rhetorical invention, specifically educational practices that valued mental landscapes and mnemonic devices for storing, retrieving, and recombining texts to meet new situations and effectively negotiate life's uncertainties.

PRAISING THE PSALMS IN THE *LETTER TO MARCELLINUS*

It is fitting that Athanasius's letter to an ailing friend should prescribe psalmody. It was a commonplace in late antiquity to refer to the Psalter as a medicine and psalmody as a therapy.[10] The Cappadocians and Origen called Christ the physician (*iatros*) of souls and employed medical analogies in their descriptions of spiritual progress (and setbacks). Evagrius described ascetical practices as *pharmaka*, or remedies. Athananius likened demons' illusory foreknowledge to the prognosticating powers of physicians. The therapy Athanasius prescribed for Marcellinus, by contrast, was more potent. He framed the advice as a "conversation with a learned old man" retold for Marcellinus' sake.[11] Whether this old man was a fiction or an actual monk Athanasius once encountered remains uncertain. For our purposes, however, the rhetorical characteristics of the speech concern us more than its origins.

The *Letter to Marcellinus* praises the riches and usefulness of the Psalter. Cast in the form of advice, it both praises and prescribes psalms. For Athanasius, the Psalter encapsulates the entire Bible, recounting key moments in salvation history, as well as containing all the appropriate responses to God's grace and mystery, the dispositions to meet every challenge in life, and the words and song to mark the events of Christ's life throughout the liturgical year. In celebrating this "garden" of all scriptural knowledge, Athanasius also offers the reader several sachets of scriptural quotations and psalm numbers to use as needed. Athanasius concludes the letter with detailed advice on the proper way to chant the psalms and preserve them from harmful embellishments. The core of the letter consists of several lists of events and situations followed by strings of apt psalm numbers. These lists, I suggest, provide the key to understanding

Athanasius's program of psalm devotion. It is worth reviewing their characteristics.[12]

The Psalms as Epitome of the Other Biblical Books (§§ 2–8)

The first list of the speech celebrates the Book of Psalms' ability to contain and complement other scriptures. To make his case, Athanasius narrates salvation history from Creation to Christ with an overview of the Christian Bible. Key episodes from Genesis, Exodus, Numbers, Deuteronomy, Joshua, Judges, Kings, Esdras, and the Prophets appear in some guise in the psalms. In addition to repeating law, history, and prophecy, the psalms foretell the events of Christ's coming, from Israel's anticipation of a redeemer to the Annunciation, the Incarnation, and Christ's persecution, passion, ascension, and exaltation. To illustrate this rapid retelling of salvation history, Athanasius quotes a psalm verse for each event, a habit he drops in subsequent lists.[13] However much the psalms echo the rest of the Bible, Athanasius insists they are no substitute. Rather, they underscore the unity of the canon. He proves his point by borrowing language from the Apostle Paul's appeal to the unity of the Holy Spirit amid the diversity of spiritual gifts (1 Cor 12:4).

Athanasius focuses more, however, on the psalms' distinctive traits. He marvels at their wondrous versatility to speak on various subjects, in various modes, and to a wide range of moods.[14] More importantly, they provide the very words to use when one's own words fail. Whereas other biblical books contain the words of patriarchs, prophets, and kings, the psalms provide one's own words. Not only do the psalms contain the themes of other scripture. "This marvel of its own," Athanasius claims, is that the Psalter teaches "even the movements of the soul" so as to "possess the image deriving from the words."[15] Although other biblical books can exhort one to bear suffering, the Book of Psalms does more. As Athanasius describes the psalms' vivid approach to suffering, "in the Psalms it is written [γέγραπται] and inscribed [κεχάρακται] how one must bear suffering, what one must say to one suffering afflictions, what to say after afflictions, how each person is tested, and what the words of those who hope in God are."[16] Thus in the psalms one "recognizes . . . [one's] own words. And the one who hears is deeply moved as though he himself were speaking, and is affected by the words of songs as if they were his own songs."[17] When reciting other books of the Bible, one repeats the words of patriarchs and prophets. But when reciting the psalms, one "is uttering the rest as his own words, and each sings them as if they were written concerning him. . . . He handles them as if he is speaking about himself."[18] In short, to know thyself is to know thy psalms.

To capture that process of internalizing the words of another to arrive at deeper self- or soul-knowledge, Athanasius likens the psalms to a mirror (ὥσπερ εἴσοπτρον).[19] This self-perception also includes an ideal image, what Athanasius calls "the perfect image for the souls' course of life."[20] By this metaphor, Athanasius shifts from temporal events (salvation history) to spatial metaphors of maps and mirrors to describe that most fragile connection between speech, emotion, and soul.[21]

That union of time and space prompts Athanasius to compare Christ to the Psalter. In both exemplars, the devout find "perfect instruction in virtue," whatever the issue. Both are exemplars and guides for any situation. As Athanasius likens the two: "Just as [the Lord] provided the model of the earthly and heavenly man in his own person, so also from the Psalms he who wants to do so can learn the movements and dispositions of the souls, finding in them also the therapy and correction suited for each movement."[22] James Ernest captures Athanasius's incarnational concerns when he describes the Psalter as the "inscripturation of the Word, as it were, that preceded the incarnation of the Word."[23] In this first section Athanasius progresses inward, from biblical narrative to epitome (Psalter) to Incarnation (Christ), then internalizing the Psalter's words such that they become one's own.

How to Talk to God (§ 14)

The next list classifies the psalms by their ability to narrate God's saving work (narrative) as well as to address God according to various modes of speech (e.g., praise, confession, thanksgiving, prayer, prophecy, petition). For each mode or combined modes, Athanasius furnishes a string of psalm numbers, without quoting from any. The page bulges with numerals: "Those in the form of prayers are 16, 67, 89, 101, 131, and 141. Those spoken in petition and in prayer and in entreaty are 5, 6, 7, 11, 12, 15, 24, 27, 30, 34, 37, 42, 53, 54, 55, 56, 58, 59, 60, 63, 82, 85, 87, 137, 139, and 142. And that in the mode of appeal and thanksgiving is 138."[24] By this list, Athanasius equips the reader with all available (and presumably comprehensive) human stances toward God.

For Every Situation, There Is a Psalm (§§ 15–25)

The longest list is ostensibly the most interior in tone and character. Here, Athanasius catalogues what he describes as the variety of "stirrings" the soul encounters in daily life along with a specific psalm number (or several) best suited to address that situation. Typically, the formula is presented as a series of scenarios beginning with "If you are . . ." and followed by "Say/sing Psalm [number x]." For instance: "If you are being persecuted by your own people and you have many who rise up against you, say the third psalm."[25] Or, "Let us say you stand in need of a prayer because of those who have opposed you . . . sing Psalms 16, 85, 87, 140."[26] There is no attempt to classify situations; the good and bad ones are intermingled. Instead, the situations follow the canonical order of the psalms. Thus the first situation requires Psalm 1. The final situation calls for Psalm 150.[27] As Everett Ferguson observes, "In substance, [this part] is a running summary of the contents of the Psalms, *seriatim*."[28]

Remembering Christ's Life through Psalms (§ 26)

Having spanned the entire Psalter, Athanasius circles back once more to generate a list of psalms cued to private commemoration of "events concerning the Savior." The fourth and final list focuses on private devotions for marking events related to the Savior, beginning with psalms foretelling "his true generation from the Father and incarnate appearance" (Psalms 44, 109) and those best suited to recalling his crucifixion, betrayal, kingship, post-Resurrection appearances, and ascension. Striking here is the repetition of roughly half the psalms in the "epitome of the Bible" list (§§ 7–8), as if to suggest that the Christian liturgical cycle is foretold in the span of all biblical time.

How to Sing the Psalms (§§ 27–29)

This section focuses on the importance of melody in the singing of the psalms, as a way to integrate the various *kinêmata,* or stirrings, of the soul. Thus in chanting the psalms one aims to bring harmony to the soul by becoming a *psaltêrion*, a harplike stringed instrument, but also the word for the Book of Psalms itself.[29] Here Athanasius returns to quoting psalms: "That which causes grief is healed when we sing psalms. *Why are you very sad, O my soul, and why do you trouble me?* That which causes stumbling will be discovered, as it says, *But my feet were almost overthrown.* With regard to what he fears, he gains strength from hope by saying, *The Lord is my helper, and I will not fear what man shall do to me.*"[30] In this section, unlike earlier lists, Athanasius omits all references to psalm numbers while preserving the pairing of situation and psalm.

Conclusion (§§ 30–33)

The final section of the *Letter* recapitulates the main points about the usefulness of the Psalter. It offers no list, except a series of three quotations from the longest psalm, Psalm 118 (119 in Hebrew). Having abandoned quoting psalms after his overview of salvation history, Athanasius quotes Psalm 118 in closing the *Letter*. He evokes memory work in "I will meditate [μελετήσω] on your ordinances; I will not forget [ἐπιλήσομαι] your words" (Ps 118:16). He evokes place: "Your ordinance were my songs in the place of my sojourning [ἐν τόπῳ παροικίας μου]" (Ps 118:54), to link memory work to path.[31]

"LEAVE NO PSALM BEHIND"

It is important to observe that the *Letter* cites every psalm at least once,[32] showing a completeness that is rare in patristic treatments of the Psalter. Very few commentaries or series of homilies on the psalms were complete. Gregory of Nyssa's treatise on the psalms focused on the inscriptions, or titles, added to the psalms.[33] Nor does it appear preachers such as Basil of Caesarea, John Chrysostom, or Asterius the Homilist managed to "cover" the entire Psalter.[34] Commentaries by Origen, Theodore of Mopsuestia, Theodoret of Cyrus, and Hippolytus focused on portions of the Psalter. Even Evagrius, for whom the Psalter was a preferred weapon in his compilation of retorts to destructive thoughts and demons, did not exhaust the Book of Psalms.[35] Although Athanasius's treatise is considerably briefer by comparison, its use of the Psalter is remarkably complete.

Scholarly studies of this *Letter* have noted Athanasius's thoroughness.[36] Charles Kannengiesser suggests that Athanasius "distinctly mention[s all canonical psalms] in order to illustrate their convenient appropriation in the daily pace of a Christian lifestyle."[37] A smaller number, if well chosen, could just as well have conveyed the chaos of any given day. More recent studies call attention to the *Letter*'s practical value in the quest for virtue. David Brakke has focused on how Athanasius promoted scriptural study as the cultivation of "embodied virtue" in both the *Letter to Marcellinus* and his festal letters, sent annually to Egyptian churches to announce the date of Easter.[38] Likewise, Derek Krueger has called attention to the *Letter's* program of psalm recitation in the larger context of monastic identity formation.[39]

More sustained attention to "embodied virtue" also guides Paul Kolbet's analysis of the *Letter to Marcellinus.* In a recent article, Kolbet opens new and fruitful interpretive approaches to this work.[40] He likens Athanasius's advice to spiritual exercises promoted by Hellenistic and Stoic philosophers. In letters of advice (*paraenesis*), philosophers prescribed regimens that promoted both a "care of the self" and the ability to internalize doctrines. In this effort to reconcile convictions with deeds, the disciple combined daily self-scrutiny with a desire to internalize dogmas and conform their actions to these ideals. Against this backdrop, Athanasius's advice to Marcellinus demands a similar internalization of the psalms as a way to order an otherwise disordered soul. For Kolbet, then, the Book of Psalms gives Athanasius a "linguistic blueprint of the drives that inhabit his soul."[41] Once internalized, its stability exposes and thereby checks the "fluidity of the human soul."

Kolbet's insights into psalmody's effect on the stirrings of a disordered soul can be pushed further. Specifically, is the soul in need of stillness? Or does it simply require clear direction? Kolbet's analysis suggests a static ideal of the soul, stilled by internalized dogma. Ancient rhetorical education, however, offered a more dynamic view of formation. In rhetoric, one acquired a fluid understanding of the soul's progress, cultivated by a program of careful memorization and generative thinking to guide its movements.

Another question this completeness raises is whether it is related to the inward movement (from Psalter to soul) found in this progression of lists. Kolbet, for instance, regards the internalization of the psalms as critical to the "caring for oneself" and as an "effective tool for introspection."[42] Also worth noting is Athanasius's attention to the entire contents of the Psalter. After all, he could have conveyed the multiple uses of the psalms with fewer selections. Instead, he chose to be concise yet complete. To what end does he need to invoke every last psalm? What precisely is being formed in this project of formation?

If we take seriously Athanasius's thoroughness in citing the Psalter, we are in a better position to understand what he assumes of Marcellinus, what he expects of him, and how he thinks it is best to help him. What he assumes is that Marcellinus has the means to use every psalm and can have access to the entire Psalter. What he expects is that he must retrieve an apt and effective psalm at the right moment to meet the situation at hand. Still, given the multitude of situations, it is unlikely he would have a Psalter in hand at the very moment he needed it. What he can retain, however, is a map consisting of numbers, the memory locations for what he needs most when he needs it. Thus the best way to help Marcellinus is to equip him with a vehicle by which to navigate the psalms mentally. Rhetorical invention is that vehicle, for it will prepare Marcellinus to scan and retrieve psalms from memory.

RHETORICAL CULTURE AND THE *LETTER TO MARCELLINUS*

Nothing in the *Letter to Marcellinus* suggests that psalmody is a bookish activity. Rather, Athanasius stresses the orality of Marcellinus's devotions: to "take up this book" means to be the "one who hears" (ὁ ἀκούων) the psalms.[43] Orality is also presumed in the negative examples Athanasius provides. His criticism of Hellenistic wisdom denounces "those legislators among the Greeks [who] possess the grace as far as speaking goes."[44] By "the grace as far as speaking goes," Athanasius is referring to those educated in rhetoric. His criticism, however, should not detract our attention from rhetorical features of the *Letter to Marcellinus*. However much Athanasius denounces Greek rhetoric, he has shown no compunction about borrowing its techniques to persuade Marcellinus. As Philip

Rousseau has shown for Basil, Christian intellectuals grappled with the relevance and worth of Greek rhetorical education, or *paideia*. To employ its tools in the very act of denouncing its moral worth was common in late antiquity.[45] As George Kennedy describes late fourth-century Christian elites, "They adopted features of classical rhetoric on an unprecedented scale. Although they regularly criticized pagan mythology and the vanity of worldly display, they put high value on education and eloquence and not only stylistic, but also structural features from sophistry."[46] In other words, Athanasius could "love the rhetoric, hate the rhetor" as he crafted his own persuasive speech to Marcellinus.

In adopting habits of rhetoric, Athanasius and the writers he strove to emulate joined a long tradition of public speaking. Rhetoric as Aristotle defines it is the ability to persuade an audience with a speech that is credible (ἦθος), emotionally stirring (πάθος), and logical (λόγος).[47] These three criteria —*êthos*, *pathos,* and *logos*—figure early on in the *Letter to Marcellinus* In his prologue, Athanasius renders himself "worthy of confidence" by framing the letter as the speech of "an old man . . . holding fast the Psalter," who addresses Athanasius (and by extension, Marcellinus) as a "child" (ὦ τέκνον).[48] Moreover, reference to this φιλόπονος γέρων, a phrase that appears frequently in the *Apophthegmata patrum,* suggests a monastic trope.[49] That his speech is *logos* is shown in Athanasius's demonstrations that the Psalter contains all other scriptures. *Pathos* is prevalent in the subsequent lists of psalm references. As Athanasius advises, certain emotions or moods (fear, joy, gratitude, humility, anger, etc.) require specific psalms. Moreover, the reading of any psalm "first calls to mind the emotions of the soul," prior to any representation of or instruction in its contents.[50] Thus *pathos* is both therapy and precondition for knowing. As Athanasius evokes the affective dimensions of psalmody in his description of the stirrings of the soul: "The one who hears is deeply moved, as though he himself were speaking, and is affected by the words of the songs, as if they were his own songs."[51]

In addition to the criteria of *êthos*, *pathos*, and *logos*, students of rhetoric were trained to memorize large bodies of works in order to gather and put forth the best selection of evidence. In this predigitized, even pre-Gutenberg world, students of rhetoric learned ways to organize and retain their materials mentally. Rhetorical education in antiquity involved the training of young orators to compose persuasive and timely speeches. The persuasiveness of one's proofs depended on the ability to repeat exactly passages from previously written works. To do so required extensive training in memory. As Mary Carruthers describes the memorization of canonical texts in rhetorical education, one had to internalize a text to the point of being able to summon the relevant passage efficiently. Rote memorization was a rudimentary step toward this goal, as it allowed one to fix syllables in the memory. What the Latins called *memoria verborum*, or rote memorization, was followed by a more sophisticated memorization technique known as *memoria rerum* (memorizing things), that is to say "converting" the canonical text into a set of images that could be rearranged and more easily scanned and "called up."[52] One needed the surety and grasp of entire texts that rote memorization furnished, but also the flexibility and resourcefulness to gather passages from texts and recombine them in speeches. If the aim of rote memorization was to become, in Carruthers's words, a "living book," the aim of rhetorical memory was to become a "living concordance."[53] Augustine, for instance, famously described his imagistic memory in the *Confessions*: "in the wide plains of my memory and in its innumerable caverns and hollows filled beyond reckoning with varieties of countless things; either through images, as of all material things. . . . Through all these I range and freely move from this to that, digging into them as far as I can and never finishing. Such is the energy of memory."[54]

Augustine's movements about those "caverns and hollows" were guided by carefully laid-out patterns of images. This schematization of memory in order to selectively roam and gather from its storage spaces is the type of mental device that would have served Marcellinus well. As Athanasius advises him, one who hears the Book of Psalms "is enabled by this book *to possess the image* deriving from the words."[55] The image to be possessed here is primarily cognitive, rather than dogmatic or theological.[56] Athanasius is pointing to what Carruthers calls the "cognitive utility" of images, "their necessity as sites upon which and by means of which the human mind can build its compositions, whether these be thoughts or prayers."[57]

What Augustine describes as roaming mental spaces to gather images was standard educational practice in rhetorical education. Students who advanced past primary education would have been introduced to the arts of memory in their rhetorical education. Students were trained in three types of oratory: forensic (courtroom), deliberative (political), and epideictic (ceremonial).[58] Each branch of oratory involved preliminary exercises (*progymnasmata*) designed to help students master skills specific to that branch. However oral this education, reading, writing, and remembering books were intricately bound up in the training of young men.[59] To produce a speech (or compose a text) required the orator to generate ideas by collecting from a well-ordered storehouse of texts (εὕρεσις; Latin: *inventio*).[60] For ease of storage and retrieval, texts were often fragmented and rearranged in mental schemata (μνήμη; Latin: *memoria*). Once re-collected, these ideas would be arranged (τάξις, οἰκονομία; Latin: *dispositio*) into a meaningful and persuasive order, rendered elegant through considerations of phrasing, expressions, and diction that go into style (λέξις; Latin: *elocutio*). Their performance was governed by rules of delivery (ὑπόκρισις; Latin: *pronuntiatio*) attentive to the use of one's voice, countenance, posture, and gestures.[61]

From these elements of rhetoric, it is easier to see how much these skills would have aided Marcellinus. However lofty his wonder at the Psalter's power, beauty, and paradoxes, Athanasius sets before Marcellinus a challenge: to assess the needs of a situation and then locate and recite the most suitable psalm. That ability to remember and summon in the moment was also a goal of rhetorical memorization. It is fruitful, then, to approach the *Letter to Marcellinus* not only as a spiritual exercise or an exegetical discourse but as a rhetorical guide to psalmody.

It is worth pausing for a moment to ask what level of rhetorical education we can presuppose for Athanasius.[62] Athanasius had some access to the rudiments of a rhetorical education, though probably not at the advanced level that Gregory of Nazianzus, Basil of Caesarea, or John Chrysostom enjoyed.[63] Yet even if Athanasius was not well versed in the standard rhetorical handbooks of his day, his writings show sufficient familiarity with those who were well trained in them. "A man of his intelligence," G.C. Stead surmises, "will have absorbed a great deal, simply by imitation, from the writings of Irenaeus, Origen and Eusebius."[64] Stead identifies standard methods of argument that surface in Athanasius's doctrinal and polemical works. For instance, all twenty-eight methods of argument that Aristotle lists in the *Rhetorica* (2.23) are exemplified in Athanasius's theological and polemical works. That Athanasius criticized rhetoric and sophistry, like so many Christian writers of his day, should not deter us from considering what debts to rhetoric surface in his nondoctrinal and nonpolemical works.[65] Whatever disparaging remarks Athanasius made against rhetoric, nothing prevented him from availing himself of its devices and techniques for persuading Christian audiences.[66]

Thanks to the pioneering work of papyrologists such as Raffaella Cribiore, we know far more today about the training of young men in rhetoric, a higher level of education normally off limits to women.[67] After completing studies with a grammarian, a relatively smaller number of young men around the age of fourteen or fifteen embarked on their rhetorical education. The student of rhetoric might devote his first year to studying theory, his second to studying exemplary prose works, and his third trying his own hand at various *progymnasmata*. Several works prescribing these compositional exercises survive from antiquity, including the handbook by the fourth-century CE rhetorician Aphthonius of Antioch. Among the exercises recommended by Aphthonius were composing a *mythos* or fable (in imitation of Aesop); a διήγημα, or narrative (to recount an event or series of events); and an ἐγκώμιον, or speech of praise (Latin: *encomium*).[68] Another, ἔκφρασις, or description, aimed to bring "what is shown clearly before the eyes."[69]

The *Letter to Marcellinus* bears traces of some of these exercises. Ἐγκώμια, or speeches of praise, were standard fare in any training in epideictic rhetoric. As historian of rhetoric Malcolm Heath describes the typical encomium, "The student takes as given the good qualities attributed to a particular person and seeks to exhibit them in a way which will excite or increase the audience's admiration." He adds, "The subject of encomium was not always a person; a place or an abstract quality such as courage might also be prescribed."[70] A standard ingredient of any encomium was a list of "excellences." As Aphthonius described the genre, it "is language expressive of inherent excellences [that] celebrate[s] persons and things, both occasions and places. . . . Collective as well as individual encomia may be given; collectively, like an encomion of all Athenians, individually, like an encomion of an Athenian."[71] The first section of the "old man's" speech can be understood as an encomium praising the Psalter's distinct excellences: its ability to encompass other scriptures, its power to capture and track the stirrings of the soul, its uncanny metamorphosis into one's own words, and, like the mirror, its ability to reflect as well as to correct. Athanasius's summary of salvation history can be interpreted as an exercise in *diêgêma,* a retelling of the events from creation to the ascension of Christ (*Letter to Marcellinus* 3–8). Athanasius also evokes *ekphrasis* in assuring that the one who hears the psalms can "possess the image deriving from these words."[72]

In addition to speeches of praise, rhetorical students were assigned exercises in impersonation, or, speech-in-character, whereby they prepared plausible speeches for another person or character.[73] More expansions than innovations, these speeches could take several forms.[74] Ἠθοποιία involved crafting speeches that famous historical personages or characters might have made in a given situation. In προσωποιία (lit. "to make a face"), one produced a speech for a mythical or literary figure. In all three varieties, one's own words became another's. Strictly speaking, Athanasius offers no formal προσωποιία. He does not instruct Marcellinus to imagine what David would have said or how Moses would have responded in a given situation. Yet Athanasius's instructions do promote a conversion of voice, a basic element of speech-in-character.[75] Whereas προσωποιία is the act of "assum[ing] another's voice," the reverse happens in psalmody: another's voice becomes one's own.[76] As Athanasius describes this fusion of voices: "He who recites the Psalms is uttering . . . [them] as his own words, and each sings them as if they were written concerning him, and he accepts them and recites them not as if another were speaking, nor as if speaking about someone else. But he handles them as if he is speaking about himself."[77] Athanasius's insistence on the Psalter's uncanny ability to become one's own words evokes the transferal of voice required for προσωποιία.

It is important to distinguish between Athanasius's praise for the psalms and the actual therapy he prescribes for Marcellinus. Here the lists upon lists of psalm numbers can aid our understanding of the therapy Athanasius prescribes. These schematic lists of needs or situations and the appropriate psalm numbers suggest the need for timely recollection. Specifically, Marcellinus must learn how to recall the right psalm for the situation at hand. To do so would require him to scan his memory and retrieve the proper psalm accurately.

Memory work was at the heart of all ancient education and was also vital to Marcellinus's therapy. As Raffaella Cribiore notes, "Whereas mnemotechnics were taught in rhetorical schools as an aid to the future orator . . . concern for improving memory and retrieval showed at every stage of education. A more capacious and elastic memory had to be nourished with tender care from the early years of childhood."[78] Invention and *heuresis* are the names ancient rhetoricians gave to a process of "creative thinking" that relied on stored memory. As Mary Carruthers describes the connection between memory and invention, "One cannot create ('invent') without a memory store ('inventory') to invent from and with."[79] Whereas we may think of our own memories as a vast (or with age, diminishing?) reservoir of personal experiences, the ancients characterized memory in more architectural terms, such as a floor plan to a house. They were taught to fragment books into images so that they could be stored in discrete locations. Students of rhetoric learned how to break down a large work into smaller units, rearrange those individual units into manageable and retrievable sizes, and devise a larger system by which to arrange and secure all those smaller units.

The need for "spaces" in which to arrange, store, and retrieve material prompted teachers of rhetoric to advise students to imagine built spaces, such as palaces, houses, or theaters to hold materials that could be divided, retrieved, gathered, and recombined. To hold those elements in place, the orator depended on backgrounds and images. Backgrounds were schemes by which the speaker stored fragments of memory in discrete sequences. Thus one might use a palace, a church, gardens, or some other structure with a roamable layout. Within these structures the mind had discrete rooms, compartments, sections in which to store the fragments of material that could be scanned as needed, retrieved, and incorporated into a new idea. Composition, then, was based on a system of learning that was locational and specifically architectural. These structures, Carruthers reminds us, "should be thought of as fictive devices that *the mind itself makes* for remembering."[80] The need for a "well-furnished and securely available memory" was at the heart of rhetorical composition.

As Jerome describes the Psalter, it is "a great house whose key is the Holy Spirit."[81] Likewise, the *Letter to Marcellinus* can be regarded as a storehouse in which to retrieve and gather psalms. The *Letter to*

Marcellinus is not concerned with retention or rote memorization. Athanasius's disregard for problems of forgetting or memory lapses suggests he is confident in Marcellinus's ability to memorize and invent. What the *Letter to Marcellinus* evokes are rhetorical tropes to aid recollection and invention.[82] Readers familiar with ancient education will recognize these inventive tropes.

In describing the Psalter as the epitome of other biblical books, Athanasius likens it to a garden twice in the *Letter*: "The Book of Psalms," he declares early on, "is like a garden (παράδεισος) containing things of all these [books of the Bible]."[83] He returns to this image in the closing remarks as he recounts the "old man's" exhortation to read every psalm, "to take benefits from these, as from the fruits of a garden on which he may cast his gaze when the need arises."[84] This image of casting one's gaze on the entirety of a garden to take benefits evokes several conventions of memory and invention. To memorize the entirety of a work required a background and scheme (garden), which one scans (gaze), in order to gather or re-collect (take benefit).[85] Another common trope in inventive memory was the house. In tracking the movements of the soul, Athanasius exhorts Marcellinus, "When consecrating your house — that is, the soul that is being received by the Lord and the somatic house in which you dwell bodily — give thanks and say the twenty-ninth and the one hundred and twenty-sixth which are among the gradual psalms."[86]

Much of Athanasius's vocabulary of the gaze centers on this mnemotechnical practice of mental scanning. In comparing psalmody to a mirror, he muses, "It seems to me, that these words become like a mirror to the person singing them, so that he might perceive himself and the movements of his soul, and thus affected he might recite them. For in fact he who hears the one reading receives the song that is recited as being about him and . . . , when he is convicted by his conscience, being pierced, he will repent."[87] This passage combines a variety of rhetorical tropes. In addition to scanning, memory work involved piercing to fix memories.[88] Memory in antiquity was likened to a wax tablet on which memories were inscribed.[89] Early Byzantine writers also drew from this metaphor in describing the lance that pierced Christ's crucified body as a writing implement. As Derek Krueger has shown, sixth-century liturgical poet Romanos the Melodist punned on the reed (κάλαμος) inserted in Christ's hand and also the reed bearing the vinegar-filled sponge to suggest that "his torture is rendered an act of inscription." Likewise the lance that pierced Christ's side connotes a reed stylus dipping into an inkwell.[90] Piercing, then, evoked both the pain to fix memories and the recognition necessary for enduring memory work.

In addition to invoking structures, locational memory depended on a clearly marked path to guide the act of memory through the buildings, palaces, and so on. Athanasius speaks of the soul's movement on several occasions. The garden invoked by Athanasius is immediately followed by a list of psalm quotations. On one level the selections rehearse the events of salvation history, from Genesis to Christ. Upon closer examination, however, the psalm verses quoted for the Pentateuch and historical books invoke a host of spaces and places. In Athanasius's words, the Book of Psalms is a garden "set to music," which

> sings the events of Genesis in Psalm 18: The *heavens* declare the glory of God; and the *firmament* proclaims the work of his hands, and in Psalm 23: The *earth* is the Lord's and the fullness thereof, the world and all that swell in it. He has founded it upon the *seas*. The themes of Exodus and Numbers and Deuteronomy it chants beautifully in Psalms 77 and 113 when it says: At the going forth of Israel from *Egypt*, of the house of Jacob from a barbarous people, *Judea* became his *sanctuary*, and Israel his dominion. It hymns the same events in Psalm 104: He sent forth Moses his servant, and Aaron whom he had chosen. He established among them his words, and his wonders in the land of *Ham*.[91]

This string of quotations maps a series of places: heavens, firmament, earth, world, and seas, Egypt, Judea, and Ham. In moving from the cosmic to the geographical, Athanasius marks a pathway for Marcellinus. The remaining quotations evoke structures and places: from tabernacle (citing the Septuagint's superscription on Psalm 28), Joshua and Judges evokes the "cities of habitation," "fields," and "vineyards" of Psalm 106, terminating in the sacred center of Jerusalem (Esdras; Ps 121): "Let us go into the house of the Lord. Our feet stood in your courts, O, Jerusalem."

This emphasis on movement along paths is characteristic of rhetorical arts of memory. Athanasius invokes the word *kinêmata* or *kinêsis* no less than a dozen times in the *Letter to Marcellinus*.[92] As Athanasius characterizes the soul, it is an object in motion. The "marvel" (θαῦμα) of the

Psalter is its unique ability to "[contain] even the movements of each soul" (τὰ ἑκάστης ψυχῆς κινήματα).[93] As a mirror, it allows one to contemplate the movements of one's own soul (τὰ τῆς ἑαυτοῦ ψυχῆς κινήματα).[94] Moreover, from the psalms one can learn "the movements and dispositions of the souls [and also] the therapy and correction suited for each movement."[95]

These movements have no hint of meandering. Rather, they are triggers to learning. "If the point needs to be put more forcefully . . . the Book of Psalms possesses the perfect image for the souls' course of life [τὴν εἰκόνα πως τῆς διαγωγῆς τῶν ψυχῶν]."[96] As Athanasius describes the process, "To the one who . . . wishes to know the life of the Savior in the body, the sacred book first calls to mind [ὑπομιμνήσκει] the κινήματα of the soul through the reading, and in this way represents the other things in succession, and teaches the readers by those words."[97] The connection between memory and movement intersects with language of the path. The path was a common device in ancient rhetorical education. One contemporary of Augustine, Fortunatianus, claimed that good invention depended on a clearly marked path, or *ductus*. Thus the "flow" of a composition relied on this *ductus* to guide the work of memory in creating and arranging the various parts of a work. As Carruthers describes it, "*Ductus* insists upon movement, the con*duct* of a thinking mind on its *way* through a composition."[98] Already in the first century CE, the theorist of rhetoric Quintilian admired Cicero's ability to choose words that guide a person through the composition. In rhetorical practice, the goal of that path, or σκοπός (from the word for a bowman's target), became an important term in meditation.[99] Both meditation and rhetorical composition, Carruthers observes, depended on "spatial and directional metaphors" to mark a *ductus*, a form of "way-finding." In her words, "Every composition, visual or aural, needs to be experienced as a journey, in and through whose paths one must constantly *move*."[100] Like the *ductus*, Athanasius invokes the διαγωγή, or "course," as when he claims that "the Book of Psalms possesses . . . the perfect image for the soul's course."[101] He also calls attention to the Psalter's arrangement (διατάξεως), structured "in such a way that whoever is praying can find the movements [κινήματα] and the condition of his own soul."[102] Just as rhetorical practices conjured an elaborate system of images and paths by which to guide the process of composition, so too the *Letter to Marcellinus* prescribed a method of psalmody bound by images and paths.

A compendium of several rhetorical cues occurs in one of the closing passages of the old man's speech: "Now, my son, it is necessary for each one approaching this book to read it in its entirety, for truly the things in it are divinely inspired, but then to take benefits from these, as from the fruits of a garden on which he may cast his gaze when the need arises. For I believe that the whole of human existence, both the dispositions of the soul and the movements of the thoughts, have been measured out and encompassed in those very words of the Book [of Psalms]."[103] The notions of approaching, scanning, and selecting as needed capture well the principles of rhetorical memory and invention, whereby one scanned and retrieved stored memories in order to progress in one's composition. The memory as inventory operates on the dual processes of fragmenting ("measuring out") the texts to be remembered and containing ("encompassing") the text in its entirety. Equally important is the ability and agility to draw from the right psalm in any given circumstance. "Let him therefore select the things said in [the Psalms] about each of these circumstances, and reciting what has been written as concerning him, and being affected by the writing, lift them up to the Lord."[104] By these words, psalmody becomes an act of selection, delivery, and emotion before an audience (the Lord).

Having focused on how techniques of memory and invention shape Athanasius's advice, I can only touch briefly here upon the remaining elements: arrangement, diction, and delivery. Determining the proper order of words and ideas and crafting an effective sequence for a speech's parts were important elements of rhetorical theory. The arrangement of the *Letter to Marcellinus* reflects elements of conventional parts of a speech: introduction (προοίμιον), narrative (διήγησις), and division (πρόθεσις), most notably into the lists. In particular, Athanasius's third list (§§ 15–25) shows special attention to arrangement. He opens this section by invoking the "arrangement" (διατάξεως) of the Psalms.[105] The list that follows — by far, the longest of the *Letter*— imagines every possible situation in which one might need to reach for a psalm. G. C. Stead calls this section the "devotional use of the Psalter."[106] As noted earlier, Everett Ferguson detects an additional underlying numerical pattern in the psalm citations: "In substance it is a running summary of the contents of the Psalms, *seriatim*, except that when later psalms in the collection deal with the same thing, they are listed with the first one which fits the description."[107] This effort to arrange situations according to the order of the Psalter suggests Athanasius paid careful attention to ordering his list. Thus the list of Christological events in § 26 can be understood as a freestanding and final list of psalm references.[108] For this final list, the narrative (*diêgêsis*) of Christ's incarnation, ministry, passion, and resurrection provides the schema by which to arrange the entire Psalter.

Athanasius's advice on diction and delivery (§§ 27–29) shows concerns for voice, embellishment, melody, what he calls, "the sweetness of sound . . . for the sake of the ear's delight" (ἕνεκεν τῆς ἀκοῆς μελῳδεῖσθαι).[109] The *Letter to Marcellinus* closes with detailed instructions on proper delivery of the psalms (melody, voice, embellishments, etc.) and general instructions on psalm recitation (to recite the Psalter in its entirety, accurately, and without embellishment or "artifice").[110]

Classical rhetoric consists of five canons: invention, arrangement, diction, delivery, and memory. As this essay has argued, Athanasius's *Letter to Marcellinus* replicates, in varying degrees, these elements both in its praise of the psalms and in its program of retrieving the appropriate psalm for any given situation. His approach to the psalms draws on metaphors of memory and the mechanics of invention, notably re-collection, locational memory, and guided composition. More than instilling a deeper appreciation for the versatility of the psalms, the *Letter to Marcellinus* conjures the necessary images and maps that will guide Marcellinus on the pathways by which he may scan the entirety of the Psalter and select the most apt psalm to meet the needs of a given situation. In doing so, the words of the Psalter become his own. And, conversely, he becomes the Psalter.[111] By employing these various mnemotechnics he can "mold" himself into an image of the psalms and thereby mold his memory into an ordering device by which to recall, reuse, and ultimately think *with* and *through* the psalms. That the complete Psalter is contained in these lists has implications for the formation of this self. By mentioning every psalm, Athanasius confined this emerging self to the boundaries of the Psalter's words. This παράδεισος had no exit, defined as it was in a "world of words," as Philip Rousseau so insightfully described

Theodoret's correspondence.[112] Thus Athanasius prescribed a memory regimen that formed Marcellinus into a self known and engaged only through the Psalter. The craft of memory, then, constituted the self as much as it contained it.

NOTES

It is a great privilege to honor Professor Rousseau's scholarly achievements as well as his friendship, intellectual generosity, and sage counsel over the years.

1. Appended to Jn 15:7; quoted in *Bible Review* (June 2002), 15. The Survival Bible also garnered attention of church publications, as in the July 2002 "Church Business" column of *Church Solutions Magazine,* www.churchsolutions mag.com/articles/271news.html. I thank Drs. John C. Adams, James Ernest, Kim Haines-Eitzen, and Derek Krueger for their insightful comments on earlier versions of this essay.

2. On Christian attitudes toward the particularity of the codex, see Rapp, "Holy Texts," esp. 197–98.

3. Petersen, "Diatessaron," 189, a point more fully developed by Tjitze Baarda, "ΔΙΑΦΩΝΙΑ–ΣΥΜΦΩΝΙΑ," 143–45. Tatian was not the first to produce a harmony; Justin Martyr, Ammonius of Alexandria, and Theophilus of Antioch were said to have created harmonies or synopses (Petersen, "Diatessaron," 189). On the use of hand-held psalters, see Athanasius, *Ep. encyclica,* ed. Opitz, *Apologien,* AW 2.5.173.18–19; Athanasius, *De virginitate,* ed. Goltz, TU 29.2.46.7, cited in Nordberg, "On the Bible Text," 123 n. 25.

4. Eusebius explains the system in his *Epistula ad Carpianum* (PG 22.1276–77), trans. DelCogliano, *Letter to Carpanius*. Tables and Greek text reprinted in Nestle andAland, *Novum Testamentum Graece*, *73–*78; for an explanation of the tables, see *69. Metzger, *Manuscripts of the Greek Bible*, 42. Brakke's introduction to Evagrius of Pontus, *Talking Back*, 3–4. Roughly a quarter of these biblical references (143 out of 498) are taken from the psalms, according to Brakke's scripture index (pp. 183–85). On the use of study devices in the Middle Ages, see Carruthers, "Mechanisms for the Transmission of Culture," 10–12.

5. Ferguson, *Encyclopedia of Early Christianity*, s.v. "Catena."

6. On Athanasius's memorization and note taking from the Bible, see Nordberg, "On the Bible Text," 121.

7. John Chrysostom, *Hom. in Jo.* 11 (FC 33.104; NPNF 1.14.38). Cyril of Jerusalem alludes to private reading when he admonished Christians to shun texts not heard in church (*Catech.* 4.36, FC 61.137).

8. Greek edition: PG 27.12–45 (available online as TLG 2035.059). On the authenticity of the letter, see Rondeau, "Épître à Marcellinus," 178–80, and *Commentaires patristiques*, 79–80. On the dating of the letter, see Ferguson, "Athanasius," 296. On Marcellinus's identity, see Kannengiesser, intro. to *Early Christian Spirituality*, 14–15; and Stewart, "Use of Biblical Texts," 190.

9. British Museum, *Codex Alexandrinus* 4: fols. 523–32b (old) = Royal MS 1 D. vii.fol. 2–11b (new). I thank Kim Haines-Eitzen for sending me copies of these pages. On this codex, see McKendrick, "Codex Alexandrinus."

10. An excellent treatment of this theme appears in Dysinger, *Psalmody and Prayer,* 104–30, paraphrased in what follows; cf. Ambrose, *Expl. ps.* 1.7 (CSEL 64.6.4–11), discussed in Daley, "Finding the Right Key," 203.

11. *Ep. Marcell.* 1; on the view that the φιλόπονος γέρων is a literary disguise for Athanasius's views, see Sieben, "Athanasius über den Psalter," 157; cf. Kolbet, "Athanasius, the Psalms," 89. On repeated interruptions to remind the reader of this nested monologue, see the opening lines of *Ep. Marcell.* 9, 30, 33. For this essay, I will refer to Athanasius as the author of the treatise (even though the bulk of the letter's contents are framed as the discourse of another).

12. Useful outlines appear in Stead, "St Athanasius on the Psalms," 66–69, and Ferguson, "Athanasius," 296–98.

13. According to James D. Ernest, the average size of a citation or quotation of the psalms in Athanasius's works is roughly 11.4 words (*Bible in Athanasius*, 201).

14. *Ep. Marcell.* 9–13.

15. *Ep. Marcell.* 10, trans. Gregg, *Life of Antony,* 108 (modified). PG 27.20.47–51: τὰ κινήματα τῆς ἑαυτοῦ ψυχῆς . . . ἔχεσθαι τὴν εἰκόνα τῶν λόγον.

16. *Ep. Marcell.* 10, trans. Gregg, 108 (modified). PG 27.21.7–11: Ἐν δὲ τοῖς Ψαλμοῖς καὶ πῶς δεῖ φέρειν τὰς θλίψεις, καὶ τί θλιβόμενον δεῖ λέγειν, καὶ τί μετὰ τὰς θλίψεις, καὶ πῶς ἕκαστος δοκιμάζεται, καὶ τίνες οἱ λόγοι τῶν ἐλπιζόντων ἐπι Κύριου.

17. *Ep. Marcell.* 11, trans. Gregg, 109. PG 27.21.36–38: ὡς ἰδίους ὄντας λόγους ἀναγινώσκει· καὶ ὁ ἀκούων δὲ ὡς αὐτὸς λέγων κατανύσσεται, καὶ συνδιατίθεται τοῖς τῶν ᾠδῶν ῥήμασιν, ὡς ἰδίαν ὄντων αὐτοῦ.

18. *Ep. Marcell.* 11, trans. Gregg, 110. PG 27.24.13–17: ὁ λέγων τὰ ἄλλα ὡς ἴδια ῥήματα λαλῶν ἐστι, καὶ ὡς περὶ αὐτοῦ γραφέντας αὐτοὺς ἕκαστος ψάλλει, καὶ οὐχ ὡς ἑτέρου λέγοντος ἢ περὶ ἑτέρου σημαίνοντος δέχεται, καὶ διεξέρχεται· ἀλλ' ὡς αὐτὸς περὶ αὐτοῦ λαλῶν διατίθεται.

19. *Ep. Marcell.* 12, trans. Gregg, 111; PG 27.24.29. On the psalms as mirror, cf. John Cassian, *Collationes* 10.11 (trans. Ramsay, *Conferences,* 385; cf. Sieben, "Athanasius über den Psalter," 164 n. 27). Unlike the flat, clear mirrors

that we encounter in modern daily life, mirrors in Athanasius's day were more likely to be convex, darker, and their images less photographic. On the association of ancient mirrors with ideal types, see Shuger, "'I' of the Beholder."

20. *Ep. Marcell.* 14, trans. Gregg, 112; PG 27.25.33–34: ἡ δέ γε βίβλος τῶν Ψαλμῶν ἔχει καὶ τὴν εἰκόνα πως τῆς διαγωγῆς τῶν ψυχῶν.

21. Athanasius's interiorizing of the psalms here bears interesting similarities to Augustine's use of the psalms in the *Confessions*, as described by Burns: "He recognizes the intense personalizing of the sacred text finding there the identification and the clarification of emotional experiences. . . . Augustine in a sense discovers himself in the text of this Psalm [4]" ("Augustine's Distinctive Use," 160, citing the work of Sieben, "Psalter").

22. *Ep. Marcell.* 13 (PG 27.25.26–30), trans. Gregg, 112 (modified).

23. Ernest, "Athanasius," 353.

24. *Ep. Marcell.* 14; trans. Gregg, 113 (PG 27.25.50–55).

25. *Ep. Marcell.* 15; trans. Gregg, 114. PG 27.28.51–53: Ἂν δὲ διώκῃ παρὰ τῶν ἰδίων, καὶ πολλοὺς ἔχῃς τοὺς ἐπαναστάντας κατὰ σοῦ, λέγε τὸν γ′ ψαλμόν.

26. *Ep. Marcell.* 17; trans. Gregg, 115. PG 27.29.28–30: Προσευχῆς σοι χρεία διὰ τοὺς ἀνθεστηκότας σοι καὶ περιέχοντάς σου τὴν ψυχήν, ᾆδε τὸν ις′, καὶ τὸν πε′, καὶ τὸν πς′, καὶ τὸν ρμ′.

27. Although this list contains the most psalm references, almost one-fifth of the Psalter is omitted here (but mentioned in other lists). Athanasius may skip a psalm or more or even reverse the order. Whatever is missing from this *seriatim* list, however, appears in at least one of other lists. The claim to completeness assumes the "psalms of ascent" (119–33) as "counted" by their collective mention.

28. Ferguson, "Athanasius," 297. In other words, for some situations one psalm alone fits the circumstances; for others, several psalms address the matter. Whether there's one or several, the first (or only) psalm reference follows numerically the first (or only) psalm number for the previous situation. To diagram this pattern, the situation is represented by an asterisk (*), first or only psalm italicized, and psalm numbers appear in order, so that chapter 15 would be rendered:* *1*, 32, 41, 112, 119, 128, * *2* * *3* * *4*, 75, 115 * *5* * *6*, 38 * *7*. Presented this way, a sequence of numbers 1 through 7 appears. To be sure, there are gaps in the serial organization; some twenty-nine psalms go unmentioned in this section (yet appear elsewhere in the letter).

29. Lampe, s.v. "ψαλτήριον."

30. *Ep. Marcell.* 28 (PG 27.40.43–49), trans. Gregg, 125, citing Ps 41:6, 11; 72:2; and 117:6 respectively.

31. PG 27.45.28–33. He supplements these verses by invoking the Apostle Paul: "Practice these duties, devote yourself to them, so that our progress may

become manifest" (1 Tim 4:15; quoted in PG 27.45.35–36). On medieval composition as "advanced *memoria*," see Carruthers, *Craft of Thought,* 74.

32. Following Ferguson ("Athanasius," 297 n. 8), who includes psalms 119–33 in the count by virtue of Athanasius's appeal to the "fifteen odes among the gradual psalms" (*Ep. Marcell.* 24; trans. Gregg, 122).

33. Gregory of Nyssa, *Gregory of Nyssa's Treatise,* ed. Heine.

34. Blaising and Harding, *Psalms 1–50,* xviii–xxvi; Rondeau, *Commentaires patristiques.*

35. Dysinger, *Psalmody and Prayer,* 136–37; Evagrius of Pontus, *Antirrhetikos,* ed. Frankenberg. By Dysinger's calculations, the collection includes ninety-one references to individual psalms, comprising almost one-fifth (19 percent) of the biblical texts cited. To illustrate how a rightly chosen psalm could repair the damage of a nagging *logismos*: "*Philargyria 23:* For the thought that our parent's house is a reflection of their greatness and makes a little cell hateful to our eyes — 'I would rather be a castoff in the house of the Lord, than live in residence in the tents of sinners.'" This formula, *"For the thought that . . . ,"* anticipates a vast array of thoughts but never pretends to put the entire psalter to use (trans. O'Laughlin, "Evagrius Ponticus, *Antirrheticus*," 250). See also Brakke, "Making Public," and his introduction to Evagrius of Pontus, *Talking Back*, 1–40.

36. Ferguson, "Athanasius," 297 n. 8; Kannengiesser, "Athanasian Understanding of Scripture," 229.

37. Kannengiesser, "Athanasian Understanding of Scripture," 229.

38. Brakke, *Athanasius*, 192–96, esp. 194, citing *Ep. fest.* 11.

39. Krueger, "Old Testament and Monasticism." In addition to his astute interpretation of this letter, Krueger calls attention to its afterlife in Byzantine psalters: "This practice of reciting psalms especially in times of distress endured throughout the history of Byzantine monasticism, as evidenced by a number of tenth- to thirteenth-century psalters that include supplementary texts recommending which psalms to recite when attacked by thoughts of despondency or lust, when remembering injuries done to one, or when held captive by an evil thought, and so forth" (citing Parpulov, "Toward a History," 268–69).

40. Kolbet, "Athanasius, the Psalms," 85–101.

41. Ibid., 95.

42. Ibid., 89, 95, respectively.

43. *Ep. Marcell.* 11 (PG 27.21.31–36), trans. Gregg, 109.

44. *Ep. Marcell.* 13 (PG 27.25.18–19), trans. Gregg, 112. Cf. his condemnation of scripture reading for the purpose of exorcism or the novelty of "fashioning phrases meant to be persuasive in the pagan style [ἔξωθεν πιθανὰ ῥήματα]" (*Ep. Marcell.* 33 [PG 27.45.5], trans. Gregg, 128), an echo of his warning against

"amplifying these words of the Psalter with the persuasive phrases of the profane [τοῖς ἔξωθεν πιθανοῖς ῥήμασι]" (*Ep. Marcell.* 31 [PG 27.41.54–55], trans. Gregg, 127).

45. On Basil's shifting ambivalence toward *paideia*, from his student days in Athens to his *Ad adulescentes,* see Rousseau, *Basil of Caesarea*, 27–37, 45–60. See also Brown, *Power and Persuasion*, 39–49; Averil Cameron, *Christianity,* 80–88. On the legacy of rhetorical education in later Byzantine periods, see Jeffreys, "Rhetoric."

46. Kennedy, *Greek Rhetoric*, 214.

47. Aristotle, *Rhet.* 1.2.3–6 (1356a), trans. J.H. Freese, LCL 22.17: "Now the proofs furnished by the speech are of three kinds. The first depends upon the moral character of the speaker, the second upon putting the hearer into a certain frame of mind, the third upon the literary speech itself, in so far as it proves or seems to prove. [4] The orator persuades by moral character when his speech is delivered in such a manner as to render him worthy of confidence; for we feel confidence in a greater degree and more readily in persons of worth in regard to everything in general. . . . Moral character, so to say, constitutes the most effective means of proof. The orator persuades by means of his hearers, when they are roused to emotion by his speech. . . . Lastly, persuasion is produced by the speech itself, when we establish the true or apparently true from the means of persuasion applicable to each individual subject."

48. "Worthy of confidence": Aristotle, *Rhet.* 1.2.4, trans. Freese, LCL 22.17. "Holding fast the Psalter": PG 27.12.16–18 φιλόπονος γέρων; cf. PG 27.17.45 Οὐκ ἀγνοῶν, "not being unwise." Translations of κατέχων τὸ Ψαλτήριον περὶ αὐτοῦ differ. Bright: "clasping the Psalter to him" (p. 56); cf. Gregg: "that old master of the Psalter." My translation remains closer to the sense of κατέχων as holding fast in one's memory or holding fast (e.g., 1 Cor 15:2, 1 Cor 11:2). BDAG3 s.v. "κατέχω." "Child": PG 27.12.22 and also, toward the end of the speech, PG 27.41.32, as if to form an *inclusio*.

49. A TLG online search of the alphabetic collection alone yielded some 1,400 citations.

50. *Ep. Marcell.* 14 (PG 27.25.39–40), trans. Gregg, 113.

51. *Ep. Marcell.* 11 (PG 27.21.36–38), trans. Gregg, 109. The ability to see a rhetorical device here also qualifies the tendency to read a budding interiority in this *Letter* (as Derek Krueger cautions about this passage in "Romanos the Melodist," 272).

52. Carruthers, *Craft of Thought,* 29–30, illustrated well in Jerome's advice to Laeta on teaching children to memorize scripture, *Ep.* 107.4 (*memoria verborum*); cf. 107.12 (*memoria rerum*). I thank Derek Krueger for calling my attention to this letter.

53. Carruthers, *Craft of Thought,* 31.

54. Augustine, *Confessiones* 10.17.26.1–13 (CCSL 27.168), trans. Carruthers, *Craft of Thought,* 31.

55. *Ep. Marcell.* 10 (PG 27.20.50–51), trans. Gregg, 108 (emphasis mine).

56. Here, my thinking is shaped by Carruthers's distinction between cognitive and doctrinal images in her discussion of Cassian, *Collationes* 10.5–7 (*Craft of Thought,* 70–74).

57. Carruthers, *Craft of Thought,* 72.

58. On this distinction, see Aristotle, *Rhet.* 1.3.1–4 (1358a–b).

59. Cribiore, *Gymnastics of the Mind*, 143. On girls' and women's very limited access to rhetorical education, see 74–101.

60. For a useful overview of the system of ancient rhetoric, see *New Pauly,* s.v. "Rhetoric," 12:530–58, esp. the table at 543–46. On the role of books and writing in ancient education, see Cribiore, *Gymnastics of the Mind*, 143–59.

61. Cicero, *Rhetorica ad Herennium* 1.3 (trans. H. Caplan, LCL 403.6 and note a); cf. Aristotle, *Rhet.* 3:1 (trans. Freese, LCL).

62. The Marcellinus addressed in the letter predates another Marcellinus, who authored a commentary to the second-century sophist Hermogenes of Tarsus's *On Staseis*, one of the standard works in later Greek rhetoric (Kennedy, *Greek Rhetoric,* 54, 58–59). Kennedy add that this commentary "seems to have drawn on a lost earlier commentary on Hermogenes by Athanasius of Alexandria" (*Greek Rhetoric*, 112 n. 55, citing *R-E* 14:1487–88).

63. Kennedy, *Greek Rhetoric,* 214.

64. Stead, "Rhetorical Method," 121. Regrettably, the *Letter to Marcellinus* is not among the works Stead surveys in this important essay. On schooling in early Byzantine Egypt, see Cribiore, "Higher Education."

65. For his criticisms of rhetoric and sophistry, see *Vit. Ant.* 72–80, cf. 20 (trans. Gregg, 83–89, 46). See also Kennedy, *Greek Rhetoric,* 208–15, citations on 209, cf. *Contra gentes* 17; *Contra Arianos* 1.11.

66. On the standard handbooks and commentaries available in late antiquity, see Kennedy, *Greek Rhetoric,* 52–103.

67. Cribiore, *Gymnastics of the Mind*, 56, 187. A notable exception is the female orator Hortensia, mentioned in Quintilian, *Inst. Orat.* 1.1.6 (trans. H.E. Butler, LCL), mentioned in Morgan, *Literate Education,* 235 n. 159.

68. Kennedy, *Progymnasmata,* 108.

69. Trans. Kennedy, *Progymnasmata,* 117. On the range of definitions (from description in general to descriptions of works of art, see Webb, "*Ekphrasis* Ancient and Modern," 8; on the use of emotional involvement of audiences and language as a "quasi-physical force" in such exercises, see Webb, *Ekphrasis, Imagination,* 103–28. See also Webb, "*Progymnasmata* as Practice."

70. Heath, "Invention," 95.

71. Trans. Kennedy, *Progymnasmata,* 108.

72. *Ep. Marcell.* 10 (PG 27.20.50–51), trans. Gregg, 108.

73. Cribiore, *Gymnastics of the Mind*, 228–30; Stowers, *Rereading of Romans*, 16–21; Kennedy, *Progymnasmata,* 47–49, 115–17, 164–66, 213–17. For *proposopoiia*, see Harrill, "Paul and the Slave Self."

74. Kennedy, *Greek Rhetoric*, 64.

75. I am indebted to James J. Paxson's thought-provoking reading of Quintilian's *Institutio* in *Poetics of Personification*, 18–19.

76. Connolly, "New World Order," 143.

77. *Ep. Marcell.* 11 (PG 27.24.13–16), trans. Gregg, 110. Such ventriloquism was not unique to Athanasius. As Dysinger describes Evagrius's attitude toward psalmody, "Texts which have been memorized through the practice of psalmody can serve as the soul's own words to God in times of temptation and affliction" (*Psalmody and Prayer,* 149). Modern commentators also note this effect. As Kugel puts it, "When someone reads the words of a psalm as an act of worship, he or she takes over, in a sense, the psalm's authorship. It may have been written by an ancient Levite, but at the moment of its recitation, its words become the worshiper's own: they speak on his or her behalf to God. . . . The true author is now the worshiper himself" (*How to Read the Bible*, 472–73).

78. Cribiore, *Gymnastics of the Mind*, 166–67.

79. Carruthers, *Craft of Thought,* 11–12, esp. 12.

80. Ibid., 13 (Carruthers's emphasis). A lucid explanation of the basic principles of *memoria* appears in Carruthers and Ziolkowski, general intro. to *Medieval Craft of Memory,* 4–8

81. *Tractus in psalmorum* I (ed. G. Morin, *Anecdota Maredsolana* 3.2:1), cited in McCambley's intro. to Gregory of Nyssa, *Commentary on the Inscriptions of the Psalms,* 1.

82. My approach adopts Jeffreys's useful distinction between "embedded compositions" and "free-standing compositions" ("Rhetoric," 831–35).

83. *Ep. Marcell.* 2 (PG 27.12.38), trans. Gregg, 102.

84. *Ep. Marcell.* 30 (PG 27.41.35), trans. Gregg, 126.

85. The language here is also reminiscent of fourth-century pilgrims' "souvenirs," or *eulogiae*. See G. Frank, "Loca Sancta Souvenirs."

86. *Ep. Marcell.* 17 (PG 27.31.57–60), trans. Gregg, 116.

87. *Ep. Marcell.* 12 (PG 27.24.28–34), trans. Gregg, 111 (modified).

88. As Carruthers observes (*Craft of Thought,* 101–3), puncture wounds played an important role in rhetoric. In the act of writing, the writer's implement often pierced or left an impression on some surface. Writing involved some physical exertion, as writing or erasing on animal skins required considerable scraping, scratching, and tearing into the surface (hence our word *punctuation,* which derives from these punctures in the animal skin).

89. On this trope in classical and biblical literature, see Carruthers, *Book of Memory,* 21–22, 74, 92; see also Small, *Wax Tablets;* Jager, *Book of the Heart*.

90. On the lance and reed in Romanos, see *Hymns* 18.7 (ed. Grosdidier de Matons) as interpreted in light of Jn 19:34 by Krueger, *Writing and Holiness*, 160–61.

91. *Ep. Marcell.* 3 (PG 27.12.41–13.6), trans. Gregg, 102 (adapted; emphasis mine).

92. *Ep. Marcell.* (PG 27.20.36, 48; 21.22; 24.30, 50, 53; 25.27, 29, 40; 28.39; 40.9, 11, 30; 41.20, 39).

93. *Ep. Marcell.* 10 (PG 27.20.36), trans. Gregg, 108 (modified).

94. *Ep. Marcell.* 12 (PG 27.24.30), trans. Gregg, 111.

95. *Ep. Marcell.* 13 (PG 27.25.29–30), trans. Gregg, 112 (modified); (τὴν ἑκάστου κινήματος θεραπείαν τε καὶ διόρθωσιν); cf. *Ep. Marcell.* 14 (PG 27.25.39–41), trans. Gregg, 113.

96. *Ep. Marcell.* 14 (PG 27.25.34), trans. Gregg, 112.

97. *Ep. Marcell.* 14 (PG 27.25.38–42), trans. Gregg, 113.

98. Carruthers, *Craft of Thought,* 77; Carruthers's emphasis.

99. Ibid., 79–80.

100. Ibid., 81; Carruthers's emphasis.

101. *Ep. Marcell.* 14 (PG 27.25.33–34) trans. Gregg, 112.

102. *Ep. Marcell.* 15 (PG 27.28.37–39), trans. Gregg, 114 (modified).

103. *Ep. Marcell.* 30 (PG 27.30.32–40), trans. Gregg, 126 (modified).

104. *Ep. Marcell.* 30 (PG 27.41.49–50), trans. Gregg, 127.

105. *Ep. Marcell.* 15 (PG 27.28.37), trans. Gregg, 114. To modern interpreter Alicia Suskin Ostriker, the idea of "arranging" the psalms is oxymoronic: "Uncontrollable, unpredictable. Scholars have tried in vain to find and orderly structure in the sequence of psalms because there is very little in the way of rhyme or reason to them. They are not rational; they are intense. Anyone who meditates knows how unruly the mind is. You try to still it and make it serene, and it fails to obey. This is what we find in the psalms as well" (*For the Love of God*, 60).

106. Stead, "St Athanasius," 67.

107. Ferguson, "Athanasius," 297.

108. *Pace* Stead, "St Athanasius," 67.

109. *Ep. Marcell.* 27 (PG 27.39.53–54), trans. Gregg, 123. Daley notes instances of patristic critique of psalmody used as magical incantation and appeals to Hellenistic musical ideals of "sweetness" ("Finding the Right Key," 192, 201).

110. *Ep. Marcell.*, 31.

111. I thank John C. Adams for calling my attention to the convergence of *mimesis* and recitation in ancient rhetorical training.

112. Rousseau, "Knowing Theodoret," 282.

PART II

Disciplines and Arenas

Chapter Six

From the Pillar to the Prison

Penitential Spectacles in Early Byzantine Monasticism

DANIEL F. CANER

"Come, gather round, and I will speak to all who have angered the Lord. Come see what He has revealed to me for your edification." Thus John Climacus, author of the seventh-century ascetic treatise the *Ladder of Divine Ascent,* introduces readers to a place called the Prison. This was a monastery of penitents, "a land of true mourners," belonging to a cenobium that John knew outside Alexandria. Built a mile away from the cenobium, it was "dark, stinking, filthy, and squalid"—"Just seeing the place," says John, "teaches complete repentance and mourning."[1] Also called the Isolation Monastery, it confined monks who, after entering the cenobium, had fallen into sin.[2] Having heard about their "strange condition and humility," John asked to visit, and what he saw there fills much of the *Ladder*'s fifth chapter on *metanoia,* that is, repentance/penance: "I saw some of those accused yet innocent men stand all night in the open, their feet never moving, driving sleep away with abuse and insults. . . . Others prayed with hands bound behind their backs, like criminals. . . . Some sat in sackcloth and ashes, beating the ground with their heads, [while] others constantly beat their breasts. . . . Often they would go to the [abbot] and beg that he place iron fetters and collars around their hands and necks, bind their feet . . . and not release them until death."

"Believe me, brothers," adds John, "I am not making all of this up."[3] These penitential ascetics embodied what he called *metanoia memerimnēmenē,* a truly serious repentance.[4] Some of them seemed to have become "completely altered in their attitude and state of concentration."[5] Indeed, after spending an entire month in that "land of *metanoia,*" John says that he returned to the cenobium "utterly changed and altered" himself.[6]

John Climacus provides our longest and most vivid description of the performance of penance in any early Byzantine monastery. No doubt he was describing a real place.[7] The use of space in cenobitic monasteries for confining unruly monks (as well as heretics, prostitutes, court officials, and adulterous aristocrats) is amply attested from the fifth century onward.[8] According to John, inmates of the Alexandrian Prison, eating only bread and chopped vegetables, were forced to pray unceasingly while a supervisor supplied them with palm leaves to weave to ward off boredom.[9] But for all such historical detail, John was not particularly interested in recording *realia*. He says little, for example, about the actual lapses that caused monks to be sentenced to the Prison: instead, he depicts all of them as holy sinners, "accused yet innocent men," who have redeemed themselves through intense mourning (cf. Mt 5:4, "Blessed are those that mourn, for they shall be comforted"). His description must be treated not as a historical account but as an example of hagiographical *enargeia,* a rhetorical construct meant to turn readers into spectators. Its purpose, notes John Chryssavgis, was to provide "an image of *penthos,* a living icon of repentance" for readers of the *Ladder*.[10]

Recent studies of early Byzantine monasticism have focused on the role of a spiritual master in hearing a disciple's confession and sharing the burden of his sins.[11] Climacus is an important witness to that relationship,[12] but the connection he draws between visualizing penitential acts and achieving "complete repentance and mourning" invites inquiry into the role of penitential spectacles in early monastic thought and practice. As is well known, Christian communities from the second to the fourth century had also featured dramatic rituals of penance that required sinners to perform confessions and prostrations before entire congregations. Public displays of humility were considered crucial to the efficacy of these rituals, providing at once both the means of acquiring, and a demonstration that one truly had acquired, contrition and repentance; indeed, the public humiliation involved was probably one reason why these rituals were abandoned in the Roman East in the late fourth or early fifth century.[13] Climacus and other sources show that they continued to be performed, at least occasionally, in monastic communities.[14] Climacus is unusual, however, in drawing attention to the effect they had on their spectators: according to him, seeing such performances helped concentrate their minds on the eternal drama of sin, Final Judgment, and its consequences.

The result is a portrayal of early Byzantine spirituality that modern readers have understandably found appalling. Unlike other ascetic writers, Climacus does not soften his descriptions of penitential punishments with depictions of heavenly rewards. To appreciate his imagery requires us to take seriously a problem he identified in himself as well as his peers: the sheer difficulty of maintaining a penitential fervor or focus. Indeed, Climacus's blend of hagiography and analysis makes his *Ladder* unusually revealing of the challenges that monastic leaders faced in turning a monastery into what Karl Heussi called a *Sonderwelt,* an environment where monks might perceive themselves as actors in a transcendent reality and drama.[15] At the same time his presentation provides an opportunity to reconsider the rationales behind some of the seemingly more eccentric, spectacular penitential practices found in earlier monastic culture, and to explain more fully why these eventually became incorporated into cenobitic regimens. Here I wish to express my debt to Philip Rousseau, whose observations on this development, as on so many others in early monastic history, have spurred me forward.[16]

PUTTING ASCETIC PENANCE ON DISPLAY

By "spectacular" practices, I mean the wearing of long hair, sackcloth, and iron collars, fetters, belts, or chains. Although the wearing of the latter are often depicted by Greek authors as a type of athleticism meant to break down the body (some chains reportedly weighed over 120 pounds!), all find precedent in Old Testament penitential behavior;[17] hence Jerome can refer to long hair and chains as "signs of sorrow" that, along with sackcloth and ashes, were appropriate to monks.[18] Though mainly associated with the Syrian-Mesopotamian milieu (where solitaries were identified as "mourners," *avilē,* rather than "recluses," *anachōrites*), monks wearing chains have been found buried in Palestine and Egypt, suggesting that such behavior was originally more widespread.[19] Indeed it may be, as Matthias Henze has argued, that long hair and chains were merely Christian expressions of a deeply rooted, Near Eastern religious sensibility based on penance and mourning.[20] At any rate it is not surprising to find them included among the "practices and poses that win [God's] philanthropy" that Climacus saw in the Prison.[21]

But such practices hardly passed without criticism when seen on display in the late fourth century. The *History of the Monks in Egypt,* for example, censures monks who wore long hair and chains on the grounds that they were exhibitionists pursuing popular acclaim (*anthrōpareskeia*): "They should wear down the body with fasting and do good in secret, but rather than do this, they make themselves conspicuous to all."[22] Jerome also warned his protégé Eustochium to avoid "men you see laden with chains, who go against the Apostle [1 Cor 11:3–16: see below] and have long hair like women, as well as a billy goat's beard, a black cloak, and bare feet braving the cold. All this is evidence of the devil. . . . Such men have made their way into houses of the nobility and deceived 'silly women laden with sins' [2 Tim 3:6–7]. . . . Feigning sadness, they pretend to fast while all night they feast in secret."[23] Similar suspicions were raised by the bishops Epiphanius of Salamis and Augustine of Hippo. Both alleged that such monks had donned an Old Testament guise in order to be esteemed more holy.[24] In response, both cite 1 Corinthians 11:3–16, where Paul states that men must keep their hair short, not only because they bear the image of God but because "nature itself teaches that if a man wears long hair, it is a "degradation" (*atimia*) for him." Paul abruptly concludes: "If anyone thinks it well [viz., by wearing long hair] to be contentious [*philoneikos*]— we have no custom, nor does God's church."

Though dealing only with long hair, Paul's passage evidently guided fourth-century church policy on all ascetic practices deemed ostentatious:

Epiphanius, for example, applies it to condemn the visible wearing of sackcloth, arguing that "Paul had rejected those who had such customs and practices because, by apostolic law and in the eyes of the Church, they are contentious."[25] No explanation for such behavior survives directly from the monks in question. Augustine, however, summarizes what he claims to have been the justifications put forth by certain long-haired monks in Carthage. According to him, these argued that Paul's prohibition against men wearing long hair did not apply to them both because they were no longer men — having become "eunuchs for the kingdom of heaven" (cf. Mt 19:12) — and because they considered their long hair a "degradation" that they had "deservedly assumed on account of [their] sins."[26] In other words, rather than reject long hair because of Paul's negative characterization of it as a dishonor for men, they kept it precisely because he had characterized it negatively as such. Augustine will have none of this. Anyone, he remarks, who has deliberately adopted an Old Testament guise "for the sake of humility," or who seeks to hide his pride beneath a "shade of feigned humility," ought to "cover his head in sackcloth" instead — that is, pull a bag over his head.[27]

It would be easy to follow these authorities and discount such behavior as mere exhibitionism, charlatanry, or as evidence of *philoneikia* — a contentious spirit of rivalry. Jerome, Epiphanius, and Augustine all allege that it was motivated simply by gain. The Carthaginian monks were a case in point: Augustine characterizes their long hair as a "venal hypocrisy" meant to remind people of Samuel and other biblical Nazirites so as to win their material support.[28] Authority was also at issue: Augustine and Epiphanius repeatedly complain that such monks were defying church custom as well as Paul. But their charges also recall polemics against *goēteia* ("religious charlatanry") that learned authors had routinely deployed to discredit radical ascetics or unlettered counterparts in the earlier Roman past.[29] Suspicions should be raised by Epiphanius's allusion to the "immoderate simplicity" of the monks in question: this suggests that he and other authorities were dealing with ascetic rationales that were unfamiliar or simply puzzling to them.[30] Augustine's charge of false humility warrants special attention. It is a way of condemning a paradox: he directs it against monks who not only have adopted a mark of dishonor as a mark of sanctity, but also claim to seek humility by drawing attention to themselves through that very mark of dishonor. Faced with this apparent contradiction between this behavior and their professions of humility, he prefers to regard their long hair as the mark of "venal vainglory" instead.[31]

Augustine's assertions aside, what is interesting is the Carthaginian monks' characterization of their long hair as a "degradation deservedly assumed on account of our sins." This implies (as Augustine's remarks indeed make clear) that they wore it to visibly dishonor and humble themselves as sinners. To move beyond the accusations of false humility and pride expressed by Augustine, we must examine the paradox he confronted and consider why late fourth-century monks would have assumed that self-humiliation and public display were appropriate for each other (rather than "inappropriate," to quote Epiphanius).[32] Was there any precedent for such ascetic behavior and logic?

There was, in the earlier church spectacles of public penance. Two hundred years before Augustine was dealing with the long-haired monks in Carthage, Tertullian, a Carthaginian Christian himself (d. ca. 225), had asserted that, to be properly humbled, a penitent must disfigure himself with "sordid apparel" (meaning sackcloth and ashes; Commodian adds long hair) and then lie prostrate before fellow church members, supplicating them to pray for him.[33] Closer to our period, in late fourth-century Cappadocia, Basil of Caesarea assigned the most dire sinners (those guilty of murder, apostasy, or adultery) to a penitential class called "mourners." These were to stand outside church gates publicly confessing their sins, while supplicating those who went in to pray on their behalf. Only after doing so for four years did these mourners graduate to another penitential class called "prostrators." These could enter the church but still had to perform genuflections before the rest of the congregation for seven years more.[34]

Tertullian and Basil remind us that, for Christians who identified themselves as dire sinners, making a penitential spectacle of oneself had long been considered both an appropriate and a necessary means of attaining redemptive humility. This penitential logic helps explain the behavior that Augustine and others criticized as exhibitionism and pride. It is notable that the long-haired Carthaginian monks come into view at about the same time that the older church rituals of public penance were falling into disuse, and at the same time that monks were becoming identified as professional penitents who could not only mourn for their own sins but also "share the pain" of the sins of others.[35] Arguably one such mourner was Symeon Stylites (d. 459), the first known pillar saint and most spectacular of all late antique monks. While Symeon's own motives for originally ascending his pillar are not documented, at least one later stylite is reported to have presented himself as a penitent on display: "Understand you not that . . . it is on account of my sins and spots and crimes that God has bound me to this stone, like a judge who puts a criminal in bonds?"[36] Symeon's case is particularly intriguing because the ceremonies that developed around his pillar seem to represent an inversion of the rituals of public penance earlier prescribed by Basil for neighboring Cappadocia: whereas in Basil's day a humble mourner would stand at the church fringe to supplicate entering congregations to pray for *him,* now, in the mid-fifth century, congregations would leave their churches to supplicate a humble mourner standing on the fringe to pray for *them*. This enabled lay congregations to observe an edifying spectacle of penance without having to humiliate any members of their own.

Symeon's performance, however, was sufficiently eccentric to provoke both charges of vainglory and outright mockery from Christian contemporaries.[37] Why, we may still ask, did his behavior eventually gain acceptance, while that of other ostentatious mourners did not? Susan Ashbrook Harvey has proposed that the ceremonial processions and liturgies that developed around Symeon's pillar not only "brought to fruitful order" his novel stylitism but also "framed and defined" the practice itself, providing the ritual context necessary to give it acceptable purpose and meaning.[38] I would also propose that such formal rituals, by making Symeon the ceremonial center of attention, would have helped Symeon himself to maintain his own concentration and vigilant watch. That this might have otherwise been a problem is suggested by two letters attributed to the fifth-century monk Nilus of Ancrya (d. ca. 430). In these letters Nilus rebukes an unknown stylite named Nicander both for making himself "conspicuous to all" and for "not wishing to contemplate heavenly things." Allegedly this stylite preferred to pass his time not by focusing on prayer but by chatting with pious ladies attracted to his pillar.[39] These letters may be satirical and Nicander apocryphal, but Nilus elsewhere expresses concern that any monk, whether praying in solitude or genuflecting before a crowd of admirers, might easily become distracted and forget what was pleasing to God.[40]

In this light the ceremonies that developed around Symeon's pillar provided the formal context necessary to ensure that he, unlike Nicander, maintained his penitential fervor and focus despite being "exposed to all as a new and extraordinary spectacle."[41] Moreover, the liturgical appropriation of Symeon's practice dignified him as an object of church ritual, thereby diminishing at once both his individualism and his eccentricity.[42] As a result his behavior, although "conspicuous to all," could not be simply dismissed as vainglorious or contentious by the Christian establishment. But it is important not to dismiss the concerns of this establishment either. It is possible to detect in its criticisms a concern that exposing such flamboyant penitential practices to public view might affect the way not only those practices but also monasticism more generally were perceived or construed. Among the monastic rules attributed to Rabbula, the early fifth-century bishop of Edessa, is one that forbids monks from wearing either long hair or chains unless they do so within the confines of a monastery. While it may be tempting to see here an episcopal effort to control ascetic enthusiasm and charisma, Rabbula's rule sought not to prohibit the monks' practices so much as to restrict their location. Its true rationale should probably be inferred from the rule that immediately follows, that forbade monks from leaving their monastery in a hair shirt lest they "denigrate the honor of the monastic garb."[43] At stake was the public perception and honor of monasticism itself.

PENITENTIAL SPECTACLES IN MONASTIC SETTINGS

What we are seeing in these early fifth-century rules and ceremonies are measures meant to put potentially distracting, destabilizing, or embarrassing devotional impulses into structured environments that would be meaningful and beneficial for both monk and community. In his own discussion of this development, Philip Rousseau has drawn attention to John of Ephesus's (d. ca. 586) depiction of the accommodations at a sixth-century cenobium at Amida, where individuals who conformed to communal norms could nonetheless acquire "more idiosyncratic status" through their great practices of standing and watching. Rousseau notes John's concern that "the wisdom of the group and the custom of the community should modify extremes of individual devotion."[44] Yet John also emphasizes the communal benefits of seeing such ascetic exertions put on display: "Even if there were a man idle and stolid and careless and lazy, he would be incited by the sight of these labours, and awake with astonishment as from deep sleep, and henceforth labour, and emulate these heavenly practices."[45] According to John, the ostentatious penitential practices performed at this Syrian monastery (standing on posts, suspension by armpits, etc.) bred, not a "deadly and destructive" rivalry among the monks, but rather "an emulation that is beautiful and good and sound." As a result, "Unremitting contrition spread over great and small . . . because everyone was looking at his fellow . . . and was eager to pass his fellow in the race of righteousness."[46]

John of Ephesus nicely anticipates John Climacus's understanding of the utility of penitential spectacles ("everyone was looking at his fellow") for stimulating and sustaining a spirit of contrition throughout a monastic community. Climacus's description of the Alexandrian cenobium (probably meant to depict the famous Metanoia Monastery on the city's eastern shore) shows how this was thought to work in an ideal institution a century later.[47] Before turning to the extreme forms of penance on display in the Prison, John devotes his *Ladder*'s fourth chapter, on obedience, to describing individual acts of penance within the cenobium itself. These range from standing and pleading at the monastery's gates for prayers from passersby, to prostrating oneself before the entire community in the monastery's church or refectory.[48] All are presented as things John considered "worthy of wonder and remembrance";[49] more to the point, he emphasizes their spectacular nature and impact by variously describing them as "a strange sight," an event in which "one could see the extraordinary coming to pass," or a "drama done to edify all."[50] Most memorable of all is a monastic ceremony reminiscent of earlier church penitential ritual. According to John, when a former bandit sought admission to the cenobium, the abbot required him to "parade" his sins before the entire community. This meant entering the monastery chapel dressed in a hair shirt, with hands bound and ashes sprinkled on his head, while attendants repeatedly hit him and the abbot rebuked him. Finally he lay face down on the floor and tearfully enumerated his sins. "By this spectacle," John says, "all were stunned." The abbot orchestrated it, he explains, not merely to save the postulant himself, but to impress the entire community with an edifying example of "salvation and energetic humility."[51]

John describes a monastery in which humility and instruction were both advanced and reinforced through dramatic performances of penance. For the penitents, "publicly parading" their sins helped release them from these sins, on the basis of the rationale that "without shame one cannot be freed from shame."[52] For the rest, it was hoped that seeing such spectacles would prompt them to confess their own sins and achieve salvation too.[53] But that was not all. As John presents it, this monastery was entirely orchestrated to heighten a monk's awareness of his participation in a drama of heavenly judgment and redemption. This is most apparent in the penitential ceremony described above, in which the penitent bandit is said to have sworn that when he heard the abbot's rebuke upon entering the church he was astonished, "for he believed he had heard thunder, not a human voice," coming from the sanctuary; another monk claimed to have seen at that very moment a fearsome apparition strike off a list each sin that the bandit confessed.[54] But John portrays all experience in this cenobium to be similarly heightened. Elsewhere, for example, he notes that its monks imagined that all the punishments imposed by their abbot were imposed not by him but by God instead, while those sentenced to the Prison lamented God's absence there, calling on him to show his face and release them from their "hell of penance."[55] The result was an environment where "action and contemplation were wonderfully combined," and "if there was any talk at all, it was always about remembrance of death and mindfulness of eternal judgment."[56]

Thus Climacus presents this monastery to readers as a *Sonderwelt* that used penitential spectacles to keep monastic minds focused on the perils of Final Judgment. One crucial element in his depiction of it as such is its close identification of the abbot with God. As explained by one whom the abbot had forced without explanation to stand for an hour in silence at a refectory table, "I thought of the [abbot] as the image of Christ and thought his command came not from him but from God. So I stood praying as if before an altar of God instead of a table of men, and because

I have faith in and love for my shepherd, I had no malevolent thoughts towards him."[57] This identification provided the monks with a figure toward whom they could direct the faith and love (*pistis* and *agapē*) that they wished to show God. But it also meant that any lapses in obedience toward the abbot were tantamount to lapses before God. It is therefore not surprising to find the Prison described as a kind of hell that is defined by the absence not only of God but of the abbot as well: John depicts its inmates as exclaiming amid their lamentations to God, "Where is our faith in our shepherd?"—that is, why had they failed their abbot.[58]

Overly dramatized though it doubtlessly is, John's depiction of the penitential regimen in this cenobium alerts us to a basic monastic concern: namely, how to maintain a penitential mind-set and fervent awareness of sin. This difficulty was related to that of maintaining compunction, a state that, as Basil observed in the 370s, was easily lost unless monks were constantly vigilant.[59] To do either required that monks acquire strong powers of imagination. The apophthegmata and related texts repeatedly advised them to imagine themselves as prisoners awaiting their judge ("Constantly contemplate this, and you can be saved"), or to visualize Judgment Day and the torments to come: "Look," the monk is told, "and never forget these things inside or outside your cell."[60]

Of course, the challenge was always to look and never to forget. "Three things are difficult for us to acquire," wrote Isaiah of Scetis in the fifth century, "and these protect all the virtues: mourning, weeping for our sins, and holding death before our eyes." The reason was, above all, forgetfulness, which "fights against us . . . continually taking down everything we erect."[61] As Dorotheus of Gaza observed in the sixth century, "The Fathers say a person acquires fear of God by holding onto the memory of death and the memory of eternal punishments . . . but we do the opposite and chase away the fear of God by holding onto neither . . . occupying ourselves with things that do not matter. . . . Little by little, these things lead to complete contempt."[62]

These basic challenges of memory and imagination help explain John's unusually graphic depiction of the penitential regimen in the Alexandrian cenobium and its prison: this most descriptive section of the *Ladder* served to fix in his readers' imagination the advice he gave them elsewhere: "Impress on yourself and never stop examining the abyss of dark fire, its cruel servants, its unsympathetic judge . . . and all such images."[63] They also help explain some of the ostentatious practices attributed to the earlier penitential ascetics surveyed above, especially their wearing of chains. Discussing a Syrian monk named Harfat who attracted much public acclaim by his wearing of chains on his neck, hands, and feet "on account of [his] sins," John of Ephesus notes that Harfat sought to mourn at "all moments" in anticipation of his condemnation on Judgment Day, when Jesus would say, "Let he who has no wedding clothes be bound on hands and feet and be cast into the outer darkness" (Mt 22:31).[64] Because Harfat's chains attracted such attention (and because "God gave no command about irons"), John insisted that he take them off. But elsewhere John commends a monk named Zacharias who secretly wore a knotted thread bound tight around his wrist as a "guardian of the remembrance of God." Its purpose, Zacharias explained, was to serve "as a guardian of my thoughts, lest they dissipate themselves in vain things, and that, if error gain dominion over my mind, and it be suddenly captured and dissipated by the sight of an object, I may remember my soul and turn to God . . . and if again, the evil of error . . . take possession of my intellect, when I see this object, I may . . . cry to God to deliver me from error." At one time he had kept another thread tied round his neck but he had eventually removed it because it caused many in his monastery to laugh. "I know," he said, "that these things are folly to many . . . but to me they are very useful, and are to me the irons of my [ascetic] servitude [*parzlē d-purlanā*]."[65] Similarly, Theodore of Sykeon is said to have put iron fetters on his feet and to have called them "an eternal bond of remembrance."[66]

Thus chains or their equivalents served as dramatic devices and reminders to help monks maintain their devotional fervor and focus. Climacus admits to being well aware of the difficulty of maintaining either of these himself. As he confides in a chapter on insensitivity (*anaisthēsia*), "I am not ashamed to admit that my powers fail here, for I myself have been sorely tried by this vice."[67] This "mother of forgetfulness," he explains, makes monks not only impervious to compunction but so unfeeling toward the sacred that they might come to regard the sacramental Host, for example, as just "plain bread." Its only remedy is contemplation of Judgment Day. John recommends praying in a charnel house so as to impress an image of its skeletons on one's heart: "Otherwise," he says, adopting the voice of the affliction, "you will never defeat me."[68]

Climacus presents the Alexandrian cenobium as arranged to ensure that its monks will remain ever mindful of and sensitive to the approaching perils of death and Judgment Day. Elsewhere he describes penitential activity itself as a means of "whipping the soul into an intense awareness" (or sensitivity, *aisthēsis*).[69] This he considered to be the basis of the fervent concentration (*synnoia*) of the monks he saw in the Alexandrian cenobium and especially in its prison. Such was the power of this fervent concentration to preserve a monk's sense of mourning, he says, that demons feared it "more than thieves fear dogs."[70]

FROM SYMEON'S PILLAR TO CLIMACUS'S PRISON

Climacus knew that the penitential asceticism he so vividly described in his *Ladder* would not be approved by all. "I once saw two people sitting out of sight and watching the toils and groans of the athletes," he says. "One did so in order to imitate them. But the other did so in order that, when the time came, he could broadcast them with reproach."[71]

While repentance, compunction, and tears were basic pursuits of Christian monasticism from the very start, the apparent rise in emphasis during the sixth and seventh centuries on penance and mourning as monastic ends in themselves warrants attention and explanation. It is notable that the Greek word *penthos* ("mourning"), so prominent in the *Ladder*, hardly appears at all in the writings of Palladius, Evagrius Ponticus, or Theodoret of Cyrus, who, when they mention mourning at all, treat it mainly as a necessary precondition for achieving contemplation and tranquillity.[72] How might we explain the emphasis on penitential mourning found in sixth- and seventh-century writers?

One explanation may be linked to the emergence of monarchical abbots like the one Climacus portrays, whose supreme role and authority in the monastery was expressed by issuing penitential commands: "After evening prayers you could see the great one sitting on a throne like an emperor, surrounded by the community, which listened to and obeyed his commands as if they were the words of God. He would order one to recite fifty, another thirty, another a hundred psalms. He would order one person to make so many genuflections, another to sleep sitting up."[73] At the same time a different historical explanation is suggested by Climacus's warning, placed near the end of his description of the Prison, against using the teachings of "godless Origen" on God's love as an excuse to be lax in seeking forgiveness for one's sins. Climacus alludes here to Origen's notion of the *apokatastasis*, which extended an assurance of mercy and redemption to all sinners, even Satan, at the end of time.[74] Its condemnation in the mid-sixth century left Christians bereft of any such assurance, it seems, apart from the regular performance of penitential gestures designed to soften a stern judge's heart.

But yet another possible reason why earlier writers such as Palladius, Evagrius, and Theodoret did not make mourning more central to their descriptions or prescriptions may have been that, to be stimulated or sustained, it seems to have required a degree of physical dramatization or communal reinforcement that did not easily fit with the notions of tranquil isolation and rational self-control that these earlier authors, all of whom were writing in a Hellenic philosophical tradition, held so dear. Theodoret, for example, writes approvingly of a bishop who persuaded Symeon Stylites to take off the irons by which he had chained himself to a rock early in his career. Symeon had initially put on the irons "in order to force himself to continually imagine heaven and contemplate things beyond heaven." The bishop reportedly convinced him that "the mind sufficed to put rational fetters on the body." But the story reveals that Symeon had felt the need to use dramatic devices to maintain his devotional fervor and focus long before he mounted his pillar.[75]

Nonetheless by mounting that pillar, Symeon helped steer monastic tradition in a direction that ultimately pointed the way to Climacus's Prison. In an apology for the saint, Theodoret explained that Symeon's "strange spectacle" had been divinely contrived so as to rouse negligent people to contemplate heavenly things.[76] Though this apology was written to defend Symeon against his many contemporary detractors, it reflects an understanding of the utility of penitential spectacle similar to that displayed by Climacus himself, whose graphic imagery was calculated to fix a "fiery blast" in his readers' hearts more memorable and effective than any other lesson they might find in his *Ladder*.[77] As he says in conclusion to his description of the Prison, "Let the holy prisoners I have called to memory stand as your rule, imprint, and image of repentance, and you will never need another book for the rest of your life."[78]

NOTES

1. John Climacus, *Scala paradisi* (hereafter *Scal.*) 5 (PG 88.764b), trans. Luibheid and Russell, *Ladder of Divine Ascent,* 121 (773b): αὐτὴν τὴν τοῦ χώρου θέαν μετανοίας πάσης καὶ πένθους ὑπάρχειν διδάσκολον. All translations mine unless otherwise indicated.

2. *Scal.* 4 (PG 88.701b).

3. All-night standing, *Scal.* 5 (PG 88.772b); binding of hands (PG 88.765a); sackcloth and ashes (PG 88.765e); collars and fetters (PG 88.772b), trans. Luibheid and Russell, 121, 122, 105, slightly adapted.

4. *Scal.* 25 (PG 88.989d).

5. *Scal.* 25 (PG 88.765c): ἐξεστηκότας τῷ ἤθει καὶ τῇ συννοίᾳ.

6. *Scal.* 25 (PG 88.776b): ἠλλοιωμένον ὅλον καὶ ἐξεστηκότα.

7. His description is sometimes cited as the earliest evidence for a medieval monastic prison; see Sellin, "Dom Jean Mabillon"; Peters, "Prison before Prisons," 27–30.

8. John of Ephesus, *Lives of the Eastern Saints* 5 (ed. Brooks, PO 17.104), and Elijah, *Life of John of Tella* (ed. Brooks, CSCO Script. Syr. III.25, Syr. 87/Lat 55); *Canons of Marutha* no. 6 exiles violent monks to another monastery for a year of "fasting and nazariteship" (ed. and trans. Vööbus, *Syriac and Arabic Documents*, 139). John provides the only clear example of an entire monastery being dedicated to that purpose. A possible parallel is the "monastery within a monastery" at the Theodosius coenobium outside Bethlehem. This was reserved for monks who had become unhinged and rebellious because of extreme asceticism. However, Theodore of Petra portrays it as a place of convalescence rather than of penance (of course, he may not have seen a difference); see Usener, *Heilige Theodosios*, 41–42. For state use of monasteries to reform lay sinners, see Hillner, "Monastic Imprisonment," and Guillou, "Monde carceral."

9. *Scal.* 4 (PG 88.701b).

10. Chryssavgis, *John Climacus,* 138. Climacus's rhetorical skills are now recognized; see Duffy, "Embellishing the Steps," and Johnsén, *Reading John Climacus.*

11. Kolenkow, "Sharing the Pain"; Bitton-Ashkelony, "Penitence"; Rapp, "Spiritual Guarantors" and *Holy Bishops,* 73–77.

12. Müller, *Konzept des geistlichen Gehorsams*, 205–95.

13. As suggested by Rapp, "Spiritual Guarantors," 125. For ancient church rituals, see Watkins, *History of Penance*.

14. See Climacus's description of the initiation of an Alexandrian brigand, below; also Vivian, "Monks, Middle Egypt," 547–71; *Rules of Saint Pachomius* 135.

15. Heussi, *Ursprung des Mönchtums,* 53–54.

16. Rousseau, "Eccentrics and Cenobites," 49, also "Monasticism."

17. For Greek authors' views on the monks' wearing of iron chains, fetters, collars, etc., see Theodoret, *Hist. relig.* 3.19, 21.8; cf. *Hist. mon.* 8.59. For these practices' precedents in the Old Testament, see, e.g., 2 Sam 3:31, Job 4:6, Dan 9:3, Jon 3:6, Mt 11:21 (sackcloth and ashes); Jer 27:2, 28:13 (collars; cf. Roman practices of putting collars on slaves); Num 6:1–21 (long hair and fasting of the Nazirites).

18. Jerome, *Ep*. 17.2 (written ca. 379; PG 22.360): "catenae, sordes et comae . . . signa . . . fletus." Cf. John Chrysostom, *Subintr.* 5 (PG 47.501), *Hom. in Eph*. 13.3 (PG 62.97). For catalogue and comment, see Peña, Castellana, and Fernandez, *Reclus syriens,* 103–7.

19. In Syria and Mesopotamia: see Palmer, *Monk and Mason,* 84–87; Vööbus, *History of Asceticism,* 282–86; Beck, "Beitrag zur Terminologie." In Palestine and Egypt: see Kogan-Zehani, "Tomb and Memorial" (fifth- to sixth-century Palestine); Butler, *Lausiac History of Palladius*, 2:215–16 (Egypt).

20. Henze, *Madness of King Nebuchadnezzar*, esp. 191–215.

21. *Scal.* 5 (PG 88.765a): ἐπιτηδεύματά τε καὶ σχήματα τὴν αὐτοῦ φιλανθρωπίαν συντόμως κατακάμπτοντα.

22. *Hist. mon.* 8.59 (ed. A.-J. Festugière, 70): ἐμέμφετο δὲ πολλὰ τοὺς τὰ σίδηρα φοροῦντας καὶ τοὺς κομῶντας· "οὗτοι γὰρ ἐνδειτιῶσι, φησίν, καὶ τὴν ἀνθρωπαρέσκειαν θηρῶσιν, δέον αὐτοὺς μᾶλλον νηστείας ἐκλύειν τὸ σῶμα καὶ ἐν κρυπτῷ τὸ καλὸν πράττειν· οἱ δὲ οὐ τοῦτο, ἀλλὰ πᾶσιν ἑαυτοὺς φανεροὺς καθιστῶσιν." Since the authors of the text (ca. 400) were from Palestine, this passage may have been meant to censure such practices there.

23. Jerome, *Ep*. 22.28 (PL 22.413): "fuge, quos videris catenatos, quibus feminei contra Apostolum crines, hircorum barba, nigrum pallium, et nudi in patientia frigoris pedes. Haec omnia argumenta sunt diaboli . . . . qui postquam nobilium introierunt domus, et deceperunt mulierculas oneratas peccatis . . . tristiam simulant, et quasi longa jejunia, furtivis noctium cibis protrahunt."

24. Epiphanius, *Panarion* 80.7.2, ed. Holl and Dummer, 3:492: οὐ γὰρ διὰ θεὸν ἡ ἀρετή, κἂν τε διὰ θεὸν ὑποληφθείη, ἀλλὰ διὰ φιλονεικίαν. Augustine, *De opere monachorum* 31.40, ed. Zycha, 591: "timent ne vilior habeatur tonsa sanctitas quam comata."

25. Epiphanius, *Pan*. 80.6.5–6, 7.4. In *De fide* 23.6, he states, "It is inappropriate [ἀπρεπὲς] to go out in visible sackcloth, as some do, and to go out in iron collars, as we have said," apparently referring to 13.8, where he censures wearing iron collars as παρὰ τὸν θεσμὸν τῆς ἐκκλησίας; ed. Holl and Dummer, 3:520, 513.

26. No longer men: see Augustine, *De opere* 32.40. Long hair as a self-inflicted degradation: see Augustine, *De opere* 31.39, ed. Zycha, 591: "ipsam ignominiam, inquiunt, suscipimus merito peccatorum nostrorum."

27. Augustine, *De opere* 31.39, ed. Zycha, 591: "obtendentes simulatae humilitatis umbraculum . . . sed si hanc ignominiam . . . pro humilitate isti appetunt, tondeant et cilicio caput velent."

28. Augustine, *De opere* 31.39, ed. Zycha, 590–91: "illi enim venalem circumferentes hypocrisin . . . ut videlicet qui eos videt, antiquos illos quos legimus cogitet, Samuelem et ceteros, qui non tondebant." Cf. Epiphanius, *Pan*. 80.6.5, ed. Holl and Dummer, 3:492: βούλεσθαι λαβεῖν ἀπὸ τῶν ὁρώντων τὸν μισθὸν καὶ τὴν χάριν. For context, see Caner, *Wandering, Begging Monks*, 117–22, 151–52.

29. See Francis, *Subversive Virtue*, 47–49; also Caner, "Nilus of Ancyra."

30. Epiphanius, *Pan*. 80.4.1, ed. Holl and Dummer, 3:488: ἀπὸ τῆς ἀμετρίας τῆς τινων ἀδελφῶν ἀφελείας; cf. John of Ephesus, *Lives of the Eastern Saints* 11 (see below, note 64).

31. Augustine, *De opere* 33.41, ed. Zycha, 591: "sub eo proponant venalem typhum."

32. See above, note 25.

33. Tertullian, *De poenitentia* 9.3–4; Commodian, *Instructiones* 2.8; discussed in Watkins, *History of Penance*, 1:114–17.

34. Basil of Caesarea, *Ep*. 217.56; cf. Watkins, *History of Penance*, 1:240–41.

35. See Rapp, "Spiritual Guarantors," 122–25, and *Holy Bishops*, 96–97; and Kolenkow, "Sharing the Pain." Perhaps the "consolations" the Carthaginian monks claimed to provide for their supporters (Augustine *De opere* 1.5) were of this nature too.

36. John of Ephesus, *Lives of the Eastern Saints* 4 ("Life of Abraham and Maro"), ed. and trans. E.W. Brooks, PO 17.68, slightly adapted. Only the later Greek *vita* interprets Symeon's practice in penitential terms; see Harvey, "Sense of a Stylite." However, the Syriac *Vita* 112 states that Symeon conceived of it during his Lenten confinement, and thus it seems to have been understood by the authors as an extension of his Lenten regimen. The iron collar that he wore, along with his head, was put on display after his death; Evagrius Scholasticus, *Church History* 1.38.

37. *Vit. Danielis Stylitis* 7; Evagrius 1.13. Theodoret characterizes Symeon's critics as φιλοσκώμμενοι ("scoffers"), suggesting that Symeon was an object of ridicule (*Hist. relig.* 14, ed. Canivet and Leroy-Molinghen, SC 257.192).

38. Harvey, "Stylite's Liturgy," 537. This article nicely complements Rousseau, "Eccentrics and Coenobites."

39. Nilus of Ancyra, *Ep*. 2.115 (PG 79.249b–d): τοῖς πᾶσι φαίνομενου ἐνδόξοι, κάτω δὲ τοῖς λογισμοῖς σύρεσθαι, μήδεν ἄξιον τῶν οὐρανίων πραγμάτων διανοεῖσθαι βουλόμενον, μόνον δὲ ταῖς γυναιξὶν ἡδέως προσλαλοῦντα. Cf. Alan Cameron, "Authenticity of the Letters," 118–19.

40. Nilus of Ancyra, *De voluntaria paupertate* 22–23 (PG 79.997–1000); *De monachorum praestantia* 22 (1084).

41. Theodoret, *Hist. relig.* 22, ed. Canivet and Leroy-Molinghen, SC 257.204, trans. Price, *History of the Monks,* 170: πρόκειται πᾶσι θέαμα καινὸν καὶ παράδοξαν.

42. Harvey, "Stylite's Liturgy," 238.

43. *Rules of Rabbūlā for the Monks* 5 and 6, ed. Vööbus, *Syriac and Arabic Documents,* 28: *d-la nzalon yaqirutā d-eskimā*. On efforts to control monastic garb and its meaning in this period, see Basil of Caesarea, *reg. fus*. 22, and Krawiec, "Garments of Salvation."

44. Rousseau, "Eccentrics and Coenobites," 45. John's depiction was meant to show unity under the Chalcedonian persecution: see Harvey, *Asceticism and Society,* 69–70.

45. John of Ephesus, *Lives of the Eastern Saints* 35 ("Of the Amidene Convents"); ed. and trans. Brooks, PO 18.612; cf. 609.

46. Ibid., PO 18.613.

47. Regarding the Metanoia Monastery, see Müller, *Konzept des geistlichen Gehorsams*, 237.

48. *Scal*. 4 (PG 88.688d, 692a, 692d, 697d).

49. *Scal.* 4 (PG 88.684d): πολλὰ αξιοθαύμαστα καὶ ἀξιομνημόνευτα ... ἑώρακα.

50. *Scal.* 4 (PG 88.684c): ξένον σχῆμα πεποίηκεν, 697b: ἦν ἰδέσθαι ὑπερφυὲς τὸ γινόμενον, 697c: δρᾶμα πρὸς οἰκοδομὴν πᾶσι πεποίηκεν.

51. *Scal.* 4 (PG 88.681d): ἐπὶ πάσης τῆς ἀδελφότητος ταῦτα θριαμβεῦσαι . . . 684a–b: ἐξ αὐτῆς τῆς θεωρίας ἅπαντας καταπλαγέντας. . . . σωτηρίαν αὐτοῦ ἐν ἁπᾶσι πραγματευομένου, καὶ τύπον σωτηρίας καὶ ἐνεργοῦς ταπεινώσεως πᾶσι παρέχοντος.

52. *Scal.* 4 (PG 88.681b): μώλωπες γὰρ θριαμβευόντες . . . ἰαθήσονται, with 708d: οὐ γάρ ἐστιν ἐκτὸς αἰσχύνης, αἰσχύνης ἀπαλλαγῆναι. Γύμνου σὸν μώλωπα . . .

53. *Scal.* 4 (PG 88.684d).

54. *Scal.* 4 (PG 88.684d).

55. *Scal.* 4 (PG 88.692b); *Scal.* 5 (PG 88.769b).

56. *Scal.* 4 (PG 88.685a–b): παῤῥησίας καὶ ἀργολογίας ἀπηλλαγμένη. . . . θαυμαστὴν κεκτημένην καὶ τὴν ἐργασίαν καὶ τὴν θεωρίαν. . . . ἦν δὲ αὐτοῖς ἄλυκτος (εἰ δέοιτο φθέγξασθαι) καὶ ἄπαυστος συλλαλία, ἡ τοῦ θανάτου ἀνάμνησις καὶ κρίσεως αἰωνίου ἔννοια. This is illustrated by reference to a monastic cook who imagined he was serving not humans but God, and that the fires of his oven were the fires of hell.

57. *Scal.* 4 (PG 88.692ab), trans. Luibheid-Russell, 98. For this doubling of God and abbot, see 684d, 688b, 693d, and Müller, *Konzept des geistlichen Gehorsams*, 241, 282–89.

58. *Scal.* 5 (PG 88.766a; cf. 680d and 776d).

59. Basil of Caesarea, *Reg. fus.* 16 (PG 31.1092d–93a); cf. Hausherr, *Penthos*, 88–120.

60. Imagining themselves in prison: see *Apophth. patr.* (systematic collection) 3.4, ed. Guy, SC 387.152: οὕτως μελετήσῃς διαπαντὸς, δύνασαι σωθῆναι. Cf. Isaiah of Scetis, *Ascetic Discourse* 14. Remembering death and visualizing Judgment Day: see *Apophth. patr.* (systematic collection) 3.5, ed. Guy, SC 387.152: ὅρα μὴ ἐπιλάθῃ ποτὲ . . . τῆς ἐκ τούτων μνήμης. Cf. 3.1, 2, 4, 40; Isaiah of Scetis, *Ascetic Discourse* 16, 27. For the early history of Christian Judgment Day descriptions, see Shaw, "Judicial Nightmares."

61. Isaiah of Scetis, *Ascetic Discourse* 7, trans. Chryssavgis and Penkett, 82. Cf. *Apophth. patr.* (systematic collection) 3.9, 15, 55.

62. Dorotheus of Gaza, *Discourse* 4.52–53, ed. Regnault and Préville, 230–32. Cf. Barsanuphius of Gaza, *Ep.* 237; *Apophth. patr.* (systematic collection) 3.55, 56.

63. *Scal.* 7 (PG 88.804c): ἀνατυπῶν ἐν ἑαυτῷ μὴ παύσῃ καὶ διερευνῶν . . . τῶν τοιούτων παντῶν εἰκόνας. He goes on to say that readers should tremble like prisoners before a judge when they pray, since their "outward appearance and inward disposition" would overcome God's anger.

64. John of Ephesus, *Lives of the Eastern Saints* 11 ("Life of Harfat"), trans. Brooks, PO 17.163–64, where John also attributes Harfat's wearing of chains to his "simplicity."

65. John of Ephesus, *Lives of the Eastern Saints* 19 ("Life of Zacharias"), trans. Brooks, PO 17.271–72, slightly adapted.

66. *Vit. Theodorii Syceonis* 28, ed. Festugière, 26: δεσμόν τινα ἀίδιον ὑπομνηστικὸν ἑαυτῷ ἐφευράμενος); cf. the Old Testament explanation for wearing tassels (the *tzitzit*), Num 15:39–40.

67. *Scal.* 18 (PG 88.933b–c), trans. Luibheid-Russell, 192. Here Climacus seems to follow Evagrius Ponticus, *Thoughts* 11 (on "the demon of insensibility").

68. *Scal.* 18 (PG 88.933d): εἰκόνα τούτων ἀνεξάλειπτον ζωγραφῶν ἐν σῇ καρδίᾳ.

69. *Scal.* 5, 764c: πλῆξις ἐν αἰσθήσει κραταιᾷ, trans. Luibheid-Russell, 121.

70. *Scal.* 805a; cf. 685c, 765c.

71. *Scal.* 4, 713c, trans. Luibheid-Russell, 112, adapted.

72. Cf. *Scal.* 7, 816d, trans. Luibheid–Russell, 145: "When we die . . . we will not be criticized for having failed to be theologians or contemplatives. But we will certainly have some explanation to offer to God for not having mourned unceasingly." For the importance of *penthos* in Climacus's *Ladder* and his relation to earlier authors, see Chryssavgis, *John Climacus*, 132–208. Hausherr, *Penthos*, remains the classic general treatment but is not historical.

73. John Climacus, *Liber ad pastorem* 14 (PG 88.1200c).

74. *Scal.* 5 (PG 88.780d), trans. Luibheid–Russell, 131: "All of us — but especially the lapsed — should be especially careful not to be afflicted with the disease of the godless Origen. This foul disease uses God's *philanthropia* as an excuse, and is very welcome to those who are lovers of pleasure." Barsanuphius, *Ep.* 600, also expresses concern that Origen's notion might prevent a monk from seeking repentence and mourning.

75. Theodoret, *Hist. relig.* 10, ed. Canivet and Leroy-Molinghen, SC 234.178–80. Cf. John of Ephesus, *Lives of the Eastern Saints* 11 ("Life of Harfat"), trans. Brooks, PO 17.164, where John persuades Harfat to replace his chains with "labours of knowledge." Cf. Price's intro. to Theodoret, *History of the Monks,* xxxiii–iv: "One is left with the disconcerting impression that Theodoret's own Hellenic Spirit of rationalism and moderation was something of a hindrance in dealing with the more extraordinary features of Syrian Christianity. . . . For in contrast to his Hellenic assumptions (which we today largely share), their lives point to a very different climate of thought. The histrionic element in Syrian asceticism reveals a mentality in which outward actions have their own value, quite apart from their influence on the soul."

76. Theodoret, *Hist. relig.* 12, ed. Canivet and Leroy-Molinghen, SC 234.188: παράδοξον ἐπρυτάνευσε θέαμα τῷ ξένῳ πάντας ἕλκων εἰς θεωρίαν.

77. *Scal.* 5 (PG 88.777b; cf. 7, 813a): πένθος γάρ ἐστιν πεποιωμένον ἄλγημα ψυχῆς ἐμπύρου.

78. *Scal.* 5 (PG 88.780d–81a): Ὅρος σοι, καὶ τύπος, καὶ ὑπογραμμὸς, καὶ εἰκων πρὸς μετάνοιαν ἔστωσαν οἱ προμνημονευθέντες ἅγιοι κατάδικοι, καὶ οὐ μὴ δεηθήσῃ βιβλίου ὅλως ἐν τῇ ζωῇ σου πάσῃ.

Chapter Seven

Cassian, Cognition, and the Common Life

CATHERINE M. CHIN

For the past few decades, much work on early Christian asceticism has focused on ascetic individuals, or holy persons, and on the strategies late ancient Christians used to create them.[1] In most of this work, the traditional boundaries of the human body have generally been taken to be the boundaries of the ascetic person, always excepting cases of miraculous intervention. Yet late ancient Christians themselves were troubled by the concepts of personhood and individuation: Trinitarian and Christological disputes are merely the most obvious examples of the problems such topics could engender.[2] Ambiguity over the boundaries between persons also extends into Christian thought about the material routines of everyday life. My specific subject in this essay is not just any kind of everyday life but the routines imagined by John Cassian for ascetics in Gaul. Cassian's *Institutes* are useful for reconsidering the categories of the individual person and the collective in late antique Christianity, since they are clearly intended to bring together collective cenobitic practice and what is often considered the individual and interior pursuit of virtue. Because it is traditional to think of ascetic practice in terms of the single individual ascetic, the specific relationship between the common life and the individual pursuit of virtue in Cassian's thought has been a point of some scholarly concern. Although Cassian seems at times to favor *anachoresis* as a superior method of seeking virtue, he also clearly lays out the pitfalls of withdrawal into the desert, pitfalls that he claims are best avoided by remaining in the common life.[3] No individual ascetic, however, can simultaneously practice both the common and the solitary life; thus a choice must be made between the two.[4]

One of the more fruitful approaches to resolving this tension in Cassian was proposed by Philip Rousseau in his 1978 study *Ascetics, Authority, and the Church in the Age of Jerome and Cassian*: that, for Cassian, "the final aim . . . is not so much union with Christ as union with one's fellows — 'to be loved by the brethren who share one's task.'"[5] Rousseau's lucid formulation of Cassian's aim as "union," and the implied parallel between "union with one's fellows" and "union with Christ," provide an excellent theoretical starting point for understanding the limits and ends of ascetic personhood in Cassian. If the aim of ascetic practice is union, either with multiple others or with a single divine other, the modern category of the individual becomes a very problematic lens through which to view the ascetic person. As an alternative, I would like to examine Cassian's notion of the ascetic person using the idea of union and the sharing of an ascetic task. The idea of the cooperative system rather than the freestanding individual as the fundamental unit of analysis is basic to modern systems theory;[6] to analyze Cassian's depiction of ascetic union and the shared ascetic task, I draw specifically on the idea of distributed cognition, in which the performance of ostensibly interior cognitive tasks is understood to be situated within specific human and nonhuman systems.[7] The integration of individual cognitive actors into a larger systemic unit in this model allows us to see Cassian's portrayals of individual and collective ascetic lives without a strict division between an interior and exterior in the activity of the mind or soul. Once this division breaks down, once multiple figures may be understood to be contributors to interior cognitive actions, the line between the "inner man" and the "outer man," and hence the line between the individual and the collective, also begins to blur. Thus a distributive model of ascetic virtue allows the cenobitic and anchoritic lives to be neither competing nor hierarchically distinct models of ascetic practice but different manifestations or processes within the same system of unification.

In brief, I will argue here that Cassian uses the framework of the Origenist *apokatastasis* as his large-scale system of unification. The creation of individualized ascetic persons as traditionally understood is not Cassian's intent. Instead, Cassian distributes the ascetic pursuit of virtue across both human and nonhuman, visible and invisible, components of a larger ascetic system. In so doing, Cassian locates the "interior" of the interior life not exclusively in the individual human body but inside the collectivity in which that body participates. Thus Cassian's notion of the ascetic person should not be limited to specific manifestations in certain monks; rather, it should be expanded into a much more complex unit of human, divine, and material convergence. My primary focus will be on the foundations of this notion in the first five books of Cassian's *Institutes*, but it will also be necessary to consider related material on the relationship of the soul to the common life in the *Conferences*.

DISTRIBUTION

The notion of distributed cognition has been complicating accounts of human intellectual activity for the last two decades, and I should begin by offering a summary of the idea before attempting to apply this distributional model to Cassian. One of the more influential studies of distributed cognition is Edwin Hutchins's 1995 *Cognition in the Wild*, an ethnography of the complex task of navigation on a naval transport ship.[8] Hutchins emphasizes both the interdependent roles of the people assigned to different navigational tasks and the important role of computational and representational shortcuts embodied in such nautical equipment as navigational charts and tide tables. The process of navigation, Hutchins argues, is undeniably cognitive, but this cognition occurs in a physically diffuse network; except in the case of sailing alone, no one person or object is the locus of navigational cognition in each navigational event.

Thus Hutchins argues that navigators are actors within "sociocultural cognitive systems":[9] people think, but do so within material contexts that structure their thought in particular ways, so that the material contexts should be considered participants in the cognitive process. As Hutchins suggests:

> The real power of human cognition lies in our ability to flexibly construct functional systems that accomplish our goals by bringing bits of structure into coordination. That culturally constituted settings for activity are rich in precisely the kinds of artifactual and social interactional resources that can be appropriated by such functional systems is a central truth about human cognition. The processes that create these settings are as much a part of human cognition as the processes that exploit them, and a proper understanding of human cognition must acknowledge the continual dynamic interconnectivity of functional elements inside with functional elements outside the boundary of the skin.[10]

The connection between interior and exterior in the distributed cognitive process is what creates the system as a thinking whole. It is not strictly speaking any one navigator who thinks through the navigation of the ship at every point; instead the entire navigational system, consisting of both human and nonhuman actors, thinks through the navigation.[11] Human navigators and their internal and external actions are merely some of the combined components in a dynamic cognitive machine.

In models of distributed cognition, then, the relationship between the apparently freestanding person and the cognitive task must be reformulated to include actors and processes "outside the boundary of the skin." D.N. Perkins has called the resulting system the "person-plus," suggesting that "any person alone is the intersect of the set of person-pluses in which that person participates. A person alone, then, becomes the queen bee in a hive of innumerable participations."[12] This expansion of the person entails a significant redefinition of personhood in terms of open dynamic systems working over time, and it allows for many kinds of interactions between the contributors to a given system, and many kinds of interactions between any one contributor and the system as a whole. In Hutchins's case study, the actors do not become in any way incapable of thought outside the navigational system — that is, they do not become automatons or lose their agency[13]— but within the parameters of the system their thought is both constrained in particular ways and enhanced by its conjunction with that of other thinking contributors. The boundaries of personhood in such cases are effectively system dependent.

A comparison of Hutchins's argument to premodern ascetic thought is illuminating. At the basic level of material interaction between the ascetic practitioner and her environment, it is a commonplace of ancient ascetic literature that the physical settings and trappings of ascetic practice play a major role in defining the character of the ascetic, hence the vital ideology of the desert, or of the enclosed space, and the classification of ascetics by material living arrangements.[14] More specifically, as Darlene Brooks Hedstrom and Caroline T. Schroeder have argued, monastic buildings could both shape and represent the state of monastic virtue.[15] This kind of dynamic interplay between the ascetic and her environment, in which the ascetic both shapes and is shaped by the physical fact of a building, a location, or an artifact, is a relatively straightforward example of ascetic personhood defined within the constraints of an open system. Cassian's configuration of the ascetic person includes this straightforward physical aspect, although, as we shall see, it also goes beyond it.

On the most obvious level, the conflation of material systems with the activity of the soul is immediately clear in Cassian's preface to the *Institutes*, in which he claims that his dedicatee, Castor of Apt, is "setting out to construct a true and spiritual temple for God not out of unfeeling stones but out of a community of holy men . . . and you also desire to consecrate very precious vessels . . . forged . . . out of holy souls."[16] Beyond simply identifying souls as vessels and building blocks for a common purpose, however, Cassian claims explicitly that the material routines of the ascetic life are necessary intellectual tools: "And, in particular, the reasoning behind what was done then could never be handed on or understood or conjured up by means of leisurely meditation or verbal teaching."[17] It is not merely the monastic life that cannot be understood by armchair ascetics, but specifically the *ratio* behind that life that is impenetrable without physical practice. In other words, ascetic *ratio* is located not simply inside the mind of the monk irrespective of routine but in the cognitive system of monk-plus-routine.[18] Cassian reiterates the dependence of the interior life on an understanding of the exterior in his opening to *Institutes* 1: "After having exposed their outward appearance to view we shall then be able to discuss, in logical sequence, their inner worship."[19] The same dependence is expressed in the first preface to the *Conferences*: "In this regard, however, if anyone wishes to give a true opinion and desires to see whether these things can be fulfilled, let him first hasten to seize upon their chosen orientation with similar zeal and by a similar way of life. Only then will he realize that what seemed beyond human capacity is not only possible but even most sweet."[20] Again, what is made possible through practice is, according to Cassian, not merely spiritual or ascetic progress but *vera sententia* about the ascetic life. This assertion, however, suggests that the foundation of ascetic experience is the system of the person and the routine, rather than what Perkins would call the "person alone." This may seem obvious (an ascetic person is necessarily a person *and* an ascetic practice), but it is important to remember that Cassian's starting point is not the individual person but the person embedded in a specific material system that extends outside the boundaries of the body.

The creation of human and material ascetic systems is clearly laid out in the first four books of the *Institutes*. Famously, Cassian opens book 1 by asking, "As we start to speak of the institutes and rules of monasteries, where could we better begin . . . than with the very garb of the monks?"[21] In fact, placing the treatment of clothing at the very beginning of a monastic treatise is quite rare in the previous tradition.[22] Cassian's source for this opening is Evagrius's *Letter to Anatolius*, the preface to the *Praktikos*.[23] Cassian also borrows Evagrius's conclusion to his discussion of clothing; where Evagrius claims that taking the habit is the first step to *apatheia* and knowledge of God, Cassian argues that monastic garb enables "purity of heart with respect to spiritual progress and the knowledge of divine things."[24] Both Evagrius and Cassian thus link material aspects of asceticism to the ability to think certain things. Cassian, however, goes further than Evagrius by emphasizing the necessary commonality of property. For Evagrius, the habit is remarkable for its visible difference from ordinary clothing;[25] but for Cassian the important aspect of monastic clothing is that "it should be different from the apparel of this world in that it is kept completely in common for the use of the servants of God."[26] His insistence on the systemic nature of asceticism is reinforced in his rationale for rejecting the use of sackcloth in monastic clothing, namely that this is a minority practice: "For the opinion of a few must not be preferred to nor must it prejudice the common practice of all. For we ought in every respect to bestow an unshakable faith and an unquestioning obedience . . . on those [rules] that were long ago passed on to later ages by innumerable holy fathers acting in accord."[27] Cassian's location of monastic difference in commonality rather than in visible distinctiveness sets his discussion apart from other ascetic discussions of clothing and suggests that, for him, clothing is more than merely a matter of ascetic representation.[28] Rather, "spiritual progress and the knowledge of divine things," to be gained, must be gained in the communal and material system that sharing the clothing creates, and not strictly within the ascetic individual.

The location of ascetic *ratio* in community and in shared physical routines continues in Cassian's accounts of communal prayer. In *Institutes* 2.10.1, Cassian describes the Egyptian synaxis as follows: "When they come together . . . to celebrate the aforementioned services . . . everyone is so quiet that, even though such a large number of brothers has gathered, one would easily believe that no one was present apart from the person who stands to sing the psalm in their midst."[29] Cassian's focus here is less on the psalms or on their content than on their potential to create a single praying entity out of many monastic presences. Similarly, the movements of the monks at prayer should be in unison: "But when the person who is about to say the prayer has arisen from the ground, all stand up at the same time. Thus no one is moved to bend the knee before he does, and no one dares to dally once he has arisen from the ground, lest anyone give the impression that he has made his own conclusion rather than having heeded that of the person who says the prayer."[30] Unlike the Pachomian Rules (at least in Jerome's Latin version), which also enjoin silence and obedience during the synaxis but without further elaboration, Cassian's account stresses the result of such obedience, namely physical and intellectual unification.[31] Clearly this aspect of the spiritual life is tied both to material routines and to the extension of those routines through the entire group.

Cassian describes the early stages of intellectual and ascetic unification between bodies in book 4 of the *Institutes* and is again explicit as to the process of expanding ascetic cognition to function outside the body. After the renunciants have joined the "body of the brotherhood," they are trained to "reveal [wanton thoughts] to their elder as soon as they surface, nor to judge them in accordance with their own discretion but to credit them with badness or goodness as the elder's examination discloses and makes clear."[32] In this way the monk "is protected not by his own but by his elder's discretion and . . . he cannot be persuaded to hide from his elder whatever promptings and fiery darts [the devil] casts into his heart."[33] Of course, the revealing of one's thoughts to an *abba* is portrayed as a common practice in other ascetic literature as well; the *Apophthegmata patrum* are full of accounts of monks freed from difficult or dangerous thoughts by revealing them to their elders.[34] What is notable in Cassian is the incorporation of this practice into an institutionalized system of thinking outside one's own body. The novice is protected by the elder's discretion in the cases of both good and bad thoughts, and while it is understandable for the vanquishing of bad thoughts to seem more pressing, the inclusion of both good and bad thoughts in the shared cognitive process reveals that the commonality of thinking is the primary aim of the practice. In fact, as Cassian will go on to argue in *Conferences* 2.10, the practice of thinking "with" an *abba*, rather than any specific guidance imparted by the *abba*, is the process by which harmful thoughts lose their force: "For as soon as a wicked thought has been revealed it loses its power . . . even before the judgment of discretion is exercised."[35] Along with the sharing of clothing and the uniform practice of common prayer, the sharing of thoughts becomes a physical practice of intellectual unification and personal expansion.

The emphatic connection in the *Institutes* between commonality and the possibility of ascetic thought indicates that Cassian is using a model of thinking or of spiritual activity that is fundamentally not grounded in the individual or aimed toward the creation of individuated ascetic persons. Thus Cassian's concern for the common life in the *Institutes* does much more than encourage charity or humility between ascetics. Instead, it is a reconfiguration of the ascetic person as such.

APPEARANCE AND ESCHATOLOGY

The theoretical key to this reconfiguration can be found in an excursus in book 5 of the *Institutes*, where Cassian begins to describe the eight principal faults. The cognitive aspects of the previous four books set the stage for Cassian's discussion of virtuous endeavor, which is, as many commentators have noted, largely understood in psychological or cognitive terms.[36] The distributed nature of cognition in books 1–4, however, also points to a distributed system of virtues. At *Institutes* 5.4.2, Cassian notes that not all ascetics, even those who are "outstanding," will possess all the virtues. "Therefore the monk who, like a most prudent bee, is desirous of storing up spiritual honey must suck the flower of a particular virtue from those who possess it more intimately. . . . For if we want to obtain all of them from a single individual, either examples will be hard to find or, indeed, there will be none that would be suitable for us to imitate."[37] This sounds commonsensical, and Cassian will return to this point in *Conferences* 14.6: "For it is impossible for one and the same person to shine simultaneously in all the virtues that I have listed above. If someone wants to strive after all of them together, in his pursuit of them he will of necessity not possess a single one completely, and he will suffer loss rather than make gain as a result of this diversity and variation."[38] But Cassian also explains in *Institutes* 5.4.2 why different monks will necessarily excel in different virtues: "The reason for this is that, although we see that Christ has not yet been made all in all . . . we can nonetheless in this fashion find him partly in all."[39] Readers of Origen will immediately recognize one of the scriptural pillars of Origen's doctrine of the *apokatastasis*, 1 Corinthians 15:28.[40] This may not seem surprising in a text that borrows heavily from Evagrius, but in fact Evagrius does not use 1 Corinthians 15 at all in the *Praktikos*, on which the *Institutes* is most closely modeled. What we see in *Institutes* 5 is not just a reuse of the doctrine borrowed from Evagrius but a deliberate deployment of it in defining the ascetic person.

In the context of Latin Origenist thought, it is easy to see Cassian's distribution of ascetic virtue throughout the group both as a way of anticipating the reunification of souls with God and as a way to redefine the individual in terms of unification and participation.[41] In fact, as Cassian explains after his citation of 1 Corinthians 15, the goal of the ascetic routine is not perfecting one's own person at all; it is creating the person of Christ as a unified system: "Inasmuch, therefore, as there is wisdom in one, righteousness in another, holiness in another, meekness in another, chastity in another, and humility in another, Christ is now divided among each of the holy ones, member by member. But when all are assembled together in the unity of faith and virtue, he appears as 'the perfect man,' completing the fullness of his body in the joining together and in the characteristics of the individual members."[42] The ascetic group is a system in which reunification happens, but it does not happen at the level of any one individual. What is more, the reunification does not produce perfected individuals at all: it produces, in startling simplicity, Christ. To return to Hutchins's study of navigation: the distribution of cognition across multiple navigators, charts, and instruments creates a sociocognitive entity that is more than the sum of its parts, an entity whose thinking results not primarily in the improvement of its members individually but in their arrival at a safe haven.[43] Cassian separates the entity assembled by the ascetic system, Christ, from the individual workings of the system's members, in the same way that individual navigators are distinct from, but necessary for, the haven toward which they sail.

This strongly eschatological passage is found where Cassian is shifting in the *Institutes* from his discussion of the shared intellectual nature of material routines to the discussion of the eight principal faults.[44] It is at this point that traditional readings of Cassian have seen a shift from the "exterior" to the "interior," although a more radical shift from outside to inside has traditionally been located between the *Institutes* and the *Conferences* and has been mapped onto the divide between the common and the solitary life. As many modern scholars have pointed out, however, any clear distinction between cenobitic and anchoritic life is difficult to sustain in Cassian's work.[45] Given the shared cognitive functions of physical monastic practice in *Institutes* 1–4, the same difficulty exists for the distinction between interior and exterior. The pursuit of virtue, which Cassian claims will lead to reunification, and which is traditionally located in the "interior" life, here does not happen individually but collectively: "Until the time comes . . . when God will be all in all, God can be such presently in the fashion that we have spoken of—that is, by virtues partly in all, although he is not yet all in all with respect to the fullness of them."[46] This means, however, that the pursuit of virtue, traditionally taken to be in the individual soul and body of the ascetic, is for Cassian also located, by extension, inside the network of souls and bodies that form the ascetic group, a group that is made ascetic not by individual ascetic acts but by its own fundamental collectivity. This shift in the location of virtue leads Cassian to his striking redefinition of the ascetic person. Ultimately for Cassian, there is only one ascetic person, Christ, a person produced by an interlocking network of ascetic contributors who serve as his "interior." The perfecting of multiple individual souls does not produce multiple virtuous persons; it produces one perfect person, distinct from but made up of them all.

Institutes 5 thus introduces the union of the visible human with the invisible divine, the union for which the distribution of ascetic thought through visible material practices serves as the foundation. Viewed nonsystemically, interactions between individual humans in a monastery must of course seem to be of a different order than interactions between the human and the divine; yet Cassian's suggestion that it is precisely through the unification of the monks that one finds Christ "partly in all" indicates that a clear distinction between types of unification cannot be maintained. Instead, Cassian's eschatological turn in *Institutes* 5 makes clear another aspect of his systemic asceticism, namely the presence in the system not merely of visible material artifacts, practices, and humans who contribute to the ascetic task but also of invisible elements: souls, spirits, and divine figures who also participate in the ascetic process. These invisible elements are not less, but also not necessarily more, a part of Cassian's distributed asceticism than the monastic clothing with which Cassian begins the *Institutes*. The shift in book 5 from apparently external to apparently internal practice, from monastic routine to the battling of evil thoughts, is primarily a shift from the visible aspects of systemic asceticism to its invisible aspects, as Cassian writes at 5.1: "so that we may worthily investigate their natures, which are so intricate, so hidden, and so obscure."[47] The eschatological emphasis on Christ "appearing" as "the perfect man" signals Cassian's turn toward making visible the invisible components of the ascetic process.

The presence of these invisible elements in the ascetic process is important to an understanding of the role of the solitary life in Cassian's distributed system, a system that might at first seem to have no place for the monk in the desert. While a detailed analysis of the *Conferences* is well beyond the scope of this essay, one point from Cassian's discussion of the solitary life should be kept in mind: the monk is not, in fact, alone in the desert. Cassian's solitaries are repeatedly called upon to display hospitality to other humans and to assist other monks (like Cassian and Germanus themselves) in their pursuit of virtue.[48] They are also, more importantly, surrounded by spirits, both good and evil: "But this air which is spread out between heaven and earth is so thick with spirits . . . that divine providence has quite beneficially withdrawn them from human sight";[49] each monk is constantly accompanied by two spirits, one good and the other bad.[50] Cassian's portrayal of the "solitary" as constantly interacting both with other monks and with spirits brings the solitary back into an asceticism that is ultimately systemic rather than individual. In the case of the anchorite, the system may be extended over a larger or more irregular geographic area (the space between the solitary and other humans), and the nonhuman contributors to ascetic virtue may be more varied, encompassing different individual settings and practices, as well as nearby angels and demons, but the profoundly interactive nature of the ascetic process remains the same. Appropriately enough, then, Cassian describes the anchoritic life as fundamentally an extension of the cenobitic life: "From this number of the perfect [i.e., the early cenobites], from what I would call this most fruitful root of holy persons, the flowers and fruit of the anchorites sprouted forth afterward."[51] The final goal of the solitary life is "to have a mind bare of all earthly things and, as much as human frailty permits, to unite it thus with Christ."[52] This unification returns us to the goal of the ascetic life as broadly conceived in *Institutes* 5, the point at which Christ becomes "all in all."

Indeed, given the emphasis on the solitary life in the *Conferences*, it is noteworthy to see the same passage from 1 Corinthians reappear here, first in *Conferences* 1.13, describing the kingdom of heaven, but in more detail in *Conference* 7 on the soul and evil spirits, and in *Conference* 10, on prayer. Each of the latter two conferences deals with a topic that may at first seem to be strictly individual and well-suited to the solitary, but in each of them Cassian argues that their subjects are embedded in a system of bodily interactions and multiple contributors. At *Conferences* 7.6.4, Cassian uses 1 Corinthians 15:28 to argue explicitly that the final reunification must be anticipated "in this flesh": "But no one will arrive at the fullness of this measure in the world to come except the person who has . . . been initiated into it in the present and who has tasted it while still living in this world; who, having been designated a most precious member of Christ, possesses in this flesh the pledge of that union through which he is able to be joined to Christ's body; who desires only one thing . . . that is, that 'God may be all in all' to him."[53] That this anticipatory union in the flesh is meant literally becomes clear as Cassian continues his discussion on the mechanics of demonic possession, material union between demons, and the question of whether a demon can physically unite with a human soul.[54] The answer to this last question is quite striking: "Nor even if a spirit is mingled with this dense and solid matter (that is, with flesh), which can very easily be done, is it therefore to be believed that it can be so united to a soul. . . . This is possible to the Trinity alone, which so penetrates every intellectual nature that it is able not only to embrace and encompass it but even to flow into it and, being itself incorporeal, to be poured into a body."[55] Where the *Institutes* describe the joining of monks into a visible ascetic system, in the *Conferences* Cassian describes the invisible, but still bodily, union of human and divine in the same ascetic system.

Cassian uses 1 Corinthians 15:28 again in *Conference* 10, to make a similar point, but expands upon it by using passages from John 17, a scriptural combination also found in Origen's speculation on the final reunification.[56] Reunification is here said, as it is in *Conference* 19, to be "the goal of the solitary" and the reason why monks "should . . . draw apart from all the turbulence and confusion of the crowd."[57] Yet withdrawal is not for the cultivation of the individual but for the monk's more perfect participation in the unifying system: "For then will be brought to fruition in us that prayer of our Savior . . . : 'That all may be one, as you Father in me and I in you, that they also may be one in us.' . . . In him we shall attain, I say, to that end of which we spoke before, which the Lord longed to be fulfilled in us when he prayed: 'That all may be one as we are one, I in them and you in me, that they themselves may also be made perfect in unity.'"[58] It is telling that Cassian places the scriptural reunification of all the disciples in his discussion of solitary prayer: like the materially unified prayer of *Institutes* 2 and 3, prayer in *Conference* 10 is the participation of the human in a more-than-human system. Where the contributors to this system are treated as visible in the *Institutes*, however, the multiple contributors to the system are invisible in *Conference* 10. The system itself is the same distributed ascetic process described in both texts, aiming toward the creation of a single transcendent figure.[59] Cassian's asceticism does not require the material cenobium to satisfy its distributional nature, since ascetic practice occurs within a crowded cosmos in which the boundaries of the person are always capable of expansion and dissolution.

The common life of Cassian's asceticism, then, is only in some cases the life of the literal cenobium. In all cases, the common life is the life of the eschatological Christ, in whom all ascetics have their end. Union with one's fellows is union with Christ, because the production of Christ as the perfect man is the task that ascetics ultimately share. Cassian's distribution of ascetic practice across multiple figures, human and nonhuman, thus represents a significant turn in several areas: in the history of asceticism, which would soon become in the West a history of monasticism; in the afterlife of Origenism; and perhaps most fundamentally, in the history of human individuation. Cassian's project in the *Institutes* challenges modern historians to understand late ancient definitions of human personhood as intersecting with, but not bound by, the limits of individual bodies and souls. The role of both material objects and collective action in carrying out Cassian's ascetic contemplation suggests much more complex structures of individuation than the historiographic model of the individual holy person easily allows. The model of the distributed cognitive system may be anachronistic, but it may also, more importantly, draw out the nuances of late ancient personhood beyond the fashioning of the self and into the complex dynamics of convergence and divergence, unity and multiplicity, in any one thinking thing.

NOTES

The title of this essay is a play on Philip Rousseau's "Cassian, Contemplation and the Coenobitic Life." I am deeply indebted to Philip for years of kind support and encouragement, beginning in my graduate student coursework and continuing into the present. My debt to his work on Cassian will be obvious in this essay.

1. As readers of this volume are well aware, Peter Brown's classic study "The Rise and Function of the Holy Man in Late Antiquity" set the tone for late twentieth-century scholarship on Christian asceticism, with its focus on the single holy figure and his relationship to the surrounding community; for retrospective assessments of Brown's impact, see the essays collected in the special issue of the *Journal of Early Christian Studies* 6, no. 3 (1998), marking the twenty-fifth anniversary of its publication; see also the essays in Howard-Johnston and Hayward, *Cult of Saints.* Brown's later *Body and Society*, incorporating insights from Foucault's *History of Sexuality*, retained a focus on ascetic practice as experienced and undertaken on an individual basis and in pursuit of an individual "self." Departing to some extent from this model, work on early Christian asceticism in the 1990s and 2000s has tended to focus on the literary representation of ascetic and holy figures, often using literary-theoretical approaches introduced to the field of early Christian studies by Elizabeth A. Clark: for such approaches, see especially E. Clark, "Ideology, History," and more recently "History, Theory, and Premodern Texts," ch. 8 of her *History, Theory, Text*. For a discussion and critique of Foucault's unfinished work on Cassian, see E. Clark, "Foucault, the Fathers."

2. See, e.g., Burrus, *"Begotten, Not Made,"* for a rich rethinking of the intersection between conceptions of divine personhood and human persons.

3. He seems to favor it, e.g., at *Conl.* 1 praef. 4. For the Latin text of the *Conferences*, I use the edition of E. Pichery; for the *Institutes*, I use that of Jean-Claude Guy. The English text quoted in this essay is that of Boniface Ramsay.

4. *Conl.* 19.3–6; for two relatively traditional accounts considering Cassian himself as an individual ascetic and as the advisor of individual ascetics, see the biographies of Jean-Claude Guy, *Jean Cassien,* and Chadwick, *John Cassian*; this tradition is also in evidence in Stewart, *Cassian the Monk*. For surveys of the complex relationship between the anchoritic and cenobitic life in Cassian, see Leroy, "Cénobitisme"; Rousseau, "Cassian, Contemplation" and *Ascetics, Authority*, 177–82; and also Markus, *End of Ancient Christianity*, ch. 12. On Cassian's audience as extending well beyond participants in the cenobitic life, see Leyser, *Authority and Asceticism*, 33–61.

5. Rousseau, *Ascetics, Authority,* 181–82, quoting *Conl.* 24.26.

6. Classically formulated by Ludwig von Bertalanffy, "Outline of General System Theory," and revisited in Bertalanffy's "History and Status."

7. Two useful overviews of the notion of distributed cognition are Giere and Moffatt, "Distributed Cognition," and A. Clark and Chalmers, "Extended Mind."

8. Giere notes the work's "canonical" status in "Role of Agency." Hayles concludes her study *How We Became Posthuman*, 288–91, with a concise summary of Hutchins's work and some of its implications; one quite useful application of Hutchins's study to an early modern cooperative venture is Tribble, "Distributing Cognition." For an account of premodern distribution of cognition

in navigation (the use of the compass rose), see Frake, "Cognitive Maps of Time," which Hutchins discusses at 99–102.

9. Hutchins, *Cognition in the Wild*, 362.

10. Ibid., 316.

11. Hutchins, *Cognition in the Wild*, 141, notes the somatic effect of navigational information on an experienced navigator: "When a knowledgeable navigator hears or sees this bearing, he may know which direction he is currently facing and may actually feel the direction indicated by the bearing as a physical sensation. For example, a navigator facing west may hear '059' and experience a sense of the direction to the right of directly behind." The physical sensation of directions is called by one navigator "thinking like a compass." This intimate connection between physical sensation, shared nautical information, and inanimate tools conveys the unity of the cognitive system as well as its specific embodiment as a system.

12. Perkins, "Person-Plus," 107. See also A. Clark, *Being There*, epilogue, on the person as "an agent whose nature is fixed by a complex interplay involving a mass of internal goings on . . . a particular kind of physical embodiment, and a certain embedding in the world."

13. The origins and location of agency in distributed systems are, however, debated: see Giere, "Role of Agency"; and Salomon, "No Distribution."

14. See especially Goehring, "Encroaching Desert."

15. Hedstrom, "Your Cell," especially ch. 3, "Relocating to Monastic Space"; Schroeder, *Monastic Bodies*, ch. 3, "The Church Building as Symbol of Ascetic Renunciation"; see also Aravecchia, "Hermitages and Spatial Analysis." For a theoretical overview of many of the issues involved, see Gieryn, "What Buildings Do."

16. Praef. 2: "uerum ac rationabile Deo templum non lapidibus insensibilibus, sed sanctorum uirum congregatione . . . aedificare disponens, uasa etiam pretiosissima Domino cupiens consecrare . . . conflata . . . animabus sanctis."

17. Praef. 4: "praesertim cum harum rerum ratio nequaquam possit otiose meditatione doctrinaque uerborum uel tradi uel intellegi uel memoria contineri."

18. Perkins, "Person-Plus," 90, calls the nonhuman parts of the environment that participate in cognition the "surround" and argues that thinking "lingers not just in the mind of the learner, but in the arrangement of the surround as well." Steven D. Driver offers an excellent analysis of the way in which Cassian structures both the *Conferences* and the *Institutes* to facilitate a transformation in the reader, so that the reader's praxis will in fact allow the content of the texts progressively to be grasped: Driver, *John Cassian*, ch. 4.

19. *Inst.* 1.1: "Quorum interiorem cultum consequenter tunc poterimus exponere, cum exteriorem ornatum sub oculorum depinxerimus obtutibus."

20. *Conl.* praef. 1: "De quibus tamen si qui uoluerat ueram proferre sententiam et utrum impleri queant desiderat experiri, festinet prius eorum proposi-

tum simili studio et conuersatione suscipere, et tunc demum ea, quae supra facultatem hominis uidebantur, non solum possibilia, uerum etiam suauissima deprehendet."

21. *Inst.* 1.1.1: "De institutis ac regulis monasteriorum dicturi unde competentius . . . quam ex ipso habitu monachorum sumemus exordium?"

22. The predecessors whom Cassian names in his preface, Basil and Jerome, with Jerome representing the Latin Pachomian literature as well, do not have anything like the treatment of clothing that Cassian advocates. Richard J. Goodrich offers a strong general account of how Cassian differentiates himself from other ascetic writers whose works were circulating in Gaul: *Contextualizing Cassian,* ch. 3, "Experientia vs. Other Builders."

23. The classic treatment of Cassian's dependence on Evagrius is Salvatore Marsili, *Giovanni Cassiano ed Evagrio Pontico;* for the *Institutes* specifically, see also Vogüé, "Sources des quatre premiers livres."

24. *Inst.* 1.11.1: "circa spiritalem profectum ac diuinarum rerum scientiam cordis puritate."

25. *Ep. ad Anat.* 1.

26. *Inst.* 1.2.1: "sic ab huius mundi separentur ornatu, ut cultui seruorum Dei in omnibus communia perseuerent."

27. Ibid. 1.2.3–4: "Generali namque omnium constitutioni paucorum non debet praeponi ne praeiudicare sententia. Illis enim debemus institutis ac regulis indubitatam fidem et indiscussam oboedientiam per omnia commodare . . . quas uetustas tantorum temporum et innumerositas sanctorum partum concordi definitione in posterum propagauit."

28. For other such discussions, see Krawiec, "Garments of Salvation."

29. *Inst.* 2.10.1: "Cum igitur praedictas sollemnitates . . . celebraturi conueniunt, tantum praebetur a cunctis silentium, ut, cum in unum tam numerosa fratrum multitudo conueniat, praeter illum, qui consurgens psalmum decantat in medio, nullus hominum penitus adesse credatur."

30. Ibid. 2.7.3: "Cum autem is, qui orationem collecturus est, e terra surrexerit, omnes pariter eriguntur, ita ut nullus nec antequam inclinetur ille genu flectere nec cum e terra surrexerit remorari praesumat, ne non tam secutus fuisse illius conclusionem, qui precem colligit, quam suam celebrasse credatur."

31. For the Pachomian rules, see *Precepts* 6 and 8, trans. Veilleux, *Pachomian Koinonia,* 2:146.

32. *Inst.* 4.5: "corpori fraternitatis." *Inst.* 4.9: "confestim ut exortae fuerint eas suo patefacere seniori, nec super earum iudicio quicquam suae discretioni committere, sed illud credere malum esse uel bonum, quod discusserit ac pronuntiauerit senioris examen."

33. *Inst.* 4.9: "Non sua sed senioris discretione muniri, et suggestiones suas uel ignita iacula, quaecumque in cor eius iniecerit, ut seniorem celet non posse suaderi."

34. See Stewart, "Radical Honesty"; Gould, *Desert Fathers*, ch. 2, "The Abba and His Disciple"; Guy, "Educational Innovation." I hesitate to put Cassian's technique into the general category of "spiritual direction," however, since that category emphasizes the act of the *abba*, whereas Cassian here emphasizes the disclosure on the part of the younger monk.

35. *Conl.* 2.10.3: "Illico namque ut patefacta fuerit cogitatio maligna marcescit, et antequam discretionis iudicium proferatur . . ."

36. The themes of contemplation and purity of heart in Cassian's discussion of virtue, and their relation to both Evagrian *apatheia* and Stoic psychology, are analyzed in Marsili, *Giovanni Cassiano ed Evagrio Pontico*; Stewart, *Cassian the Monk*, ch. 3; Driver, *John Cassian*, ch. 6; Sheridan, "Controversy over *Apatheia*"; Rousseau, "Cassian, Contemplation"; Chadwick, *John Cassian*, ch. 3.

37. *Inst.* 5.4.2: "Et idcirco monachum spiritalia mella condere cupientem uelut apem prudentissimam debere unamquamque uirtutem ab his qui eam familiarius possident deflorare. . . . Cunctas namque si ab uno uolumus mutuari, aut difficile aut certe numquam idonea ad imitandum nobis exempla poterunt repperi."

38. *Conl.* 14.6: "Inpossibile namque est unum eundemque hominem simul uniuersis quas superius conprehendi fulgere uirtutibus. Quas si quis uoluerit pariter affectare, in id incidere eum necesse est, ut dum omnes sequitur nullam integre consequatur magisque ex hac inmutatione ac uarietate dispendium capiat quam profectum." Cf. also *Conl.* 19.9.1.

39. *Inst.* 5.4.2: "quia, licet necdum Christum omnia factum . . . uideamus in omnibus, tamen hoc modo possumus eum, id est per partes in omnibus inuenire."

40. Used, e.g., in *De Princ.* 1.6.4, 1.7.5, 2.3.5, 3.5.6, 3.6.1–3, 3.6.6–9.

41. See E. Clark, *Origenist Controversy*, 249–50; more broadly, her "New Perspectives."

42. *Inst.* 5.4.3: "Dum ergo in alio sapientia, in alio iustitia, in alio sanctitas, in alio mansuetudo, in alio castitas, in alio humilitas repperitur, membratim Christus per unumquemque nunc sanctorum diuisus est. Concurrentibus uero uniuersis in unitatem fidei ac uirtutis redditur in uirum perfectum, plenitudem sui corporis in singulorum membrorum conpage ac proprietate perficiens."

43. Hutchins, *Cognition in the Wild*, chs. 6 and 7, discusses the individual training and learning that can go on in a distributed system but locates this learning within the performance of the overall task.

44. Chadwick, *John Cassian*, 43–45, argues that this section, 5.4, although it is likely by Cassian, is an interpolation from other Cassianic material, since the previous section, 5.3, introduces the topic of gluttony, and the subsequent section, 5.5, recommences with gluttony. While I agree that 5.4 may not belong between 5.3 and 5.5, it nonetheless seems closely connected to 5.1–2, on the number and necessary disclosure of the vices. If a scribal change has occurred here, it may simply be a transposition of 5.3 and 5.4.

45. See note 5, above.

46. *Inst.* 5.4.3: "Donec ergo ueniat illud tempus quo sit Deus omnia in omnibus, in praesenti potest hoc quo diximus modo, id est per partes uirtutum esse in omnibus Deus, licet nondum plenitudine earum omnia sit in omnibus . . ."

47. Ibid. 5.1: "ut . . . naturas eorum tam minutes, tam occultas tamque obscuras inuestigare condigne . . ."

48. On the practical interactions between anchorites and the outside world, see Goehring, "World Engaged"; see also Gould, *Desert Fathers*, ch. 3, "The Monk and His Neighbour," for the ideology of personal interaction in the desert.

49. *Conl.* 8.12: "Tanta uero spirituum densitate constipatur aër iste qui inter caelum terramque diffunditur . . . ut satis utiliter humanis aspectibus eos prouidentia diuina subtraxerit." Cf. 8.15 on the corresponding angels. On demons and spirit presences in monastic thought, see Brakke, *Demons,* and G. Smith, "How Thin Is a Demon?"; on angels in ascetic literature, see Muehlberger, "Ambivalence."

50. *Conl.* 8.17.

51. *Conl.* 18.6: "De hoc perfectorum numero et ut ita dixerim fecundissima radice sanctorum etiam anchoretarum post haec flores fructusque prolati sunt."

52. *Conl.* 19.8: "exutam mentem a cunctis habere terrenis eamque, quantum humana inbecillitas ualet, sic unire cum Christo."

53. *Conl.* 7.6: "Ad cuius tamen mensurae plenitudinem nemo perueniet alias in futurum, nisi qui . . . inbutus ea fuerit in praesenti eamque adhuc in hoc saeculo positus praelibarit, Christique membrum pretiosissimum designatus arram conpaginis illius, per quam corpori eius ualeat copulari, in hac carne possederit, unum dumtaxat desiderans . . . id est sit ei deus omnia in omnibus."

54. *Conl.* 7.9–15.

55. *Conl.* 7.13: "Nec enim si crassae huic solidaeque materiae, id est carni, spiritus admiscetur, quod fieri facillime potest, idcirco et animae quae itidem spiritus est ita uniri posse creditur. . . . Quod soli est possibile trinitati, quae sic uniuersae intellectualis naturae efficitur penetratrix, ut non solum circumplecti eam atque ambire, sed etiam inlabi ei et uelut incorporea corpori possit infundi."

56. *De Princ.* 1.6.2–4, 2.3.5, 3.6.1, 3.6.4–6.

57. *Conl.* 10.7: "Haec igitur destinatio solitarii." *Conl.* 10.6: "ab omni inquietudine et confusione turbarum . . . secedamus."

58. *Conl.* 10.7: "Tunc etiam perfecte comsummabitur in nobis illa nostri saluatoris oratio . . . ut omnes unum sint, sicut tu pater in me et ego in te, ut et ipsi in nobis unum sint. . . . In illum, inquam, peruenientes quem praediximus finem, quem idem dominus orans in nobis optat inpleri: ut omnes sint unum sicut nos unum sumus, ego in eis et tu in me, ut sint et ipsi consummati in unum."

59. It is worth noting that *Conl.* 13 also seems to depict ascetic agency as distributed across a system of multiple persons and actions: "Thus it is that the

God of the universe must be believed to work all things in all, so that he stirs up, protects, and strengthens, but not so that he removes the freedom of will that he himself once granted." The difference at the heart of the "semi-Pelagian controversy" may be the question of whether agency can or cannot be distributed across more than one person, whether that person is human or divine. For discussion of Cassian's role in the controversy, see especially Weaver, *Divine Grace*, ch. 3; and Casiday, *Tradition and Theology*, chs. 1 and 2.

Chapter Eight

Gender, Eros, and Pedagogy

Macrina's Pious Household

VIRGINIA BURRUS

"I want to defend here the contention that Gregory of Nyssa's *Life of Macrina* describes more a 'pious household' than anything 'institutional,'" asserts Philip Rousseau in the opening salvo of a 2005 essay.[1] A decade earlier, he writes of the special role and status of educated women like Macrina, raising the question of "the 'learned' woman's relationship with what we might loosely call 'the servant class'" and going on to suggest an increase in "the perceived usefulness or purpose of instructed insight among women, not least by the women themselves."[2] Building on these arguments, I would like to reflect further on the implications of the emergence of a distinctly female culture of learning and teaching within the late ancient Christian household. In particular, I would like to consider the relational and affective dynamics thereby engaged, as these leave their traces on the ascetic literary imagination.

Susanna Elm argues that "fourth-century women ascetics adopted organizational patterns and forged institutions via a complex process involving both the transformation of the given model of the family and a reaction against that very model." She adds: "Women did so in concert with men."[3] Rousseau would have us resist the temptation to see every instance of household asceticism as a nascent form of monastic institution forging, and rightly so; yet the process of imaginative transformation (even, possibly, of "reactive" transformation) still demands attention, as does the way in which men as well as women are implicated in the changes taking place within a household like Macrina's. Gregory's innovative hagiography shows us how one man uses his sister to think about his own transformed familial identity, even as he also gives voice to hers. By reconstructing the traditional patriarchal household as an eroticized pedagogical community of women, the *Life of Macrina* simultaneously creates space for Gregory to reimagine the erotics of male receptivity, via performed reversals of gender. Allowing Macrina to take the lead as teacher, parent, and lover, Gregory turns the traditionally feminine necessity to submit into a desirable masculine virtue. In so doing, he decisively queers the family values conveyed by the ascetic household.

PAIDEUSIS, EROS, OIKOS

This reading of the *Life of Macrina* will be lightly situated within the intertwined histories — or perhaps better, metahistories — of education, sexuality, and the family. Here I can, of course, offer no more than a rough sketch of some of the more prominent features of those histories, as commonly construed.[4] We may begin by recalling that ancient Greeks notoriously considered the *oikos* not only inferior to, but also potentially in tension with, the *polis*; if the former provided the basic necessities of life, the latter existed so that at least some men might live *well* (Aristotle, *Pol.* 1.2). The educational formation of a noble citizenry was not, then, primarily a familial or household function but took place within the realm of warfare, politics, and/or philosophy, where mastery of others and self — in short, the fulfillment of manhood — was the goal. Pederasty, the erotic relationship of an older man (*erastēs*) with a youth (*eromenos*), seems to have been central to the process of male socialization in many parts of Greece and indeed became a commonly noted feature of Greek culture. As Henri Marrou observes (with some skittishness) in his classic *History of Education in Antiquity*, "This type of love was essentially educative." He elaborates: "The establishment of a closed masculine community from which women were excluded had an educational significance, and in a certain sense derived from an educational impulse"—namely, the need to reproduce manhood.[5] Yet however pervasive and pedagogically effective "Greek love" was, pederasty could also be a source of anxiety, as Michel Foucault has argued more recently, with specific reference to classical Athens. Was the submission of the boy to his older lover seemly, or did it, on the contrary, compromise the very manhood that it also promised to instill? "The role of the boy was the focus of a good deal of uncertainty, combined with an intense interest."[6]

Plato's writings, however idiosyncratic, are among the best-known reflections of a widespread (and, needless to say, androcentric) Greek tendency to exalt the love of boys over the desire for wives, the pursuit of philosophy or politics over the care of the household. They also reflect a degree of problematization of traditional pederastic practices, insofar as these practices presume a fixed hierarchy and a strict corresponding distinction between active and passive roles. David Halperin argues that Plato borrows from conceptions of feminine desire in order to promote an understanding of male homoerotic desire that is reciprocal, rather than unidirectional, and (pro)creative, rather than dominating or acquisitive. This is especially evident in the *Symposium*, where Socrates' teacher in the art of eroticism is represented as a woman, namely, the prophetess Diotima (*Symposium* 201d).[7] According to the Platonic model, the overflowing desire of the lover evokes a responsive or "countering" desire (*anterōs*) in the beloved, and the result of this mutual (though nonsymmetrical) erotic excitement is not physical pleasure or social conquest but rather the "birth" of philosophic insight—begotten by the lover yet also conceived within the soul of the beloved. Thus, in "Platonic love," the educational aspect of pederasty is intensified even as the sexual aspect is, to a degree, sublimated. As Foucault puts it, Plato structures "the love relation as a relation to truth," and he does so in part by "reversing the role of the loved young man, making him a lover of the master of truth."[8]

Roman tradition was biased against a pederasty deemed suspiciously "Greek," but this bias was due less to differences in erotic sensibilities keyed to gender or age — the homoerotic cult of youth being shared by Romans and Greeks — than to an even greater discomfort with regard to free youths, as opposed to slaves, taking on "passive" sexual roles.[9] At the same time, the rise of the Hellenistic and Roman empires was also accompanied by a broader shift in elite attitudes toward marriage. As Foucault has argued, in this later period marriage came to be defined less exclusively in relation to the social and economic functioning of the household. It "appeared more and more as a voluntary union between two partners whose inequality diminished to a certain extent but did not cease to exist."[10] Corresponding to the increased attention to marriage as a source of more or less egalitarian companionship as well as a central site of moral self-fashioning was "the fact that the love relation between men ceased to be the focus of an intense theoretical and moral discussion."[11] Thus the tension between the marital sexuality of the household and the erotics of masculine friendship was reduced, as the marital relationship came to be imbued with some of the values of friendship, learning, and eros formerly associated more exclusively with relationships between men. This shift coincided with the rise of Rome as an empire and the consequent constriction of the scope of political power available to the men of the Mediterranean cities. As Paul Veyne frames it: "In the first century B.C. a man was supposed to think of himself as a citizen who had fulfilled all his civic duties. A century later he was supposed to consider himself a good husband; as such he was officially required to respect his wife."[12]

A case could be made, however, that the tension between the household and marital sexuality, on the one hand, and a sublimated, nonmarital erotics, on the other, reasserted itself elsewhere in the Roman imperial period. Ascetic tendencies emerging as early as the first century culminated in later antiquity with the flourishing of Christian monasteries, rabbinic study houses, and philosophical schools. Existing alongside the marital institutions also sustained by Christian, Jewish, and pagan cultures, the space of the monastery, study house, or school was distinguished not only by its privileging of male homosociality — erotically charged to varying degrees — but also, paradoxically, by a certain permeability of the very boundary established by the masculine gendering of this space.[13] Ascesis, textual study, and philosophical contemplation were all practices of self-formation to which some women had access. Women who engaged in such practices might thereby be rendered virtually masculine, a transformation in status that opened up possibilities for friendships with men as well as with other women — erotically charged to varying degrees.

The egalitarian model of male-female friendship was at odds with the traditional gendered and class-inflected hierarchy of household relations, while at the same time it colluded with contemporaneous trends toward infusing marriage with intellectual friendship and eros. There was, then, a fundamental ambiguity with regard to the positioning of learned women as either proper to the household or disruptive of its boundaries. Transgressions of gender roles might be least evident in the rabbinic context, yet even the Babylonian Talmud had its Beruria, whose scholarship put the men to shame: she "studied three hundred laws from three hundred teachers in [one] day" (Pesachim 62b); not only crossing from household to the study house, she also crossed in the other direction, turning her household into a study house when she used her exegetical skill to challenge her husband's behavior (Berachot 10a).[14] Less legendary figures may be more telling: papyri and non-Jewish sources give scattered testimony to the fact that some Jewish women were not only literate but even possessed of sophisticated educations, as Tal Ilan has shown.[15] Among pagans, Rousseau mentions the case of Plotinus's follower Gemina, in whose house the philosopher dwelt (Porphyry, *Life of Plotinus* 9); the intellectual partnership of Porphyry and his wife Marcella (Porphyry, *Letter to Marcella*); and the famous female philosophers Sosipatra (Eunapius, *Lives of the Sophists* 6.6–10) and Hypatia (Socrates, *Church History* 7.15), the first of whom outshone her husband and the second of whom was not embarrassed to keep the company of men.[16] Among Christians, we will turn shortly to the example of Macrina, though others could obviously be named: Rousseau's own list of learned Christian ladies, mostly unmarried or widowed, also includes the *cento*-writer Proba, Ambrose's sister Marcellina, Augustine's mother Monica, John Chrysostom's friend Olympias, and Jerome's friends Paula and Marcella, among others.[17]

Focus on the potential transgressiveness of women's crossings from the household to the realm of extrafamilial friendship and study or, correspondingly, on the exclusively masculine context of young men's education should not obscure the fact that the household itself always encompassed educational roles, relationships, and processes, or that the passage from household to school was somewhat fraught even for boys. In elite families, an infant of either sex would typically be assigned to a wet-nurse (*tithēnē / tropheus* or *nutrix*), usually a female slave. Either she or another nanny would often extend her care into the nursling's childhood, if not beyond; the nurse, along with the parents, would thus be among the child's earliest teachers.[18] In the case of a boy, a male slave referred to as a pedagogue (*paidagogos* or *paedagogus / educator*) would also offer oversight and moral tutelage. As Keith Bradley puts it: "The pedagogue's job was to instill in the child social graces and to provide rudimentary academic knowledge, but in addition, and more importantly, to guide the child through the early years in the capacity of moral custodian."[19] Following etymology, the pedagogue was the one who *led the boy*, not only mediating his transition away from the female portion of the household but also accompanying him as he was delivered to the public instruction of grammarians, rhetoricians, and philosophers. Guiding the boy in his movement beyond the household, the pedagogue also extended a form of familial care into the public sphere. In the Roman context, the eroticism that was acknowledged to underlie the homosociality of masculine education aroused notable anxiety, and the pedagogue was expected to protect the young boy's moral purity in that treacherous realm of social formation.[20] At once the boy's alien slave and his intimate familial protector and guide on the journey to adulthood, the pedagogue evoked deep affection and sometimes also considerable hostility, particularly in response to his disciplinary interventions.[21] The social and emotional complications and contradictions attending this relationship were enhanced in the ambiguous space between household and the public sphere onto which the relationship was mapped — a space that must often have been charged with excitement, anxiety, and erotic tension.

Although some girls were provided with male pedagogues, this seems to have been rare; references to female pedagogues are even rarer.[22] There was typically no sharp demarcation between the nurturance of the early caregiver, whether mother or nurse, and the processes of socialization by which a young girl became a woman; indeed, a nurse was not unlikely to continue to care for a girl into her adolescence.[23] Was there then less tension, and thus less sharpness of erotic charge, accompanying the formation of girls within the elite household, or attending the relations of teaching and learning between women? Was the learned woman of late antiquity, however transgressive of her gender role in certain respects, always haunted by her own inevitable domestication? Where, if anywhere, might we detect lingering echoes of Sappho's classroom, in which, as Marrou puts it, "education, like the men's, was lit up by a blaze of passion that united mistress and disciple in bonds forged by its heat"?[24] Such expansive questions will here be addressed in a circumscribed way, through the reading of a single fourth-century text.

EDUCATING VIRGINS

In relating his sister's life, Gregory is "conscious of having produced the history of a family," notes Rousseau.[25] In this history, Macrina's mother (who is never called by name in the text) provides a kind of narrative matrix. The mother is also, of course, Gregory's, but this is an awareness gently suppressed by the text: Gregory's relation to the maternal is almost entirely mediated by his older sister. At any rate, the story of a mother appropriately begins with the birth of her first child. As Gregory describes it, this is no common birth. Shortly before the delivery, the mother falls into a deep sleep, during which she dreams that she is holding "in her arm [*dia cheiros*] the one who is still encompassed within her [*to eti hypo tōn splagchnōn periechomenon*]," while a larger-than-life heavenly being addresses the infant three times by the name of the virginal Thecla. Thus is revealed the secret identity and destiny of one who will be known publicly by her paternal grandmother's name, Macrina (*Life of Macrina* 2).[26] Although the infant Macrina is subsequently given her own nurse (*tithēnē*), it is her mother who most often nurses the young child "with her own hands" (*en tais chersi tais idiais*), according to Gregory (3). And also with her own breasts? We might consider this possibility, remembering the advice of the physician Soranus: "Other things being equal, it is better to feed the child with maternal milk, for this is more suited to it, and the mothers become more sympathetic towards the offspring, and it is more natural to be fed from the mother after parturition just as before parturition" (*Gynaecology* 2.18). Yet in this particular text, hands or arms (*cheires*) are perhaps even more evocative of maternal nurturance than breasts. We recall the mother's dream of holding "in her arm" her yet-unborn baby.

As Macrina grows, her mother tends her mind as well as her body: she "was eager that the girl be educated [*paideusai*]." However, the mother eschews the usual "external" (i.e., non-Christian) curriculum for youngsters — namely, the myths of the epic poets and playwrights — on the grounds that such literature is full of shameful tales, most especially shameful tales of women. Instead, the textbook employed by Macrina's mother is scripture alone: the Psalter is Macrina's faithful and ever-present companion (3). No "outsiders," whether teachers, siblings, friends, or strange books, are seen to intrude on this mother-daughter dyad. The piety of the family is defined by the exclusiveness of both its curriculum and its relational bonds — standards set by its women.

When the girl matures into an adolescent beauty, her father finds her a husband. Happily, the death of her fiancé thwarts this well-intended but wrongheaded paternal plot (4). Henceforth, Macrina firmly resolves "never to be separated from her mother, not even for a moment of time." Indeed, it is as if the mother's delivery-bed vision had now been reversed, so that the child who is already born appears to be still within the womb: "Often her mother used to say that she was pregnant with the rest of her children for the usual time, but this one she carried in herself constantly, always, so to speak, encompassing her within herself [*tois splagchnois heautēs periechousa*]," reports Gregory. Moreover, just as Macrina's mother has slaved as nurse to her daughter, so Macrina now slaves as attendant (*therapaina*) to her mother. "The benefits were mutual," Gregory assures us. "For the one looked after the girl's soul, and the other looked after the mother's body." The daughter even makes bread for her mother "with her own hands" (*tais idiais chersi*), much as her mother once nursed her by taking her "in her own hands" (*en tais chersi tais idiais*). The blurring of class roles effected by the women's performance of servants' tasks thus intensifies the intimacy of this female household. Her father having died (a fact that Gregory mentions in passing), Macrina comes to serve as virtual husband to her mother, in all things sharing "her mother's toils, dividing her cares with her, and lightening her heavy load of sorrows," even as the two train each other in what Gregory refers to as the life of "philosophy" (5).[27]

Made of sterner stuff than the older woman, Macrina is the one who directs the transformation of their household, urging her mother to give up her luxurious lifestyle so as to relate to the servants as "sisters and equals" rather than "slaves and subordinates" (7), guiding and "preparing her to become equal in honor to the full community [*plērōma*] of virgins" (11). If her mother is no longer occupied with "the care of child-rearing and education and the establishment of her offspring" (11), it is partly because Macrina herself has taken on those duties. Her mother's youngest child, Peter, is born just as his father dies. "Tearing him almost immediately from the breast of the one nursing him, she [Macrina] raised him herself and led him to all higher learning. . . . She became all things to the youth — father, teacher [*didaskalos*], pedagogue, mother, counselor of every good." Thus nurtured, Peter becomes his sister's and mother's collaborator in the pursuit of the angelic life: he is particularly good with his hands — skilled at every kind of craft *dia cheiros* (12). When the time comes for their mother to depart from life, she does so embraced by the arms of Macrina and Peter —*en tais amphoterōn tōn teknōn chersi* (13).

Such is the "pious household" depicted in Gregory's initial account of Macrina's life, which covers the first fourteen out of thirty-nine chapters of the hagiography. Within its confines, Macrina is at once the child who never left her mother's womb and all the husband her mother could want, her mother her own nursemaid, and she both her mother's maidservant and her brother's father. Conjunctions, displacements, and reversals of parent-child, husband-wife, and master-slave relations thus accumulate, intensifying and complicating the intimacy that envelopes a family now reconfigured as a feminine community of pedagogical formation — a pleroma of virgins (drawn from "what we might loosely call 'the servant class,'" as Rousseau puts it), their female teacher, and a fraternal handyman.

Having thus set the scene, it remains for Gregory to recount his final meeting with Macrina in this household of maidens and to tell of her death and funeral — Peter being conveniently absent, having taken the wrong road in setting out to meet his brother. As the author for the first time intrudes directly into the narrative of his sister's life, the narrative, paradoxically, becomes for the first time hers. Gregory now depicts Macrina as recounting the story of her own life as if she were recording everything "in a written account" (20; *epi suggraphēs*), much as he has formerly described his own composition as a letter extended "into a lengthy written account" (1; *eis suggraphikēn makrēgorian*).[28] And as soon as Macrina takes control of the pen, so to speak, she writes the long absent Gregory back into the household of women.

She has already begun to do so, one might say, before he even arrives on the scene. Still a day's journey away from the family estate, Gregory is visited by a vision in his sleep. "I seemed to hold [*pherein*] martyrs' relics in my hand [*dia cheiros*], and there came from them a light such as that from a bright mirror placed facing the sun, so that my eyes were dazzled by the radiance of the beam" (15). The vision appears three times, and Gregory confesses that he has difficulty interpreting it when he first receives it. The knowing reader has no such difficulty. Pregnant not with Macrina's virginal flesh (thrice hailed as "Thecla" in the mother's dreamed vision) but with her resplendent corpse (thrice apparent as holy relics in the brother's), Gregory, like his mother before him, already holds in his hand what has not yet come to be.[29] His sister's history conscripts him unwittingly, even unwillingly: Macrina's mother bore her life, but he is to be the bearer of her death.

In the meantime, Macrina pauses long enough on the threshold of eternity to welcome her brother home. Like the Socrates of Plato's *Phaedo*, she delivers inspired discourses on her deathbed concerning the mysteries of the mortal body and immortal soul (18).[30] When she sends Gregory off to rest, he overcomes his own reluctance to leave her by embracing the disciple's pleasure of "being seen to obey the teacher [*hē didaskalos*] in all things" (19). Meeting again later in the same day, the siblings engage in more familiar talk; indeed, it is talk of the family. Night passes in prayer, and the day that will be Macrina's last dawns. His sister now appears to Gregory like an angel. If she is no longer of this world, it is because she is already racing toward another one, where her divine lover awaits her (22). Like an athlete, she strains to reach the finishing line and attain the victory crown — like an athlete, but no longer the "invincible" one who refuses to "give way before the assault of misfortune," as she is earlier represented (14). Now dispassionate endurance cedes to the impatient passion of an actively desiring bride: "As she approached the end, contemplating the beauty of the bridegroom," reports Gregory, "she rushed toward the desired one with more urgent haste" (23).[31]

As Macrina thus achieves the consummation of her desire in death, Gregory is undone both by the sight of his sister's eerily beautiful and virtually bridal corpse — upon whose face he rests his own grief-stiffened hand (*cheira*)— and by the sound of the weeping of her virgins. "Suddenly a sharp and unrestrained cry broke out, so that my mind no longer remained settled, but as if submerged in an overflowing stream, it was swept away by emotion and I, neglecting the tasks at hand, gave myself over wholly to lamentations." Here Gregory makes Macrina's virgins' voice his own. Justly, as it seems to him, they bewail the withdrawal of their teacher: "The lamp of our life has been extinguished; . . . the safety of our lives has been destroyed; the seal of our incorruptibility has been removed; the bond of our union has been demolished." Gregory adds that "the ones who called her mother and nurse were more seriously distraught than the rest" (25–26). Is Gregory not among them? It is, after all, he who has given us the portrait of a daughter inseparable from, very nearly fused in identity with, her mother and nurse — his mother too, we recall.

Cries of lamentation must finally be transformed into hymns of praise, Gregory insists. Even as he mourns with the virgins, he rejoices with his sister — indeed, he does so in explicit appropriation of his sister's stern eschewal of grief (27)— while marveling at her luminous transformation as a bride at once submissive to Christ her bridegroom and active in her own intense desire to be made one with him. Gregory himself must ready his sister for her wedding, in compliance with her demand: "She ordered that her body be prepared by your hands [*tais sais chersi*]," the deaconess Lampadion tells him (29). As he dresses the corpse in fine linen of his own, he is assisted by the beautiful and well-born Vetiana, who has chosen Macrina as the "guardian and pedagogue of her widowhood," making herself a frequent visitor in the household of virgins (28). Indeed, much as Macrina herself has cleaved to her mother after the death of her fiancé, so has Vetiana cleaved to Macrina since the death of her husband soon after their marriage, as she explains. Much as Macrina has cared for her mother's body, so has Vetiana cared for Macrina's. Now she pushes aside the saint's garment and guides Gregory's eye to a tattoo-like mark on Macrina's breast, which was left, she explains, as a divine sign of a miracle of healing performed through her mother's requested intervention. In this charged scene of transgressively intimate viewing,

Gregory is ushered into an inner sanctum of female flesh and divine power. Where a mother has made the sign of the cross with her own hand (*idia cheiri*), placing her hand (*tēn cheira*) on her daughter's breast, God has marked that breast with a transformative stigma (31). Macrina carries the stigma of Jesus on her body: "I too was crucified with you," she has proclaimed to her bridegroom with her dying breath (24). Mother and daughter are joined in the flesh, joined at the site of the stigma, joined through the bridegroom. Macrina and Vetiana are joined there too, united across death, for it is Vetiana who bears — and now lays bare — the secret of the mark, as Gregory gives witness.[32]

The funeral takes place on the next day, after a night of vigil. Gregory leads the slow processional to the family crypt in the Church of the Holy Martyrs, accompanied by crowds of local folk. Having just barely brought his grief under control, now he is overcome by fear at the prospect of viewing his parents' exposed and corrupted bodies — too much flesh for this son to handle. He resolves his dilemma by contriving that the bodies be covered by a linen cloth before they can be seen. Then he and the local bishop, "lifting the holy body from the bier, lay it to rest by the side of the mother, thus fulfilling the prayer shared by both." As he explains, both Macrina and her mother "for their whole life begged God with one voice that their bodies might be mingled with each other after death and that their communion in life should not be broken apart in death" (35). Does one not hear an echo of the Gospel? "What God has joined, let no human part" (Mark 10.9). Before Gregory leaves, he throws himself on the tomb and embraces the dust, as the mysterious union of women recedes from his grasp (36).

Has Macrina finally schooled Gregory in Christian family values? Hailed repeatedly as *hē didaskolos*, Gregory's grammatically androgynous sister is perhaps equally well dubbed *hē paidagogos*, as she skillfully leads him, along with the (other) virgins, toward the ultimate teacher, Christ. Having drawn the young men of her family away from the beguiling comforts and emotional entanglements of worldly pursuits to take part in the austere life of philosophy and prayer, she also reminds the now-mature priest that the endless path of virtue not only begins but also ever begins *again* at home. There the women live like angels. Calling Macrina "mother" and "nurse," "guardian" and "pedagogue," they reach out to her with longing arms. She pulls them close by slipping away, racing onward toward the endlessly elusive bridegroom, falling backward into the infinitely alluring maternal embrace. As the virgins are thus led by their queerly nurturant pedagogue toward union with the beloved (whoever he or she might be!), Gregory too is swept up in the passion of erotic transformation.

THE TEACHER'S GENDER

Like Diotima, Macrina teaches the art of loving.[33] Yet we recall that Plato's *Symposium* is staged as an erotically charged conversation from which women are explicitly excluded, and Diotima's discourse is received secondhand through Socrates. Gregory's hagiography, in contrast, depicts an erotically charged family of women into which he is allowed to enter, and Macrina's teaching comes less through her discourse than through the hands-on desire embodied in her pious household. Halperin has suggested that Diotima must be a woman "because Sokratic philosophy must borrow her femininity in order to seem to leave nothing out and thereby to ensure the success of its own procreative enterprises, the continual reproduction of its universalizing discourse in the male culture of classical Athens."[34] Macrina's case is both similar and different. Her femininity must itself be revised if it is to be borrowed by Christian ascetics like Gregory: *it must seem to leave nothing out.*

Macrina can indeed teach Gregory how to love Christ like a woman, receiving the divine bridegroom's passion so as to overflow with it in turn. She can do so because she has already discovered the "usefulness of instructed insight among women," to recall Rousseau's phrasing. In the *Life of Macrina*, instruction in love begins and ends with the *mother*; in the meantime, it swells in a pleroma of virginal desire that unites "mistress and disciple in bonds forged by its heat," as Marrou imagines Sappho's classroom. In the *Life of Macrina*, instruction in love begins and ends with desire for an *other;* this desire knows no beginning or end, no bottom or top, no holding or being held, no living or dying. No fear of dissolution. Such love may be more than Gregory can yet handle, which is why he needs a teacher — and why his teacher must be a woman.

NOTES

1. Rousseau, "Pious Household," 165.
2. Rousseau, "Learned Women," 145.
3. Elm, *Virgins of God,* viii.
4. This is an understatement. Nor will I pretend to provide thorough annotation, which would swiftly swamp these (im)modest paragraphs. The contribution of this paper lies with the reading of the *Life of Macrina*, while the initial invocation of longer, larger histories provides a framing to set off certain features of that reading.
5. Marrou, *History of Education*, 29–30.
6. Foucault, *Use of Pleasure*, 217.
7. Halperin, "Why Is Diotima a Woman?," 257–308.
8. Foucault, *Use of Pleasure*, 242.
9. C. Williams, *Roman Homosexuality,* 72–77.
10. Foucault, *Care of the Self*, 75.
11. Ibid., 190.
12. Veyne, "Roman Empire,"36.
13. With reference to the eroticism haunting the lives of ascetic Christian men, see, e.g., Burrus, *Sex Lives of Saints,* 19–52, 161, and Krueger, "Homoerotic Spectacle," 99–118. With reference to the rabbinic study house, see Boyarin, *Unheroic Conduct*, 127–50.
14. Boyarin, *Carnal Israel,* 167–96, comments on the Beruria legends, suggesting that there was more scope for "studying women" in Palestinian than in Babylonian contexts.
15. Ilan, "Learned Jewish Women," 175–90.
16. Rousseau, "Learned Women," 117–21.
17. Ibid., 121–47.
18. Bradley, *Discovering the Roman Family*, 23–29.
19. Ibid., 55.
20. Ibid., 53. See also C. Williams, *Roman Homosexuality*, 76, on Roman perceptions that "not only teachers but also their older classmates posed a potential threat to beautiful boys."
21. Bradley, *Discovering the Roman Family*, 53–55.
22. Ibid., 27, 48–49.
23. Ibid., 25–28.
24. Marrou, *History of Education*, 35.
25. Rousseau, "Pious Household," 171.
26. The Greek edition used is Gregory of Nyssa, *Vie de Sainte Macrine*, ed. Maraval, SC 178. English translations are my own. See also Gregory of Nyssa, *Ascetical Works*, trans. Callahan, 163–91.

27. Harvey, "Sacred Bonding," 27–56, discusses similar representations of intense mother-daughter bonds in Syriac hagiography.

28. On the language of inscription, see Krueger, "Writing and the Liturgy," 483–510.

29. Cf. P. Miller, *Dreams in Late Antiquity*, 237: "Thus Emmelia's dream was a mirror of the ascetic vocation of her daughter, herself a mirror of the great Thecla, just as Gregory's dream mirrored the beatific result of that vocation."

30. Allusion to the *Phaedo* is even more noticable in Gregory's other Macrinan work, the dialogue *On the Soul and the Resurrection*; see Apostolopoulos, *Phaedo Christianus.*

31. This bridal eroticism is the focus of my discussion in Burrus, *Sex Lives of Saints*, 69–76.

32. On the stigma, see G. Frank, "Macrina's Scar," 511–30, and Burrus, "Macrina's Tattoo," 103–17.

33. For a discussion of the resonances of Gregory's Macrinan works with Plato's *Symposium*, see Burrus, *"Begotten, Not Made,"* 112–22.

34. Halperin, "Why Is Diotima a Woman?," 288.

Chapter Nine

Waiting for Theodosius, or The Ascetic and the City

Gregory of Nazianzus on Maximus the Philosopher

SUSANNA ELM

This is a book that was written in some ways backwards: not as a search for roots, but as the exploration of . . . the ordered discovery of attitudes (above all on authority) gradually accumulated in the minds of Christians . . . after Constantine. The book is about ascetics, but the inquiry began [and ends] with bishops. . . . What reputation could [these men . . .] acquire? What hold did [they] have over the imagination [of their audience]?

— Rousseau, *Ascetics, Authority, and the Church*

Asceticism, authority, and the church, the individual and the community as illuminated through "exploration of [their] literary heritage," are among the themes that fascinate Philip Rousseau.[1] Focusing on a broad cast of characters, ranging from Sidonius Apollinaris via Jerome, Augustine, and Pachomius to Basil of Caesarea and Theodoret of Cyrus, Philip Rousseau has repeatedly explored whether these ascetics of great authority displayed in their literary legacy "an understanding of the human heart and what was required in those who wished to form and guide it."[2] That capacity, rather than, say, the institutional ramifications of the organizations and communities created by and reflected in this literary legacy, is Philip Rousseau's litmus test for authority. What did the individuals in question do or write to ensure that their community would be both lasting and humane? The answers are rarely straightforward. After all, many of these persons were "rather odd" (e.g., Basil), "tentative and gradual [in shaping the] alliance among men and women" whom they sought to guide. Mistakes were made.[3] As ascetics, these men were not "secluded and self-protective," but, having carefully assessed "the relation between the pursuit of philosophy, as [they] interpreted it, and engagement with the pastoral life," they "made a definite commitment, and stuck with it."[4] Maximus the Philosopher might therefore be a man at least somewhat after Philip Rousseau's heart insofar as he too was rather odd and engaged in consciously assessing the relationship between philosophy and "pastoral care." The same cannot so confidently be said for his literary impresario, Gregory of Nazianzus, whom Philip Rousseau had in mind when making the remark cited above. Gregory had not made a definite commitment to the pastoral life and stuck with it (or so it could easily appear). His literary legacy, moreover, certainly encourages readings that portray him as a reclusive "theologian of the inner life of the Trinity" whose concerns regarding the κοινωνία, its longevity and humanity, were secondary to theological concerns.[5] No wonder that Gregory of Nazianzus features less in Philip's oeuvre. Still, not all is lost, and perhaps even Gregory may be brought closer to Philip's standards. Those for whom Philip Rousseau is an admired mentor know how high these standards are. Philip's "understanding of the human heart," his wisdom in knowing what is required when forming and guiding, is a precious inspiration.

Maximus the Philosopher, or Maximus of Constantinople, as portrayed by Gregory, was at the very least not frail as "a spider's silk swinging widely at the slightest breeze, [nor] too tender for this tumbling world of mountebanks, and quacks and gobs."[6] Gregory's picture of the man may, however, suggest that Gregory, by contrast, was not suited to action and leadership but was easily duped by others more at home in the world and ready to make commitments and stick with them. Yet his portrayal of Maximus of Constantinople was, as so often in his work, a calling card: to praise and then to condemn Maximus let others know what Gregory considered the true ascetic life, how he interpreted the pursuit of philosophy, and what that implied for the situation in which Gregory found himself. Gregory's philosophy was an active one in which service (λειτουργία) to the community was the raison d'être. This community was the οἰκουμένη of the Romans, metaphorically and literally represented by the "city" (Constantinople), an earthly city intrinsically tied to "the city above" (Gregory Nazianzen, *Or*. 19; 26.17).

"THE NOBLEST OF THE NOBLE"

Maximus the Philosopher is a figure integral to Gregory's time in Constantinople, the intense two years between his arrival in 379 to lead a small Nicene community and his retirement to his estate near Nazianzus in 381. These years witnessed his accession as bishop of Constantinople thanks to Theodosius I, his presidency of the ecumenical council, his resignation, and his subsequent retirement. Gregory delivered his "panegyric on philosophy" (*Or*. 25.1) to Maximus in the spring or early summer of 380. This period has received a great deal of scholarly attention, since it marks the period between Theodosius's famous law known as "*cunctos populos,*" issued in February 380, and his arrival in Constantinople in November of that year.[7] In this edict the emperor declared that he wished all his subjects to follow the religion Peter had brought to the Romans as exemplified in the teachings of Damasus of Rome and Peter of Alexandria; that the followers of these teachings should be known as Catholics while dissenters were to be considered "infamous" protagonists of heresy; and that dissenters' meeting places should be denied the name *churches*. "They are to be smitten first with divine vengeance, and afterwards also by punishment on our initiative, which we shall have taken up on the basis of the judgment of heaven."

On the face of it, this law appears to be an unambiguous declaration of imperial intent. Scholars have indeed long read it as such, following the opinion of Sozomen, the only church historian to mention it at all. Sozomen placed the edict into the context of Theodosius's illness and subsequent baptism and considered it advance notice from the emperor, still at Thessalonica, to his subjects in Constantinople "so that he would not seem to be acting with such violence if he gave instructions to worship contrary to their way of thinking."[8] The Constantinopolitans would have been justified in being startled. If the law was indeed reflecting the intent to establish his definitive religious views prior to his arrival in the city, Theodosius would have been the first Christian emperor to have done so for quite some time. Constantius II and Valens, for example, had been much more circumspect, leaving a great deal of room for their advisors and bishops to juggle for positions and modify competing views before taking any religious position, never mind issuing unequivocal laws.[9] Indeed, R. Malcolm Errington and Neil McLynn have recently given nuance to our perception of Theodosius the lawgiver, the nature of his religious policy, and hence the *cunctos populos*. Gregory's orations on Maximus should therefore be reread in the context of these revisions.[10]

WAITING FOR THEODOSIUS

Issued in Thessalonica and addressed to the people of Constantinople, the law *cunctos populos*, as scholars have noted, remained largely without effect (leading Ritter, for example, to read it as programmatic and without legal impact).[11] Not only do historians such as Rufinus, Orosius, and Theodoret fail to mention it, but events in the city show that even Errington's suggestion, following Sozomen, that the edict was intended to prepare the local clergy for the behavior the emperor expected cannot be sustained.[12] First, it is evident that the emperor did not intend to take action against the heretics; such action was postponed until decreed appropriate by the "judgment of heaven," that is, indefinitely. Second, the edict began by indicating Theodosius's wishes, an emphasis our most contemporary source also notes. Gregory of Nazianzus stated in his *De vita sua* 1304 that Theodosius had intended to convince all people gently, "making his wishes into a written law of persuasion." But Gregory did more. In a speech delivered during that waiting time (rather than in the retrospective poem *De vita sua*), he challenged his opponents by asking them a series of questions, the fifth of which was: "What disregarding of a royal decree did we jealously resent?" (*Or*. 33.13). A peculiar question, since its reference to what Stephen Williams and Gerard Friell have called "one of the most significant documents in European history" is strangely subdued.[13] Indeed, Claudio Moreschini, the most recent editor of the oration, thought that this remark referred to another edict entirely, since Gregory could not possibly have made so little of an imperial document potentially so advantageous for him.[14] However, Gregory did refer precisely to this law and in so doing revealed that he and his contemporaries understood the law to be the most provisional of all commitments, permitting Theodosius a great deal of room to maneuver upon arrival in the city prior to making a more definitive move and sticking with it.

Gregory's attack in *Oration* 33, delivered in his church, the Anastasia, after Easter 380, was ostensibly directed against "Arians" but was in fact a defense of his own position vis-à-vis critics among his own "Nicene" community. First he had to justify why he was the right person to lead them even though, second, he decisively rejected the zeal of some in his audience who engaged in ferocious battles for the faith and consequently accused him of not doing enough.[15] Among the strategies Gregory employed to make his points was to decry the murderous cruelty of the previous regime in contrast with his own and the new regime's moderation (*Or*. 33.3–5). He had not "contested churches . . . [or] money" with his adversaries. His "Arian" interlocutors, acting as foil for the critics among his own people (cf. *De vita sua* 679–702), remained in fact safely ensconced in their meeting places. And it was precisely this "inactivity" that his opponents decried as madness (*Or*. 33.14), this restraint from using the courts and other drastic means that reflected — so the import of the oration — the new emperor's stance (as conveyed by his edict): moderation and persuasion. In other words, Theodosius's edict was not understood as a call for action. Neither the clergy nor the magistrates used the nine months in which they waited for the emperor to deprive anyone of their meeting places (a move for which at any rate no enforcement was provided), and no member of the clergy not covered by the new label *Catholic* was deprived of his privileges. Waiting for Theodosius was thus much like what waiting for his precursors had been like. No one appears to have been certain what the future would hold; there was no clear Nicene agenda. All leaders (the Nicene ones included) within the Eastern Christian churches and in Constantinople were therefore tensely preparing for the imperial presence, jostling to position themselves so that they would be able to influence the emperor once he arrived.[16] Or, to quote Caroline Humfress, "Theodosius' legislation had to be played out in actual disputes."[17]

Such a pressure-cooker atmosphere demanded, as a consequence, initiative of a particular kind: everyone had to be sure to put his best foot forward. All had to present their version of the truth and the nature of the Trinity to the best of their respective abilities and to demonstrate with all the means of rhetoric that they were of the stuff leaders were made of. To wait was not to be inactive, and of course, Gregory's "inactivity" consisted precisely of such initiatives. In the late spring and early summer of 380 Gregory delivered his so-called *Theological Orations* and presented his paragons of true Christian leadership, Cyprian of Carthage (actually a composite character), in *Oration* 24 and Athanasius of Alexandria in *Oration* 21 in May 380. He also, according to *De vita sua* 858–62, got in touch with Peter of Alexandria, Athanasius's successor, to ascertain his support.[18] Peter of Alexandria on his part appears to have presented to Gregory at some point in 380 one of his fellow Egyptians then in Constantinople, Maximus the Cynic, also known as Heron. Maximus quickly became Gregory's confidant and advisor.[19] Given the tensions within his "own" community, Gregory evidently appreciated the support of a person directly endorsed by Peter of Alexandria, who was in turn endorsed by Theodosius.[20] By the summer of 380 Gregory had dispatched Maximus as his emissary to Alexandria, either to ascertain Peter's support in the form of "the σύμβολοι of his function" to which *De vita sua* 862 refers or to thank him for this recognition. *Oration* 25 was Gregory's farewell speech delivered on the eve of Maximus's departure, which functioned also as a letter of intent indirectly addressed to Peter. Asceticism, authority, and the church were the themes of this panegyric on philosophy to impress upon his local audience what kind of men should be their leaders: men such as Maximus, or rather, Gregory himself.

However, in the hands of Maximus and Peter of Alexandria, *Oration* 25 became a prime exhibit for the law of unintended consequences.

Maximus and Peter of Alexandria — I suggest — read it (or could easily have pretended to read it) as Gregory's endorsement of Maximus's superior leadership qualifications, making him the perfect candidate to lead the Nicenes at Constantinople. Upon his return to Constantinople shortly thereafter, while Gregory was out of town (it was summer), Maximus and several Egyptian bishops accompanying him celebrated a service in the Anastasia during which they consecrated Maximus as bishop. Local members of the community, including clergy, supported the consecration, and Maximus in turn ordained members as priests.[21] As Gregory later pointed out, the ordination of Maximus had to have been invalid (in his view) because it was disrupted by a crowd. The composition of this crowd, was — still according to Gregory — much like the one that earlier in the year had attacked Gregory and the community in the Anastasia, consisting of high-ranking officials, Homoians and other opponents of the Nicenes, and "those on the outside" (i.e., pagans; so much then for the effect of Theodosius's law, *De vita sua* 901–2). Those who rejected and sought to prevent Maximus's consecration were mainly those who also opposed Gregory's increasing visibility as Nicene leader. They, as John McGuckin has noted, were quite convinced of Maximus's legitimacy as a powerful, Alexandria-backed player in the waiting game and hence wanted to put a brake on his rise in status.[22]

Maximus's opponents (including Nicenes loyal to Gregory) were successful. He left the city for Thessalonica to appeal directly to Theodosius, "hoping," according to Gregory's later apologetic poem *De vita sua*, "to obtain the episcopal see by imperial decree," only to be chased away "like a dog [κυνός]" (1005–7). Maximus and Peter, those seeking to expand Alexandrian interests in Constantinople too actively, had misread Theodosius. Though endorsing Peter of Alexandria, the emperor in Thessalonica had no intention of creating a fait accompli in favor of one particular group. Theodosius's dual endorsement of both Peter and Damasus proves that he was fully aware of the schisms that divided those commonly known as Nicenes into those allied with Peter of Alexandria versus those loyal to Damasus of Rome, such as the bishop of Thessalonica, Acholius, tensions also apparent in the microcosm of Gregory's Anastasia community. Thus, by suggesting to the people of Constantinople that he wished to see the teachings of both men followed and by postponing any direct action vis-à-vis those who did not follow those teachings, Theodosius signaled that he, like his imperial precursors, would wait and see what the Eastern bishops had in store before deciding whom to establish as bishop of the capital.

Maximus for his part also was aware that the waiting game was far from over. He returned to Alexandria and then went on to Milan with another letter by Peter to elicit the support of Ambrose. Ambrose was convinced of Maximus's orthodox credentials and the legitimacy of his consecration and wrote to Theodosius conveying his view that Maximus ought to be confirmed as bishop. Damasus of Rome, meanwhile, assured Acholius in Thessalonica that his rejection of Maximus had been entirely the right move. He also voiced his opposition to the rising star of Gregory.[23]

After Theodosius finally arrived in the capital, Gregory carried the day (after Demophilus, the actual bishop, had refused Theodosius's offer to remain *in situ* on certain conditions). As is well known, he did not carry the day for all that long; barely a year later, he was back in Nazianzus, composing the poem *De vita sua* to present his view of the affair of Maximus, his interaction with Theodosius, and of course, his role in the council of 381. Gregory defined our understanding of Maximus as the feckless villain, as he had already presented him in *Oration* 26. However, even though *De vita sua* and *Oration* 26 have absorbed the majority of scholarly interest — they are the principal accounts of the "scandal" — the Maximus eulogized in *Oration* 25 and the one vilified in *Oration* 26 are not that far apart; invective is after all the inverse of panegyric. Both present what Gregory considered to be the essential characteristics of the ideal Christian leader under Theodosius. The unintended "success" of *Oration* 25 and the real success of Gregory, the winner, in turn shed light on what Theodosius appears to have considered "right teachings." In other words, both *Oration* 25 and *Oration* 26 serve as good indications why Gregory was so adept, in the end, at playing the waiting game.

ORATION 25

Gregory's panegyric praising the "noblest of the noble" (*Or*. 25.3) upon his departure from Constantinople to Alexandria is a so-called λαλιά or μελέτη, a demonstration of the meaning of philosophy. This genre, according to Menander, was ideally suited to showcase the orator's deliberative as well as epideictic qualities. Here he could praise a person of authority as virtuous and good and also exhort "the entire city, the entire audience, and all representatives of the highest authority" with many good counsels. The genre was structurally looser than most others, allowing the author to let his fantasy roam without a prescribed plan. Thus the author could use whatever he deemed appropriate, with the sole proviso that the treatise should be fairly brief.[24] The departing philosopher (never called by name) was a true philosopher, praised by one who was at least a true servant of wisdom. Both shared the same essential trait: they placed their love of philosophy above all else, so much so that they incurred the "hatred" of others. To praise Maximus, then, was itself uplifting. By living such an exemplary life, the philosopher offered his panegyrist an opportunity to contemplate beatitude, the aim of all serious men. Maximus was "the best and most perfect" philosopher because he was "an exemplar of virtue, both in θεωρία as well as in πρᾶξις" (25.2). He recognized that "each of us was not born for himself alone but for all, given that we participate in the same nature and are created by the same being for the same end" (*Or.* 25.4 and 5). Even though he cultivated philosophy in a different guise, wearing the habit of the Cynic, Maximus's philosophical life was perfect because he practiced the highest form of philanthropy: once purified, he devoted himself to bringing the benefits of contemplation to all for the greater public good. That was "the function and objective of philosophy, to bring good to our lives" (25.1). Therefore, as a "citizen of the world," the true philosopher acted within the city, because *only* by so doing might he, through his "active" engagement, affiliate the many as close as humanly possible to God, who had created everything and everyone. Hence, the true philosopher actively engaged in bringing all to the one created harmony and unity in imitation of the one God who had united mankind and aligned it with his divinity through his divine φιλία (*Or.* 25.5).[25]

Maximus the Cynic had been an authentic defender of the Trinity and a champion of orthodoxy, as demonstrated by his near martyrdom (25.3). His willingness to die for the truth was fundamentally different from that of other so-called philosophers, who sought a noble death only to achieve glory among man, such as the Stoic "martyrs," and therefore died "nobly" only for their selfish interests. Maximus would have died selflessly for Christ alone. Such selflessness was already apparent in the manner in which he, the cosmopolite, acted as citizen of Alexandria. He was firm in the faith, as other prominent Alexandrians had been — Athanasius, praised shortly beforehand in *Oration* 21, comes to mind. As a young man, Maximus had been propelled by natural inclination toward philosophy, and Alexandria's Christian fervor had cemented that inclination. He disdained luxury, fortune, and power. "Modest in appearance, but heightened by his deeply hidden depth that leads toward God" (25.4), he had chosen the "middle way" of a philosophy that "was good for him as well as for all Christians" by living in a detached way within the city (*Or*. 25.3 and 6). "He recognized that the eremitic and solitary life, practiced separately and isolated from the masses, is great, elevated and superior to human affairs; but it is, on the other hand, reserved exclusively for those who can practice it as it must be practiced, and furthermore, it contradicts the communal and philanthropic character of charitable love, which is, as he knew, the first of all virtues" (25.5). Such solitary life without active charitable love was not for Maximus because it neglected the first duty of the philosopher, to bring about actively οἰκείωσις πρὸς θεόν, the "kinship with the divine" "through which God cemented his universal love towards all" (25.5). Such οἰκείωσις, for which Gregory had coined the neologism θέωσις in his *Oration* 4 against Julian, was the principal duty of the philosopher: active engagement for the benefit of all understood as unity and harmony prefigured in the Trinity.[26]

Such philosophical life was predicated upon a correct understanding of λόγοι, of the teachings of all philosophers, so that their insights could be properly utilized to comprehend and teach the Trinity, while soundly rejecting the noxious aspects of Greek learning. Maximus, the "old dog," had "in the Cynic philosophy repudiated atheism" but had adopted its frugality, poverty, frank speech, purity of spirit, and the quest for the good (25.6 and 7). Thus he had chosen the "true" philosophy from the beginning and had practiced philosophical purification ever since. As a consequence he could employ the techniques of the "Peripatetics, the Academics, the venerable Stoa, the . . . atomism and hedonism of the Epicureans" to refute what needed refuting. Without imagining "cities of words drawn in the sky" (Pl. *Resp*. 3.1–6), he created true cities based on deeds (25.6). This demanded a defense of the laws and of justice against unjust magistrates, the capacity to resist the madness of crowds, to oppose those in power who divided families and threatened the good order, to help the old, the infirm, the widows, and the orphans. Last but not least, it meant to challenge those without education and those full of pride in an education wrongly achieved (pagans, Eunomians, and other Homoians, 25.7). In sum, Maximus's philosophical life allowed him to use the good in the "philosophies on the outside" to recognize true teachings regarding the Trinity, and then to defend those to the point of martyrdom against Julian, Valens, and their representative bishops in keeping with his fellow citizens, Athanasius and Peter (25.6–14).

MAXIMUS THE CYNIC, A.K.A. GREGORY THE TRUE PHILOSOPHER

Beyond doubt, Maximus the Cynic from Alexandria had been an impressive person in his own right, as his endorsement by Gregory as well as by Ambrose proves. Jerome also knew him as a prolific anti-"Arian" or anti-Homoian writer and as a staunch supporter of Athanasius, and he attributes to him a treatise "against Arians" dedicated to Emperor Gratian.[27] The "Maximus" of *Oration* 25, however, is none other than Gregory in disguise. The allusions to Maximus's actual youth and formation in Alexandria and to his Cynic pedigree thinly veil the quintessential Gregorian themes. *Oration* 25 reads like a synopsis of Gregory's *Orations* 4 and 5 against Julian, to cite but the most obvious comparative example.[28] The praise of the Stoic notion of οἰκείωσις πρὸς θεόν, affiliation with the divine understood as voluntary submission of the purified philosopher to the common good in order to guide all through his mediation to the divine as the philosopher's highest ideal; the correct parsing of Greek philosophy (λόγοι) so that the good could be used properly, while the bad denoted *Hellens*, or pagans; near martyrdom as the hallmark of the true philosopher not out for worldly glory; resistance against Arians and others; and above all the call for the middle way, the rejection of extremes in favor of creating unity and well-ordered harmony that would guide the οἰκουμένη of the Romans to salvation: Maximus embodied all of Gregory's favorite characteristics. When sending off Maximus to Peter, then, Gregory not only sent a trusted advisor who had joined him at the altar (*Or*. 25.2) but made him the envoy of the maxims of the clerical leader as a moderate, restrained, active philosopher engaged in the city for the good of the οἰκουμένη of mankind united as one — a message of conciliation and compromise that was nevertheless not so flexible that it would ever deny its version of the truth of the Trinity. It was appropriate for an emperor who had just issued a "written law of persuasion" firm enough in its commitment to the Nicene version of orthodoxy but flexible enough to chart a conciliatory course for the greater good of the realm.

ORATION 26

Such a claim for Gregory's sophistication in weathering the waiting period could easily be falsified by *Oration* 26 and indeed the entire "scandal" of the "affair of Maximus." Scholars have traditionally read the episode as attesting to Gregory's political naïveté, his lack of decisive leadership, and the kind of bumbling that foreshadowed his inevitable failure when presiding over the ecumenical council.[29] Other readings consider *Oration* 26 in particular as yet another exhibit of Gregory's stance regarding classic philosophy by placing Gregory firmly on the side of theology and orthodoxy versus "hellénisme et hérésie."[30] But in fact *Oration* 26 promotes, this time through Maximus as negative foil, the same characteristics of Gregory's philosophical life (26.9–13). It also, of course, underscores Gregory's quality as leader. Delivered probably prior to Theodosius's rejection of Maximus's claims, the oration was in fact Gregory's bid to regain and solidify his control of the divided flock of the Anastasia. It was a situation with which he had had prior experience: wolves in sheep (or dog's) clothing had snuck in, and "foreign hands" had ordained leaders in opposition to the true shepherd — much as they had done in Nazianzus in the 360s when his father had been the bishop (*Or*. 26.3; cf. *Or*. 1, 2, 6, and 18). Then Gregory had proposed *his* definition of the middle way, of the royal road as the sole "compromise" to reunite the community rendered by schism; now he proposed the same. While the intruders had been aggressively "active" and "decisive," Gregory had been a "timid and circumspect shepherd," giving rise to accusations of laxity and inactivity (*Or*. 26.4). But what inactivity and what laxity? Gregory had never misused the community's finances, a misdeed with which he now charged Maximus, nor had he paraded around in fine clothes (the same accusation) or otherwise given in to the corruption of the theaters and the social whirl (26.1 and 4–5). As I have shown elsewhere, in cases of a competitor's doctrinal soundness — and Maximus's anti-Arian and pro-Alexandrian credentials were unassailable — accusations of fiscal misconduct often proved to be the favorite weapon of those disputing the legitimacy of leadership claims, and Gregory was not above using the same tactic.[31] The entire beginning of the oration anticipates, furthermore, a move Gregory would repeat in *Oration* 42: it is a form of "certificate of discharge" in which the public official about to depart gives an account of the manner in which he has dispensed of the public funds; equitably and soundly in this case, of course (*Or*. 26.6–8).[32] Indeed, after the synopsis of the ideal philosopher as actively involved, self-contained, and imperturbable as a rock on the shore of the sea (26.9–13), Gregory pronounces a series of charges with which he can, in effect, not be threatened. Sending him into exile means nothing since he is a true cosmopolite, at home everywhere and nowhere, since his fatherland is not of this world. Taking away his "throne"? What throne does he occupy? None — at least not for his pleasure (and in effect none in Constantinople as yet). To deny him even access to the altar? He knows what altar to worship truly. To seize his property? He owns nothing. To expel him from the city? Never from the one above (*Or*. 26.14–17). In sum, he is unassailable. Nothing can threaten him, since he, as true philosopher, is immune to the passions roiling lesser mortals — the classic qualification of the ideal leader ever since Plato. And when it comes to true Cynic philosophers, true cosmopolitans who disparage all worldly ambition and revel in their outsider status, *voilá*, Gregory is the man. "If an army of enemies were to set up camp against me, my heart would not fear; even if the battle rages against me, I have confidence" (*Or*. 26.18).

To be guided by a self-contained yet publicly engaged philosopher bravely facing off against enemy combatants — what more could anyone ask for? More to the point, a person who could turn a potentially damaging incident into a personal triumph by showcasing his imperviousness to attack even — indeed especially — from "his own" while at the same time refraining from activism that would jeopardize the relation to the power on the throne must be considered good leadership material. As McGuckin and others have suggested, the affair of Maximus may have damaged Gregory's position; if it did, then those who mattered were not among the doubters. Rather than reflecting a crucial misstep, the "affair of Maximus" as it emerges from *Orations* 25 and 26 showcased a man at the top of his game. That the bishops of Alexandria and Rome were also no mean players is another matter — the "affair of Maximus" as Gregory presented it in the *De vita sua*, overshadowed by his retirement from the council and the "throne," reflects that. While waiting for Theodosius, however, Gregory remained firmly in the city, poised to occupy the throne and to guide the οἰκουμένη to salvation.

NOTES

The chapter's epigraph to Rousseau's *Ascetics, Authority, and the Church* is taken from p. 1.

1. Rousseau, "Pious Household," 165–86.
2. Rousseau, *Pachomius*, xiii.
3. Rousseau, *Basil of Caesarea*, xii, and, *Pachomius*, xxv.
4. Rousseau, *Pachomius*, xxv, and *Basil of Caesarea*, 85–86.
5. McGuckin, *Saint Gregory of Nazianzus*, xxvi.
6. Ibid., xvii.
7. *CTh* 16.1.2, with analysis by Escribano, "Ley religiosa," 143–58; S. Williams and Friell, *Theodosius*, 53. It is important to keep in mind that the law as preserved in the code is a collage.
8. Sozomen, *Historia ecclesiastica* 7.4.5–6; Errington, "Christian Accounts," 411.
9. Elm, *Sons of Hellenism*, 28–50, 435–72
10. Errington, "Church and State," 21–72, and "Christian Accounts," 398–443, in particular; and McLynn, "Genere Hispanus," 77–120, and "Moments of Truth," 215–39.
11. Ritter, *Konzil von Constantinopel*, 28–31.
12. McLynn, "Moments of Truth," 221–23; Errington, "Christian Accounts," 410–16.

13. S. Williams and Friell, *Theodosius*, 53.

14. Moreschini and Gallay's intro. to *Grégoire de Nazianze, Discours 32–37*, SC 318.21–22; McLynn, "Genere Hispanus," 81–82.

15. This speech does not indicate that Gregory already considered himself a shoo-in for the bishopric or that this was an elaborate defense against Arian-inspired prosecution. McGuckin, *Saint Gregory of Nazianzus*, 256–62; Gautier, *Retraite et le sacerdoce*, 364. The speech was given after an attack against the Anastasia.

16. McLynn, "Genere Hispanus," 83–84.

17. Humfress, "Roman Law," 144–45.

18. Gregory of Nazianzus, *Or*. 21 and 24; on *Or*. 24, see Mossay's intro. to *Grégoire de Nazianze, Discours 24–26,* SC 284.9–31, 88–107; Gómez Villegas, *Gregorio de Nazianzo en Constantinopla*, 105–12; McGuckin, *Saint Gregory of Nazianzus*, 311–25; Gautier, *Retraite et le sacerdoce*, 363–73.

19. Gregory does not mention the philosopher by name in *Or*. 25 or 26 but refers to a Heron in *De vita sua* 810 and 1037; lines 954–67 of *De vita sua* indicate that Maximus and Heron are the same. Thus the identification of the philosopher addressed in *Or*. 25 and 26; Mossay's intro. to *Grégoire de Nazianze, Discours 24–26,* SC 284.120–27; Mossay, "Note sur Héron-Maximine," 229–36.

20. Snee has the most extensive reconstruction of Maximus's career and of his time with Gregory ("Gregory Nazianzen's Constantinopolitan Career").

21. These ordinations were then cancelled by can. 4 of the Council of 381.

22. McGuckin (*Saint Gregory of Nazianzus*, 313) also wonders whether *Or*. 25 gave Peter the idea; at the very least it offered the perfect foil.

23. Ambrose, *Ep. Extra coll*. 9.13, is a slightly later letter implying the existence of an earlier one; and see Damasus *Ep*. 5. For the fate of Maximus after his rejection in Thessalonica, see especially Errington, "Church and State," 67–70; but also Mossay, "Note sur Héron-Maximine," 229–36. For the event in Constantinople and ensuing events, see also McGuckin, *Saint Gregory of Nazianzus*, 311–25; Gómez Villegas, *Gregorio de Nazianzo en Constantinopla*, 105–12; McLynn, *Ambrose of Milan*, 111, 142; Gautier, *Retraite et le sacerdoce*, 363–73.

24. Menander Rhetor, *De genere demonstratio rhet. Gr*. 3. 388, quoted in Mossay's intro. to *Grégoire de Nazianze: Discours 24–26,* SC 284.108–12; Dagron, "Empire romain d'Orient," 42.

25. Dagron, "Empire romain d'Orient," 43.

26. Elm, *Sons of Hellenism*, 176–81, 413–22.

27. Jerome, *Vir. il*. 127.

28. Elm, "Gregory of Nazianzus's Life," 171–82, and "Translating Culture."

29. See Gautier, *Retraite et le sacerdoce*, 363–77, for further bibliography; also Mossay's intro. to Gregory of Nazianzus, *Grégoire de Nazianze: Discours 24–26,* SC 284.137–41; Gómez Villegas, *Gregorio de Nazianzo en Constantinopla*, 110–12; McGuckin, *Saint Gregory of Nazianzus*, 310, 314–25.

30. Plagnieux, *Saint Grégoire de Nazianze théologien*, 11–28, analyses the content of *Or*. 25 and 26 primarily from the perspective of Gregory's presentation of the relationship between "profane" philosophy and Trinitarian heresies on the one hand and Nicene orthodoxy on the other, characterized as "héllenisme et christianisme," "hellénisme et hérésie," and "hellénisme et orthodoxie."

31. Elm, "Dog That Did Not Bark," 68–93.

32. Elm, "Programmatic Life."

PART III

Landscapes (with Figures)

Chapter Ten

Remembering for Eternity

The Ascetic Landscape as Cultural Discourse in Early Christian Egypt

JAMES E. GOEHRING

In a fascinating volume entitled *The Age of Homespun*, Laurel Thatcher Ulrich explores the origins, contributions, and persistence of the American myth of homespun through an analysis of eleven late seventeenth- to early nineteenth-century objects from New England representing rural life and household production: an Indian basket, two spinning wheels, a niddy-noddy, a woodsplint basket, and an unfinished stocking. The objects were collected and saved in the latter half of the nineteenth century, a period of rapid industrialization and urban growth, and their preservation reflects the cultural response of individuals longing for a simpler and more authentic life left behind. Ulrich's study unravels the idealizations inherent in the myth of this more idyllic past, revealing the complex economic and social structures that shaped the history of preindustrial America.[1] In the process, she reveals as well the persistent power of historical myth to influence American lives and culture.

In uncovering the historical realities of rural life and household production, Ulrich lays bare the selective nature of memory in the construction of the myth of homespun. Horace Bushnell, for example, who christened the Age of Homespun in a speech at the Litchfield, Connecticut, County Centennial in 1851, constructed an alternative vision of history by focusing on the common people instead of simply repeating the usual recitation of famous men and events.[2] Declaring the latter "to be commonly very much a fiction," he offered up instead the rural families who had cleared the forests, built the cabins, and spun and woven the clothes as the real founders of Litchfield County.[3] "You must not go to the burial places," he proclaimed, "and look about only for the tall monuments and the titled names. It is not the starred epitaphs of the Doctors of Divinity, the Generals, the Judges, the Honourables, the Governors, or even the village notables called Esquires, that mark the springs of our success and the sources of our distinctions. These are rather effects than causes; the spinning-wheels have done a great deal more than these."[4] He drew a picture of a rural Eden where an industrious and religious family life centered the individual. "Daily work created . . . spontaneous pleasure," and neighborliness offered connectedness.[5] Spinning and sewing bees supplied the kind of recreation that "pleased them, this to them was real society."[6]

Bushnell's vision of the past, of course, was as idealized as those he sought to replace. He created his "lyrical and cohesive rendering" of the myth in part by avoiding "the dark underside of New England history . . . by removing events from his story."[7] The indigenous people, for example, disappear from Bushnell's landscape. He refers to them but once, "early in his speech when he suggested that spinning and weaving marked a stage in the evolution of humankind from savagery to civilization."[8] While, as Ulrich shows, the indigenous people continued to play a significant role in the economics and culture of New England, there was simply no place for them in the ideal rural landscape that Bushnell constructed. He fashioned his myth by excising those troubling elements that confounded his vision of the Age of Homespun.

What interests me here in Ulrich's work is the way history is transformed into cultural myth through a process of selective remembering. She directly notes this aspect in her conclusions, observing that "people make history not only in the work they do and the choices they make, but in the things they choose to remember."[9] Authors like Bushnell participate in and add momentum to the process. The historical myth that emerges fashions the past both as an ideological haven that offers release from the pressures and anxieties of the present and as a value-laden tableau that works to conform the present culture to its own particular vision of history. By presenting its artificial world as given and inevitable, the myth naturalizes its cultural and social construction of the world within the world.[10] In an ongoing dialectical process, culture produces out of its own past the very myth that creates its own future. Myth, history, and culture perform a dance of cultural change.

The interaction of history, memory, and culture evidenced by Ulrich in the nineteenth-century creation of the myth of homespun finds significant parallels in the fourth-century Christian creation of the myth of the desert. Through a process of selective and often purposeful memory, ascetics, believers, and authors elaborated on figures and events of the recent past to fashion "one of the most abiding creations of late antiquity."[11] The myth drew its power in part from its association with historical figures, an association that increased the believability of its claims by linking them to factual events. In its preserved memory, however, the myth enhanced the concept of withdrawal from society through its emphasis on the spatial imagery of the desert, increased the spiritual stature of the ascetics through miracle stories and a process of selective memory, and purified their landscape through the equation of monasticism and orthodoxy. The myth of the desert that emerged served not only to recruit new ascetic disciples but also to buttress the values of the larger Christian culture through the example of the desert saints whose angelic lives provided evidence of the power inherent in the new faith. Their stories served as guidebooks for ascetic and lay Christians alike. They played a central role in the development of late antique Christian spirituality and, perhaps even more impressively, have continued to influence Christian culture through the centuries until today.

In the following pages, I would like to explore three examples from antiquity that illustrate the role played by selective memory, whether conscious or unconscious, in the production of the myth of the desert. These include Athanasius's *Life of Antony*, the *Life of Shenoute*, traditionally attributed to his disciple Besa, and the recent evidence of a Manichaean ascetic community emerging from the Dakhleh Oasis.[12] I will focus on the role of memory in the formation of the myth of the desert by exploring the creation of a physical space of otherness in Athanasius's *Life of Antony*, the production of the ideal ascetic in the *Life of Shenoute*, and the general cleansing of the ascetic desert of heresy suggested by the documents discovered in the Dakhleh Oasis. In these analyses, I use the concept of memory broadly not only to include what is remembered over time as opposed to what is forgotten but also to represent what is chosen by a storyteller or author from the past as the focus of his or her story as opposed to what is played down or ignored. A cultural myth, of which the myth of the desert represents a case in point, arises over time as the latter process transforms itself into the former. That which was left out or ignored for whatever reason is eventually forgotten. The original authorial focus of the stories comes to define the cultural memory of the past and through it to shape the cultural agenda for the future. As such, myth plays a fundamental role in cultural change. Created by human agency, it becomes the agent of human change.

ATHANASIUS'S *LIFE OF ANTONY*

The publication of the *Life of Antony* by Athanasius shortly after the ascetic's death in 356 marked a seminal stage in the emergence of the myth of the desert.[13] While the discovery of the Egyptian desert as an ascetic arena by figures like Antony obviously predated Athanasius's effort, it was his *Life of Antony* that captured the moment, translating the historical practice of a relative few into a social and spiritual force that far transcended the direct reach of the individual ascetics. In Athanasius's hands, Antony became the ideal ascetic, and through the *Life of Antony* the ideal ascetic became a desert monk.

Much of the cultural power of the *Life of Antony* lies in its forceful linkage of the concept of ascetic renunciation with the actual physical practice of withdrawal into the desert. Athanasius connects ascetic progress and perfection to the ascetic's increasing separation from the world of the average Christian. The reader follows Antony as he withdraws from his home in the village to places close by the village, from there to a nearby desert cemetery, from the cemetery to a deserted fortress beyond the river, from the fortress to the upper Thebaid, and from the Thebaid to his inner mountain retreat near the Red Sea.[14] Each withdrawal increases Antony's ascetic authority and fame, which in turn encourages those from the civilized world to follow him out into the desert, undoing his solitude and forcing his retreat further into the desert. In the *Life of Antony*, in fact, Antony's final retreat near the Red Sea becomes the *telos* or final goal toward which his successive withdrawals lead. In describing Antony's earlier move to the deserted fortress, for example, Athanasius writes, "Intensifying more and more his purpose [τὴν πρόθεσιν], he hurried toward the mountain."[15] The spiritual *telos* of ascetic practice is here joined to the physical *telos* of withdrawal into the desert. The reader of the *Life of Antony* sets the book down with a clear understanding of the link between Christian asceticism and the call of the desert. Withdrawal, which had earlier indicated a person's renunciation of certain culturally expected patterns and behaviors, came increasingly to include a spatial dimension that connected the true athletes of such renunciation with the concept of relocation beyond the immediate reach of civilization.[16]

The positive formulation of this connection between asceticism and the desert gains additional strength in the *Life of Antony* as the more familiar urban forms of ascetic practice fade into the background. Recent scholarship has underscored the prevalence of urban (city, town, and village) asceticism in Egypt,[17] and there can be little doubt that Athanasius knew and interacted more closely with such urban ascetics than with true desert figures like Antony.[18] Given this fact, there is considerable irony in the possibility that Athanasius composed the *Life of Antony* during his exile under Constantius (356–62), hiding on occasion in the homes of urban ascetics in the city of Alexandria.

Antony died on January 30, 356.[19] Less than a month later, in the early morning hours of February 8/9, Athanasius went into hiding in Alexandria. Condemned the previous summer at the Council of Milan, he had outmaneuvered the Arian opposition within his own see until that night. Meeting in vigil in the Alexandrian church of Theonas in preparation for holy communion the following day, Athanasius and his followers were scattered by a large military force under the control of the dux Syrianus. Surrounding the church and urged on by Arian sympathizers, they eventually broke down the doors and stormed inside. Many died in the attack. Athanasius escaped, spirited away by a group of monks and clergy.[20]

While he must have moved frequently during his exile to avoid capture, and probably spent considerable time in the deserts of Lower Egypt, various accounts suggest that female ascetics within the city played a significant role in protecting the fugitive archbishop.[21] The most famous and most legendary account is that of Bishop Palladius of Helenopolis. In the monastic history that he dedicated to Lausus (*Historia lausiaca* 63), he reports that Athanasius remained hidden in the city for the entire six years of his exile in the home of a young and beautiful virgin, who, apprehensive at first, eventually took him in, cared for his bodily needs, and borrowed books for his use. Fanciful as the story sounds, aspects of it gain credibility from the brief reports of these years preserved in the *Festal Index*.[22] There it is indicated that Athanasius remained hidden within the city, somehow avoiding the oppressive searches for him conducted by the authorities.[23] The index further reports that in the year 359–60 the prefect Faustinus and the dux Artemius entered a private home that contained a small cell in search of the archbishop. If Athanasius had been there, he had already flown. The confidence of the officials in their information, however, is suggested by the fact that they proceeded to torture the apparent owner of the home, the dedicated virgin Eudaemonis.[24] While Palladius has elaborated the story, it seems evident that Athanasius found support among and was occasionally concealed by urban ascetics in Alexandria during his years (356–62) as a fugitive.

The possibility suggested in the Pachomian corpus that he sought refuge in one of their monasteries in Upper Egypt, even if it is reliable, only reinforces the point.[25] While Pachomius is often associated with Antony and Amoun as one of the founders of Egyptian monasticism, his coenobitic innovation was in fact a form of village, not desert, asceticism. Antony and Amoun represent desert ascetics. Pachomius and the communities of his *koinonia*, on the other hand, illustrate the continuing and innovative expansion of asceticism within towns and villages.[26] If Athanasius did find refuge among the Pachomians, it would once again underscore the role played by urban ascetics in protecting the archbishop, the very ascetics whom he essentially ignores in his *Life of Antony*.

The juxtaposition of Athanasius's composition of the *Life of Antony* with his rescue and concealment by both urban and desert ascetics suggests something of the draw of the desert landscape in the formation of the late antique myth of the desert. Valiant urban ascetics filled the archbishop's world, yet when he sought to encapsulate the goals of the ascetic life in a single story, he turned to the desert anchorite Antony, about whom his knowledge was limited.[27] Athanasius recognized that the ascetic ideals of renunciation and withdrawal, forged in the urban environment of Christian origins, acquired in the desert a spatial dimension that resonated for the storyteller and audience alike. The desert supplied the indispensable elements of the heroic figure and the exotic location on which any good story, romance, or myth depends.[28] As the earlier persecutions had spawned a literature centered on the struggles of heroic Christians in strange and exotic places (prisons, coliseums, and arenas), inhabited by fierce adversaries and wild beasts, so now the ascetic's story could be told in similar terms. The exotic desert became the new arena for heroic conflict, and the renunciations and struggles of the monk, portrayed as realistic battles with demonic beasts, replaced the external torments imposed upon the martyr. In the process, the desert was refashioned as a literary landscape of Christian trial and perfection.

In his focus on Antony and the desert, Athanasius virtually ignores the familiar urban ascetics that filled his own environment. The dedicated virgins to whom Antony entrusts his sister and the old solitary ascetic in the neighboring village, both of whom appear at the beginning of the story, serve but to anchor what follows in a reality known to its readers.[29] The average Christian, after all, knew and had frequent contact with the urban and village ascetics who populated their immediate landscape. In the *Life of Antony*, however, these ascetics fade into the background as Athanasius fashions an alternative picture that locates the spiritual otherness of the ascetic visibly in the physical otherness of the desert. He unbalances the classical view of the city as center by presenting the desert as an emerging alternative city of God on earth, imbuing its ascetic inhabitants with a semblance of biblical saints and angels.[30] The otherness of the desert serves to enhance the otherness of the ascetic in the minds of the reader.

The spatial localization of this otherness witnessed in the *Life of Antony* supplies the setting for the myth of the desert.[31] Myth operates in an alternative space, and the desert supplied that space. Urban ascetics were simply too close at hand and too familiar a part of the landscape to elicit a sense of otherness. While they continued to play a vital role in

Christian society and surely always outnumbered their true desert counterparts, they slowly lost their place in the history of asceticism as the literary tradition fostered by Athanasius's *Life of Antony* took hold.[32] Urban ascetics were simply forgotten, or, like Pachomius, who had developed a form of village asceticism in Upper Egypt, were drawn into the interpretive sphere of the desert. Over time, the success of the *Life of Antony* transformed Athanasius's focus on the desert into a cultural memory. The myth of the desert became the story of Egyptian monasticism.[33]

THE LIFE OF SHENOUTE

If the otherness of the desert served to locate the myth of the desert in a space beyond the usual boundaries of human habitation and history, the portrayal of the ascetic heroes who populated the landscape conformed them increasingly to the biblical and angelic ideals of the myth.[34] In the case of historical figures like Shenoute, the process begins with the natural tendency to focus memory on and often exaggerate the positive elements in a person's life after his or her death. Rarely in a eulogy does one hear of the shortcomings or faults of the deceased. Rather, the speaker chooses what to remember in order to extol his subject's life. For ascetic heroes, this process was augmented by the religious function of the remembered stories as spiritual guides for those who heard and read them.[35] Episodes were chosen and shaped so as to encourage the appropriate virtues and beliefs in the present. As a result, the ideologies (ascetic, spiritual, religious, ecclesiastical, and/or political) of the storytellers and authors informed their particular elaboration of the saint's memory. Exaggeration and the use of interpretive metaphors enhanced the effectiveness of the stories and with it the stature of the saint, widening further the growing gulf between his or her life and that of the living. Superhuman regimens, conflicts with demons, clairvoyant abilities, and miraculous feats configured the saint more and more in the image of the biblical prophets and the angels. The narrative process transfigured the historical ascetic into the mythical saint. While his past existence grounded the myth in history, the incredible elements of the story generated the myth's effective power.

The Bohairic *Life of Shenoute* offers an interesting case in point,[36] for just as the existence of documentary evidence of urban ascetics has allowed scholars to see behind the literary sources' emphasis on the desert, so the extant writings of Shenoute permit one to weigh the evidence of the *Life* against the actual words of the ascetic in question.[37] While the *Life* is no longer attributable to Shenoute's successor Besa, a fact that distances it from its subject matter, its inclusion of three references to Shenoute's discourses, rules, and/or letters indicates that its author(s) knew the very texts to which scholars are turning with renewed interest today to recover the "true" history of Shenoute's monastery.[38] The author(s) and/or editors had access to Shenoute's corpus, but the history they sought to write was different. Drawing on the memory of the saint, which was shaped already by hagiographical interests in the oral and liturgical tradition after Shenoute's death, the creators of the *Life* fashioned their history so as to present Shenoute as the new Elijah, linking him with Jesus and the prophets, apostles, and saints of the past through an array of mystical and magical abilities.

The reader of the *Life* learns that Shenoute, like Jesus, was different from other people already in his youth. While he was still a boy, a shepherd observed his rigorous ascetic practice and saw his fingers burning like ten flaming lamps.[39] When his parents learned of his abilities, they entrusted him to the ascetic Pcol, under whose care he exorcised demons and received the mantle of Elijah, delivered by an angel at night.[40] As abbot, he was clairvoyant and possessed the ability of miraculous travel.[41] When required, he could multiply grain or loaves, bring forth plentiful harvests, or limit the ash output of the community's ovens.[42] He could intercede with God to bring on the annual flooding of the Nile or sink an island whose owners exploited its farmers.[43] He could himself miraculously rescue captives from the Blemmyes or, by giving a military leader (dux or comes) his girdle as a token, grant success in war against the barbarians.[44] Even the animals recognized his stature. Ferocious lions bowed down before him, and a camel responded to his plea to accept and feed its rejected foal.[45]

The author uses the miracles to link Shenoute's way of life with that of Jesus, the prophets, and the apostles. "For my father Apa Shenoute of good memory," he writes, "whose [feast] we celebrate today, is worthy to have his good works related, and also his asceticism, his way of life, his admirable virtues, and the great and incredible signs, just like those of the holy prophets and the apostles of the Lord."[46] Various episodes echo the miracles of Jesus: Shenoute's exorcism of a demon at the beginning of the *Life*, multiplication of loaves, increase of the grain in a mill to the point where the brothers were unable to gather it up.[47] Accounts of Shenoute's visions of and conversations with Elijah, Elisha, Jeremiah, Ezekiel, the twelve prophets, King David, Mary, John the Baptist, Jesus, the twelve apostles, and Paul reveal his true colleagues and set him apart from the living monks.[48] As "the new Elijah," he is a latter-day embodiment of the biblical saints.[49] He is the perfect monk and monastic leader, a representative of the effective power of the ascetic life.[50]

While in general one can agree with the English translator of the *Life* who wrote, "Besa is obviously more interested in narrating miraculous and marvelous stories to augment his hero's reputation than in providing historical data for the use of later scholars," it is perhaps more instructive to explore the way in which the author uses the historical evidence to effect his purpose.[51] There is, after all, history in the *Life of Shenoute*. Various historical patterns and events known from Shenoute's own writings are echoed in the *Life*. The historical evidence, however, is used selectively and is inevitably clothed in the miraculous. Episodes of famine relief, interaction with lay and ecclesiastical authorities, and opposition to pagans and heretics, all of which find their parallels in the Shenoutean corpus, function in the *Life* to enhance Shenoute's otherness. The feeding of the hungry villagers during a great famine recorded in the *Life*, for example, reflects the social efforts of the monastery evidenced in Shenoute's account of its relief services for the lay community.[52] But whereas Shenoute's account illustrates the organizational and economic power of the community, the author of the *Life* uses the episode to reveal Shenoute's miraculous power to multiply the community's insufficient stores to meet a greater need.[53] Shenoute plays the role of Jesus in the multiplication of the loaves. So too, the historical fact of Shenoute's journey to Constantinople with the Archbishop Cyril becomes, among other things, a vehicle to extol the saint's miraculous power. Denied passage on Cyril's ship back to Egypt, Shenoute beats the archbishop home by traveling on a cloud.[54] A final interesting example occurs in the story of Shenoute's breaking and entering into the house of Flavius Aelius Gessius, a former governor of Thebais, to uncover and destroy idols that he kept in his home. The account of the events in the *Life* appears to derive from an account of the incident preserved in Shenoute's own writings.[55] The claim in the *Life* that "the doors of the house opened immediately one after another until they came to the place where the idols were" appears modeled on Shenoute's assertion, made in his own defense, that the various doors into the house and second floor private chamber opened easily.[56] Denying any inside help, he credits Jesus for the ease of entry, noting that last door to the upper room fell off its hinges when he grasped it.[57] While the ease with which the doors opened could be seen in miraculous terms, the *Life* does not directly assert that claim. It does, however, add to the sense of the miraculous by reporting that when Shenoute and his party crossed the Nile to conduct the raid and again to return to the monastery, they did so "without any ship or sailor," a claim that situates Shenoute alongside other early monastic heroes capable of miraculous travel.[58] The *Life* expands on the sense of the miraculous. History, as we understand it, survives in the *Life* in the service of myth.

None of this is to deny that the myth ultimately depends on the reality of Shenoute's organizational abilities and success as a charismatic leader. He was, of course, set apart *in* this life, and that fact became the starting point for the evolving myth that sets him apart *from* this life. The use of the miraculous to set Shenoute apart, however, represents but part of the story. The idealization of his life requires as well the submersion of those elements that conflicted with the ideal. While, as Rebecca Krawiec has shown, the "narrative world" of the *Life* can capture Shenoute's self-presentation as one "having a close and trusted relationship with God, which granted him special status in the human world," it cannot, given its purpose, report on the internal debates over various controversial practices that one finds in Shenoute's own writings.[59] The beating of erring monks, the death of a monk at Shenoute's hands, the conflict over expulsion, and various challenges to Shenoute's authority do not fit the portrait of the perfect monk.[60] Where they do appear, as for instance in the story of an expelled monk, there is no hint of discord. The effectiveness of Shenoute's decision is underscored by the repentance and return of the expelled monk.[61] There is no problem here. There is no disputing the correctness of Shenoute's decisions in the *Life*. Everything works, as one would expect, to his glory. While conflicts and complexities were a natural part of the White Monastery experience, they could not survive in the "narrative world" of the *Life*. They are as unnatural to the ideal world of the desert myth as they are natural to the actual experience of monastic life under Shenoute.[62]

The *Life of Shenoute* further participates in the myth of the desert by connecting the otherness of the perfect ascetic Shenoute with the otherness of the desert. Shenoute's historical use of the desert made the connection relatively easy. In addition to the location of the White Monastery in the desert at the edge of the fertile zone, the evidence from Shenoute's own writings suggests that as abbot he continued to live as a solitary hermit in the desert some distance from the monastery.[63] His withdrawal to the desert undoubtedly set him apart and enhanced his power. In the *Life*, Shenoute seems to reside in the monastery but withdraws to his desert cell on occasion to pray and seek God's intercession in certain matters.[64] Shenoute's intimate connection with the desert functions in the *Life* to link him once again with his biblical predecessors, the prophets, who found God in the desert.[65]

One story, in particular, underscores this theme.[66] It begins with Jesus informing "the prophet Apa Shenoute" that his friends, who live in the desert (ⲛⲉⲕϣⲫⲏⲣ ⲙⲡⲟⲗⲓⲧⲉⲩⲧⲏⲥ ⲉⲧϩⲉⲛⲡϣⲁϥⲉ), will be coming to the monastery that night to see the monks he has gathered under him. Shenoute summons the monastery's leaders and informs them of the expected visit. At the assembly that night, Shenoute enters with the three monks (ⲙⲙⲟⲛⲁⲭⲟⲥ) from the desert. After the brothers pay their respects, the visitors depart. The next morning the curious monks ask Shenoute to reveal the visitors' identity. "They walked with majesty and wisdom," the monks say, "and their garments were glorious. They were different from other living men, but were like angels of God."[67] Shenoute accedes to their wishes and identifies the visiting desert monks as John the Baptist, Elijah the Tishbite, and Elisha. In this single story, the desert, the biblical prophets, and the angels are effectively bound together to fashion the portrait of the perfect monk. Shenoute, as the visitors' friend and the one who withdraws to the desert, fits the portrait. His mystical and miraculous abilities evidenced throughout the *Life* mean that he too is "different from other living men, . . . like an angel of God."

As the perfect monk, a miracle-working embodiment of the biblical prophets and angels, the Shenoute of the *Life* has taken on mythic proportions, becoming the perfect inhabitant of the desert myth. In his otherness, literarily distanced from the world of the living, he corresponds perfectly with the otherness of the desert. As myth operates in an alternative space, so it inhabits that space with otherworldly figures.[68] As the desert supplies the alternative space in the myth of the desert, so the literary portraits of figures like Shenoute supply the otherworldly inhabitants who populate the myth. While their ascetic skills and charisma surely set them apart from the average monk during their lives, their postmortem elevation conformed them more and more to the figures of the biblical past and the angelic future than to those of the world of the living.[69] It is, in fact, little wonder that later monks so often bemoaned the decline of the monastic life. Whether the decline was real or not, the literary creation of the early ascetics as perfected monks meant that those who followed in their footsteps necessarily fell short in this life of their perfection. Be that as it may, the lives of the desert saints served as spiritual guides, promoting and shaping the ideals toward which the individual and the culture strove. As the culture gave rise to and developed the myth of the desert, so the myth worked to conform the culture to its ideals. Myth and culture supported one another in the formation of a Christian world.

THE MANICHAEAN COMMUNITY IN THE DAKHLEH OASIS

In fashioning the ideal monk as the latter-day embodiment of the biblical saints, the myth of the desert necessarily aligned the monk with the prevailing orthodoxy of the dominant church, which served finally as the repository of the myth. The perfection of the saint precluded his or her accidental or intentional association with those suspected of schism or heresy. Chosen by God in their youth, the saints were steered away from error. When Pachomius first embarked on the solitary life, for example, he was confused by the overtures of the Melitians and Marcionites until God answered his prayers.[70] Authors and editors fashioned their heroes as unquestionably orthodox. Athanasius portrays Antony as "truly wonderful and orthodox." He perceived the wickedness of heretics and schismatics from the start, never held communion with the Melitians, and never professed friendship toward the Manichaeans or any other heretics. He chased away the Ariomaniacs who came to his mountain retreat, and he returned to the city to rally the orthodox against them.[71] So too in the *Life of Shenoute*, Shenoute accompanies his archbishop to the Council of Ephesus, where he rebukes Nestorius and strikes him on the chest with the Gospels, causing him to fall from his chair and be possessed by the devil.[72]

The point here is not to challenge the orthodoxy of the early ascetics but rather to recognize the simplified, dualistic presentation of orthodoxy and heresy as another element in the literary production of the myth of the desert. As in old American westerns, the good guys and the bad guys do not overlap. They are immediately recognizable as such, and one knows from the start whom to root for and who will come out on top in the end. As the old westerns fostered allegiance to the cultural values represented by the good guys, the dualistic stories of the myth of the desert fostered individual and cultural conformity to the prevailing orthodoxy of the dominant church. The myth retained this power over time by constantly realigning its heroes' orthodoxy with that being professed by the church. The editor of the first Greek *Life of Pachomius*, for example, added an anti-Origenist episode, absent in the Coptic tradition, that established his hero as cognizant of the problem before the problem existed.[73] The *Apophthegmata patrum*, on the other hand, accomplished the same result by effectively erasing the more speculative elements from the teachings of many of the monks whose sayings it preserved. In the myth of the desert, these monks come to support the very orthodoxy that condemned them in their lifetime.[74] Beyond such specific literary examples, it is worth noting as well that the myth updates itself in the mind of readers or listeners through the assumed equation of the ascetic hero's orthodoxy with their own.

While such dualistic clarity serves a literary function in the desert myth, it fails to capture the complex realities that swirled around the profession of faith in the desert. The story of Pachomius's initial encounter with Melitians and Marcionites, whether apocryphal or not, hints at the diversity available in ascetic circles at the beginning of the fourth century. With respect to the Melitians, for example, while the major literary sources have "chiseled" their memory out of the history of monasticism, documentary evidence confirms their widespread participation in the ascetic movement of the day and indicates that they continued to live in some ascetic communities together with "orthodox" monks at least into the sixth century.[75] A late account of Archbishop Damian's (569–605) expulsion of the Melitians from the monasteries in Scetis, while meant to praise his orthodoxy, reveals as well a continuing Melitian presence in that community well into the second half of the sixth century.[76] Such evidence not only underscores the exclusion of those who do not fit the "orthodox" mold from the emerging myth of the desert but also belies the simplicity of the myth's dualistic division between orthodoxy and heresy. While Athanasius's Antony never held communion with the Melitians or professed friendship toward the Manichaeans or any other heretics, in reality various "orthodox" and Melitian ascetics continued to practice their asceticism in related monastic communities in Egypt well into the sixth century. One suspects that others did too. Since, however, they served no purpose in the developing myth of the desert, they were simply not "remembered."

The reality of this selective remembering and shaping of the past has been underscored once again by the evidence of Manichaean ascetics emerging from the village of Kellis (Ishmant el-Kharab) in the Dakhleh Oasis.[77] Prior discoveries of Manichaean manuscripts have supplied literary texts whose contents have permitted scholars to better understand Manichaean teaching and history free from the biased accounts contained in the writings of their opponents. What those texts have done for our understanding of Manichaean history, teaching, and ideology the Kellis texts now promise to do for our understanding of their daily lives and social location.[78] Rather than relying on opponents' accounts whose efforts aim to identify differences and sow division, scholars now have access to letters and documents that open a window into the private lives of members of a Manichaean community. While this is not the place to enter into a detailed discussion of the evidence, the religious elements in the texts raise fascinating questions concerning the interaction between the so-called Manichaeans and their neighbors.

The published letters, dated circa 355–80, belong to members and associates of extended families resident in Kellis.[79] While most were composed in Kellis, a few derive from family members who were living in the Nile Valley at the time. None of the letters offer any evidence of formal governmental or ecclesiastical origin. The editors identify them as "domestic and informal productions intended solely for a local and immediate readership."[80] Specific references in a few letters, particularly Makarios's religious instructions to his son Matthias, offer convincing evidence of their Manichaean origin. While examples of the Manichaean cosmology are rare, as one would expect in personal correspondence, mention of "our lord Paraclete," "the teacher," "the light Mind," "the Light Soul," "light angels," "the God of truth," "the knowledge of truth," "the elect," and "the catechumen" support their Manichaean connection.[81] Nonetheless, while the Manichaean context of most of the letters is clear, the editors observe that "in general and with notable exceptions . . . , a casual reading of these documents might note little beyond a warm Christian piety."[82] While there is nothing in any of the letters that precludes Manichaean authorship, much of the terminology, from the opening epistolary greeting (ⲭⲁⲓⲣⲉⲓⲛ) to the concluding farewell "in God" (ϩⲙ̄ ⲡⲛⲟⲩⲧⲉ) or "in the Lord" (ϩⲙ̄ ⲡϫⲟⲉⲓⲥ), would be at home in any Christian context.[83] Had various of the letters been found individually and out of context, one can only guess that they would have been interpreted simply as late fourth-century Christian letters.[84] As the editors make clear in their conclusion, the Kellis texts dispel various common misconceptions about the perceived relationship between so-called Manichaeans and Christians. The authors of these letters did not understand themselves as a dualistic alternative to Christianity but rather simply "as Christians, the true (and perhaps more effective or spiritual) church."[85] They were but one of the flavors of Christianity in the oasis.[86]

An agricultural account book found in the same area adds to this impression.[87] It appears to derive from one of several agents (*pronoetai*) in charge of a portion of a large estate and offers valuable evidence on the economy of the oasis.[88] Included in the list of accounts are two references to a bishop, four to presbyters, who also appear under the title of "father," one to a deacon, and four to two different monks, who appear both with and without the title *monachos*. The account also contains three references to a church and refers intriguingly to a *topos Mani*, which appears to be a Manichaean residence.[89] In one entry, the monk Petros makes a payment "in place of Mani," that is, for the *topos Mani*.[90] The evidence currently in hand does not permit the identification of any of the religious figures, other than the monk Petros, or of the references to the church as either Manichaean or non-Manichaean. Archaeological excavations have uncovered two churches in Kellis, a small west church located near the find site of the Manichaean texts and a larger east church, which may represent the non-Manichaean Christian community.[91]

While conclusions must remain tentative, the mixture of Manichaean and non-Manichaean Christians in Kellis seems clear and challenges the sharper division of the two often suggested in the heresiological literature. As the editor of the Kellis agricultural account book has observed, "Such a dualism, however welcome it eventually may have been to both sides, may not be a realistic description of the situation in the fourth-century Dakhleh Oasis — or, for that matter, elsewhere in Egypt. It is very possible, even likely, that those who used Manichaean language and read Manichaean texts in Kellis thought of themselves as members of the Christian communion — albeit a group with special interests and insights not shared by all their neighbors."[92] The matter-of-fact references to the *topos Mani* and the Manichaean Christian monk Petros further suggest that the Manichaeans lived as a recognized and accepted part of the wider community. There is no certain evidence of open hostility between the various Christians in the oasis. The Manichaean Christian houses show no sign of having been destroyed. They appear simply to have been abandoned as part of the general decline of the Kellis community.[93] While non-Christian temples were shut down, neither of the two churches shows any evidence of destruction.[94] It would seem that the various flavors of Christianity evidenced in the Kellis discoveries managed to exist side by side for at least most of their existence in the Dakhleh Oasis.[95] This need not preclude religious competition of some sort between the two groups, but it does suggest that despite it all neighbors remained neighbors. While some of the letters suggest their authors' concern about mounting opposition and threats of persecution in the Nile Valley, such pressures do not yet seem to have reached into the Dakhleh Oasis.[96] One suspects that the situation in Kellis, isolated as it was from the trends in the valley, reflected the earlier and more natural pattern of peaceful coexistence.

While this discussion has taken us some distance from the usual monastic settings of the myth of the desert, it illustrates once again how the myth shapes its "history" of monasticism through a process of selective memory. As the discovery of manuscript collections and documentary papyri increasingly underscores the diversity of Christian options available to ascetics in fourth-century Egypt, the portrait of the ideologically pure monastic movement presented in the myth has become less and less convincing. While Antony may never have professed his friendship to a Manichaean or any other heretic, as Athanasius asserts, it would seem that many Christians probably did.[97] Religious orientation did not of itself, particularly in a recently pluralistic culture, preclude social interaction or even friendship with those of a different persuasion. Surely there were rigorous monks like Shenoute from the start who favored the form of Christianity represented in the myth as orthodoxy. It is clear, however, that there were as well Manichaean and Melitian monks, Hieracite and so-called Gnostic ascetics, and others, whose lives and teachings attracted numerous followers. Where ascetic practice brought such people together, as in the sixth-century communities that housed Melitian and "orthodox" monks or in the isolated Dakhleh Oasis, religious difference, while noted and perhaps confrontational at points, did not inevitably preclude peaceful interaction. Yet as Christian culture developed, it came to define itself in terms of a more rigorous orthodoxy that demanded singular allegiance.[98] The myth of the desert, with its strictly orthodox ascetic heroes, participates in and lends support to this development. It is both a product of the emerging Christian culture of orthodoxy and an important player in its success.

In explaining her analysis of the myth of homespun, Laurel Thatcher Ulrich wrote, "My purpose is not to debunk the sentimental vision of the late nineteenth century, but to trace its origins, exploit its contributions, and perhaps in the process explain its persistence."[99] So too, my intentions are not to debunk the romantic, spiritual vision of the late antique myth of the desert but to understand its origins, explore its contributions, and appreciate its persistence as a cultural myth. While comparison of the myth's formulation of history with that reconstructed from less tendentious sources reveals its mythic character, the historical role of the myth in the formation and support of Christian culture through the centuries remains unchallenged.

In terms of its origins, the myth of the desert, no less than Bushnell's "Age of Homespun," fashioned its "lyrical and cohesive rendering" of history in part by removing events from the story.[100] It framed the desert as the landscape of Egyptian asceticism by ignoring the more common urban ascetics. It molded its heroes as biblical saints and angels by, among other things, disregarding much of the evidence that united them more closely with the actual world of Egyptian monasticism. And it fashioned a more purely orthodox asceticism by either expunging the record of heterodox monks or transforming them through a process of selective memory into orthodox ascetics. The resulting myth of the desert, while obscuring much of the history that modern historians seek, became in the long run for Christian culture a more effective history of asceticism. While Shenoute's own writings offer better entrée into the complex social world of the White Monastery and were known in a very limited way throughout Egypt, it is the *Life of Shenoute* that preserves the saint's memory in Coptic (Sahidic and Bohairic), Arabic, Ethiopic, and Syriac versions.[101] While the survival of Antony's *Letters* in Coptic, Syriac, Georgian, Latin, Arabic, and Greek is impressive, the number of surviving manuscripts and their state of preservation betray their more limited influence when compared to the manuscript tradition of Athanasius's *Life of Antony*.[102] Later monks and laity knew the famous ascetics primarily through the fanciful lives that located them in the myth of the desert.[103]

The reconstruction of the complex and multifaceted social world of the early Egyptian ascetics remains a desideratum of modern scholarship. Much remains to be done, as the current interest in and publication of the *Discourses* and *Canons* of Shenoute, and studies based upon them, make abundantly clear. Yet as we unravel history from myth, it is well to remember that it was through the weaving together of history and myth that the culture of Christianity came into its own. Through the myth of the desert, the power of early Christian asceticism transcended the immediate confines of the human experience to become a cultural model working to conform society to its ideals. As ascetic performance served both to deconstruct an individual's old identity and to inaugurate a new subjectivity that integrated him or her into the new Christian culture, so the myth of the desert translated the individual experience into a broader cultural one.[104] The stories of the desert ascetics confirmed the value and attainability of the Christian virtues and promises. They deconstructed the cultural expectations of the classical world, working to inaugurate a new cultural subjectivity that integrated the culture's expectations with those of the emerging church. While the myth of the desert converted many to and guided them in the ascetic life, it played a broader role as well in the creation of Christian culture.

As I began with a modern example of cultural myth, let me close with one as well. John Muir's publication of *The Mountains of California* in 1894 ushered in the conservation movement in this country by creating a new vocabulary to describe the natural world.[105] In his introduction to the 2001 Modern Library edition of Muir's book, Bill McKibben writes, "It was a language unfamiliar to those Americans used to reading about the outdoors, a language of ecstasy and exuberance that calls to mind the religious mystics like Francis or Theresa of Avila."[106] McKibben further observes,

> It is worth remembering . . . that John Muir could have described his experiences in an entirely different way. After all, he was often in danger, cold, wet, or somewhat lost. . . . But none of that crosses your mind while reading Muir, and none of it appears to have crossed his mind either. That's what makes this, his first, such a watershed book. In it he invents, by sheer force of his love, an entirely new vocabulary and grammar of the wild, a language that powered the conservation, and later the environmental, movement through the first century of their respective existences.[107]

In a sense, as we seek to recover the actual history of early Egyptian monasticism, we are describing it in an entirely different way than those who composed the myth of the desert. As Muir drew from his real experiences to "invent, by sheer force of his love, an entirely new vocabulary and grammar of the wild," so those who fashioned the myth of the desert drew from history to create, by sheer force of their love, a new vocabulary and grammar of asceticism. And as Muir's new vocabulary and grammar powered the conservation and environmental movements in their first century of their respective existence and beyond, so the myth of the desert has played its part in powering the movement of Christianity.

None of this is to deny the value in recognizing the realities that lie behind the myth. Quite the contrary. To enter a wilderness after reading Muir's book unaware of the dangers is to risk death from cold, dampness, and the loss of one's way. To fully appreciate Muir's Sierra Nevada, the visitor should know their geology, their flora and fauna, their seasons and storms, their beauties and their dangers. It was Muir's knowledge of these realities and his selective use of them that gave strength and power to his "myth," and it was through the myth that he attracted his and later generations to the mountains. Knowing the realities behind the myth permits one to better appreciate the processes whereby the myth's cultural power is generated. To step back and recognize the origins of the modern environmental movement in the creative spiritual vision of such figures as Henry David Thoreau, John Muir, and Ansel Adams is simply to see into the process of cultural change. It is the same with the myth of the desert.

NOTES

This essay, in an earlier form, was presented at the "Living for Eternity: Egyptian Monasticism" conference held at the University of Minnesota, March 6–9, 2003. It is my distinct pleasure to offer it here in honor of Philip Rousseau, a scholar whose work has influenced me deeply and whose friendship I have valued through the years.

1. I purposely avoid the sharp division between history and myth that is often assumed in standard Western definitions. I understand myth broadly as those stories arising within a culture that serve to shape and define its identity. A culture's production of history functions in this way no less than its production of myth.

2. Bushnell, "Age of Homespun." Ulrich's introduction to her *Age of Homespun* (11–40) employs Bushnell's speech to define the nature of her study and prepare the reader for the following eleven chapters that explore the specific individual objects.

3. Bushnell, "Age of Homespun," 378–79; Ulrich, *Age of Homespun*, 15.

4. Bushnell, "Age of Homespun," 380; Ulrich, *Age of Homespun*, 15.

5. Ulrich, *Age of Homespun,* 24.

6. Bushnell, "Age of Homespun," 386; Ulrich, *Age of Homespun*, 24.

7. Ulrich, *Age of Homespun*, 17 and 24.

8. Ibid., 24; cf., Bushnell, "Age of Homespun," 376, 381.

9. Ulrich, *Age of Homespun*, 414.

10. See Goehring, "Dark Side of Landscape." The process is, of course, complex, since through interpretation the same myth can serve various ideological positions. See, for example, Ulrich, *Age of Homespun*, 414.

11. P. Brown, *Body and Society*, 216. The myth naturally drew on the desert imagery prevalent in various biblical accounts.

12. The recent work of Nina Lubomierski has clearly established that Besa did not author the *Life*. Nina Lubomierski, *Vita Sinuthii* and "Coptic Life of Shenoute."

13. *Vie d'Antoine,* Bartelink's intro., 27; *Life of Antony*, Gregg's intro., 2–3; and *Life of Saint Antony*, Meyer's intro., 8.

14. *Vit. Ant.* 3, 8, 12, and 46.

15. *Vit. Ant.* 12, trans. Gregg, *Life of Antony*, 40. The statement describes Antony's preparation to move across the river to the deserted fortress.

16. Goehring, "Encroaching Desert." On the earlier patterns of asceticism, see Emmett, "Female Ascetics," 513; Goehring, "Through a Glass Darkly"; Choat, "Development and Use."

17. Goehring, "Encroaching Desert," "Withdrawing from the Desert," and "Hieracas of Leontopolis"; Wipszycka, "Monachisme égyptien."

18. The best study of Athanasius's interaction with and use of ascetics is Brakke, *Athanasius*.

19. The date of 356 is generally accepted (*Vie d'Antoine*, Bartelink's intro., 27; *Life of Antony*, Gregg's intro., 2; *Life of Saint Antony*, Meyer's intro., 7). Timothy D. Barnes (*Athanasius and Constantius*, 97) cites Antony's death as ca. 355. January 30 is Antony's feast day in the Synaxarion.

20. Barnes, *Athanasius and Constantius*, 118–20.

21. Ibid., 121. In his chronology for Athanasius (xii), Barnes lists "In hiding in Alexandria and elsewhere in Egypt" for the years 356–62. Brakke (*Athanasius*, 130–31) suggests that "while Athanasius spent most of his six years in the villages and desert, he made sporadic clandestine trips into the city." That Athanasius did not spend the entire time in the city is made clear by his own statements in his *Letters to Serapion* (*Ep. Serap.* 1.1, 33 (PG 26.530a, 605c); cf. Shapland, trans., *Letters of Saint Athanasius,* 59 n. 3. Gregory of Nazianzus (*Orationes* 21.19.6) similarly places him in monastic cells in the desert during this exile.

22. Barnes (*Athanasius and Constantius*, 121) describes it as "a picturesque story." But see Badger, "New Man," 209–11.

23. *Festal Index* 29 (356–57 CE) reports that Athanasius "had fled and was sought for in the city with much oppression"; *Festal Index* 30 (357–58 CE) records that he "lay concealed in the city of Alexandria." *Festal Index* 35 (362–63) does report his flight to the Thebaid, but this occurs only after his ini-

tial pardon and return under the Emperor Julian. He is forced subsequently to flee from the city as a result of Julian's renewed order against him. Athanasius, *Select Writings and Letters*, trans. Robertson, 505.

24. *Festal Index* 32. Sozemen (*Historia ecclesiastica* 4.10) reports that Athanasius initially took refuge with acquaintances in the city, being hidden underground. There is no mention of a virgin in this story, but rather a serving woman who eventually revealed his whereabouts, forcing him to flee to the country.

25. Brakke (*Athanasius*, 130–31) notes that "this search [for Athanasius] extended (probably without good reason) even to the Pachomian monasteries in the Thebaid."

26. Goehring, "Withdrawing from the Desert."

27. It seems likely that his sojourn in the deserts of Lower Egypt in this period gave him access to stories about Antony. It may also have focused his interest on the desert ascetics, which bore fruit in the *Life of Antony*.

28. Gregg's intro. to Athanasius, *Life of Antony*, 3.

29. *Vit. Ant.* 3.

30. *Vit. Ant.* 14.

31. Note here the connection with the classical world's association of exotic peoples with remote places. See, in particular, G. Frank, *Memory of the Eyes*, esp. ch. 2; for the classical elements, Romm, *Edges of the Earth*; François Hartog, *Mirror of Herodotus*.

32. The nature of the desert and the ascetic's location in it relative to the settled land are important considerations. Many ascetics, like those in Shenoute's White Monastery, were located only nominally in the desert, at the edge of the fertile valley. They continued to function as an integral part of the broader social and political world in which they lived. On the use and meaning of the term *desert,* see Cadell and Rémondon, "Sens et emplois." Regarding the growing prestige of desert asceticism, note, for example, the effort by Jerome to "outdistance" Antony's withdrawal in his *Vita Pauli*. The desert withdrawal is carried to an extreme in the Coptic *Life of Onnophrius* (Paphnutis, *Histories of the Monks,* trans. Vivian); see also Goehring, "Dark Side of Landscape."

33. Many questions remain, of course, as to the precise nature and development of this association across time and geographical boundaries. One suspects, for example, that the urban ascetics faded from memory more rapidly as the stories moved outside Egypt, where the readers' contact with and knowledge of the Egyptian urban ascetics did not exist.

34. G. Frank, *Memory of the Eyes*, esp. chs. 5–6; P. Frank, *Angelikos Bios*; Nagel, *Motivierung der Askese*; P. Miller, "Desert Asceticism"; Muehlberger, "Ambivalence."

35. On the book as spiritual guide, see Valantasis, *Spiritual Guides*.

36. Leipoldt, *Sinuthii vita Bohairice* (CSCO 16); Bell, trans., *Besa.* On Besa, see K.H. Kuhn, "Besa" and "Fifth Century Egyptian Abbot"; Cauwenbergh, *Études sur les moines,* 137–53.

37. As a parallel example, recent discussions of the *Letters* of Antony suggest a much closer linkage to the ideas of Origen than is suggested in Athanasius's *Life of Antony*. Rubenson, *Letters of St. Antony* and "Christian Asceticism."

38. On the erroneous attribution of the *Life* to Besa, see Lubomierski, *Vita Sinuthii* and "Coptic Life of Shenoute"; for earlier discussions, see Emmel, "Shenoute's Literary Corpus," 13; cf., Ladeuze, *Étude sur le cénobitisme*, 116–27. The three references in the *Life* are *Vita Sinuthii* 11, 98, 173.

39. *Vita Sinuthii* 4; cf. *Apoph. patr.*, Joseph of Panephysis 7.

40. *Vita Sinuthii* 5–8.

41. On his clairvoyance, see *Vita Sinuthii* 13, 33–36, 42, 75, 77, 131–32. On miraculous travel, see *Vita Sinuthii* 18–19, 58–63.

42. *Vita Sinuthii* 27–28, 138–43 (multiplication of loaves); 162–71 (miraculous harvest); 29 (limiting the ash).

43. *Vita Sinuthii* 102–5 (Nile flood); 85–86 (sinking island).

44. *Vita Sinuthii* 89–90, 107–8, 135–37.

45. *Vita Sinuthii* 136, 161; on the common nature of this hagiographic *topos*, see Elliott, *Roads to Paradise*, 144–67.

46. *Vita Sinuthii* 2.

47. On the exorcism of the demon, see *Vita Sinuthii* 6; cf. Mark 1:21–28. On the multiplication of loaves, see *Vita Sinuthii* 27–28, 138–43; cf. Mark 6:30–44; 8:1–10; and parallels. On the miracle at the mill, see *Vita Sinuthii* 20; cf. Luke 5:1–11.

48. *Vita Sinuthii* 115–18 (Elijah and Elisha); 94 (Jeremiah); 95–97 (Ezekiel and the 12 prophets); 91–93 (David); 150 (Mary); 115–18 (John the Baptist); 22, 25, 30, 70, 115, 121, 154 (Jesus); 124 (the twelve apostles); 138 (Paul).

49. In the early sections of the *Vita Sinuthii*, Shenoute, as a young boy, receives Elijah's mantle from an angel (*Vita Sinuthii* 8), his life and intentions are described as being like those of Elijah (10), and Archbishop Cyril addresses him specifically as "our holy father, the new Elijah" (19).

50. Krawiec, *Shenoute and the Women*, 75.

51. Bell's intro. to *Besa*, trans. Bell, 6. Bell, writing before Emmel, "Shenoute's Literary Corpus," and Lubomierski, *Vita Sinuthii* and "Coptic Life of Shenoute," assumes Besa's authorship. On the author's use of historical evidence, see Emmel ("Shenoute's Literary Corpus," 13), who notes that "the Bohairic *Life of Shenoute* requires complete reevaluation in light of Shenoute's own writings."

52. The *Life's* account is in *Vita Sinuthii* 27–28.

53. On Shenoute's account, see Emmel, "Historical Circumstances"; Leipoldt, *Schenute von Atripe*, 166–75; B. Layton, "Social Structure," 27 n. 12, 33, 45.

54. The *Life of Shenoute* reports two separate journeys with Cyril to Constantinople to confront Nestorius (*Vita Sinuthii* 17–19, 128–30). One suspects that they both depend on Shenoute's participation in the Council of Ephesus in 431 CE. Bell, *Besa,* 97–98 n. 22; Leipoldt, *Schenute von Atripe*, 89–91.

55. For the account in *Vita Sinuthii,* see §§ 126–27, cf. § 88. On the account in Shenoute's own writings, see Emmel, "From the Other Side" and "Shenoute of Atripe." Emmel's discussion of the whole affair is fascinating. He argues convincingly that Gessius was in fact a crypto-pagan. See also Behlmer, "Historical Evidence"; Thissen, "Zur Begegnung von Christentum." It is worth noting that Shenoute's curse of Gessius recorded in *Vita Sinuthii* § 88, "His tongue shall be bound to the big toe of his foot in hell!" (trans. Bell, *Besa,* 68), is paralleled in Shenoute's *The Lord Thundered* (in *Oeuvres de Schenoudi*, ed. Amélineau, 1.379). Caroline Schroeder kindly pointed out this parallel to me.

56. *Vita Sinuthii* § 126; translation from Bell, *Besa,* 78.

57. Emmel, "From the Other Side," 104–5, and "Shenoute of Atripe," 168–69. The apparent claim in the earlier translation that Shenoute and his monks put their shoulders to the upper door to open it fell away when the negative was restored in the Coptic transcription (see Emmel, "Shenoute of Atripe," 196 n. 237).

58. *Vita Sinuthii* §§ 125 and 127; Bell, *Besa*, 78. For other accounts of monks' miraculous travel, see, for example, the case of Apa Bessarion in the alphabetical collection of the *Apoph. patr.*, Bessarion 2.

59. Krawiec, *Shenoute and the Women*, 74.

60. Krawiec (in ibid., 74–77), in a fascinating few pages on the *Life of Shenoute*, uncovers a hint of discord and argues that "while the *Life* lacks any account of beatings, or of any monk's death at Shenoute's hands, Besa's narrative world seems indifferent to a high level of violence as a source of sin and as a path to salvation" (76). Yet the story in question, that of a confessed murderer sent by Shenoute to confess his sin to the duke in Smin so as to be executed and saved, hardly sets the narrative world apart in terms of violence from that of many another Christian storyteller. No one reading the *Life* would suspect discord, beatings, or deaths at Shenoute's hands unless he had additional information.

61. *Vita Sinuthii* 98–107.

62. In the *Panegyric on Apollo,* ed. and trans. Kuhn, CSCO 395.4.18), he is referred to as "the perfect lawgiver and model of all virtue."

63. Emmel, "Shenoute's Literary Corpus," 799; B. Layton, "Social Structure," 27–28. For a history of the monastery, see Coquin and Martin, "Dayr Anba Shinudah."

64. *Vita Sinuthii* 102, 122, 154.

65. On the wilderness theme in the Bible, see Mauser, *Christ in the Wilderness*.

66. *Vita Sinuthii* 115–18.

67. Translation from Bell, *Besa,* 76.

68. See P. Miller, "Jerome's Centaur."

69. As P. Brown (*Cult of the Saints*, 81) noted, the hagiographer recorded "the moments when the seemingly extinct past and the unimaginably distant future had pressed into the present."

70. *Epistula Ammonis* 12; for a discussion, see Goehring's notes on the text in Ammon, *Letter of Ammon,* 230–32.

71. *Vit. Ant.* 68.

72. *Vita Sinuthii* 128–30. The story appears in the *Panegyric on Macarius* 12.8 (ed. and trans. Johnson), where Shenoute has an angel standing by his side strike Nestorius, sending him into torment for three hours.

73. *Vita Prima Graeca Pachomii* 31; Vivian, *St. Peter of Alexandria*, 5–6.

74. Goehring, "Monastic Diversity"; Rubenson, *Letters of St. Antony*, 38–39, 188; Cassian's silence with respect to these same figures, including Evagrius Ponticus, his single most important influence, while necessitated by the fierce anti-Origenism of the time, resulted in influential ascetical writings that reconstituted the ascetic past as free from Origenism. Stewart, *Cassian the Monk*, 11–12.

75. On Melitians' participation in the ascetic movement, see Bell, *Jews and Christians*; Kramer and Shelton, *Archiv des Nepheros*; Goehring, "Melitian Monastic Organization." On their living in communities with "orthodox monks," see *Trinity College Dublin Papyrus* D 5 and *SB* I 5174–75; Sayce, "Deux contrats grecs"; Krause, "Apa-Apollon-Kloster"; McGing, "Melitian Monks at Labla"; Goehring, "Monastic Diversity."

76. Evetts, *History of the Patriarchs*, 473–74.

77. The excavations and publications are ongoing. The results are being published in the Oxbow Monograph Series of Oxbow Books. The two published volumes most important for the present discussion are Gardner et al., *Coptic Documentary Texts,* and Bagnall, *Kellis Agricultural Account Book*.

78. Gardner and Lieu, "From Narmouthis."

79. On their dating, see Gardner et al., introduction to *Coptic Documentary Texts*, 73. The Manichaean material in general occurs in the context of contracts and coins dated between 301 and 390 CE (Gardiner and Lieu, "From Narmouthis," 161).

80. Ibid., 4–5; given the ongoing nature of the excavations and preliminary state of publication, conclusions drawn from the evidence are set forth cautiously.

81. Ibid., 75–80.

82. Ibid., 80; the uncertainty in assigning certain letters is noted on 72.

83. Ibid., 72–74.

84. Such evidence raises questions about many letters and documents. While scholars in general look for evidence of nonstandard Christian belief be-

fore assigning a text to that category, it seems clear that the lack of such evidence is insufficient in itself to assume that the text belongs to the mainstream.

85. Gardner et al., introduction to *Coptic Documentary Texts*, 73.

86. Bagnall, *Kellis Agricultural Account Book*, 84.

87. On the find context, see Hope, "Find Context."

88. Bagnall, *Kellis Agricultural Account Book*, 77; on the official position of the *pronoetai*, see Bagnall, *Egypt in Late Antiquity*, 152.

89. The precise nature of the topos Mani remains unclear. It should not, however, be understood as a monastery. Dubois, "Y a-t-il eu des moines."

90. Bagnall, *Kellis Agricultural Account Book*, 81–82; Gardner et al., introduction to *Coptic Documentary Texts*, 76; cf. Koenen, "Manichäische Mission."

91. Hope, "Find Context," 12–13; Bagnall, *Kellis Agricultural Account Book*, 81.

92. Bagnall, *Kellis Agricultural Account Book*, 84; cf. Gardner and Lieu, "From Narmouthis," 167.

93. Hope, "Find Context," 14; confirmed by Iain Gardner, e-mail, February 9, 2003.

94. Hope, "Find Context," 12–13. It may be that the presence of a common "enemy," namely the non-Christians, allowed the various flavors of Christianity to emphasize their shared elements rather than their differences.

95. In an e-mail of February 9, 2003, Iain Gardner wrote with respect to the oasis, "It is certainly my understanding from the evidence that 'Catholics' and 'Manichaeans' co-existed openly from the 350s onwards."

96. Gardner et al., introduction to *Coptic Documentary Texts*, 81–82; Gardner and Lieu, "From Narmouthis," 166–67. Elsewhere, Gardner theorizes that Manichaean success in the oasis occurred through the conversion of a largely pagan population, before the Catholic Church and its institutions gained a firm hold. Gardner, introduction to *Kellis Literary Texts*, xi, and "Manichaean Community at Kellis," 7–9.

97. Athanasius's assertion is in *Vit. Ant.* 68.

98. Goehring, "Monastic Diversity."

99. Ulrich, *Age of Homespun*, 7.

100. Ibid., 17 and 24.

101. On the reception of Shenoute's writings, see Stephen Emmel ("Shenoute's Literary Corpus," 39), who notes, "For knowledge of Shenoute's writings, we depend almost entirely on the manuscript tradition of his own monastery." For the remaining meager evidence of Shenoute's writings, see Emmel, "Shenoute's Literary Corpus," 12–13, 727–71. On the many versions of the *Life of Shenoute,* see Lubomierski, *Vita Sinuthii*, 8–113; Bell, *Besa,* 3–6.

102. For the *Letters*, see Rubenson, *Letters of St. Antony*, 15–34; for the *Life of Antony*, see Bartelink's intro. to Athanasius, *Vie d'Antoine*, 77–101.

103. It is intriguing to wonder about the relationship between an individual Egyptian ascetic's knowledge of the historical figure and his writings, and his embracing of the mythic saint. The dichotomy that our modern critical culture draws between history and myth surely does not apply.

104. On ascetic performance, see Valantasis, "Theory of the Social Function."

105. Muir, *Mountains of California*. For a fascinating study of social memory and the production of landscape, see Schama, *Landscape and Memory*; see also P. Miller, "Jerome's Centaur," 209–10.

106. McKibben, introduction to Muir, *Mountains of California*, xiii.

107. Ibid.

Chapter Eleven

Xeniteia According to Evagrius of Pontus

ROBIN DARLING YOUNG

The condition of being a *xenos* — a stranger — fascinated the authors of ascetic culture in the mid-fourth century. The novelty and experimental arrangements of monastic settlements outside and around cities and villages prompted anxious discussion of what kind of voluntary exile —*xeniteia*— was tolerable and what kind was controversial and intolerable. A few earlier Christians had used the term and had admired exemplary wanderers like Abraham, Paul, or Jesus; but monastic writers recording their new project had the more difficult task of distinguishing between good *xeniteia* and its menacing imitation. Ultimately, some came to abjure the footloose monks whom they labeled and forbade in the course of describing monastic life but to retain the practice of *xeniteia* metaphorically, replacing actual travel with an intellectual voyage for the journeying mind. I dedicate the following discussion of this process in one notable monastic to my friend and colleague, Philip Rousseau.

Uneasily at times, the ascetic culture of late fourth-century Egypt played host to a genuine stranger in the person of the cosmopolitan intellectual Evagrius of Pontus, now practitioner of the monastic life under the tutelage of local masters in the exurbs of Alexandria. Taking up residence in Nitria and then in Kellia, Evagrius learned the arts of the ascetic life from the great teachers there, among whom were Macarius the Great and Macarius the Egyptian. Yet at nearly forty, Evagrius came as one already trained at the highest level of the late ancient curriculum, and as an ascetic philosopher he would outstrip his previous teachers — Rufinus and Melania, Gregory Nazianzen, and Basil of Caesarea. Like them, he knew and loved the books of ancient philosophers and scientists; but his affinity for the works, and the thinking, of Clement of Alexandria and Origen drew his own thought closer to an earlier era, when the Christian sage could freely mingle traditional sources with Christian scriptural ones.

Evagrius was a notable *xenos* who left Neocaesarea for Constantinople, Constantinople for Jerusalem, and finally Jerusalem for the "desert" southwest of Alexandria, but like his teachers he interpreted Christian *xeniteia* as an internal stance rather than a geographic dislocation. His teachings on the topic often appear in scholarly treatments of monastic wandering or voluntary exile. This doxographical approach fundamental to the history of ideas, however, is not much help in describing the climate of thought among the men and women who wrote about *anachoresis*, withdrawal, and *xeniteia* in the ascetic life. No attention has yet been given to how Evagrius's views were formed by Clement of Alexandria, who addressed the subject in his own controversial interpretation of a rival gnostic's teachings. Evagrius evidently followed the lead of Clement in framing his own discussion of *xeniteia* by elevating it to a virtue — and placing it within the long tradition of stories of wandering, seen in both its temporal and its otherworldly meanings. As a philosopher Evagrius contributed little to the actual regulation of ungovernable monastics, but he did ensure that Clement's portrait of the gnostic and wise man would persist as a template for the elite, intellectual Christian ascetic. Through Evagrius, Clement's fusion of scriptural and Hellenic (Clement's own term) imagination reached into the ascetic life and survived among Evagrius's ascetic legatees.

XENOS AND *XENITEIA* IN CLEMENT

Antoine Guillaumont has already demonstrated Evagrius's acquaintance with the works of Clement of Alexandria, and a more thoroughgoing comparison would help account for why Evagrius seems as indebted to Clement as to Origen in many respects.[1] In specifically discussing *xeniteia*, though, Evagrius shares Clement's evident aim to convey esoteric teachings through pedagogical and exegetical works; as the leader of an esoteric group himself, one still prizing gnôsis, he may have found Clement's works to be a model for encoding a program of *paideia* in a language already enriched with Hellenic allusions and snippets of ancient authors given new meaning by the practice of allegorical exegesis. In addition, Evagrius may have had his own difficulties with dualist rivals, a situation that allowed him to see in Clement's work analogies to his own situation. Where Clement wrote against interpreters like Basilides and Valentinus, Evagrius may have written against the Egyptian disciples of Mani.[2]

It was in just such an encounter that debate concerning the meanings of *xenos* and *xeniteia* had already arisen among esoteric Christian teachers. In the late second century, Basilides' *Exegetica* spurred Clement to clarify numerous points of esoteric teaching for the philosophically inclined among his Christian students. In the discussion of one such point, the problem of *xeniteia* arose. Clement raised the term *xenos* in at least two places in his writing. In both of these passages, he seems to have intended to use it to wrest another and related term from his rival in Alexandria, something he consistently did in his teaching.

For Clement and Basilides, the term really at issue was not *xenos* per se but *eklogê*, "choice" or "election." Valentinus, Theodotus, and Basilides had all used the term to describe the "seed," that is, the spiritual ones whose natural destiny was beyond that of the rest of the human race, out of whom they had been chosen. Clement cited Basilides in particular as having interpreted election as a consequence of nature; whereas earlier Christian interpreters had asserted that God had shifted his choice of a people from Israel to the followers of Christ, Basilides and others, reflecting on Providence through a Platonist lens, interpreted election as a kind of intellective affinity for the divine. Basilides was himself interpreting Paul, who in Romans 9:11 and elsewhere discussed God's election of Israel and expanded its meaning. Basilides may have known Logion 23 of the *Gospel of Thomas*, which quotes Jesus as saying, "I shall choose you, one out of a thousand and two out of ten thousand, and they shall stand as a single one." Basilides may not have understood these passages to signify a kind of natural determinism, but he was interpreted by Clement as having said so.

According to Clement, then, Basilides taught that election results not from faith, "the rational assent of a soul possessing free will," but from "nature and substance," a definition making "the commandments of both the old and the new covenants . . . superfluous."[3] Clement himself held a restricted notion of election, but he expressed it in two lengthy passages in which he proposed that *eklogê* depended upon choice. Thus he disputed Basilides, while retaining his approach in acknowledging two levels of election:

> All the faithful, then, are good and godlike, and worthy of the name by which they are encircled as with a diadem. There are, besides, some, the more elect of the elect, and so much more or less distinguished by *hauling themselves to safety, like ships onto the sand, out of the surf of the kosmos*; not wishing to seem holy, and ashamed if one call them so; hiding in the depth of their mind the unutterable mysteries, and disdaining to let their nobility [*eugenian*] be seen in the world; whom the Word calls "the light of the world" and "the salt of the earth" (Mt 5:13–14). This is the seed, the image and likeness of God, and his legitimate child and heir, sent as it were on some *xeniteia*, by the great economy and proportion of the Father, by whom the visible and invisible things of the world were created; some for their service, some for their discipline, some for their instruction; and all things are held together so long as the seed remains here; and when it is gathered, these things shall be quickly dissolved.[4]

Clement, in other words, understands the truly "elect seed" as the gnostics, for whom the visible world exists, and thinks that the visible world will cease to exist when the gnostic elect ones are gathered back out of it. Their *xeniteia* is an ocean voyage that ends with their homecoming — an image that Evagrius will in turn find useful, along with the assignment of *xeniteia* to the "more elect of the elect."

Clement disputes the views of Basilides from another angle in his *Stromateis* and in a much longer passage feels it necessary to defend the body as an organ of intellection and therefore as a means used by the gnostic to teach others among the elect. The elect are similar enough in body and soul to "stand as a single one" and thus it is possible for those in the lower ranks to advance to the upper; but the gnostic, as the preeminent example of the elect, is in the world as a stranger and considers the body to be inferior to the soul, even though the body is the soul's abode, temporarily. Clement writes, "The soul of the wise man and gnostic, as being in voluntary exile in the body [*epixenoumenê*], conducts itself toward it gravely and respectfully, not with inordinate affections, as about to leave the tabernacle if the time of departure summon."[5] He cites Genesis 23:4 and Psalm 39:12, already part of the Christian interpretive tradition relating to Christ: "I am a stranger in the earth, and a voluntary exile with you." Indeed, the soul does come down from heaven, but this descent is not a catastrophe — the soul has a choice, and "he who is in a state of knowledge, being assimilated as far as possible to God, is already spiritual, and so elect," and thus can choose to exchange "earth for heaven."[6]

In two places in this long interpretive argument with Basilides, Clement makes observations about *xeniteia* that will appear as the field of interpretation through which Evagrius understands his own, later version of the term. The first place is in the middle of a passage in which Clement cites Basilides in order to engage him in disputation:

> Basilides says that he apprehends that [those of] the [divine] election [*eklogê*] are strangers to the world, being supramundane by nature. But it is not like this — for all things are of one God. And no one is a stranger [*xenos*] to the world by nature, their essence being one, and God one. But the elect man dwells as a voluntary exile, knowing all things to be possessed and disposed of. . . . The body, too, as one sent on a distant pilgrimage, uses inns and dwellings by the way, having care of the things of the world, of the places where he halts; but leaving his dwelling-place and property without excessive emotion; readily following him that leads him away from life; by no means and on no occasion turning back; giving thanks for his sojourn, and blessing for his departure, embracing the mansion that is in heaven.[7]

Finally, at the very end of the fourth book of the *Stromateis,* and at the end of his discussion of *xeniteia,* Clement once more constructs, with selections from scriptural and philosophical authors, a composite image of the gnostic, proposing that the gnostic is not only an imitator of God but a likeness of God for others to behold. Just as the prophet Isaiah knew that the gnostic could be seen in his works (62:11), so did the poets "call the elect godlike and gods, and equal to the gods, and equal in sagacity to Zeus." Euripides, Clement writes, anticipated the elect's flight to heaven in saying, "I shall go aloft into the wide ether, to hold converse with Zeus," but, says Clement, "I shall pray the Spirit of Christ to wing me to my Jerusalem. For the Stoics say that heaven is properly a city. . . . And we know Plato's city placed as a pattern in heaven."[8]

Evagrius may already have had Clement's understanding of election and *xeniteia* in mind when he undertook his own writings about the gnostic ascetic, or he may have turned to Clement as an aid to interpretation when he went to Nitria and heard of *xeniteia* as a monastic pattern. In either case, as we shall see, he could draw on Clement both to interpret *xeniteia* as a practice and to use actual *xeniteia* as an allegory for the intellectual journey whose goal was noetic *endêmia*— a homecoming after a long voyage at sea. In this way he too fused gnostic ideas with an allegorical interpretation of ancient sources including epic to provide a way of thinking about the untrammeled *xeniteia* already troubling the communities of Egypt when he arrived.

XENITEIA AS A PROBLEM FOR SCHOLARS

Discussions of *xeniteia* in fourth-century monastic literature usually cite the first-century texts collected in the New Testament as the beginning of the Christian use of the term. The recent treatment of its use began with Campenhausen, who was disputing the early twentieth-century claims of Wilhelm Bousset and Richard Reitzenstein to have found the origins of monasticism in, respectively, philosophical movements and mystery religions.[9] In the view of Campenhausen, the term originated, not in groups external to earliest Christianity, but in the Bible itself. He distinguished a "figurative" state of exile described in 2 Corinthians 5:6 from literally "living and existing in an alien land, as an alien [*xenos*] . . . leaving one's own land," as the traveling teachers of the first century did; and he argued that the practice of literal *xeniteia* was a later, less legitimate development that was somehow passed down as a form of Christian life from the first century to ascetics in the third and fourth centuries.[10] Unfortunately, in Campenhausen's view, fourth-century Christian ascetics had perverted Paul and the early apostles' understanding of *xeniteia*: "For there is only one genuine way of absolute abandonment of self, which is the direct personal service of others, and this way cannot be found by one who flees to a strange land and to the desert. Like any other ascetic ideal, that of abandonment of country has its nobility, but, fundamentally, it is a demonic and despairing distortion of the Christian reality."[11] The difficulty with the subsequent scholarly discussion of *xeniteia* is that it tends to assume that the term has a genealogy, in which usage passes down from one author to another in a kind of evolutionary inheritance, and — along with other theological terms — becomes singularly and exclusively Christian once it has found a place in Christian theological discussion. Gerhart Ladner is an apposite example, even though he takes a more neutral stance than Campenhausen and is more inclined to see *xeniteia* as a phenomenon continuous over time; he writes that "the topoi of *xeniteia* and peregrination, of pilgrimage, of homelessness, of strangeness in this world, are among the most widespread in early Christian ascetic literature, and not a few ascetics, monastic and otherwise, practiced it by voluntary and migratory exile from their fatherland."[12] Thus scholars have often assumed a direct inheritance from scriptural terminology to the ascetic literature beginning with the *Life of Antony*.[13]

More recently scholars have taken a historicist approach to the term, arguing that its meaning arises from a particular context. Philip Rousseau wrote in 1978 that when ascetics moved into the Egyptian hinterlands there was "a shift in the meaning of xeniteia, exile, or pilgrimage." Although the word among ascetics "implied withdrawal from society, and from family ties," it came to mean — ironically — stability and was "combined with an emphasis on the inner life." It became a cessation from restlessness and an adoption of privacy, introspection, and even community life.[14]

Daniel Caner, though interpreting monastic *anachoresis* and *xeniteia* in their social context, followed Campenhausen and Ladner: "The term," he wrote of *xeniteia*, "originated from scriptural references to Christians as 'strangers and travelers on earth' (e.g. Hebrews 11:13, 1 Peter 2:11).... Antony himself wrote that Abraham's departure (Gen 12:1) from home and family 'is the model for the beginning of this way of life.... Wherever and whenever souls endure and bow to it, they easily attain the virtues, since their hearts are ready to be guided by the Spirit of God.'"[15] Caner also proposed that the rapid transformation of *xeniteia* to a mental or spiritual state in the late fourth century was the result of restrictions on personal mobility during this period, a reflection of the anxieties of the late empire. The spiritualization of *xeniteia* was a solution to this problem:

> Xeniteia was the term that became used for the voluntary alienation by which ascetics sought release from material and social circumstances that might hinder their ability to trust in God and make spiritual progress thereby. Christians had traditionally achieved *xeniteia* in Egypt by withdrawing to the confines of their homes or to the outskirts of their villages. Over time, however, increasing numbers sought a more dramatic fulfillment by relocating, like Antony, to the stark otherworld of the desert. Here, beyond the sights and sounds of the world, it was believed a monk might find spiritual stillness or tranquility (*hesychia*).[16]

Caner describes Evagrius's views on *xeniteia* as responses to contemporary stories and debates about an earlier generation of wandering monks who lived in remote deserts and confronted extraordinary perils and privations. For instance, he cites Evagrius's opposition to *xeniteia* in the *Antirrhetikos*:[17] "Against the vain thought that persuades us to extend our discipline beyond what is appropriate by putting sackcloth on our loins, setting out for the desert, living continuously under the sky, and tending wild plants; and that advises us as well to flee from the sight of human beings who comfort us and who are comforted by us: Do not be very righteous or especially wise, lest you be deceived (Eccl 7:16)."[18] Yet by *xeniteia* Evagrius does not primarily mean "wandering." Sinkewicz has translated the word as "voluntary exile" when it is used in a positive sense and as "exile" when it seems to be negative, as in *[To Eulogius] On the Vices as Opposed to the Virtues:* "Sadness [*lupê*] is one who dwells over loss, who is familiar with frustrated acquisition, a forerunner of exile, remembrance of family."[19] Overall, though, Evagrius more often uses the term in a positive sense.

It is more judicious not to assume that Evagrius's works are examples of some broader meaning of the term *xeniteia* in use across a wide variety of monastic literature. In particular, as the historiography of ancient monasticism has developed, a kind of general definition of *xeniteia* has formed. According to this discussion, *xeniteia*, with its origins in the first- and second-century reflections on Christ as *xenos* or the *xeniteia* of Abraham, means "voluntary exile"— the uprooting and resettlement outside one's own country as a response to a divine order.

Xeniteia undertaken in the later monastic movement then necessitates travel, but travel stands in opposition to the need for stability, which itself also resists the custom of pilgrimage, now eagerly undertaken by many toward the end of the century. As Brouria Bitton-Ashkelony observes, citing Evagrius's *Letter* 25, Evagrius's place in the "debate on Christian pilgrimage" belongs to those who "internalize" pilgrimage to the holy places, making actual departure unnecessary.[20] In John McGuckin's treatment, though, Evagrius "does not make monastic stability synonymous with xeniteia."[21] Neither does the term, for Evagrius, mean "pilgrimage," "exile," or "alienation." It is, rather, "the spiritual allegorization of the exilic journey" and means, in a positive sense, "living in the condition of being foreign or alien among one's neighbors." *Xeniteia* is "largely rhetorical in its origins," not biblical, and it has been brought into the descriptions of the education of the Christian sage from neo-Stoic "detachment-theory" attributed to Democritus the Philosopher.

Like his teacher Gregory, Evagrius, according to McGuckin, was "a consummate philosopher and rhetorician," and *xeniteia* in his writings is not to be taken literally; rather, it is a metaphor for "the process of a philosopher-theologian who moves toward a more purified and thus more potent form of discourse." Again, like Gregory, Evagrius used *xeniteia* to make "claims to authoritative discourse."

McGuckin has grasped an important aspect of Evagrius's purpose in composing monastic discourses — Evagrius's description of the practice of *xeniteia* means to represent the sage as a voice guiding the movement of the intellect to its destination of *hesychia*, or stillness. Although this description can and does enlist scriptural images, it does not begin in the

Christian sacred text — it begins in a rhetorical practice that requires the alternation of speech and silence.

Finally, although Evagrius has been enlisted in numerous scholarly treatments of *xeniteia*, it has to be asked whether his remarks on the topic have much to do at all with the matter for debate in monastic literature of the fourth century. We have seen that Evagrius draws on a much earlier and premonastic writer, Clement, for a discussion of *xeniteia* that proposes authentic gnostic and esoteric readings of scripture. Practical considerations of whether the practice of self-exile was in conformity with scripture were far from Evagrius's business. But then what was his business in taking up the term? I suggest below that his interest in *xeniteia* was usually not a way of engaging in the lengthy debates about a practice that was controversial at the time. Instead, it provided him with a way to imagine himself and his readers in continuity with a certain kind of Christian gnostic, which allowed the further possibility of imagining ascetics as undertaking the voyages of epic poetry, the primary myth for all educated persons in the late ancient world, Christian or not. If Odysseus was a man of travel, so was the monastic *xenos*.

This rhetorical practice, in which Evagrius had been schooled by, among others, his beloved teacher Gregory, was itself an appropriation of certain aspects of the education of the *grammatikos* and the *didaskalos*. In the case of *xeniteia*, the allegorization of the term made possible its enrichment with much older meaning — specifically, the ancient sense of *xenos* as "guest-friend" and *xeniteia* as the state of being such a person, released from social obligation by a very old social obligation itself — and protected as such by the divinity. Since, as we saw earlier, Evagrius made room for the wisdom of "outsiders," it is no surprise to encounter him enlisting Odysseus as an example of *xeniteia* — and it is even less surprising to note that he does so only allusively, and only in a treatise directed to a friend and advanced student, Eulogius.

However *xenos* might have been applied to Christ, the term appears first in Jewish Greek literature — in particular, in the Septuagint at Wisdom 18.3, in Aristeas, in Philo, and in Josephus.[22] These uses suggest that Jewish authors adopted the term in connection with emigration and diaspora, constructing it from a verb *xeniteuô*, itself connoting the verbal form of *xenos*, that is, "to be a stranger." Whereas the last two words are ancient in Greek literature, and will be discussed below, *xeniteia* appears in works of the Hellenistic period and later.

The influence of the Septuagint and other Jewish authors may well have provided the context for the earliest Christian use of the term, in which Christians had taken over a specifically Jewish word for exile and in an allegorical reading had transferred its meaning to a spiritual, pre-eschatological state. For Hellenistic Jews, Judaea was home, and other lands were lands of *xeniteia*; for Christians, the kingdom of God was home, and this earth was a land of *xeniteia*.

Yet with the development of distinctively Christian exegesis, thanks to which the Christian sacred text could be interpreted alongside other sacred texts and with the instruments of grammatical and rhetorical interpretation, it seems possible that *xeniteia* could take on an added, older significance — a significance that would reflect pagan literature and its philosophical interpretation. It was here that Clement of Alexandria became a good example for a practice that Evagrius would later adopt, of regarding certain hallowed pagan authors as sources for revelation — or, if not to the extent that Clement thought, at least to the extent that would allow them to illustrate and influence the significance of specifically Christian texts. Thus Clement's view of Homer as a sage and a privileged source of wisdom about the soul and about God could well have allowed him, or others of his students, to link words in scriptural texts with the same or similar words in respected pagan texts.

Those commentators might have looked back through the Christian and Hellenistic Jewish term *xeniteia* and recognized in it the state in which Odysseus dwelt through his long wanderings as described in the *Odyssey*. Here they would have had the benefit, not only of the figure of Odysseus as an ancient moral and philosophical example, but of Platonic and Stoic interpretations that justified and made him available as a parallel sage.

Such a reading, available in schools attended by both Christians and pagans, is likely to have been responsible for a second appropriation of Homer among Christian writers in the mid-fourth century. The two most obvious examples of such an appropriation are Basil of Caesarea and Gregory Nazianzen, each of whom recommends and uses Homer differently. There is no reason to think that the learned monks of Nitria and

Kellia, themselves alumni of the late ancient school curriculum, would have known the figure of the stranger, or the state of wayfaring, only from their Christian scriptures. With minds furnished early in boyhood by the epic of Homer and the journey of Odysseus, it seems reasonable to conjecture that they hardly stopped thinking respectfully of the hero when they began their lives of askesis.

It might have been much easier for these monks — Evagrius's teachers and his later students alike — to have returned to Homer as a source for Christian speculation once Porphyry, in *On the Cave of the Nymphs*, had come to refer to Homer as "the theologian."[23] He did this thanks to a "Neoplatonic hermeneutic program" that allowed him, in his *On the Cave of the Nymphs*, to understand a particular passage of Homer's epic as part of "a poem about the fate of souls . . . [and] the progress of one single soul through the realm of matter (genesis), the sublunary realm of coming to be and passing away."[24] In section 79 of the essay, Porphyry interprets the passage as follows: "Homer says that all outward possessions must be deposited in this cave and that one must be stripped naked and take on the attire of a beggar and, having withered the body away and cast aside all that is superfluous and turned away from the senses, take counsel with Athena, sitting with her beneath the olive, to learn how he might cut away all the destructive passions of his soul." According to Robert Lamberton, Porphyry understands himself to be continuing the philosophy of Numenius in understanding the *Odyssey* as "a poem about the fate of souls." For Porphyry, Lamberton writes, it relates the story of a single man who also symbolizes all people in that he is "passing through the successive stages of genesis and so being restored to his place among those beyond all wavecrash and 'ignorant of the sea,' i.e. the material universe."[25]

If allegories of Homer, present in Porphyry at the beginning of the fourth century, and in Proclus at the end of the fifth, were "proliferating all over the intellectual life of the Roman empire," then it is possible to think of Evagrius and his company as reading the Christian ascetic philosophical journey and Odysseus's journey in a similar fashion.[26] As Porphyry writes, "When one takes into consideration the ancient wisdom and the vast intelligence of Homer, along with his perfection in every virtue, one cannot reject the idea that he has hinted at images of more divine things in molding his little story."[27]

XENITEIA AS AN EVAGRIAN WORD OF ART

Evagrius frequently uses the term *xeniteia* or synonyms for the state of being away, temporarily or permanently, from one's native land. Indeed, the first of his letters, and the only one preserved completely in Greek, presents itself as a rationale for his departure from a community for a foreign destination in order to gain further teaching from Gregory.[28] Two treatises contain the longest discussions of the term and practice; and it appears scattered elsewhere in his kephalaia and letters.

In *Foundations of the Monastic Life*, a work of basic instruction for the monk just learning the *praktikê*, Evagrius recommends initial rules: ways of handling money and property, as well as the customary human relationships that would either impede or promote stability in the beginner. Then (in section 6), he cautiously raises the possibility of *xeniteia* and devotes a long paragraph to it. In a carefully structured section, he details a state of traveling that simultaneously requires serious reflection and uses the Stoic language of *prothesis* to denote the beginning of a movement toward *xeniteia*: "If you are unable to cultivate stillness [*hesychia*] with ease in your regions, direct your purpose toward *xeniteia* and apply your thinking to this with diligence. Be like a very good businessman, evaluating everything with regard to the cultivation of stillness and always retaining those things that are peaceful and useful in this regard (*cf.* 1 Thess 5:21)." Note that here *xeniteia* has two aspects: the direction of purpose and the application of thinking — it is at the same time a movement and a state of the soul and mind (*nous*). To the latter belongs the admonition to be a "very good businessman," with the implication that the monk trades what is necessary for *hesychia*.

Evagrius takes his admonition further, however, when he continues: "Indeed, I tell you, love *xeniteia*, for it separates you from the circumstances of your own country and allows you to enjoy the unique benefit of practicing stillness" (§ 6). *Xeniteia*, then, is a positive therapy, even a medicine for those afflicted with an imbalance of affection toward their own region and, possibly, for their families.

The rest of the passage in *Foundations* gives details about the balancing act that follows upon this decision. It urges the monk to "avoid stays in the city, persevere with your stay in the desert," thereby following the example of "the holy one," that is, David in the Psalms, and adds, "Do not enter a city at all, for you will behold there nothing of value, nothing useful, nothing beneficial to your way of life." Evagrius concludes, "Therefore, go after places that are secluded and free from distractions" (§ 6).

Yet evidently nowhere fits this description. Completely abjuring the city in pursuit of quiet is an invitation to opposing forces: the demons and the *logismoi*, or twisted reasonings, that they induce in the mind.[29] Evagrius writes: "Do not be afraid of the noises there. If you see there fantasies of demons, do not be scared and do not flee the stadium of our profit. Endure patiently without fear and you will see the marvels of God, the assistance, the solicitude, and every other assurance of salvation" (§ 6).[30]

Indeed, Evagrius's prose reflects the balancing act that he thought *xeniteia* in the desert required. Fear and discouragement need the remedies of scriptural quotations (and their interpretations) that Evagrius cites, and David is the source of these remedies: "For the blessed man says: 'I waited for the one who saves me from discouragement and the tempest' (Ps 54:9)" (§ 6). When the innocent mind is in a state of discouragement, the "desire for roving" may strike and may pervert it. Evagrius ends the section by stating: "On this account temptations are many. Fear for a fall and be steadfast in your cell."

Although Evagrius has named not Odysseus but David, the pattern of the siren-beset sailor still provides the underlying structure for this section. The Psalms may provide remedies for the fear that must be driven away by the monk pursuing *xeniteia*, but the overall picture of the wayfaring monk owes more to the sailor than to the Psalmist. For the discussion of *xeniteia* follows sections on how the cultivation of stillness may be imperiled by a variety of tempting distractions: possessions and the care of them (including "a serving-boy," who should not be acquired "lest the adversary provoke a scandal against you through him and trouble your thoughts with concerns over expensive foods"[§ 5]); by relationships and the concerns of communities of men who are "material-minded" (§ 5); by family concerns; by life in cities, where conflicts predominate; and by the pleasures of the table. In this section, there seem to be no literary allusions and only one reference to a philosophical term beyond the standard virtues listed. References to biblical texts abound here, as they do in the entire treatise; they constitute both a moral form of interpretation and, in some cases, a strongly literal interpretation.

The lack of literary and philosophical references in *Foundations* suggests that *xeniteia* is important but that Evagrius has decided not to disclose its origins in non-Christian philosophy. Neither does he make the life of Jesus as *xenos* an example for the requisite *xeniteia* of the monk. Although *xeniteia* was an established teaching received from his teachers, Evagrius saw its deeper interpretation as meant only for an advanced monastic student: only such a student could properly catch allusions to Odysseus, who longed for home but had to remain a *xenos* until his trials were completed and his dangers vanquished.

In *To Eulogios: On the Confession of Thoughts and Counsel in Their Regard*, Evagrius's discussion of *xeniteia* is more explicit. Eulogius is no beginner, as *Foundations* envisioned its reader, but a "mystic initiate in the virtues." "You can strip off the weight of the flesh by collecting your thoughts," Evagrius tells him, "for you know that the matter of the flesh constitutes the nourishment of thoughts." Evagrius addresses him first on the subject of *xeniteia* but expresses some trepidation in venturing to advise such an advanced practitioner, and in doing so casts himself as a kind of Odysseus: "If it were not foolhardy to break an injunction of charity, I would refuse to sail on this voyage." Writing on the subject is perilous, Evagrius says, but silence about it would be worse. There follows, in this longest of ascetic treatises, a discussion of the vices and virtues that Eulogius should know of.

In the first line of the treatise, Evagrius implies that Eulogius is of those who "hold the land of heaven as their own by ascetic labors." These labors, then, will propel mystic initiates back toward their homeland. Indeed, "homecoming," another mark of the Homeric epic, is a strong theme throughout *To Eulogius* and, as it turns out, a constant theme in the ascetic works of Evagrius generally.

> The first of the illustrious contests is *xeniteia*, especially when to this end one should go abroad alone, like an athlete stripped of homeland, family, and possessions. For if in this way someone should find himself engaged in the most demanding competitions, preserving this *xeniteia* safe and sound by the goal of perseverance, with the gilded wing of virtue he will take flight from his own familiar haunts and make haste to fly away towards heaven itself (*cf.* Ps 54:7). But the author of evil contrives to cut off the wings of this way of life and attempts to cast it down by

> means of various contrivances, and in the beginning he restrains it for a little while until he observes the soul overcome by seasickness at his afflictions; then the dark owl brings on the night of thoughts and casts darkness upon the soul by robbing it of the ray of the superior goods.

It is a consistent observation in Evagrius that the *psychagogia* of the monk, his or her progress toward the goal of the illumination possessed by the gnostic, is also a kind of warfare or athletic contest; the devil, or demons, or their instruments the *logismoi*, troublesome thoughts, are the opponents. So in the passage just quoted, "competitions" already signals that the "gilded wing of virtue" is endangered. The boat in which the "mystic initiate" such as Eulogius sails is also thus a bird with wings, where wings often can stand for the sails of a ship. Here is the signal that the Phaedrus (246c) is being invoked as the interpretive filter for the *Odyssey*— the hero's return home is at the same time the shedding of the flesh in the promotion of illumination.

Yet the soul, having regained its wings, is faced in its return to heaven by Satan, who ranges "various engines of war [*mechanais*]" against it. This "nausea" caused by such afflictions can also be translated as "seasickness," a word that preserves the double imagery of wings and sails — and once seasick, the soul encounters its enemy, a raptor, the *nyktikorax*.

The darkness that the nocturnal raptor casts over the soul brings up the opportunity for the devil to display his own rhetorical skill. Recall that Eulogius is a "mystic initiate," so that he is hearing advice given to one who has already made significant progress. Nonetheless, the technique brought forward plays upon memory and nostalgia:

> But if all alone one should stand ready in the wrestling school of the desert and if the body should in some way happen to be impaired by illness, then does the devil present *xeniteia* to the soul as especially difficult, suggesting that the tasks of virtue can be formed not in a particular place but by a manner of life, and that at home with the consolation of family it could attain the prizes of freedom from possessions with less weariness; there it would have a pleasant service for its weakness and not misery and painful despondency as it now has, because the zeal for hospitality is especially lacking in the brotherhood. Therefore, he quickly says, "Go away, carry yourself off, you who are the joy and glory of

your family!—to those you have without compassion left behind an unbearable sorrow, for most people have lighted upon the virtues in the midst of their family, without having fled their homeland."

Throughout his letters and treatises, and perhaps most notoriously where he is quoted in his biography in the *Lausiac History,* Evagrius inveighs against family and ties to family as the enemy of the project of the ascetic. His harsh (and possibly legendary) response to the news of his father's death was "Stop blaspheming, for my father is immortal!"[31] Thus it is consistent that he makes the devil the advocate for a return home by presenting a reasonable opinion—it is not the topos, but the tropos, that provides the appropriate place for a virtuous life. Furthermore, "the brotherhood" does not extend "hospitality" to *xeniteia*—a passage that recalls the ancient connection between the status of a stranger-guest and the obligatory hospitality on the part of one who receives the stranger.

In the next paragraph, in keeping with the motif of voyaging, the speech by the devil here is glancingly alluded to as a storm at sea:

> But he who is clothed in the purple of afflictions, that is, in perseverance, in the battle line of *xeniteia*, and is surrounded with faith in regard to hopes in ascetic labours, will with unceasing thanksgiving shake off the raindrops of these thoughts from his inner self; and, the more they should compel the heart to turn back, all the more shall we still flee and chant against them: "Behold, I have fled far away, and taken lodging in the desert; I waited for God, who saves me from faintheartedness and tempest" (Ps 54:8). For the thoughts bring on temptations, they coax [the heart] into turning back and they afflict it with reproaches so as to drain it of its resolution and to cut it off from its perseverance in thanksgiving; and so they then set their "snares" abroad with complete freedom beyond what is seemly.

By referring to the "battle line" of *xeniteia,* Evagrius wants Eulogius to think of a later meaning of the term *xeniteuô*, "to serve as a mercenary in an army." The wanderer who has renounced his citizenship here enters military service, in which his purple (imperial) clothing signifies leadership, and the imagery of the sea quickly gives way to that of the desert because that is the setting of Psalm 54. The turbulent setting of

Psalm 91 also stands behind this passage, where the "fowler" is already interpreted as the one who sets snares for Christ and the latter stands for the imperiled monk.

Several other passages in Evagrius's writings describe *xeniteia,* though they are not always marked by the term itself. One occurs again in *Eulogius*, where the topic is the *praktikê*:

> He who through his experience makes known the error of the thoughts will not be recognized by all, except for those with experience, for experience constitutes the path towards the gnostic life at this stage. The ground for both of them is the practical life; and if we lay hold of this with greater ascetic effort, we will come to know ourselves, we will pass judgement on thoughts and we will come to know God. As for the person experienced in the emigration of the practical life and the homecoming of the gnostic life (2 Cor 5:8–9), who anoints the simple with the skill of the thoughts — let him watch out, let him not boast about the gnostic life to make a show for his own glory. But if a thought steals in to exalt him, let him take for his assistance the newcomer Jethro who gave to Moses, the great prophet, a wise counsel and discerning judgement inspired by grace (Ex 18:13–27).

Here as elsewhere in the writings of Evagrius, *apodêmia* and *endêmia* describe the Odyssean journey as the course of the intellect. The sage does not name Homer as the source of meaning of the term *xeniteia*, but Eulogius would certainly have recognized Evagrius's adoption of Homeric vocabulary and his evocation of the homeless but homebound soldier. And for Evagrius, the return to "essential knowledge," those "natural seeds" shared with philosophers from "outside," is like the movement of a river into the sea: "When minds flow back into [God] like torrents into the sea, he changes them all completely into his nature, color and taste. They will no longer be many but one in his unending and inseparable unity, because they are united and joined with him. And as in the fusion of rivers with the sea no addition in its return or variation in its color or taste is to be found, so also in the fusion of minds with the Father no duality of natures or quaternity of persons comes about" (*Ad Melaniam* 6). Perhaps Evagrius's conception of the ocean as the unity of being suggested to him his extensive and frequent use of the figure of Odysseus upon the ocean to describe the monk traveling from the state of *praktikê* to that of the gnostic *theôria*; he does not say.

Evagrius has also invoked Odysseus's journey, and Homeric nautical voyages more generally, as a model for the storm-filled voyage of monastic life. Perhaps he knew of the terrifying storm at sea that made Gregory Nazianzen dedicate his life to Christ, either because he read about it in Gregory's writings or because Gregory told Evagrius the story. In any case, Gregory's student uses the image of the "storm at sea" as a parallel to that of the battle in the desert and regularly alternates the two.

So, for instance, in his treatise *On the Eight Thoughts*, Evagrius uses the storm at sea to describe the mental turbulence of an unbalanced mind. In the section on *porneia*, fornication, we read that "the force of the waves batters a ship without ballast in a storm; the thought of fornication will act similarly on the intemperate mind" (2.3). The section also draws on this imagery in its extended descriptions of male-female encounters that threaten to become consummated sexually:

> 13. A ship caught in a storm hastens toward a harbour; a chaste soul seeks solitude. The former flees the waves of the sea that threaten danger, while the latter flees the forms of women which give birth to ruin.
>
> 14. A prettily adorned form overwhelms worse than a wave, for it is possible to plunge through the latter out of desire for life, but the deceitful form of a woman persuades one to disregard life itself.

Further, in the following section, on avarice, a series of three instructions likens "a monk with many possessions" to a ship carrying too much cargo that "easily sinks in a storm at sea. Just as a very leaky ship is submerged by each wave, so the person with many possessions is awash in his own concerns." It is interesting that Evagrius follows this with the observation that "the monk free of possessions is a well-prepared traveler who finds shelter in any place" (3.3–4). Anger is another vice whose dangers are portrayed by images of storm and shipwreck:

> If someone abstains from food and drink but rouses his irascible part to anger by means of evil thoughts, he is like a ship sailing the high seas with a demon for a pilot (*Thoughts* 13).

Like a strong south wind on the sea, so irascibility in a person's heart. (*Monks* 36)

Finally, demons may cast solitary monks into "inconsolable sorrow," then predict to them in dreams "the shipwrecks of the monastic life, throwing down from high ladders those who are ascending" (*Thoughts* 3).

Occasionally, Evagrius makes a comparison between the monastic desert and the sea:

> 23. Just as a wilderness area is brought under cultivation with diligent dedication to work, so a soul that has gone wild in its sins can be tamed if it shall conduct itself by the law of God.
>
> 24. Just as a rock in the sea stays fixed and unshaken even when buffeted by waves, so too the person accomplished in the virtues and utterly caught up in them cannot be buffeted by the devil.

In all these *kephalaia*, the common feature is a stormy sea; various features may represent the stability that protects an ascetic. Like Odysseus, the ascetic sets out in order to go home — overcoming the distance created by the separation of rational beings from the divine Monad that occurred before his birth and undergoing both warfare and a journey by sea while living in the desert. To portray this voyage Evagrius has recourse to images that evoke the common experiences of the similarly voyaging monastics to whom he writes. And he additionally recalls another storm at sea — the sea of Galilee (Mark 4:35–40).

The letters of Evagrius build on, and include, his interpretation of his life in the "desert" as a Homeric journey over the sea. They do this somewhat differently, however, than his treatises do. If in his treatises Evagrius addresses a general readership about the problem of remaining steady in the monastery and the importance of pursuing a course from the *praktikê* to the *theoretikê*, in his letters he speaks to one particular ascetic alone.

One of Evagrius's eight letters extensively employs the image of a ship in a storm at sea. *Letter* 6 is one of the few letters that has been translated into any modern language.[32] There is no indication in the manuscripts of the letter's addressee, but internal indications point to John of Jerusalem, bishop of Jerusalem from 387 to 417.

The salutation of the letter signals Evagrius's troubles. "Without knowledge," he begins, "we passed by your holiness when we came to Palestine before, and we could not receive the provisions of salvation for the road placed before us." He compares himself to the sterile field in the parable of the sower: "Perhaps we were off the path and seized by a bird," where the bird is a demon, most probably. "Or we were a rock, and caused to dessicate the sprouting plant. Or we were full of thorns and the Word in us was choked." Underlying his evocative reenactment of the parable is a gnostic interpretation in which, ironically, he portrays himself as a nongnostic.

The body of the letter, though, is an illustration of the troubled state in which Evagrius finds himself, and which he uses to exemplify difficulties in the monastic life. He illustrates the problem by means of a storm at sea — except this storm becomes one in which there is a further turbulence, this one raised by an ancient monster, the dragon in the narrative of Bel and the Dragon. Evagrius has here combined the story in Matthew of the calming of the storm with an image from the Septuagint Isaiah to portray himself not as the passenger of the ship but as the ship itself — the ship that is menaced by Satan but should be steered by Christ.

Evagrius writes:

> I ask you to forgive me this sin, and pray about the rest of my transgressions. For we go forth on a sea full of winds and waterspouts, and I fear the danger as we fight on our way toward faith, knowledge and righteousness. In these matters, our Lord lies sleeping within us, and our mind, which is able to hold him through the virtues, is not awake. The fugitive dragon is lifted high above us — sometimes he entices with his tail, and other times he bites with his mouth. . . .
>
> Who will be a Daniel, and who will receive help from the holy Gabriel? For when Daniel made a band of pitch and hair and fat, he ripped the dragon apart (Bel and the Dragon 27). I myself am unable, for I am guilty of the temptations [presented to Christ]. I have entrusted the whole ship to the shipmaster, since our trust is not in ourselves, but in God, because he rebukes the wind and commands the sea, and carries those who are on the ship to the land by his will, so that we gaze upon him. (*Letter* 6, 2–3)

Here, in a letter whose recipient is known only as "a friend," Evagrius, in his portrayal of temptation, imagines himself both as a ship in a tempest and as the prophet Daniel in combat with the dragon. In doing so, he mingles Homeric allusions and biblical imagery to enrich his self-portrait as a wayfarer.

A second letter, numbered 52 in his collection, is a letter of warning. It shows an equal fascination with the problem of impending shipwreck and similarly mingles the biblical with the implicitly Homeric. Again, to a friend whose name is not known, Evagrius writes:

> Often I have written to you of contradictory matters: remain seated in the desert, miserable one, imploring God with fasts and prayer; look not at the world, which "in many times and in many ways" (Hebrews 1:1) has made you miserable. Recall to yourself your ancient shipwreck, remember yourself in the storm, as many times you have been tested. Do not forget the sea and the wild waves. Do not forget yourself, even though your ship has arrived in the harbor of chastity, and be grateful for what you have undergone for chastity. Don't you know that your ship may founder on the rocks of your own hardening, so that the keel of your vessel might burst, the water of resentment might rush into it, and, swamping everything, destroy your prayer?

The rest of the letter makes clear that Evagrius is recalling for his correspondent his own experience of *xeniteia* and the dangers of losing one's chastity, a fate imagined in terms of shipwreck and destruction. Since elsewhere he has portrayed the sirens as the thought of *epithumia,* sexual appetite, it seems fair to propose that here, too, the monk is meant to be Odysseus at the mast.

NOTES

1. Guillaumont, "Gnostique chez Clément."
2. The well-known presence of Manichaeans in fourth-century Egypt may have prompted Evagrius to warn against heretical teachings in *To the Monks* 126 and *To a Virgin* 54.

3. Clement, *Stromateis* 5.3.2–3 (ed. Stählin, Früchtel, and Treu).
4. Clement, *Quis dives salvetur* 36 (italics added).
5. Clement, *Stromateis* 4.26.13.
6. Clement, *Stromateis* 4.26.13.
7. Clement, *Stromateis* 4.26.14.
8. Clement, *Stromateis* 4.26.14, www.earlychristianwritings.com/text/clement-stromata-book4.html.
9. Campenhausen, "Ascetic Idea of Exile."
10. Ibid., 236.
11. Ibid., 251.
12. Ladner, "Homo Viator," 235.
13. Guillaumont, "Dépaysement."
14. Rousseau, *Ascetics, Authority,* 48.
15. Caner, *Wandering, Begging Monks,* 25 n. 24; for Evagrius's view of wandering, see 34–37. For the more developed theological meaning of the term, see also Chryssavgis, *John Climacus,* 73–74.
16. Caner, *Wandering, Begging Monks,* 25.
17. Ibid., 36.
18. Evagrius of Pontus, *Antirrhêtikos* 1.37 (trans. Brakke, *Talking Back*). Similar admonitions can be found at 6.24, 26 and 33, 53 and 57, all having to do with the temptation to wander as a response to listlessness.
19. *To Eulogius* 4 (trans. Sinkiewicz, *Evagrius of Pontus,* 63).
20. Bitton-Ashkelony, *Encountering the Sacred,* 171–72. For a discussion of Evagrius's views of *xeniteia* and *hesychia*, see 153–58.
21. McGuckin, "Aliens and Citizens," p. 21.
22. For a discussion of the term's later Christian uses, see T. Miller, *Birth of the Hospital*, 25–28.
23. Lamberton, "Neoplatonists." For a longer treatment of the allegorization of Homer's epic and its characters, see his *Homer the Theologian*, and his translation of Porphyry's *On the Cave of the Nymphs*.
24. Lamberton, "Neoplatonists," 127.
25. Porphyry, *On the Cave of the Nymphs* 79, quoted in Lamberton, "Neoplatonists," 127.
26. Quotation from Lamberton, "Neoplatonists," 133.
27. *Porphyry on the Cave of the Nymphs* 31 (trans. Lamberton, 40).
28. Evagrius of Pontus, *Ep.* 1 (the "*Epistula fidei*"), in (ps-)Basil *Epistula* 8 (ed. Gribomont, "*Epistula* 8").
29. The translation "reasonings" for *logismoi* is Kevin Corrigan's (*Evagrius and Gregory*, 73–102), and the English word seems to capture their duration, their stages, and their tenacity better than the more common translation "thoughts."

30. See Brakke, *Demons.*

31. Palladius, *Historia Lausiaca* 38, my translation; cf. Socrates, *Historia ecclesiastica* 4.23.

32. Bunge, *Briefe aus der Wüste*. Luke Dysinger has produced an English translation of *Letters* 1–10, 55–57, 59; see www.ldysinger.com/Evagrius/11_Letters/ 00a_start.htm.

Chapter Twelve

Adam, Eve, and the Elephants

Asceticism and Animality

PATRICIA COX MILLER

Around the year 400 or perhaps shortly thereafter, a Christian artist of unknown provenance carved an ivory diptych whose left leaf features a nude Adam seated in a languid position.[1] Located in the upper, central-right register of the diptych leaf, Adam looks out with a dreamy expression, not quite making eye contact with the viewer. Remarkably, he is accompanied by a cascade of animals who tumble down the leaf: to Adam's right there is an eagle, followed by a smaller bird, and then a leopard, a lioness, a roaring lion, a bear, a boar, a fox, a cartwheeling elephant, a horse, a goat, a lizard, a serpent, an ox, a grasshopper, a sheep, and finally a stag and doe, who are placed just above a representation of the four rivers of paradise.[2]

In the guise of Orpheus charming the animals with the magic of his song, Adam floats in space in a topsy-turvy frolic with the beasts of paradise. What is Adam's role here in this leaf of the Carrand diptych? Is he part of a "force-field of desire" for natural harmony?[3] Does he, like

Carrand diptych,
ca. 400, left leaf.
Photo courtesy
of Hirmer Fotoarchiv,
Munich.

animals, exist in the world "like water in water," as Georges Bataille suggested?[4] That is, is Adam's intimacy with the world so profound that there is a natural continuity between the human and the animal? As Bataille, again, remarked, "The animal opens before me a depth that attracts me and is familiar to me. In a sense, I know this depth: it is my own."[5] Bataille's perspective supports an Orphic reading of the figures in this image, including Adam, as an idyll of cavorting animal life.

While most art historians acknowledge the indebtedness of this bucolic scene to artistic images of Orpheus, most would reject the animal-human symbiosis implied by the phrase "like water in water."[6] This is because the presumed scriptural referent of this scene, Adam naming the animals in Genesis 2:19–20, is understood, by an intertextual sleight of hand, in concert with Genesis 1:26, the passage in which God gives humankind dominion over the fish, the birds, and the domestic and wild animals. In art-historical interpretation, this scene thus positions Adam, on top and larger even than the elephant, as one who controls the animals rather than harmonizing with them.[7] The gesture of Adam's right hand, in this perspective, does not point to the roaring lion in wonder but instead establishes Adam's dominance and superiority. Such a view of the dominical Adam separates the human from the animal rather than placing the human in a continuum with the flesh-and-bones materiality of the natural world.

The intertextual reading that understands naming as a being-over rather than a being-with is indebted to a certain strain of patristic commentary on Adam and the beasts. Especially in the Hexameron tradition as exemplified by Basil of Caesarea, Ambrose, and John Chrysostom, Adam's dominion over the animals as namer is attributed to his creation in the image of God: only humans have reason and hence are superior to the irrational beasts.[8] As Basil of Caesarea put the case for animals, "There is only one soul of brute beasts, for there is one thing that characterizes it, namely, lack of reason [ἀλογία]."[9] As for Adam, Chrysostom was especially enthusiastic about the exalted status of the human: "Do you see the unrivalled authority? Do you see [Adam's] lordly dominance?"[10] Noting that Genesis specifies that Adam gave names to all the cattle, all the birds of heaven, and all the beasts of the earth, Chrysostom continues: "Notice, I ask you, dearly beloved, his independence of decision and the eminence of his understanding, and don't say he didn't know right from wrong. I mean, the being that has the ability to put the right names on cattle, and birds, and beasts without getting the sequence mixed up, not giving to wild beasts the names suited to the tame ones nor allotting to the tame animals what belonged to the wild ones, but giving them all their right names — how could he not be full of intelligence and understanding?"[11] Adam knew his animals! But in this kind of literal reading, the animals do not open on a depth shared by human beings but are reduced to an inferior reality.

For patristic authors, however, animal bodies were not only literal dumb flesh but also, and especially, signs that carried a complex value.[12] Discussion of Adam and the animals typically — and quickly — becomes a zoological mapping of the human being, body and soul. First, the body: uses of animals to characterize the human body could be quite negative, particularly in ascetic contexts that devalued pleasures associated with the flesh. As Ingvild Sælid Gilhus has shown, especially in her analysis of Christian texts from Nag Hammadi, "Animality was intimately intertwined with the sexual aspect of the body."[13] Human being and animal shared the negative space of the sexed body. In the *Paraphrase of Shem,* for example, demonic animality lay "at the very root of the cosmos and nature," including human nature.[14] Not everyone reduced the human body only to its bestial habits, however. Philip Rousseau, the honoree of this volume, has argued with regard to Basil that "he did not think that the Fall had destroyed nature in any fundamental way."[15] Just as animals possess "natural instincts" for self-preservation, "we also," wrote Basil, "possess natural virtues."[16] As Rousseau argues further, nature (φύσις) was for Basil "the hidden presence of God's creative word" in animal as well as human bodies.[17] Of course, even though Basil did not demonize human physicality with animal images, he was not completely positive about our animal selves; we share their earthly "humiliation," and he thought that the flesh has "whims" that, when they overtake the mind, become the source of evil.[18]

As for the zoological mapping of the soul, Chrysostom, for example, remarked that "just as there are tame and ferocious animals, so in the soul some of our ideas are more lethargic, others savage"; such "wildness of thought" needs to be "transformed into natural human mildness."[19] This connection between the wild beasts and "disturbing passions" can also be found in Basil's *Hexaemeron,* where, for example, Basil discusses "the herds":

> The herds are earthy and are bent toward the earth, but the human being is a heavenly creature who excels them as much by the excellence of his soul as by the character of his bodily structure. What is the comportment of the quadrupeds? Their head bends toward the earth and looks toward their belly and pursues its pleasure in every way. Your head stands erect towards the heavens; your eyes look upward, so that, if ever you dishonor yourself by the passions of the flesh, serving your belly and your lowest parts, "you are compared to senseless beasts, and are become like to them" (see Ps 49.13).[20]

In this passage, a human being's correct or incorrect use of his "bodily structure" quickly becomes a cipher for soulful self-control or lack thereof. Such a metaphorizing of passions with animals appears with an interesting twist in Ambrose's treatise on paradise, in which the beasts and birds are Adam's "irrational senses" "because beasts and animals represent the diverse emotions of the body." God put the passions of the body, the animals, in paradise so that Adam might have control over them.[21] Had Ambrose seen the left leaf of the Carrand diptych, he would have seen in effect a diagram of the psyche rather than an Orphic idyll.

What logic of the self do these animals embody? Ambrose's position is significant because it reveals that, in regard to the beasts, there was in late ancient Christianity not only a zoological mapping of the soul but also an anthropological mapping of animality. The self in question here was the self of ascetic striving, in which body and soul were inseparable and in which control of physical and emotional passions was paramount. I want to underscore the point that measuring the self through the lens of animals shows a different self than, for example, measuring the self by comparison with angels, as Theodoret and others did.[22] While angel images show a human self transparent to its own spiritual radiance, animal images often show a darker, more tortuous self. Again, whereas images of light-filled angels convey a sense of human transcendence, images of animals convey a psychic earthiness that might otherwise remain concealed.

The following remarks of Evagrius of Pontus are telling in this latter regard: "Among the impure demons some tempt the human person as a human being; others trouble the human person as an irrational animal. The first, when they visit us, instill within us mental representations of vainglory or pride or envy or censoriousness — these do not touch any irrational beings. When the second class of demons approaches us, they move our irascibility or concupiscibility in a manner contrary to nature. These are the passions which we have in common with irrational beings but which remain hidden by our rational nature."[23] In this passage, animals are a clue to a complex self, "contrary to nature" (παρὰ φύσιν), which is hidden by our rationality. Learning how to discern such bestial representations was, of course, central to Evagrius's goal of achieving a mature contemplative self.[24]

The medium provided by animal images is thus crucial to the message. Animals need to be named: that is, they need discrimination. Animals provided a means for sorting out the riddle of the human being; they were, to echo Foucault, a technique or hermeneutics of the self.[25] As W. J. T. Mitchell has pointed out about images in general — a point that I apply here specifically to animal images — if images "teach us how to desire, they also teach us how to see — what to look for, how to arrange and make sense of what we see."[26]

When late ancient Christians mapped an anthropology with animal images as the road signs, they ensured that an intimacy with the flesh — with those beastly depths that are both familiar and difficult to fathom — would occupy an important part of human transformation. Animal images keep the flesh — whether literal or figurative — in the forefront of the ascetic endeavor. In what follows, I will explore this theme of the transfiguration of the flesh through animal stories, bearing in mind Blake Leyerle's caution that "we must not make the mistake of dismissing stories about animals, no matter how unnatural, as simply naïve."[27] In other words, they are not just fancies with no substance. As we have already seen, theoretical musings, as in the Hexameron tradition, about the relation between the human and the animal are visceral enough, with their dumb dogs, foolish asses, and greedy leopards, to cite some of Chrysostom's images.[28] But in stories, the force field of animal desire is *really* earthy and embodied. Below is one such story that reads the human with an animal eye.

The story to be considered shortly is part of a collection of (mainly) animal stories known as the *Physiologus,* a text written in the late third century.[29] As Alan Scott has aptly summarized its gist, the *Physiologus* claims "that the proper understanding of the marvelous properties of beasts showed how nature itself contained clues to the mysteries exposed in scripture and Christian theology."[30] Among the many stories about animals that constitute this text, which is marked by the increasing ascetic fervor of the period in which it was written, there is a curious tale about elephants.[31]

> There is an animal called the elephant whose copulating is free from wicked desire. If the elephant wishes to produce young, he goes off to the east near paradise where there is a tree called the mandrake. And he goes there with his mate, who first takes part of the tree and gives it to her husband and cajoles him until he eats it. After the male has eaten, [they join together] and the female immediately conceives in her womb. . . . The male guards her while she gives birth because of the serpent who is an enemy to the elephant. . . . The great elephant and his wife represent the persons of Adam and Eve. While in a state of virtue (that is, while they pleased the Lord), before their transgression, they had no knowledge of copulation, nor any awareness of the mingling of their flesh. When, however, the woman ate of the tree (that is, the intelligible mandrake) and gave to her husband, she became big with evil; because of this act they were expelled from paradise.[32]

The story continues at some length to detail the plight of an elephant that falls because of a hunter's trick and recounts that many elephants try but fail to raise up the elephant who fell: one very large elephant, the Law, followed by twelve more elephants, the prophets. Finally a tiny elephant, "the holy intelligible elephant (that is, the Lord Jesus Christ)," succeeds where the others have failed.[33]

Besides its obvious references to the Old and New Testaments, this fantasia on the elephant was indebted to Roman zoological lore. Pliny the Elder, for example, thought that elephants were close to humans in intelligence and that they possessed virtues — honesty, wisdom, and justice — rare even in human beings.[34] According to Aelian, not only do the gods love elephants, but elephants themselves are religious, waving their trunks and branches in obeisance to the sun and moon.[35] Indeed, in an aside that appears to be critical of humankind in light of elephant behavior, Aelian remarked that "elephants for their part worship the gods, whereas human beings are in doubt whether in fact there are gods, and, if there are, whether they take thought for us."[36] In the view of this ancient zoological literature, elephants embody high ethical ideals and are fitting vehicles for religious reflection, and the testimony of the story of Adam, Eve, and the elephants in the *Physiologus* bears this out.

The most obvious aspect of elephant lore adopted by the *Physiologus* was the ancient naturalists' discussion of elephants' sexual propriety. According to both Pliny the Elder and Aelian, elephants are chaste and modest; they do not commit adultery, and they live in continence with their mates. In fact, they engage in intercourse only once in their lives and do so in private, away from the gaze of other animals.[37] The Christian appropriation of elephant lore in the *Physiologus* is ultimately a Christological allegory, but a central focus of its curious story, even though the analogy is inexact, is precisely the chaste mating behavior of the elephants. In a break from the overall allegorizing aspect of the story, the sexual chastity of the elephants is not mirrored in the sexual behavior of Adam and Eve, whose mingling of the flesh is so tinged with "wicked desire" that Eve becomes "big with evil." Here, instead of standing as metaphors or symbols of base human desires, as was so typical of late ancient Christian texts, the animals turn the tables: in the mirror of these ascetically correct elephants, it is *human* behavior that is shown to be in need of proper embodiment.

Stories like this one from the *Physiologus* that recommend a specifically ascetic human identity seem paradoxical, since, as I have noted, animal images, especially scriptural ones, were so often used by ancient Christian authors to denote the fallenness of carnal life — the base passions and evil thoughts, like Basil's angry camels, that hold sway over human behavior.[38] But was the frequent use of animal signs to develop an ascetic view of human being-in-the-world really a paradox? Here a brief digression into ancient animal psychology is in order.

From Plato and Aristotle through the Roman Stoics, and with the sole exceptions of Plutarch and Porphyry, animals were said to be lacking in reason.[39] In Plato's view, for example, animals' souls are courageous and appetitive, but they lack the human soul's rational element.[40] Similarly for Aristotle: devoid of reason, animals live "for the most part by nature [φύσει], but to some degree by their habits as well."[41] Thus according to this tradition, as Gillian Clark has noted, "Human reason can outclass any animal skill."[42] Theodoret, for example, admonished his flock not to envy spiders for their skill in weaving.[43] On the other hand, animals were accorded a sagacity that was natural and connected to instinct.[44] Animals, whose basic nature was summed up in the terms φύσις and αἴσθησις, were distinguished by their "possession of the faculty of sensation."[45] In fact, as Augustine thought, "many beasts surpass us in sensing" because "the soul of beasts is more attached to the body."[46] From the perspective of ancient theorists, then, animals live in their bodies "like water in water," to recall Bataille's phrase.

To return from my digression to the question posed just above: Was the frequent use of animal signs to develop an ascetic view of human identity really a paradox? No: precisely because animals *were* so connected to the sensuous and the material, they were perfect vehicles for ascetic reflection. Their sheer physicality was aligned with the "animal" human bodies on which so much of ascetic practice was focused. As Blake Leyerle has remarked with regard to desert ascetics and the beasts, "Animals were a powerful way in which monks thought and spoke about the encounter with the body."[47] In short, in some early Christian texts, animals were active mirrors and models *for* human behavior (both negative and positive) and not simply passive metaphors *of* it. This is why, in a text like Basil's *Hexaemeron,* which I will examine shortly, the animals form a force field of desire. Rather than playing on the opposition between bestiality and reason, texts like the *Physiologus* envisioned a transfiguration of the body through animal signs, based on a nostalgia, a paradisal wish to be like the elephants, a desire for a chaste intimacy with what animals know best, the body.

Basil certainly read the human with an animal eye in his *Hexaemeron*. Although this work is not usually considered to be a member of the canon of ascetic texts from Christian antiquity, I will consider it to be so here, for the following reasons. Basil purported to be writing about what he saw as the beauty and wondrousness of the created world.[48] Eschewing allegory for the plain sense of scripture, he wrote, "When I hear 'grass,' I think of grass, and I do the same with plant, fish, wild animal, and ox. I take everything just as it is said."[49] Yet as he detailed the natural characteristics and behaviors of the various birds, beasts, and creatures of the sea, Basil frequently introduced interjections in which he used animals to measure humans. These punctuations in the text have largely to do with Basil's shaping — or perhaps better — *re*shaping of human ethical subjectivity, largely along ascetic lines of the control of the passions: "Let the passions of the incontinent," he wrote in the seventh homily, "be restrained and trained by these examples from land and sea."[50] In Basil's handling of the earth's creatures, one sees what I would call a therapeutic use of animal-pictures to craft an ascetic self devoted to an ethic of poverty, self-control, and charity.[51]

Along with such overt appeals to ascetic values, there is the broader perspective on Basil's later works provided by Philip Rousseau, who has noted that "the importance of self-knowledge, the need for inner purification, the ideal of a freedom that rises above the enslavement of property and fame — all occur again and again in the teaching of the mature Basil."[52] Such achievements, Rousseau continues, were "not limited to an ascetic life but considered the only worthy goal of any human."[53] On Basil's extension of an ascetic mode of life to all Christians, Rousseau remarks further: "Genuine authority, he said, sprang from the self-possession and the inner control achieved by the holy ones. But the Church itself was involved in that victory: by siding with the traditions of the fathers, by adopting an ascetic mode of life, by remaining 'sons of the bride of Christ,' Christians could share with the Church a dominion over the whole world."[54]

That penchant for extending ascetic values to all human beings is certainly evident in the *Hexaemeron,* which demonstrates particular concern for evil stemming from "thought sacrificed to the whims of the flesh."[55] A particularly striking example, tinged with a not-so-concealed eroticism in Basil's telling, involves the crab whose characteristic desire *in extremis* (ἐπιθυμία) for the flesh of the oyster leads it to engage in deceitful and wicked behavior in order to devour it.[56] As Basil told the story, the crab is frustrated by the hinged shells of the oyster, against whose tight fit its claws are of no avail. So what does it do? "When [the crab] sees [the oyster] pleasantly warming itself in spots sheltered from the wind and opening its valves to the rays of the sun, then, stealthily inserting a small pebble, he prevents it from closing and gains through inventiveness what he fell short of by strength." Basil concluded: "Now, I want you, although emulating the crabs' skillfulness and industry, to abstain from injury to your neighbors."[57]

The story of the crab conforms to a significant feature of much of the *Hexaemeron*'s animal lore. For Basil what we share with the animals is not only the body but also behavior, imitable or not. As he remarks about creaturely psychology, "The soul of animals is," as we might expect by now, "something earthy" (γεηρά τίς), and animals have natural instincts that human beings often might do well to imitate.[58] The differentiated senses of mimesis in the *Hexaemeron* suggest that animal stories function there as a *technē* of the ascetic self. What I wish to explore, however, is not simply the fact that animal behavior is pedagogical but that it is pedagogical as a shame-inducing exemplum. Like the *Physiologus*'s story of the ascetically correct elephants who function as a reproach to Adam and Eve's lust, Basil's therapy of the human by means of the earth's creatures was frequently based on shame. For example, when describing the migratory patterns of fish, Basil wrote:

> I have seen these wonders myself and I have admired the wisdom of God in all things. If the irrational animals are able to contrive and look out for their own preservation, and if a fish knows what it should choose and what avoid, what shall we say who have been honored with reason, taught by the law, encouraged by the promises, made wise by the Spirit, and who have then handled our own affairs more unreasonably than the fish? Even though they know how to have some foresight for the future, yet we, through hopelessness for the future, waste our lives in brutish pleasure. A fish traverses so many seas to find some advantage; what do you say who pass your life in idleness?[59]

Similarly, in another striking story about crows that serve as bodyguards for flocks of storks and about the storks' care for their elderly ones, Basil chides his (human) flock: it is shameful "to be inferior in virtue to irrational birds" who, lacking reason, nonetheless practice "the laws of hospitality."[60]

In such pictures of animal behavior, shame is ascetic in its effect because it induces a desire to embody the sorts of virtuous behavior that lead to salvation; if we can't even imitate the brute beasts who take care of their lives, Basil wrote, "we'll be condemned."[61] In images such as these, we see the way that images "refunction our imaginations, bringing new criteria and new desires into the world."[62] Such a refunctioning of the imagination in Basil's *Hexaemeron* is often achieved by the effects of his shame-inducing animals. In her recent book entitled *Saving Shame,* Virginia Burrus has noted that shame need not be "a sheerly destructive or paralyzingly inhibiting force."[63] "There is no escape from shame," she continues, "but there may be many possibilities for a productive transformation of shame and through shame."[64] "In shame, desire, whatever its object, is not so much decisively blocked as tantalizingly arrested, caught like a deer in the headlights of (self-) scrutiny."[65] Indeed, shame is "the place where the question of identity arises most originarily and most relationally."[66] Shame, desire, self-scrutiny, and the question of identity form a set of interrelated concerns that well describe the function of the shaming animal stories in Basil's *Hexaemeron* as well as in the *Physiologus*.

In terms of this essay's focus on the usefulness of animal images for ascetic self-understanding and (trans)formation, Burrus's comments on the relations among shame, the senses, and the body are pertinent: "Shame is an affect closely linked with sensation, and this in itself binds it tightly to the flesh. Psychologist Helen Block Lewis remarks on the unusual intensity and breadth of shame's sensory register, noting that shame 'seems to rest on an increase in feedback from *all* perceptual modalities' and observing that it 'usually involves greater body awareness than guilt.' Shame plays across our senses, then; indeed, it is largely an effect of heightened *sensitivity*."[67] The shaming animal images in late ancient Christian texts offer glimmers of intimacy with our animal darkness;[68] they are the crux of transformation, as indeed John Chrysostom realized when he wrote that scripture gave animal names to human passions "in the hope that eventually they [human beings] may feel ashamed of this behavior and turn back to their true nobility."[69] Playing across the senses, then, the animal effects the emergence of the noble self, ascetically in control of the passions.

Crafting an ascetic ideal on the bodies of animals takes one into a deep intimacy with the animal, and there is where the process of transformation takes place. Many animal images can fruitfully be read, not as essences, but rather as activities of the self that require inspection and cultivation for the knowledge they disclose. Such images "both express desires that we already have, and teach us how to desire in the first place."[70] I will close with a final story, this one from the literature of desert asceticism, that presents the transformative power of knowing the animal. The *Historia monachorum in Aegypto* tells the story of the holy anchorite Theon, who had practiced silence for thirty years. "One could see him with the face of an angel giving joy to his visitors by his gaze and abounding with much grace." "They say he used to go out of his cell at night and keep company with wild animals, giving them to drink from the water that he had. Certainly one could see the track of antelope and wild asses and gazelles and other animals near his hermitage. These creatures delighted him always."[71] This was possibly a Christomimetic scenario, for it was when Christ was in the wilderness with wild beasts that angels ministered to him (Mark 1:13). But perhaps Theon was more like Adam in the Carrand diptych: like Adam, Theon existed with the animals in the world like water in water, in an intimacy so profound that the animal and the angel were one.

NOTES

1. For the dating of the Carrand diptych, now in the Museo Nazionale del Bargello, Florence, see Maguire, "Adam and the Animals," 365 n. 15. The provenance of the diptych has been variously suggested to be Constantinople or Italy.

2. As noted by Konowitz, "Program of the Carrand Diptych," 484, the left leaf of the Carrand diptych presents the earliest known artistic representation of Adam with the animals in Eden.

3. I have appropriated this phrase from Mitchell, *What Do Pictures Want?*, 59.

4. Bataille, *Theory of Religion*, 24.

5. Ibid., 22.

6. See, for example, Konowitz, "Program of the Carrand Diptych," 485; Toynbee, *Animals in Roman Life*, 294; Kessler, "Diptych," 505.

7. See, for example, Konowitz, "Program of the Carrand Diptych," 488; Maguire, "Adam and the Animals," 364–66; Toynbee, *Animals in Roman Life*, 294, allows for some mutuality in the image by noting that several of the animals "are open-mouthed, as though they were answering to the name assigned to them." Note that Orpheus, as tamer of the beasts, has like Adam been read as a dominical

figure: "The gentle imagery of Orpheus and the beasts represents a world of animals in ancient art in which humans are very much in control, and the animals are idyllically at peace with one another" (Morris, "Animals into Art," 198).

8. Basil of Caesarea, *Hex.* 10.6–7, 19 (ed. Smets and Esbroeck, SC 160.179–83, 217–19); Ambrose, *Hex.* 6.43 (PL 14.272c–274b; trans. Savage, FC 42.256); John Chrysostom, *Hom. in Gen.* 9.8 (PG 53.78; trans. Hill, FC 74.110, 121–22). See also the discussion of various passages in Augustine's works that follow this line of thought regarding Adam in G. Clark, "Fathers and the Animals."

9. Basil, *Hex.* 9.3 (ed. Giet, SC 26.488; trans. Way, FC 46.138). Note: since the numbering of this text in Way's translation does not always coincide with that in Giet's edition, I have followed Giet's numbering and have given page numbers for the English translation.

10. John Chrysostom, *Hom. in Gen.* 14.19 (PG 53.116; trans. Hill, 191).

11. John Chrysostom, *Hom. in Gen.* 14.20 (PG 53.116; trans. Hill, 191).

12. See Leyerle, "Monks and Other Animals," 151, for the reference to "the value of the sign of their [the beasts'] bodies." See also Maguire, "Adam and the Animals," 363–65, for an analysis of early Christian understandings of paradise and its inhabitants as literal, spiritual, or both.

13. Gilhus, *Animals, Gods and Humans*, 213. As she notes, however, there are also positive uses of animal metaphors in Nag Hammadi texts; see 219–20 for examples.

14. Ibid., 217.

15. Rousseau, *Basil of Caesarea*, 337.

16. Basil, *Hex.* 9.4 (ed. Giet, 497; trans. Way, 141).

17. Rousseau, *Basil of Caesarea*, 339.

18. On the humiliation of human and animal earthiness, see Basil, *Hex.* 8.2 (ed. Giet, 435–37; trans. Way, 119), and Rousseau, *Basil of Caesarea*, 340–41, for discussion; Rousseau refers to the "whims of the flesh" on 336.

19. John Chrysostom, *Hom. in Gen.* 9.7 (PG 53.78; trans. Hill, 121). On the psychological use of scriptural animal images in earlier patristic writing, see P. Miller, "Adam Ate," and "Origen on the Bestial Soul."

20. Basil, *Hex.* 9.2 (ed. Giet, 487–89; trans. Way, 138).

21. For "disturbing passions," see John Chrysostom, *Hom. in Gen.* 12.10 (PG 53.101–2; trans. Hill, 162); see also the anthropocentric representation of animals as signifying various human qualities in *Hex.* 9.3 (ed. Giet, 489–91; trans. Way, 138–39). For Ambrose, see *Parad.* 11.51 (PL 14.316c; trans. Savage, 329). For discussion, see Konowitz, "Program of the Carrand Diptych," 486–87.

22. For discussion of ascetics and angel-images, see P. Miller, "Desert Asceticism."

23. Evagrius of Pontus, *On Thoughts* 18 (ed. Géhin, Guillaumont, and Guillaumont, SC 438.214; trans. Sinkewicz, *Evagrius of Pontus*, 165.

24. See Sinkewicz, intro. to *On Thoughts* in *Evagrius of Pontus*, 136–53, for discussion.

25. See, among others, Foucault, "About the Beginning."

26. Mitchell, *What Do Pictures Want?*, 72.

27. Leyerle, "Monks and Other Animals," 157.

28. John Chrysostom, *Hom. in Gen.* 12.10 (PG 53.102; trans. Hill, 162–63).

29. On the date of the *Physiologus*, see Scott, "Date of the *Physiologus*."

30. Scott, "Zoological Marvel," 81. For a discussion of allegory and Christology in the *Physiologus*, see P. Miller, "*Physiologus*."

31. On the ascetic cast of the *Physiologus*, see Scott, "Zoological Marvel," 85.

32. *Physiologus* 20 "On the Elephant" (ed. Carmody, 117–19; trans. Curley, 29–31).

33. This use of animals to tell (or retell) the story of Christian salvation history is typical of many of the chapters of the *Physiologus*.

34. Pliny the Elder, *Nat.* 8.1.1 (ed. and trans. Rackham, LCL, 3:3).

35. Aelian, *De natura animalium* 7.2; 4.10; 7.44 (ed. and trans. Scholfield, LCL, 2:97, 1:225, 2:159); see also Pliny, *Nat.* 8.1.1 (ed. and trans. Rackham, 3:3) and Plutarch, *Moralia* 17.972 (ed. and trans. Cherniss and Helmbold, LCL, 12:397).

36. Aelian, *De natura animalium* 7.44 (ed. and trans. Scholfield, 2.161). The humans that Aelian appears to be disparaging vis-à-vis religious devotion may have been Epicureans; see *OCD*, s.v. "Aelianus (1)," 13.

37. Pliny, *Nat.* 8.5.13 (ed. and trans. Rackham, 3:11); Aelian, *De natura animalium* 8.17 (ed. and trans. Scholfield, 2:201). For discussion and multiple citations, see Scullard, *Elephant,* 208–31, and Newmyer, "Paws to Reflect," 121–24.

38. Basil, *Hex.* 8.1 (ed. Giet, 435; trans. Way, 119).

39. For a full discussion, see Sorabji, *Animal Minds,* 7–106. See also Renehan, "Greek Anthropocentric View," 239–59, and Newmyer, "Animals in Ancient Philosophy," 158–67.

40. Plato, *Resp.* 441b, discussed in Newmyer, "Animals in Ancient Philosophy," 159.

41. Aristotle, *Pol.* 1332b3–5, quoted and discussed in Newmyer, "Animals in Ancient Philosophy,"160.

42. G. Clark, "Fathers and the Animals," 70.

43. Theodoret, *Provid.* 5.553c–554a (PG 83.632–33), cited in G. Clark, "Fathers and the Animals," 70–71.

44. For discussion and examples, see Dickerman, "Some Stock Illustrations." Animals whose instinctual behavior was especially admired were ants, bees, spiders, and birds.

45. Renehan, "Greek Anthropocentric View," 242.

46. Augustine, *De animae quantitate* 28.54 (PL 32.1066), cited in G. Clark, "Fathers and the Animals," 76.

47. Leyerle, "Monks and Other Animals," 163.

48. Basil, *Hex*. 1.11 (ed. Giet, 135–37; trans. Way, 19).

49. Basil, *Hex.* 9.1 (ed. Giet, 481; trans. Way, 135). On Basil's skittishness about allegory in the *Hexaemeron*, see Lim, "Politics of Interpretation."

50. Basil, *Hex*. 7.6 (ed. Giet, 421; trans. Way, 114–15).

51. In the *Hexaemeron* as in other works, one of Basil's chief concerns was "the moral discipline of good works," in Rousseau's words (*Basil of Caesarea*, 181). For an overall view of Basil's extension of ascetic ideals to all Christians, see Gribomont, *Histoire du texte*.

52. Rousseau, *Basil of Caesarea*, 55.

53. Ibid., 55 n. 124.

54. Ibid., 181–82.

55. Ibid., 336.

56. Basil, *Hex*. 7.3 (ed. Giet, 405–7; trans. Way, 109–10).

57. Basil, *Hex*. 7.3 (ed. Giet, 409; trans. Way, 110).

58. Basil, *Hex.* 8.2; 9.4 (ed. Giet, 435, 497; trans. Way, 119, 141). See Rousseau, *Basil of Caesarea*, 221–22, on "the concept of nature (φύσις)" as key to Basil's thought, including that "it was by nature that [humans] brought their logos to bear upon the passions, schooling them to a life of virtue."

59. Basil, *Hex* 7.5 (ed. Giet, 415; trans. Way, 113).

60. Basil, *Hex*. 8.5 (ed. Giet, 453–55; trans. Way, 125–26).

61. Basil, *Hex.* 9.3 (ed. Giet, 491; trans. Way, 139). See the comment by Rousseau, *Basil of Caesarea*, 191: Basil intended "to touch his audience at the level of motive, self-image, guilt, and confidence; to awaken in them a desire for spiritual and moral growth."

62. Mitchell, *What Do Pictures Want?*, 92.

63. Burrus, *Saving Shame*, xi.

64. Ibid., xii.

65. Ibid., 2.

66. Ibid., 3.

67. Ibid., 45, quoting Lewis, "Introduction: Shame," 16–17.

68. This sentence contains a play on the following quotation from Bataille, *Theory of Religion*, 22–23: The animal "is never entirely reducible to that kind of inferior reality which we attribute to things. Something tender, secret, and painful draws out the intimacy which keeps vigil in us, extending its glimmer into that animal darkness."

69. John Chrysostom, *Hom. in Gen.* 12.10 (PG 53.102; trans. Hill, 163).

70. Mitchell, *What Do Pictures Want?*, 68.

71. *Hist. mon.* 6, "On Theon" (ed. Festugière, 44; trans. Russell, *Lives of the Desert Fathers*, 68).

Chapter Thirteen

The Consolation of Nature

Fields and Gardens in the Preaching of John Chrysostom

BLAKE LEYERLE

Preaching in the urban churches of Antioch and Constantinople at the end of the fourth century, John Chrysostom often dilated on the beauties of creation.[1] Occasionally scripture prompted this theme, but at other times the preacher seems to have deliberately introduced it. In this respect, he was not wholly idiosyncratic. As Philip Rousseau has shown, Basil too paid close attention to the natural world. It was a way, Basil believed, for a person to come to self-knowledge and, most crucially, to the knowledge of God.[2] The investigation of nature was thus a religious act that demanded asceticism and, when rightly done, led to wonder and praise. In homage, then, to Philip, from whom I have learned and continue to learn so much, I offer the following essay on Chrysostom's view of nature and the proper response of humans to their environment, and on the preacher's rhetorical use of pastoral imagery. Like other forms of pastoralism, I argue, Chrysostom's bucolic imagery represents an attempt to resolve the conflict between nature and civilization. In the late fourth-century church, this conflict necessarily engaged the debate over the practices and prestige of asceticism.

THE HYGIENIC COUNTRYSIDE

On the most basic level, the countryside is presented as a place of healthful simplicity. Chrysostom assumes that everyone would agree that life in the country is healthier than that in the city. This is the result, in the first instance, of cleaner air.[3] Rural inhabitants live far from the smell of open sewers and cesspits that pervades urban life.[4] The clear streams and bubbling springs of the countryside are indisputably purer than the piped water of the cities. People moving to the city take care to inquire about the air quality before taking up residence.[5]

A simple diet and regular strenuous work also contribute to the robust health of rural inhabitants. Countrywomen are demonstrably stronger than their urban counterparts. Fancifully, Chrysostom suggests that in a wrestling contest rural women would easily defeat urban men.[6]

Because it is healthier, country living is more pleasurable. Thus, whenever they can, elite urbanites leave their city residences and go out into the countryside; in town, they take delight in constructing private "lawns and gardens."[7] Some of these are quite elaborate, with "flowing springs and fountains, covered walkways, and trees swaying in the wind."[8] If it were a matter of choice, Chrysostom opines, the rich would prefer to have "trees and the comfort of meadows in the upper rooms of [their] houses . . . rather than golden roofs and magnificent walls."[9]

Part of this delight in the rural stemmed from the elite preference for agricultural wealth. From Chrysostom's praise of the patriarchs, it would seem that the preacher shared this preference. He describes Abraham's wealth as "more desirable, more satisfying, more useful, more secure, more just, more religious, more fit for a man, less onerous, less exposed to loss, and not liable to change or reversal." And in his praise of Job he goes even further. Because Job's wealth was primarily agricultural, the preacher characterizes it as "legitimate wealth, natural commerce, in which God himself was involved."[10] In the hygienic countryside one experiences more fully the productivity of nature.

NATURE'S PLENITUDE AND ORDERLINESS

While Chrysostom exclaims over the diversity of seasons, terrains, animals, and plants, he is especially struck by the variety of trees. Carefully he distinguishes the position, height, fragrance, foliage, fruit, season, and usefulness of various species.[11] Poplars, for example, demand a lot of water, and cypresses must be transplanted, but conifers are beautiful year-round.[12] If fruit-bearing trees "make no secret of their usefulness," others contribute timber "for building houses and making countless other things."[13] Such astute observation suggests a real engagement with nature or the mentality of a collector.[14]

Chrysostom's pleasure in contemplating natural diversity is indissociably tied to an appreciation of the productivity of the earth, in which "no part is useless." Even land that seems infertile yields valuable commodities: "It bears iron, bronze, gold, silver, not to mention spices and medicines of all sorts and varieties. Who could tell the usefulness of water both potable and brackish, the advantages of the mountains, the mines of the various rocks, the springs to be found in them, the trees suitable for roofing and building? All this is the fruit of wilderness [ἡ ἐρῆμος]."[15] Indeed, in its productive diversity, the earth's terrain resembles the human body. As a body consists of bones, nerves, and flesh, so the earth boasts mountains, ravines, and rich farms. But the fertility of the earth far exceeds that of humans. After a woman has given birth, milk flows to her breasts so that she can feed her offspring; but the earth "puts forth breasts all over" in the form of rivers, springs, and rains for the nourishment of orchards and gardens.[16] In paradise Adam rejoiced, beholding this natural abundance: "Consider, after all, how great a thrill it was to see the trees groaning under the weight of their fruit, to see the variety of the flowers, the different kinds of plants, the leaves on the branches, and all the other things you would be likely to chance upon in a garden, especially a garden planted by God."[17] The remarkable productivity of the earth comes, not from the toil of farmers, but from God.[18]

Intimately connected with nature's plenitude is its orderliness. Chrysostom celebrates the dance of days and nights, of seasons, and of years, the intermingling of elements, and "the vast array of stars."[19] This harmonious sequence underscores the worth of every person, no matter how humble, since for his or her sake God made the sun to rise, the moon to illuminate the night, and "the variegated band" of stars to shine.[20] The "beauty, magnitude, arrangement, permanence, and splendor" of creation also prove the providential presence of God.[21] For if, Chrysostom reasons, a small hut, pitched in the vineyards during harvest time, falls into disrepair after being left vacant for only two or three days, "How could the workmanship of a world, so fair and marvelous . . . continue unbroken . . . without some kind of providence?"[22] Thus the great marvels of creation should be admired, not in themselves — this was the error of paganism — but as indicators of the nature of God as creator and sustainer.[23] By observing the regular progression of winter to spring, and the necessary decay of seeds before their germination, people "come to sound thinking about the resurrection."[24]

Nature, when thus properly understood, is a more powerful and accessible form of teaching than that found in books:

> If God had taught by means of books and letters, the educated would have learned what was written, but the uneducated would have gone away without benefiting from it. . . . And the wealthy would have bought the book, but the poor would not have been able to acquire it. Again, whoever knew the language would know what the letters meant, but the Scythian, the Barbarian, the Indian, the Egyptian, and all those who lacked that language would have gone away having learned nothing. But this cannot be said of the heavens. . . . For not by ears, but by sight, it bursts into our understanding.[25]

Creation prompts observers "to thanksgiving, to hymnody, to praise, to giving glory," but this does not exhaust its "forceful teaching."[26]

Nature also teaches moral lessons — above all, the necessity of restraint.[27] When the avaricious person observes the day yielding to the night, "like two sisters dividing their patrimony with much affection, and without the least squabbling," he will learn to share his goods equitably; and the arrogant will cede their place of prominence to others.[28] The spectacle of the raging sea restrained by the shore will give the lustful person "strength to quell his raging passions."[29]

Thus, despite the astuteness of many of Chrysostom's observations on the natural world, what he offers is a very idealized picture. Nature is characterized chiefly by superlative abundance, peaceful orderliness, and wholesome simplicity. These features derive, in large part, from the traditions of Greek literature, especially those of bucolic poetry and of the Golden Age.[30] But these tropes have been recast in interesting ways.

PASTORAL IDYLLS AND THE GOLDEN AGE

The Golden Age, as it was classically construed by Hesiod, among others, was a time characterized above all by its difference from contemporary life.[31] It was a time of ease, plenty, and beauty. Fields and trees spontaneously produced abundant, nourishing food. People lived long, healthy lives and enjoyed a close relationship with the gods. No laws were necessary to regulate commerce, to restrain greed, or to redress aggression.[32] Because there was no need for weapons or coins, mining was unknown. Society was complete in itself and needed no addition; indeed, a static quality was inevitable, since any "change would result in a degree less of perfection."[33] Such a narrative, as Ruth Levitas has noted, is motivated by desire, the desire for the ideal, livable community.[34]

Chrysostom is certainly familiar with this construct; in his early treatise *On Virginity*, he specifically alludes to the Hesiodic version.[35] In the beginning, he too insists, there was no gold, and money came into being only later, as a result of envy.[36] Craft, trade, commerce, and slavery followed.[37] From the market and law courts, cities arose.[38] Thus they are rife with "causes and compulsions to discouragement and grief, to conceit and desperation." Living in the city, no one can escape being wounded by fear, grief, desire, and anger.[39] In the country, however, things are quite otherwise. There one remains "far from commotion and disturbance."[40] Rural life reflects more closely the original happy state of humanity.[41]

Indeed, even the sight of nature makes people more virtuous. Whereas covetousness and wealth cloud vision like smoke, dust, and noxious vapors, eyes become keen-sighted when exposed "to the delicate breeze, to the light air, to things heavenly and high."[42] If people want to refresh themselves, they should go to "parks [παραδείσους] . . . lakes and . . . gardens [κήπους] and listen to the cicadas [τεττίγων] sing."[43] There they can show their sons "the sky, the sun, the stars, the flowers of the earth, and meadows."[44] Such sights and sounds bring health to the body and benefit to the soul.

Many of these associations are deeply conventional, but Chrysostom has introduced some notable variations. The first and most striking divergence is the profile of the typical rural inhabitants. They are not the simple, virtuous farmers with their strong, fertile wives that we expect, but rather monks. The second variation is temporal: instead of a lost landscape, shadowed by a sense of belatedness, Chrysostom's golden age is yet to come.

ASCETIC VARIATION: MONKS AND MARTYRS

When Chrysostom draws the contrast between urban and rural life, he repeatedly presents the countryside as populated by monks. Monks are those "who having been released from the clamor of the marketplace and having fixed their huts in the wilderness . . . practice wisdom confidently in the calm of that quiet life . . . and enjoy great security."[45] In addition to respite, wilderness grants them philosophical perspective: "the possibility of surveying the whole world from on high and of reviewing one's values."[46] Humility comes readily to monks, who "pay attention only to the wilderness, and see birds flying, and trees waving, and a breeze blowing, and streams rushing through ravines."[47] Unlike the jostling urban masses, monks "hold everything in common — earth, springs, pastures, mountains, glens" — and, like the animals, migrate (μεταστήσεται) contentedly from one place to another.[48]

Part of the pleasure of monastic life derives from the healthful benefits of a vegetarian diet. "No streams of blood flow among them, nor cutting up of meat, nor heaviness of head, nor rich sauces, nor unpleasant smells, nor disagreeable smoke, nor rushing about, clamor, commotion, and oppressive shouting, but bread and water: the latter from a pure stream and the former from honest toil." In short, they eat at the table of angels.[49] Here, as so often, it is lack that defines utopia.[50] When addressing parents grieving their son's decision to become a monk, Chrysostom labors the benefits of simple rural life.

> Now, then, in regard to health, who is better off? Is not your son vigorous and healthy in body like the wild animals, since he enjoys the pure

> air and healthy streams and flowers and groves and pure sweet smells, whereas the [wealthy] person, as if he were lying in a cesspool, is rather soft and sickly? And if your son has first place in health, clearly he enjoys superior pleasure as well. For who do you think lives in greater luxury, the one who lies on the high grass beside a clear stream, under the shade of enormous trees, and who feasts his eyes on the sight and keeps his soul purer than the heavens and far from commotion and disturbance, or the person who is shut up in his house? For marble stones are not purer than the air, nor is a mosaic pavement more beautiful than a patch of multicolored flowers.[51]

The luxurious indolence of this imagined scene is striking. In Chrysostom's description, the young monk inhabits, rather than works, the land. He enjoys pristine leisure in an unchangingly verdant landscape that recalls the static perfection of the Golden Age.[52]

Elsewhere Chrysostom describes the monks at work. "They themselves light their fire, split wood, cook, and serve those who come to them."[53] They work the fields, "toiling laboriously over the earth, dragging the plough and cutting furrows in the field, scattering the seeds and entrusting them to the folds of the earth."[54] They carry water and irrigate their plants.[55] They make baskets, weave sackcloth, and practice other handiworks. Such labor was not unworthy of philosophers: even Plato "spent his time in the garden of the Academy, watering, sowing, eating olives, laying out a cheap table, and being free of . . . vanity."[56] This life of simple honest toil links monks to the insect world, and in particular to ants and to bees.[57] Like the former, they have acquired a love of hard work;[58] like the latter, they have developed "a taste for beauty . . . and a sense of sharing [κοινωνικόν]."[59]

But even in these georgic descriptions, monastic toil differs from other work: it seems less laborious and remains almost entirely uncontaminated by conflict.[60] The only strife that ruffles monastic calm is the competition over humility, as each seeks to cede his place to others. "There, no one is heard insulting, nor seen insulted, no one commanded, or giving commands; but all serve each other, and each one washes the feet of strangers — and over this there is much contention. . . . There, no one is great or little. What then? Is there confusion? Not at all! But the highest order. . . . There, a person is great who eagerly seizes upon the humble task."[61] This eager giving way resembles, not the competitive jostling of human society, but the harmonious order of the universe where day yields to night. And like the heavens, the mere sight of monks can lead the unlettered to virtue.[62] The erasure of conflict, as Moses Finley remarked, is an essential aspect of narratives of the Golden Age.[63] It is one means, among many, of evoking the "originary landscape and timescape," of inscribing divine presence in the land.[64]

The monastic countryside deviates from expectations of the blessed Golden Age, however, in that it is not rife with spontaneous production:[65] trees do not drip with abundance, and fields do not bear multiple harvests a year. Such excess would be at odds with monastic restraint and Chrysostom's admiration for virginal barrenness. Paradisal landscapes have, in fact, always had an uneasy relationship with morality, as uncontrolled, luxuriant overproduction often acquires sinister overtones, suggesting physical and moral debility.[66] In ascetic contexts, Chrysostom condemns luxuriance and excessive moisture as choking growth and producing only spindly plants. As waterlogged land generates only worms, and as overwatered plants "decay at the root," so pampered flesh loses strength and begins to rot.[67] A good yield depends upon appropriate aridity and pruning; and monks are expert pruners. The ascetic goal is productivity without luxuriance, constant labor without the creation of material surplus.[68] The landscape inhabited by monks is thus marvelously adequate rather than abundant.

Metaphors of luxuriant fertility were appropriate for another group of Christians. These were the martyrs, whose virtue could be imagined as creating lush vistas. At the sight of their trophies, Chrysostom's heart leaps as at the sight of fields of roses, irises, lilies, and "other spring flowers of varied and diverse forms."[69] Pleasing to the eye and nose, these spiritual gardens are also productive. As in the gardens of the wealthy, fruit trees and vines flourish among the flowers.[70] But unlike regular fruit trees, whose productivity diminishes over time, the aged martyr Eleazer is laden with fruit. "Now at its peak is this spiritual olive tree! Although its branches are elderly, it has provided us with mature fruit. For the plants of the earth are not of the same kind as the trees of the Church. I mean that, when the former reach old age, they then shed the majority of their leaves and, whatever fruit they bear, they produce out of season and undersized. But when these trees reach old age, it is then especially that they sink under the weight of their fruit."[71] Chrysostom's contention that the blood of the martyrs is essentially fertilizing may reflect the common practice of cultivating cemetery gardens (κηποτάφια), in which vegetables, flowers, and fruit trees were planted around tombs.[72] But his use seems more often metaphorical, as in his claim that when churches are well watered with the blood of martyrs, they grow, bloom, and multiply more than irrigated orchards.[73] Bare wood sprouts "lovely buds."[74]

Such luxuriant imagery was fitting for martyrs, who had little to fear from paradisal abundance. The record of their struggles and perseverance shielded them from any suspicion of enervation or moral laxity. By virtue of their death, they could be safely imagined as inhabiting a hyperverdant paradise. For unlike the Golden Age of classical literature, the paradise of Christianity was not only a retrospective landscape. Its imaginative reconstruction might owe many of its images to the lost Eden, and some might even now enjoy its plenitude, but on the whole, paradise remained an otherworldly and predominantly future reality. In this sense it was utopian rather than retrospective.[75]

UTOPIAN ETHICS AND THE PASTORAL PREACHER

By definition, the country lies outside the city, but the clarity with which Chrysostom opposes urban and rural life increases this notional distance. It seems a remote, ideal society, "located at the edge of mapped spaces," a place of bounty and repose.[76] It remains an imagined landscape, which cannot be seen and which the preacher does not inhabit, but which, for that very reason, can be invoked to critique observed reality. Like other utopian ideals, its description is a form of civic discourse that addresses urban, rather than rural, concerns.[77] And it does so by deliberately encouraging a kind of double vision.[78]

We see this doubling in Chrysostom's description of the physical space in which he preached. Given the crowded and filthy conditions of late ancient cities, the experience of being in church on a hot summer's day was inseparable from the sensation of a crush of bodies and the smell of sweat.[79] Chrysostom acknowledges the discomfort. Occasionally, his rejoinder is bracing: no matter how uncomfortable it is in church, it is no hotter or dirtier than at the market, the racetrack, or the theater, and yet no one complains about frequenting those venues.[80] But more often, his response is consoling and imaginative. He invites his congregation to see the church as a well-watered, green space — a meadow filled with flowers and the scent of roses — open to anyone who wishes to enjoy its refreshing delights.[81]

The landscape Chrysostom celebrates here is pleasant rather than majestic. He dwells on the verdant bank, the rippling stream, the shady tree, the sweet-smelling flowers of spring, and the burgeoning vine. Each of these features is deeply traditional. In E. R. Curtius's classic summary, the lovely landscape consists of "a beautiful, shaded natural site. Its minimum ingredients comprise a tree (or several trees), a meadow, and a spring or brook. Birdsong and flowers may be added. The most elaborate examples also add a breeze."[82] This countryside serves as a backdrop for human labor: for sowing, reaping, and herding.[83] In this exploited landscape, Chrysostom presents himself as a herdsman or a farmer. These images stem, in part, from the New Testament agricultural language and the ideal of the Good Shepherd, but their development looks as much to the canons of Theocritus and Callimachus as to scripture.

Consider, for example, Chrysostom's claim that for him the explication of scripture is a "frolicking [σκιρτῶντες] in some meadow."[84] This image conveys a joyful heart, but it also gestures toward the classical trope of the shepherd, as the privileged friend of the Muses. From this divine relationship comes knowledge, especially knowledge of the past, which allows the shepherd to speak the truth.[85] And it is as a shepherd that Chrysostom imagines himself. Grouping himself with other preachers, he says, "We, like shepherd boys, pipe on our slender flute [λεπτῷ τῷ καλάμῳ συρίζομεν], sitting in the shade of these sacred buildings as if under an oak or poplar tree."[86] Every element in this description points to bucolic poetry and promises an exchange of song.[87] Chrysostom plays with this expectation, noting that after the presbyters' simple piping on their reed flutes, the bishop, "having tuned his golden lyre, arouses the entire assembly with the harmony of his playing."[88] Here the element of contest is almost — but not quite — suppressed; in his focused remarks on the duties and difficulties of priesthood, however, Chrysostom dwells on the agonistic aspect of preaching.[89]

The first concern for any shepherd must be the well-being of his flock. Chrysostom thus delights in the sight of his congregation "as a cowherd rejoices to see his herd of cattle prospering and healthy."[90] In addition to leading his animals to good pasture, the shepherd must protect them from predators.[91] The preacher, too, must "take up tools and build a fence" to protect his flock.[92] But the enemies he fears are not the expected small-scale raiders of pastoral societies but rather vices, or the attraction of other religious groups.[93] Thus an extended metaphor opens the fourth discourse against Judaizing Christians:

> As long as no wild beast disturbs the flock, shepherds, as they stretch out under an oak or pine tree and play their flutes [τῷ καλάμῳ συρίζουσιν], let their sheep go off to graze with full freedom. But when the shepherds feel that the wolves will raid, they are quick to throw down the flute and pick up their slingshots; they cast aside the pipe of reeds [σύριγγα] and arm themselves with clubs and stones. They take their stand in front of the flock, raise a loud and piercing shout, and oftentimes the sound of their shout drives the wolf away before he strikes.[94]

To us, the imagery seems inflammatory; by assimilating Jews to wild animals intent on bloodshed, it debases them. But the language is highly conventional. As Stephen Hinds comments, "A sense of threat to harmony . . . is a constitutive feature of the landscape tradition at large."[95] The effect of this vivid pastoral evocation may thus have been restful: a kind of ekphrastic showpiece meant to divert, entertain, and refresh. Indeed, we might compare Chrysostom's rhetoric to the practice, common among wealthy urbanites, of decorating their city villas with wall paintings of the verdant countryside.[96] Both forms of art suggest an appreciation for stylized pastoral scenes and involve invitations to see.[97] Both, furthermore, use rural images as a way of thinking about city life.[98]

Elsewhere, Chrysostom prefers similes that liken the preacher to the plowing or reaping farmer. These look to Jesus' parables, especially that of the sower in Matthew 13, but they also tap into the traditional prestige of rural labor. Like a hardworking farmer, Chrysostom toils without remission. He clears away choking thorns and makes the congregation into "clean, tilled land."[99] He builds retaining fences and digs drainage ditches.[100] He sows seed and tends the young plants.[101] Sometimes the yield is immediate,[102] and the skill and diligence of the laborer is patent from the fact that "the vines are luxuriant with leaves, heavy with fruit, and walled on all sides with fences and palings."[103] At other times, repeated sowings are necessary to produce even a single crop, and then one that remains vulnerable to blight, drought, or other pests.[104] Even when the prospect is exceptionally poor, "the sower sows . . . the farmer does not stop farming."[105] And when harvest is great, the labor also increases: "When a farmer has harvested the whole vine, he does not cease working until he has also cut off the stems of the bunches. Since therefore, even now I see, as if hidden under leaves, some thoughts still concealed under the letters, come now, let us harvest these also very thoroughly, using this sermon in place of a sickle. Once a vine is harvested, it stands bare of fruit, with only leaves remaining, but the spiritual vine of the divine scriptures is different. If we take everything we can find, the greater part still remains behind."[106] The inexhaustible fertility of scripture elevates Chrysostom's labor by making of it a Herculean task: no matter how hard he works, more fruit remains to be harvested.

The preacher also encourages his listeners to see themselves in agricultural terms. In the first instance, they should regard themselves as farmers and their wealth as just so much seed grain. If they keep it shut up inside, "they lose it by surrendering it to worms and maggots, whereas if they scatter it in the furrows, not only do they keep it but they turn it into more."[107] The ideal place to sow is "the pinched belly" of the poor.[108] When giving alms, they should feel like a field hand sowing: "Scattering his seeds and emptying his stores, he is not vexed or saddened, but considers his actions profit and income, not outlay."[109]

In the second instance, Chrysostom's listeners should regard themselves as arable fields.[110] In terms of crops, the preacher recommends trees.[111] Their strength and resilience — and perhaps even their slow growth — commend them as images of virtue.[112] Prayers arising from compunction are like trees with deep roots:[113] irrigated with tears they "climb up to the greatest height."[114] But the preacher does not admire lofty oaks, whose grand height and showy foliage yields only acorns for animals.[115] Instead, people should plant in their flesh "useful and fruit-bearing trees."[116] Depending on their growth, some trees may need eventual transplantation,[117] but for all, pruning is essential.[118]

In these passages, Chrysostom's ascetic agenda comes sharply into focus. Only the ceaseless toil of clearing, pruning, and judicious watering can release the natural fertility of creation. Images of natural luxuriance are thus always in the service of ethical restraint. His most beautiful pastoral evocation comes in a homily praising patience. The soul of the long-suffering person, he says:

> is like some mountain peak with its fine air and pure sunshine, its limpid gurgling springs and multitude of lovely flowers, while the spring meadows and gardens are lush with trees, and flowers, and rippling streams. And if there is any noise, it is sweet and brings great pleasure to those hearing it. For either the song birds, perching on the topmost branches of the trees, join the cicadas, nightingales, and swallows in pouring forth one harmonious melody, or the west wind, softly rushing through the leafy branches, makes the pine and fir whistle [lit. "pipe" συριζούσας] like swans, or the meadow, deep with roses and lilies rippling and darkening in turn, recalls the dark and gently-billowing sea.[119]

This description brings pleasure, but delighting his congregation is not the preacher's goal: "I did not embark upon this simile simply to sketch a meadow or to make a rhetorical display."[120] His aim, rather, is to change their eyes and thus also their behavior. He wants his listeners to see that associating with virtuous people is even more beneficial and pleasurable than frequenting lovely places, that the apparently barren life of monks and martyrs is the most fertile one imaginable, and that the steadfast refusal to store up surplus is the strategy most in harmony with prodigal nature. As Finley remarks, "Every significant Utopia is conceived as a goal towards which one may legitimately and hopefully strive, a goal not in some shadowy state of perfection but with specific institutional criticisms and proposals."[121] Giving alms, persevering in prayer and repentance, and practicing ethical restraint are the preacher's concrete proposals.

With these highly conventional and beautifully realized vignettes, the preacher has, in effect, created a pastoral world within the church.

Interior gardens were widely admired and commonly adopted in late antiquity. Even modest city residences might have a few plants staked out or a verdant scene painted on an inside wall. More typically, urbanites combined actual and artificial greenery. By planting flowers, bushes, and trees in front of realistic pastoral frescoes, they created green vistas. From a bed of real ivy, painted ivy might appear to climb a garden wall, itself a compositional element of a lush artistic paradise.[122] Exceptionally beautiful natural scenes could, in turn, be described as pictures.[123] The interplay of reality and illusion thus deeply characterizes urban greenspace.

Bucolic poetry and theories of the Golden Age were also artifacts of the city.[124] And it was the city that made their creation necessary. For, as Bettina Bergmann has observed, every mode of pastoralism is informed by "a perceptible conflict between nature and civilization," and it is this conflict that pastoralism resolves through representation.[125] In pastoral landscapes, it is quite typical to find a balanced contrast of urban and rural elements, where distant buildings "serve as foil to the natural locale, defining its quality of escape, confirming its difference."[126]

The conflict, which John Chrysostom's bucolic imagery both acknowledges and mitigates, is the growing divide between ascetic and nonascetic Christians in late antique society. By their lifestyle as well as the prestige it commanded, monks were increasingly separated from "regular" urban Christians. Younger contemporaries, like Theodoret, make clear the outré wildness of many Syrian ascetics, but this is not how they emerge from Chrysostom's writings. Although inhabiting a pristine world of streams, grassy banks, and towering trees, monks live a moderate and orderly life. Indeed, their communal interdependence links their society to that of the city, albeit in startlingly purified form. The glory of their calling, the preacher avers, remains inferior to that of urban clergy.[127] Equally insistent is Chrysostom's emphasis on the "pastoral" vocation of all Christians. By focusing on the far vista and restraining their desires, members of his urban congregation can enjoy the sweet air and peaceful fruit of paradise as surely as the monks. The only difference that separates the regular Christian from the monk is that one is married and the other is not: all else is the same.[128] In this sense, the fields and gardens lauded by Chrysostom do not belong to a distant Golden Age but to a pressing contemporary problem — and one that troubled the city more than the country.

In conclusion, then, Chrysostom's abundant use of natural imagery sprang, in the first instance, from an awareness that anyone in his congregation "would skip at the sight of meadows."[129] This pervasive delight in greenspace arose in the first instance from an appreciation for the healthful benefits of the countryside. Instead of the rank smells, mounds of garbage, and crush of people that characterized the city, rural life was marked by sweet breezes, clear streams, and the songs of birds. While sharing this sense of the superior health advantages of the country, the preacher's appeal to nature extended well beyond hygienic appreciation. With elaborate descriptions of nature, he conveyed doctrinal messages about the majesty and providence of God. In the harmonious interplay of nature, Chrysostom read, above all, the necessity of restraint.

It is this ascetic agenda that most deeply shapes the preacher's use of bucolic language. Thus he adapts motifs of the Golden Age. Instead of the expected denizens — the simple farmers and their virtuous wives — the preacher populates his lush landscapes with martyrs and monks. The ascetic life emerges as one either of peaceful leisure or of pleasurable and harmonious cooperation. Self-renunciation is neither waste nor barrenness, but has uniquely fertilizing properties. To the extent, moreover, that his listeners can change their eyes and cultivate ascetic habits in their urban lives, he promises that they will reap the same bountiful harvest as rural monks.

Chrysostom's deft manipulation of classical motifs also elevates his own status and that of his office. It implies either that preaching is not real work — it is the leisured activity of a shepherd piping under a leafy tree or skipping through a meadow — or that if it is real work, it is at least the noble labor of the agricultural specialist. The clever evocation of pastoral imagery draws attention to the homilist's own erudition, even as it insists that the honor of the priesthood, in general, surpasses that of monasticism.

In every case, these lovely vignettes offered his congregation moments of respite and repose. Like a well-situated villa, or a trompe l'oeil fresco, they afforded a vista, a view onto both the urgent needs of the late antique city and the far-off, utopian gardens of paradise. The inevitable sense of conflict between these realities and, indeed, between their expected inhabitants finds resolution through representation. Rural ascetics are presented as living in an ideal harmonious society, and urban Christians as working the land as noble farmers. These are the images — at once, productive, orderly, and salvific — with which the preacher guided and consoled his congregation.

NOTES

1. Wendy Mayer has directed considerable attention to the question of dating Chrysostom's works (*Homilies of St John Chrysostom*). Her research has resulted in greater precision in dating some homilies, and greater caution with respect to others. In general, however, the bulk of his homilies and treatises still appear to date from his time in Antioch. I have noted where homilies are of either unknown or Constantinopolitan provenance.

2. Rousseau, *Basil of Caesarea*, 323–26.

3. *Hom. in Matt.* 2.5 (PG 57.29). The wilderness "is more suited to the health of the body, providing purer air to breathe" (*Exp. in Ps.* 9.2 [PG 55.123], trans. Hill, *Commentary on the Psalms*, 1:180–81). Chrysostom himself was tempted to stay longer in the countryside to "gain my body's health from the clean air" (*De paen.* 1.1 [PG 49.277], trans. Christo, *On Repentance and Almsgiving*, 2).

4. See Leyerle, "Refuse, Filth."

5. "If you are about to take up residence in a city, you make many inquiries about the air quality, whether or not it is salubrious, temperate, dry" (*Exp. in Ps.* 4.13 [PG 55.60], trans. Hill, *Commentary on the Psalms,* 1:72).

6. *Hom. in Hebr.* 29.3 (PG 63.206). Mayer assigns most of the homilies on Hebrews to Constantinople (*Homilies*, 472).

7. *Hom. in Hebr.* 29.3 (PG 63.206); *De virg.* 68.4 (SC 125.342). See also Libanius's acknowledgment of the delight of gardens (*Or.* 11.17).

8. *In illud: Ne timueritis* 7 (PG 55.510), trans. Hill (as *First Homily on Ps. 49.16*), *Old Testament Homilies*, 3:102; Hill places this homily in Constantinople; cf. *In illud: Ne timueritis* 1 (PG 55.514). Jashemski, *Gardens of Pompeii*, esp. 25–54.

9. *Adv. oppug.* 2.5 (PG 47.338), trans. Hunter, *Comparison,* 105.

10. ἀλλὰ τὸν ἔννομον πλοῦτον, τὴν φυσικὴν εὐπορίαν, ἣν αὐτὸς ὁ θεὸς εἰργάζετο (*Comm. in Job* 1 [PTS 35.7], trans. Hill, *Commentaries on the Sages,* 1:19; Hill finds no evidence for dating this work).

11. *Exp. in Ps.* 9.2 (PG 55.123–24). Libanius also singles out trees in his praise of Antioch (*Or.* 11.19–20).

12. *Hom. in Acta apost.* 22.4 (PG 60.176); *De Anna* 3 (PG 54.656). The homilies on Acts mostly derive from Constantinople (Mayer, *Homilies*, 471).

13. *Exp. in Ps.* 148.3–4 (PG 55.490), trans. Hill, *Commentary on the Psalms*, 2:370; cf. Pliny on the plane tree (*HN* 12.6).

14. Bergmann notes the equally careful depiction of species in Roman garden frescoes ("Staging the Supernatural," 59).

15. *Exp. in Ps.* 9.2 (PG 55.123), trans. Hill, *Commentary on the Psalms*, 1:180–81; *Exp. in Ps.* 148 (PG 55.490); *Hom. in Gen.* 7.5, 10.5 (PG 53.67, 87); cf. Libanius, *Or.* 11.25–26. Peregrine Horden and Nicholas Purcell draw attention to the importance of uncultivated, or "waste," lands in their discussion of the Mediterranean economy (*Corrupting Sea*, 418).

16. *Exp. in Ps.* 9.2 (PG 55.123), trans. Hill, *Commentary on the Psalms*, 1:180–81.

17. *Hom. in Gen.* 14.3 (PG 53.114), trans. Harkins, 187.

18. *Hom. in Gen.* 5.4, 6.4 (PG 53.51, 58).

19. For language of the dance, see *De stat.* 9.2 (PG 49.106); *In illud Isaiae* 2 (PG 56.145). Hill places this latter homily in Chrysostom's Constantinople period. The high degree of overlap between this homily and the ninth homily *On the Statues* suggests the recycling of homiletic material to which Chrysostom alludes in *On the Priesthood* (*De sacerd.* 5.1 [SC 272.282]). Theophrastus also remarked upon the harmony of the universe (French, *Ancient Natural History*, 102), as did Libanius (*Or.* 11.29). The rhythms of the days and seasons provide alternating periods of work and rest (*Hom. in Gen.* 11.1 [PG 53.91–92]).

20. *Contra ludos et theatra* (PG 56.265–66), dated certainly by Mayer to Constantinople (*Homilies*, 509); cf. *De Laz.* 6.2 (PG 48.1029).

21. *Exp. in Ps.* 110.2 (PG 55.282); *De stat.* 9.2–4 (PG 49.106–9).

22. *De stat.* 10.3 (PG 49.114); see also *De stat.* 9.4 (PG 49.108–9). Both the human body and creation "excite admiration of God" precisely because they are fragile and corruptible (*De stat.* 11.2 [PG 49.122]).

23. "God made the heavens so that we might see the work and adore the Creator, but the Greeks made of the work a god" (*De s. Phoca* 3 [PG 50.703], trans. Mayer, *Cult of the Saints*, 84, who dates the homily to Constantinople); see also *Hom. in Gen.* 6.3–4, 7.4 (PG 53.58, 66); *De Anna* 1 (PG 54.634–35).

24. *Exp. in Ps.* 110.3 (PG 55.282), trans. Hill as Psalm 111, *Commentary on the Psalms,* 2:40.

25. *De stat.* 9.2 (PG 49.106). "Do you not see, instead of written material, the whole of creation shouting aloud everywhere?" (*Comm. in Job* 37 [PTS 35.180], trans. Hill, *Commentaries on the Sages*, 1:185). See also *In illud Isaiae* 2 (PG 56.145); *Exp. in Ps.* 110.2 (PG 55.282); *De Anna* 1 (PG 54.634–35); *Exp. in Ps.* 145.3 (PG 55.522).

26. *Exp. in Ps.* 110.3 (PG 55.283), trans. Hill as Psalm 111, *Commentary on the Psalms,* 2:41. Everything in nature is useful, because everything leads to knowledge of God (*Comm. in Job* 40 [PTS 35.196], trans. Hill, *Commentaries on the Sages*, 1:200).

27. Restraint is the dominant message of creation, where "each thing remains fast as if by a kind of bridle and fetter" (*De stat.* 9.4 [PG 49.109]; cf. *Comm. in Job* 37 [PTS 35.180], trans. Hill, *Commentaries on the Sages,* 1:184).

28. *De stat.* 9.2 (PG 49.106); cf. *In illud Isaiae* 2 (PG 56.144–45), trans. Hill, *Old Testament Homilies*, 2:28. The wrathful should imitate "the great obedience" of fire (*Hom. in Gen.* 12.3 [PG 53.101]).

29. *Exp. in Ps.* 110.3 (PG 55.282), trans. Hill as Psalm 111, *Commentary on the Psalms,* 2:40. The great dragon of the deep, although large and fierce, stays in the unnavigable part of the sea to which it was assigned (*Exp. in Ps.* 148.4 [PG 55.490]).

30. "All *loca amoena* in the Greco-Roman tradition can be referred back intertextually to the *topoi* of the Golden Age" (Hinds, "Landscape with Figures," esp. 122–30, quotation on 128).

31. *Op.* 109–20. "Utopian authors set out to critique their own society and throw it into relief by describing a world in which specific institutions, inequalities or vices do not exist" (Evans, *Utopia Antiqua*, 1).

32. *Panchaia*, invented by Euhemerus in the early third century, was the location for his depiction of an idealized society that eliminated hierarchy and private property, money and slavery, and contained an abundance of natural bounty: all varieties of trees, plants, and flowers, vines, fruits and nuts, and health-giving springs (Diodore Siculus 5.42–46, 6.1.4–10). For a discussion of Euhemerus's influence, see T. Brown, "Euhemerus and the Historians."

33. Evans, *Utopia Antiqua*, 6. Typically, the static quality of these societies is conveyed seasonally: it is always spring (37).

34. Levitas, *Concept of Utopia*, 8.

35. *De virg.* 14.5 (SC 125.142); Hesiod, *Op.* 197 ff.

36. *Hom. in Jo.* 65.3 (PG 59.364).

37. In Eden there were no cities, crafts, houses, or clothes (*De virg.* 14.5, 15.2 [SC 125.140, 146]). When God led the Jews through the wilderness, he fed them on manna; they practiced no trade or craft or commerce (*Nemo se laed.* 13 [PG 52.473–74]). In "natural society" there was no slavery, which arose as a consequence of sin (*De inan.* 71 [SC 188.172]).

38. *De Laz.* 4.1 (PG 48.1007–8).

39. *De Laz.* 3.1 (PG 48.992), trans. Roth, *On Wealth and Poverty*, 59.

40. *Adv. oppug.* 2.5 (PG 47.338), trans. Hunter, *Comparison,* 105; *De Laz.* 3.1 (PG 48.992).

41. The current ferocity of wild animals shows the effects of the Fall (*Hom. in Gen.* 9.4 [PG 53.79]).

42. *Hom. in Hebr.* 17.5 (PG 63.134); cf. *Hom. in Matt.* 2.5 (PG 57.29).

43. *Hom. in Matt.* 37.6 (PG 57.428); cf. *Hom. in Acta apost.* 6.3–4 (PG 60.61). The cicada is an integral part of the *locus amoenus* tradition, often serving as a figure for the sage or the poet. See Davies and Kathirithamby, *Greek In-*

sects, 113–33; Beavis, *Insects and Other Invertebrates*, 91–103; Borthwick, "Grasshopper's Diet"; Dihle, "Poem on the Cicada."

44. *De inan*. 59 (SC 188.156–58); cf. 78 (SC 188.180). Unlike urban sights, the beauty of nature gladdens the eye, and the pleasure from that enjoyment is pure (*Hom. in Gen*. 14.3 [PG 53.114]; cf. *De stat*. 9.2 [PG 49.106]; *In illud Isaiae* 2 [PG 56.144]).

45. *De Laz*. 3.1 (PG 48.992); cf. *Hom. in Matt*. 68.3 (PG 58.643).

46. *Catech*. 8.6 (SC 50.250); cf. *Exp. in Ps*. 9.2 (PG 55.123–24). "While we are spending time in the city, it is not very likely that we will reflect on [the transitory nature of life] and think philosophically" (*De s. Dros*. [PG 50.684]).

47. *Hom. in Matt*. 72.4 (PG 58.672).

48. *Adv. oppug*. 2.5 (PG 47.337), trans. Hunter, *Comparison*, 104; cf. *In illud: Ne timueritis* 7 (PG 55.517).

49. Fruit (ἀκρόδρυα), Chrysotom adds, is their only luxury (*Hom. in Matt*. 69.3 [PG 58.653]; cf. 70.3-4 [PG 58.659–61]). "His food is garden vegetables, herbs, and breads from many places" (*Adv. oppug*. 2.5 [PG 47.337]). Hymns of thanksgiving follow their simple dinners (*Hom. in Matt*. 55.5 [PG 58.545]).

50. Evans, *Utopia Antiqua*, 79. As Finley comments, "Ancient . . . Utopias had perforce to accept scarcity of goods as a datum, and therefore to stress simplicity, the curbing of wants, asceticism, and a static society" ("Utopianism Ancient and Modern," 13). See also Poggioli, *Oaten Flute*, 4–9; *De virg*. 70–71 (SC 125.344–48).

51. *Adv. oppug*. 2.5 (PG 47.338), trans. Hunter, *Comparison*, 105. Cf. *Hom. in Matt*. 68.3 (PG 58.643).

52. Hinds, "Landscape with Figures," 124–25. Thus Chrysostom describes the state of Adam and Eve in the garden: "As a limpid stream gushing from a pure source, so they were adorned by virginity in that place" (*De virg*. 14.3 [SC 125.140]). Abraham still lived in this idyllic state: "He covered his roof not with gold, but having fixed his hut beside the oak, he was content with the shade of its leaves" (*De stat*. 2.5 [PG 49.40]). Monastic life recaptures that of Adam before his sin (*Hom. in Matt*. 68.3 [PG 58.643]); it "affords complete leisure" (*De virg*. 77, 79.1–2 [SC 125.368, 376–78]). Occasionally, Chrysostom criticizes monks for an excessive concern for their own leisure (ἀνάπαυσις) (*De compunct*. 1.6 [PG 47.403–4]).

53. *Hom. in Matt*. 72.3 (PG 58.671).

54. *Catech*. 8.3 (SC 50.249).

55. *Adv. oppug*. 2.2 (PG 47.333), trans. Hunter, *Comparison*, 97.

56. *Adv. oppug*. 2.5 (PG 47.339), trans. Hunter, *Comparison*, 106. Monks also spend their time reading and discoursing: their conversation is "constantly on spiritual topics," and a holy Bible in their hands (*Hom. in Gen*. 6.6 [PG 53.61]). While they may appear to know "nothing loftier than farming and taking care of the earth," they in fact have "exact knowledge of things which the philosophers,

who regard their beard and staff so highly, have never even been able to imagine" (*Catech*. 8.6 [SC 50.250]).

57. "As bees will never alight in an unclean vessel . . . so it is with the Holy Spirit" (*Hom. in Ephes*. 15.1 [PG 62.105]; see also *Exp. in Ps*. 41.2 [PG 55.157]). The homilies on Ephesians are hard to date; Mayer concludes that there is no secure basis for assigning them to either Antioch or Constantinople (*Homilies*, 471); see also the comments of Liebeschuetz, *Ambrose and John Chrysostom*, 181–84. Monks are like bees hovering around the honeycombs of the holy books (*Hom. in Matt*. 68.5 [PG 58.646]). Bees are "gentle to everyone" (*Exp. in Ps*. 49.10 [PG 55.256]). "Let us not imitate flies, but emulate bees" (*De proph. obscuritate* 2 [PG 56.192]).

58. *De stat*. 12.2 (PG 49.129); *Exp. in Ps*. 110.3 (PG 55.282). "The various species of ants . . . held a great fascination for the ancients, and they were noted for the qualities of intelligence, hard work, good organisation, and harmonious social life" (Beavis, *Insects and Other Invertebrates*, 198–209, quotation on 198); Davies and Kathirithamby, *Greek Insects*, 37–46.

59. *Exp. in Ps*. 110.3 (PG 55.282), trans. Hill as Psalm 111, *Commentary on the Psalms,* 2:40. The bee is especially praised for its cooperative labor done on behalf of others (*De stat*. 12.2 [PG 49.129]). Bees endorse hierarchy (*Hom. in Rom*. 23.1 [PG 60.615]). Along with cicadas, honey bees were the most popular insects in classical antiquity; see Davies and Kathirithamby, *Greek Insects*, 47–75. Aristotle noted the complexity and harmony of the society of bees; to him it indicated a divine element (*GA* 761b); see French, *Ancient Natural History*, 68.

60. God gave Adam the work of tilling and guarding the garden as "a stabilizing influence," to prevent him being unsettled by too much relaxation and freedom from care. (*Hom. in Gen*. 14.3 [PG 53.114], trans. Hill, *Homilies on Genesis,* 185). The picture is not wholly dissimilar from the Golden Age, as described by Aratus. In Evans's words, "by eliding the labour involved in agriculture" it represented "an idyllic middle way, neither labour-free nor labour-intensive" (*Utopia Antiqua*, 35). See also Loraux, "Ponos."

61. *Hom. in Matt*. 72.3 (PG 58.671).

62. *Hom. in Matt*. 72.4 (PG 58.672).

63. Finley, "Utopianism Ancient and Modern," 6–7.

64. The terms are those of Hinds ("Landscape with Figures," 128).

65. A trope, Evans remarks, of the Golden Age (*Utopia Antiqua*, 17).

66. Ibid., 20–22.

67. *Hom. in Hebr*. 29.4 (PG 63.208); *De stat*. 1.4 (PG 49.22); *Hom. in Acta apost*. 22.4 (PG 60.176).

68. Any surplus goes for the support of the needy (*Hom. in Matt*. 68.3 [PG 58.644]).

69. *De s. Phoca* 1 (PG 50.699), trans. Mayer, *Cult of the Saints*, 78; *In s. Ignatium* (PG 50.587). Spring flowers are particularly apt for virgin martyrs, as they are associated with virginal purity (Hinds, "Landscape with Figures," 133). Roses, lilies, and irises (along with violets) were among the most popular garden flowers because of their use in making garlands (Jashemski, *Gardens of Pompeii*, 271, citing Varro, *Rust*. 1.16.3); cf. Chrysostom, *Hom. in Acta apost*. 6.3–4 (PG 60.61).

70. Jashemski, *Gardens of Pompeii*, 28–32. *De proph. obscuritate* 2 (PG 56.192). Hannah was like "a vine [that, although] fixed in one place, extends its branches widely, and the bunches of grapes hang down at a great distance and touch the root" (*De Anna* 3 [PG 54.652, 655], trans. Hill, *Old Testament Homilies*, 1:96, 100).

71. *De Eleazaro et septem pueris* 1 (PG 53.523), trans. Mayer, *Cult of the Saints*, 121. The death of the Maccabean martyrs is thus described as a "harvesting of the entire tree" (*De Maccabeis* 2.2 [PG 50.625], trans. Mayer, *Cult of the Saints,* 151). "Just like a tree's root that has two shoots standing on either side" was the woman martyr with her two virgin daughters (*De ss. Bernice et Prosdoce* 6 [PG 50.638], trans. Mayer, *Cult of the Saints,* 172).

72. Chrysostom reproves his congregation for going out to the *martyria* frivolously: "Do you want to spend time in gardens and meadows and parks? Don't do it now, while there's such a crowd, but on another day" (*Hom. in martyres* [PG 50.665]). See also Purcell, "Town in Country," 188, citing Latin inscriptions (*CIL* VI, 13823, 31852, 15993). Jashemski, *Gardens of Pompeii*, 141–54.

73. *In Juventinum et Maximum martyres* 1 (PG 50.573).

74. *De ss. Bernice et Prosdoce* 1 (PG 50.629).

75. "Broadly speaking, utopias are often projected into the future, while the Golden Age usually exists in the past" (Evans, *Utopia Antiqua*, 6).

76. Ibid., 7. See also Poggioli, *Oaten Flute*, esp. 1–33. Speaking of the *Odes* of Theocritus, Krevans notes: "The pastoral world is repressively safe, a place where nature is unnaturally benign and the only human sorrows are erotic. It stands in implicit or explicit contrast to the world of the reader, a world filled with modern urban anxieties" ("Is There an Urban Pastoral?," 141).

77. "Utopian ideas and fantasies, like all ideas and fantasies, grow out of the society to which they are a response" (Finley, "Utopianism Ancient and Modern," 6). As Purcell comments, the landscape consciousness of the Romans "definitely included — if it did not indeed center on — the city" ("Town in Country," 196).

78. Kumar, *Utopianism*, 96.

79. *Si esurierit inimicus* 2 (PG 51.174–75).

80. *Si esurierit inimicus* 2 (PG 51.174–75); *Adv. Jud*. 5.7 (PG 48.897).

81. Flowers: *De stat*. 6.6 (PG 49.90); *De proph. obscuritate* 2 (PG 56.192); *De Anna* 3 (PG 54.652, 656); *Hom. in Hebr*. 17.5 (PG 63.134); *De s. Phoca* 1

(PG 50.699); *Hom. in Matt.* 72.4 (PG 58.672). Streams: *In illud: Ne timueritis* 1 (PG 55.512); *De Anna* 5 (PG 54.671).

82. Curtius, *European Literature,* 195, quoted in Hinds, "Landscape with Figures," 123. Compare Chrysostom's extraordinary evocation in *Hom. in Acta apost.* 6.3–4 (PG 60.61).

83. This preference for the exploited landscape was typical of Chrysostom's time. See the remarks of Purcell, "Town in Country," 202.

84. *Adv. Jud.* 4.1 (PG 48.871); *De Anna* 4 (PG 54.661).

85. A view found already in Hesiod and Homer. See the remarks of Gutzwiller, *Theocritus' Pastoral Analogies*, 29–35. The herdsman was, as she remarks elsewhere, "good to think with" ("Herdsman in Greek Thought").

86. *De paen.* 5.5 (PG 49.314). Plato had noted how herdsmen can soothe a flock with music (*Plt.* 268b, *Ion* 540c).

87. The use of λεπτός to describe the reed pipe or pen evokes the Alexandrian tradition of pastoral poetry. Callimachus prefers the slender Muse, the simplicity of children, and the lightness of insects (*Aetia* 1.23–38), and Athenaeus recalls Aristophanes' desire for "the cicada, caught on a slender reed" (*Deipnosophistae* 4.133b). My thanks to Albertus Horsting for pointing out these parallels. The exchange of song, as Nita Krevans notes, lies at the heart of the bucolic genre ("Is There an Urban Pastoral?," 137).

88. *De paen.* 5.5 (PG 49.314).

89. *De sacerd.* 5.8 (SC 272.298–304).

90. *De proph. obscuritate* 2 (PG 56.175), trans. Hill, *Old Testament Homilies*, 3:25.

91. For an extended analogy comparing Flavian, leading his congregation out to a suburban *martyrium*, to a shepherd taking his flock to its summer pasture, see *De s. Droside* (PG 50.683).

92. *Adv. Jud.* 4.1 (PG 48.871). For the analogy between guarding sheep and guarding knowledge, see Gutzwiller, *Theocritus' Pastoral Analogies*, 30–31, 25–27.

93. On the vices as enemies, see *De sacerd.* 2.2–3 (SC 272.106–8).

94. *Adv. Jud.* 4.1 (PG 48.871), trans. Harkins, *Discourses against Judaizing Christians,* 71–72. Theocritus established the *syrinx* as the metonymic symbol of bucolic poetry (Hunter, "Virgil's ECL. 1," 264).

95. Hinds, "Landscape with Figures," 131.

96. Jashemski, *Gardens of Pompeii*, 55–87. Chrysostom seems to allude to this custom when he exhorts his congregation to paint scriptural scenes on their walls (*De Laz.* 4.2 [PG 48.1008]) or to engrave crosses on walls (*Hom. in Matt.* 54.4 [PG 58.537]), or even the flying sickle, as he understands it, of Zech 5.1–3 (*De stat.* 9.5 [PG 49.110]).

97. For parallels between literary and painted landscapes in ancient Rome, see Leach, *Rhetoric of Space*; Bergmann, "Exploring the Grove," 21–46.

98. To describe the melancholy appearance of Antioch after the riot of the statues, Chrysostom uses the image of a garden whose irrigation system has failed and of a mighty forest that has been clear-cut (*De stat.* 2.1–2 [PG 49.35–36]).

99. *Hom. in Gen.* 13.1 (PG 53.105); *De paen.* 8.1 (PG 49.336).

100. *Adv. Jud.* 4.1 (PG 48.871–72).

101. *Hom. in Gen.* 9.1, 13.1 (PG 53.76, 105); *Hom. in Matt.* 42.4 (PG 57.456); *Catech.* 1.47 (SC 50.132); *In illud: Ne timueritis* 1 (PG 55.499); cf. *De inan.* 37 (SC 188.128). "I throw down the seeds. If you who receive the seeds are fertile land, you yield mature ears of grain. If you are sterile rock, it's nothing to do with me" (*De s. Phoca* 2 [PG 50.703], trans. Mayer, *Cult of the Saints*, 83). At one time, the monks till the earth and, at another "they take in hand the plough of teaching and deposit the seed of divine learning in the souls of their disciples" (*Catech.* 8.3 [SC 50.249]).

102. *Hom. in Oziam* 4.1 (SC 277.136), trans. Hill, *Old Testament Homilies*, 2:80; *De proph. obscuritate* 2 (PG 56.176).

103. *De beato Philogonio* 3 (PG 48.752), trans. in Mayer and Allen, *John Chrysostom*, 190. For fences in gardens, see Jashemski, *Gardens of Pompeii*, 49–51.

104. *Hom. in Jo.* 18.1 (PG 59.113); *Hom. in Gen.* 17.7 (PG 53.144).

105. Although he may not feel the same eagerness (*De Laz.* 6.2, 7.1 [PG 48.1029, 1045]; *Hom. in Gen.* 6.1 [PG 53.55]); cf. *Hom. in Gen.* 2.4 (PG 53.31).

106. *De Laz.* 4.1 (PG 48.1007), trans. Roth, *On Wealth and Poverty,* 79.

107. *In illud: Ne timueritis* 3 (PG 55.515), trans. Hill (as *Second Homily on Ps. 49.16*), *Commentary on the Psalms,* 1:110.

108. *Hom. in Acta apost.* 22.4 (PG 60.176).

109. *De eleemosyna* 5 (PG 51.268); cf. *De non it. conj.* 6 (SC 138.198).

110. *Hom. in Gen.* 2.1 (PG 53.26).

111. Theophrastus decided to take a single kind of plant as an exemplar for the rest, choosing it apparently for its perfection. He chose the tree (*HP* 1.1.6, cited in French, *Ancient Natural History*, 94).

112. *Hom. in Ephes.* 21.4 (PG 62.154).

113. *Exp. in Ps.* 129.1 (PG 55.373), trans. Hill (as Psalm 130), *Commentary on the Psalms,* 2:191.

114. *De Anna* 3 (PG 54.652, 656).

115. *De Laz.* 6.4 (PG 48.1032). Oak trees describe people "wholly involved in commerce" (*De Laz.* 6.5 [PG 48.1033]), and therefore also prostitutes (*De paen.* 8 [PG 49.338]); on this association, see Leyerle, "John Chrysostom on Almsgiving."

116. *Hom. in Hebr.* 29.4 (PG 63.208); *Hom. in Gen.* 13.4 (PG 53.110); *De paen.* 3.1 (PG 49.291). Here "fruit" means concrete practices.

117. Samuel, for example, needed transplantation to the temple "where there were constant sources of spiritual irrigation" (*De Anna* 3 [PG 54.656]).

118. *De Maccabeis* 2.2 (PG 50.626), trans. Mayer, *Cult of the Saints*, 153; *De stat*. 1.4 (PG 49.22). According to Theophrastus, cultivated plants that are neglected and left unpruned become so inferior that their natures change. Thus, for him, a wild fig has no greater relationship to a cultivated fig than to any other plant (*CP* 1.9.2; 1.18.4, 3.2.1; discussed in French, *Ancient Natural History*, 96–98).

119. *Hom. in Acta apost*. 6.3 (PG 60.61).

120. ἐπίδειξιν τὸν λόγον (*Hom. in Acta apost*. 6.4 [PG 60.61]).

121. Finley, "Utopianism Ancient and Modern," 6.

122. See the remarks of Bergmann, "Staging the Supernatural," esp. 58–69.

123. Pliny the Younger wrote: "It is a great pleasure to look down on the countryside from the mountain, for the view seems to be a painted scene of unusual beauty rather than a real landscape, and the harmony to be found in this variety refreshes the eye wherever it turns" (*Ep*. 5.6.13, trans. Betty Radice, LCL, quoted in Bergmann, "Staging the Supernatural," 55).

124. A point made by Krevans about Theocritus ("Is There an Urban Pastoral?," 145–46).

125. Bergmann, "Exploring the Grove," 42. Other contradictions animating the pastoral tradition would include complex and simple, urban and rural, urbane and sophisticated, real and manufactured, vain and humble, temporal and eternal (Pinto, "Pastoral Landscape and Antiquity," 194).

126. Rosand, "Pastoral Topoi," 163.

127. *De sacerd*. 6.5–7 (SC 272.320–26); *De beato Philogonio* 3 (PG 48.752).

128. *Hom. in Matt*. 43.5 (PG 57.464) and 55.6 (PG 58.548); *De Laz*. 3.1 (PG 48.992). Liebeschuetz, *Ambrose and John Chrysostom*, 185–204; Brottier, *L'appel des "demi-chrétiens"*; Maxwell, *Christianization and Communication*, 144–64.

129. *De s. Phoca* 1 (PG 50.699), trans. Mayer, *Cult of the Saints*, 78; *Hom. in martyres* (PG 50.665).

PART IV

Founding the Field

Chapter Fourteen

Adolf Harnack and the Paleontological Layer of Church History

CLAUDIA RAPP

The nineteenth century was an exciting period for the study of antiquity in Germany. Karl Lachmann (1793–1851) had recently pioneered the modern philological method of textual analysis that aimed to establish the "Urtext" by peeling away the layers that had accumulated and obscured it in the process of textual transmission—a method that he applied to the Iliad as much as to the New Testament. The Monumenta Germaniae Historica series for the edition of all kinds of sources relevant to the late antique and medieval history of Germany was founded in 1819; late antique texts were added in the Auctores Antiquissimi subseries in 1876.[1] The Corpus Scriptorum Historiae Byzantinae was started in 1828. The first volume of the *Realencyclopädie der classischen Altertumswissenschaft* was published by August Pauly in 1839, based on the recognition that material artifacts are as relevant to the study of antiquity as the classical authors. Schliemann "discovered" Troy in 1871, the German Archaeological Institute in Athens was established in 1874, and excavations began in Pergamon in 1878. The Academy of Sciences in Berlin became home to large-scale collaborative projects: the *Prosopographia Imperii Romani*; the *Thesaurus Linguae Latinae* (a joint project of several academies), the *Corpus Nummorum* of Roman coins, and the *Corpus Inscriptionum Latinarum*— all thanks to the initiative of Theodor Mommsen, who also edited, together with Paul Krüger, Justinian's *Digest* (1868–172) and the *Codex Theodosianus* (published 1905, two years after Mommsen's death).[2] These scholarly endeavors were riding on the tide of a new impetus to invigorate education at schools and universities proposed by intellectuals and politicians in the Kingdom of Prussia.[3] The study of Latin and classical Greek became the centerpiece of the "humanistisches Gymnasium" in the expectation that the mastery of the ancient languages, especially of Greek, would shape the mental faculties of the future German elite and that familiarity with classical culture and history would equip them with a moral compass and cultivate their aesthetic senses. Education, or better, formation in the classics became the pedagogical ideal for a fully realized humanity and thus acquired quasi-religious status, a "neuhumanistische Bildungsreligion," in the apt phrase coined by the German social historian Hans-Ulrich Wehler.[4] The Friedrich-Wilhelms-Universität (now Humboldt-Universität) in Berlin was founded in 1809, and instruction began in the following year in the four divisions (*Fakultäten*) of law, medicine, philosophy, and theology.

Through all these initiatives, the methodological triad of philology, archaeology, and history was established as the key for gaining a detailed and complete knowledge of the ancient world. The focus of this enterprise was, first and foremost, classical Athens — the seminal period that had been the inspiration for generations of Germans and the object of the romantic longings of the German *Bildungbürgertum* ever since the days of Goethe and Schiller, reinforced by the educational ideal of Wilhelm von Humboldt.[5] Roman history, if it was the object of academic study at all, was entirely focused on the republican period as a model for a structured and balanced society. In all these pioneering efforts, one phenomenon was awkwardly out of place: the Christian religion, the way it gained a stronghold in (some might even say a stranglehold on) the society of the Later Roman Empire and its rapid permeation of Greek and Latin literary production.

In the following, I wish to explore how one eminent German scholar, Adolf von Harnack, approached the methodological challenge posed by the study of Christianity. His historical vision of its development led him to emphasize the importance of the third century, which he labeled the "paleontological" layer. This choice of terminology, as I shall argue, not only points to the degree to which recent scientific discoveries in geology and biology shaped the language of the "soft" sciences but also shows that Harnack's scholarship evolved in close dialogue with colleagues abroad, especially Edwin Hatch in Oxford.

Adolf Harnack (1851–1930) may with some justification be called the father of patristic scholarship in Germany.[6] He was professor of church history in Berlin from 1888 to 1921 and creator of the series Die Griechischen Christlichen Schriftsteller (GCS) of the Academy of Sciences in Berlin, which will concern us again later. He was the author of the hugely influential *Lehrbuch der Dogmengeschichte* (1886) and of *Die Mission und Ausbreitung des Christentums in den ersten drei Jahrhunderten* (1902). But Harnack's range of activity and radius of influence extended far beyond the study of church history. He was director of the Preussische Staatsbibliothek from 1905 to 1921 and in this role advocated that women should be able to pursue careers in library work, not merely hold jobs. His daughter Elisabeth took a PhD in "Nationalökonomie," and his daughter Agnes was the first woman to hold a position in a Prussian ministry, as organizer of the women's assistance program during World War I. She would later write her father's biography.[7] On the occasion of the bicentenary of the Academy of Sciences in Berlin, Harnack wrote a two-volume work on the history of this venerable institution that predates the foundation of the Humboldt University in Berlin by over a century.[8] He devoted considerable energy to the creation of infrastructures that would facilitate large-scale collaborative research. Thus he was instrumental in the foundation of the Kaiser-Wilhelm-Gesellschaft (now the Max-Planck-Gesellschaft) that aimed to facilitate research in the sciences in interaction with industry. Active in politics, he was on friendly terms with Kaiser Wilhelm II, who conferred on him hereditary nobility in 1914,[9] but after the end of World War I, Harnack was quick to support the Weimar Republic. Indeed, in 1921, he was even asked to serve as Germany's ambassador to the United States — an invitation that he declined, somewhat disingenuously, as we shall see, on the grounds of his insufficient mastery of English. When he died in 1930, the only student who spoke at his funeral was Dietrich Bonhoeffer, who would later make his name as a theologian and end his life in April 1945 in the Flossenburg concentration camp, executed as one of the Protestant opponents of the Nazi regime. Harnack's written output, which includes monographs, articles, book reviews, and all sorts of speeches and pamphlets, is immense: the published bibliography of his work contains 1,611 entries.[10]

Like many German intellectuals of the nineteenth and twentieth centuries, Harnack's background was the "protestantisches Pfarrhaus": his father Theodosius Harnack (1817–89) was "Professor der praktischen Theologie" and author of an important work on the theology of Martin Luther.[11] After completing the Gymnasium with the traditional curriculum in Latin and Greek, Harnack took up the study of theology. This apparently needed some justification, as theology was at that time considered less a scholarly discipline than a preparation for the pastoral duties of a minister. Harnack thus felt compelled to explain in a letter to a classmate that his motivation was not a strong faith but rather an abiding curiosity about the evolution of Christianity as a cultural force. His approach to theology, in other words, was from the beginning informed by a historical perspective.[12] This was a novel approach at the time. As a theologian with historical interests, Harnack in the earlier decades of his career met with skepticism from the Protestant establishment as well as from the academic world, not to mention the anguished disapproval of his own father.[13]

After his studies in Leipzig (where he founded the *Theologische Literaturzeitung* with his friends Oskar von Gebhardt and the Judaist Ernst Schürer), Harnack held his first appointment in Giessen. His innovative efforts to study the development of the church did not go unnoticed. In 1885, he was offered a post at Harvard but chose to take up a position in Marburg instead, where he spent two years from July 1886 to September 1888.[14] Only a year later, he was invited to join the Faculty of Theology at the Humboldt University in Berlin, although the protest by the Evangelischer Oberkirchenrat (which accused him of undermining faith in the text of the New Testament through his philological work) was so strong that it took a whole year and required the intervention of several politicians, including Otto von Bismarck, before the Prussian Ministry of Culture finally implemented his appointment.[15] Even though the Protestant Church's opposition to Harnack's professorship was overcome, the resistance to him as a scholar remained. Until the end of his life, he regretted that he was never invited to participate in the examinations for future Protestant ministers. Harnack was only the fifth professor of church history at the recently founded university in Berlin (1810). As Kurt Aland put it: "Harnack was the one who established church history as a scholarly discipline at the university in Berlin."[16] His legacy at the university was continued by his pupils Karl Holl (1906–26) and Hans Lietzmann (1924–42).

Soon after his arrival, in 1890 to be exact, Harnack was accepted as a member of the Academy of Sciences in Berlin. Again, he was among the first in his discipline to blaze a new trail. He was only the third theologian, after Friedrich Schleiermacher and the latter's disciple August Neander, to be accepted into their ranks. Indeed, theologians as such had been specifically excluded from membership in the Academy since its reorganization under Frederick II "the Great" in 1744, unless they recommended themselves on the basis of other merits. In Harnack's case, it was his firmly historical approach to the study of early Christianity that redeemed him, though just barely.[17] Still, five years later, the majority of academicians refrained from electing Harnack as their general secretary because he was tainted with the "horrific name of theologian" (*Schrecknamen Theologe*).[18] The legitimacy of theology as an academic enterprise was still very much in question. Over time, Harnack was able to rise above these suspicions because of his interest in the evolution of Christianity, its beliefs and institutions, within the context of the Later Roman Empire.

Harnack's deliberately historical approach gained him allies and supporters. He owed his position in Berlin to the influential Roman historian Theodor Mommsen (1817–1903), who not only advocated his appointment to the professorship at the university but also submitted the formal request for his acceptance to the Academy of Sciences. Mommsen especially valued his eagerness to subject the constitutive texts of this period to rigorous methods of *Quellenforschung*.[19]

Mommsen was a major figure in Berlin. As a leading member of the Academy since 1858 and professor of Roman history since 1861, he initiated and secured funding for the long-term, collaborative projects mentioned earlier. The impetus for these enterprises was the desire to establish a firm body of evidence for the study of antiquity. The work of the historian could not be done without the prior editorial work of the philologist, or without the collecting and editing activity of the epigrapher. Mommsen was also a pioneer because he pushed the boundaries of the study of antiquity. In the nineteenth century, Roman history was overshadowed by the study of classical Athens, which served as a model and inspiration for the intellectual and political elite. Berlin, after all, liked to style itself as "Athens on the River Spree" (*Spree-Athen*). If Rome was studied at all, the main period of interest was the Roman Republic. Mommsen changed that by expanding his interest to the Roman Empire all the way to its collapse in the West. Within this widened chronological range, Christianity as a historical phenomenon and cultural force could no longer be ignored.

The third dominant figure in Berlin was Ulrich von Wilamowitz-Moellendorff, equally indebted to Mommsen. Professor of classics from 1897 to 1921, he was married to Maria Mommsen, the daughter of his admired teacher. Wilamowitz advocated the unity of all *Altertumswissenschaft,* the integration of history, philology, and what we would today call "material culture." Rather unconventionally, his interest as a philologist in the development of the Greek language extended also to postclassical and Christian authors.

Harnack, Mommsen, and Wilamowitz — the theologian, the historian, and the philologist — soon found themselves collaborating in a major project for the edition of Christian authors. It was the brainchild of Harnack but was supported by Mommsen from the start. Both men were scholars as much as they were managers of scholarship. Mommsen highlighted this aspect in his written application for Harnack's membership in the Academy in 1889, when he characterized Harnack's vision for future scholarship as *Grosswissenschaft,* in analogy to *Grossindustrie*— that is, large collaborative, long-term projects that also included younger colleagues.[20] The great project that Mommsen proposed was the creation of a Corpus Patrum Graecorum Antenicaenorum.[21] Mommsen emphasized the urgent need for this project, which he declared to be a "duty of honor," because the Academy in Vienna had already in 1864 founded the Corpus Scriptorum Ecclesiasticorum Latinorum with the aim of producing new, reliable editions in place of those of the Maurists, but without any further interpretive or methodological agenda.[22] While the CSEL concentrated on Latin authors and published the prefatory materials in Latin, the projected series in Berlin was devoted to Greek authors and offered prefatory material in German. The aim of this project was, after all, to be modern. It soon was to be known as Die Griechischen Christlichen Schriftsteller der ersten drei Jahrhunderte (GCS) and the committee that set to work on it as the Kirchenväterkommission.

Harnack was the director of the Kirchenväterkommission for thirty-nine years until his death in 1930, with Mommsen as a close colleague in the beginning. Wilamowitz joined the team in 1897, immediately after his appointment as Professor Ordinarius in Berlin.[23] The collaborators included historians, philologists, and patristic scholars, for whom the project represented different aims: historians hoped to bring to light additional sources for the history of the Roman Empire, philologists expected insights into the development of the Greek language throughout the centuries, and patristic scholars sought to employ the methods of modern scholarship to uncover the earliest layer of Christianity.[24]

The exact definition of this foundational layer remained an ongoing question that engaged Harnack throughout his academic career. The encyclopedic and totalizing approach of *Quellenforschung* in the context of the GCS soon led to the realization that the works of the Greek fathers of the first three centuries were often accessible only in translations into languages other than Greek, or in redactions or citations by authors of later periods. Already at its first meeting, the Kirchenväterkommission discussed the possible inclusion of George Synkellos, the Byzantine church historian of the early ninth century.[25] Soon a general decision was made to include later authors if they preserved material that was relevant for the study of earlier Christian writing.[26] In 1902, thanks to the initiative of Wilamowitz, a formal decision was taken to extend the publication program to the first five centuries, a removal of chronological barriers that was to be reflected much later in the 1945 adoption of the abbreviated series title, which is still current: Die Griechischen Christlichen

Schriftsteller.[27] The original discussions about the time frame covered by the publication project were thus primarily the result, not of historical interpretations, but of philological concerns that arose in conjunction with its editorial work.

Harnack's historical interests, however, always pulled him back to the second and third centuries, as the pivotal period of church history and the entry point to understanding all prior and subsequent developments. In Harnack's view, the third century was the key period when Christianity forged a synthesis with Hellenism, which facilitated the growth and expansion of Christianity within the existing intellectual and political framework of Greco-Roman antiquity.

Harnack dubbed this the "paleontological layer" of church history. This expression has become something of a buzzword among Harnack scholars, as it encapsulates his entire conception of church history.[28] Harnack readily acknowledged that the period from 300 to 450 was crucial for the melding of Christianity with the forces of antiquity that gave shape to later medieval culture, with repercussions to the present day. But to him, the Greek authors after 300 lacked originality and largely replicated ideas that resulted from debates and dialogues between Greco-Roman culture and Christianity that had taken place in the second and third centuries. A further argument for the importance of the third century was based on the internal development of the Christian Church, since this was the period when its organizational structure, liturgical practices, and faith traditions were streamlined and solidified. Hence Harnack's emphasis on the need to dig deeper than the reign of Constantine, to reach the layer where the life of Christianity, in the form of its dogma and its institutions, had its origin — his "paleontological layer."[29]

Harnack first employed this expression in an official context in 1916, in a report on the GCS series before the Academy, but he had already used it in print in 1883, as we shall see below. A decade later (1927), in a similar report, Harnack elaborated on his view of the "layers" of Greek Christian literature. The oldest layer, he argued, reached to about 150 and was constituted by the New Testament and contemporary writings. The second and most significant period extended from the mid-second century until the time of Eusebius and Constantine. And the third and richest layer included all Christian literature until Iconoclasm in the eighth and ninth centuries.[30] With perceptive complexity, Harnack explained the relative merits of these layers for understanding the evolution of Christianity. The earliest layer presented the unique message of Christianity. By the time of the third layer, patristic literature gave definitive shape to all branches of scholarship and science and provided the foundation for the later development of national literatures in East and West. But only the second layer allowed for the detailed study of the evolution of Christianity to the point where it was able to spread into the subsequent periods. This second period, Harnack's "paleontological" layer, represented much more than merely a fossilization of the materials of the first, or the sediment on which the third was built. It was in and of itself the *formative* period in which Christianity separated from its Jewish roots and came to a full awareness of its own uniqueness; it was the time when it gave itself an external, institutional framework and strengthened its inner life through the formulation of its own belief system, in order to assert its existence in the context of the Greco-Roman world. Harnack's second and third layers combined thus correspond exactly to the most common chronological bookends currently *en vogue* for late antiquity. But it cannot be emphasized enough that our current periodicizations are usually driven by attention to historical and social phenomena, while Harnack's approach was that of an archaeologist of textual traditions, informed by his understanding of the evolution and transmission of Christian writing.

It is interesting to do some digging of our own and to pursue Harnack's use of the concept of paleontology further, as this shows that he did not work in intellectual or geographical isolation. In the mid- and late nineteenth century, the sciences gave great impetus to the historian's task of searching for origins and causes. Geologists such as Charles Lyell in England, who published his *Principles of Geology* in 1830, had begun to study the different layers of sediment, which offered insight into historical progression. Charles Darwin published *The Origin of Species* in 1859—the fruit of research that began on his voyage on the HMS *Beagle* in 1831–36. It was especially the study of the fossils in South America in their relation to living wildlife that eventually gave rise to his theory of evolution. Darwin's work quickly gained recognition abroad. Within four years of its publication, the *Origin of Species* was translated into German (1863). Ernst Haeckel (1834–1919), professor of zoology and later pro-rector of the University of Jena, became a great promoter of Darwin's work in Germany (and eventually revoked his own membership in the Protestant Church), and it was thanks to him that, in 1868, Darwin was awarded the order *Pour le Mérite* by the King of Prussia. In that year, Harnack completed his high school education. I have not found any evidence that Harnack himself, for all the parallels he liked to draw with paleontology as a method, was an admirer of Darwin's theories. It would seem doubtful that, theologian and devout Christian that he was, he would have entirely approved. Moreover, Harnack was a close friend of the physician and public health advocate Rudolf Virchow, who was skeptical about Darwin's idea of the origin of species and was himself a strong opponent of Darwin's foremost German admirer, Ernst Haeckel.

The use of vocabulary from the sciences was not unusual among nineteenth-century humanists, including scholars of late antique history, religion, and culture. Many of them entertained an enduring personal fascination with scientific observation and the possible applications of new scientific methods to their own field. Take the example of Friedrich Preisigke, who is best known for his meticulous study of the Greek language in the Egyptian papyri but who spent his professional life in the postal service, culminating in his appointment as *Kaiserlicher Telegraphendirektor* in Strassburg before he was granted an honorary professorship at Heidelberg after World War I. He published a small treatise in which he explained early Christian popular views on the working of the Holy Spirit by recourse to analogy with the effect of electricity that could be physically experienced, yet was invisible in its movement until it found an outlet.[31] Harnack's student Karl Holl had a lifelong fascination for astronomy, published a treatise in 1922 entitled *Anleitung zur Himmelsbeobachtung mit kleinen Fernrohren* (A Guide to Observation of the Sky with Small Telescopes), and still late in life regaled students with explanations of the night sky from the balcony of his flat in Berlin-Wilmersdorf.[32] Karl Krumbacher, the first holder of the Chair in Byzantine Studies at the University of Munich (1897), whose magisterial work on the history of Byzantine literature Harnack greatly admired, was intrigued by the potential of photography for the study of ancient manuscripts.[33]

In the Harnack family, too, the study of the sciences was encouraged. Adolf Harnack's twin brother Axel became a mathematician, and his younger brother Erich a physician and pharmacologist. Harnack's own fascination was with the disciplines of geography and mathematics. Already as a schoolboy, he seized every opportunity to study maps, an interest he shared with his mother.[34] Later, he himself drew all the maps in his *Mission und Ausbreitung des Christentums in den ersten drei Jahrhunderten*.[35] He also was highly competent in mathematics. His students in Giessen noticed that the edition of Tertullian that he used in his seminars had mathematical equations written on the inside because he had used it at the Gymnasium.[36] His mathematical acumen seems never to have left him. Erhard Schmidt, a mathematician and fellow-academician in Berlin, noted with admiration after Harnack's death that the great scholar had always been able to follow difficult mathematical equations.[37]

Scientific observation of individual phenomena and their interpretation as part of a complete whole became Harnack's leading principle for scholarly enterprise. In a letter to Mommsen, Harnack emphasized the value of "striving for complete induction, going back to the genuine and pure sources that are not muddled by doctrine."[38] Harnack's use of the notion of "complete induction" may well have been indebted not only to contemporary philosophical thought but especially to the mathematical concept of induction.[39] New developments in the sciences since the 1850s demonstrated for Harnack the value of the specialized study of discrete bodies of evidence, but always with a view to applying the insights gained by such focused study to an understanding of the whole. "The biologist studied primarily the lowest organisms, the psychologist became a psychophysicist, the philosopher of language became a physiologist of sound, and the historian an economic statistician or a diplomatist."[40]

In conversation, as reported by his admiring biographer and daughter Agnes, Harnack often referred to fossilized animals to show that scientific observation of traces from the distant past allowed conclusions about larger issues, a method that could be extended to the theological enterprise: "When I deduce from the eye and the ear of a fossilized animal that there was light and sound, that the sun was shining and the wind was blowing, then I deduce with the same justification on the basis of our disposition toward God and eternity that there is only one reality that corresponds to it."[41]

Harnack was not the first, however, to invoke the notion of paleontology or to advocate the method of induction in the context of church history. That was the merit of Edwin Hatch, Anglican priest, vice-principal of

St. Mary's Hall in Oxford (which was absorbed into Oriel College in 1874), and from 1885 onward a reader in ecclesiastical history at Oxford University.[42] In 1880, Hatch was elected to present the Bampton Lectures at Oxford. He chose to speak on the subject of "the organization of the early church." While he was standing for election to hold these lectures, in 1878, he wrote to a friend: "My subject is the early organization of Christianity. I have gone over the whole ground for a series of articles for Smith's Dictionaries, and I have a good deal to say which, as far as I can make out, has not been said before. Indeed the subject could not be treated in the comparative method until the recent thorough investigation of the internal organization of the Roman Empire by Marquardt, Mommsen, Kuhn, and others: I have added to what they have done an independent investigation of all post-Christian Greek and Roman inscriptions, which has given some important results."[43] The integration of church history with the history of the Roman Empire especially as evidenced in material culture, in this instance epigraphy, was a guiding principle for Hatch as much as it was for Harnack and indeed for Mommsen.

Hatch's Bampton Lectures so impressed Harnack that he took it upon himself to translate the work into German.[44] His excitement about Hatch's research was such that he could not refrain from adding thirty pages of his own commentary and later referred to this publication as *Hatch-Harnack, Gesellschaftsverfassung der christlichen Kirchen*.[45] It is in this translation of Hatch, published in 1883, that the word *paleontology* first flows from Harnack's pen. In one of several passages that mention paleontology, Hatch explains his method thus: "The palaeontologist, for example, makes his inferences partly by putting together all that he can find about the fauna and flora of each stratum, and partly by tracing each type of animal or plant through successive strata, so as to arrive at a conclusion respecting the order and succession of life upon the earth."[46] Paleontology for Hatch here serves to illustrate the historical methods of synchronic and diachronic research, as we would now call it. To address questions of methodology, Hatch made frequent reference to fossils and paleontology in his speeches and writings.[47] Eight years after the Bampton Lectures, in 1888, he gave the Hibbert Lectures in Oxford and London, entitled "The Influence of Greek Ideas and Usages upon the Christian Church." It was Harnack's student Erwin Preuschen who translated these lectures into German in 1892. Harnack wrote a short postscript to the volume, and it is not unreasonable to assume that the translation was made at his suggestion.[48]

Harnack initially followed Hatch in his reference to paleontology. It was a convenient and modern way to refer to a historical method that proceeded with purpose and precision, collecting scraps of evidence from different chronological layers. The historian's skill consisted in their assembly, juxtaposition, and sequencing, which allowed him to make assumptions about the progression and evolution of ideas and institutions on the basis of his speculation about their origins — a perfect exercise in the method of induction. Everything depended on the availability of evidence. The vagaries of the survival of evidence were of particular concern to Harnack in the context of the editorial enterprise of the GCS. Long before *paleontological layer* became a key term for Harnack as a methodological metaphor for the study of church history, he referred to fossils in order to illustrate the uneven pattern of the survival of early Christian texts. Interestingly, he did so in his *Geschichte der altchristlichen Literatur* with reference to Hatch's Hibbert Lectures (delivered in 1888 but published in 1897): "It [Christian literature] tells us about some parts of the Christian world, but not about others. It represents a few phases of thought with adequate fullness, and of others it presents only a few fossils." What Hatch had intended as a comment on the fragmentary nature of historical evidence, Harnack developed further from the perspective of his editorial work: "The correct question is not, why one or the other ancient Christian text is no longer extant, but why it survived."[49]

Harnack's appreciation of Hatch was immense, and after a long literary acquaintance the opportunity for a meeting offered itself on the occasion of Hatch's visit to Giessen in 1887, while Harnack held a post in nearby Marburg, shortly before his move to Berlin. At this time, both scholars had embarked on similar research projects: Hatch was preparing the Hibbert Lectures, while Harnack was working on the *Lehrbuch der Dogmengeschichte,* and thus the conversation flowed back and forth with great ease, each man providing a sounding board for the other.[50] Harnack later acknowledged that he counted his friendship with Hatch as "one of the greatest possessions in my life."[51] After Hatch's death, he wrote in a letter to another Oxford theologian, Thomas Kelly Cheyne:

> I loved and respected Hatch. I saw in his activity the future of Church historical studies in England. . . . I have never found a Church historian whose judgment I so much trusted as his, and never have I met with a fellow-worker whose ways of looking at things harmonized so much with my own. Although our course of development was as different as the lands in which we dwelt, the circle of our interests, our method, and our goal was the same. When we spoke together of early Church history, our thoughts met with wonderful regularity in all chief points. It seldom happened that we were of a different opinion; and when this did occur, we were soon at one again. In conversation, I saw myself helped forward in the best manner, without being compelled to give up my independently won conviction. He was a great writer. Few books have been written so masterly as his Lectures. But above all, he was a glorious man, whose loss I shall never cease to mourn.[52]

The similarity in academic approach and the affinity of thought and outlook between Harnack and Hatch were quickly recognized by others as well. Already in 1894, the American theologian Henry Clay Sheldon entitled a segment regarding the origins of the episcopate in his *History of the Christian Church* "The Hatch-Harnack Theory of Early Christian Organization."[53] Stewart Chamberlain, the British-born Germanophile intellectual of the turn of the twentieth century, remarked in a letter to Harnack on February 22, 1919, that Hatch was "next to you . . . the most important, most free and most deep personality, capable of great vision and cautiously bold."[54]

Harnack's notion of a paleontological layer in the development of Christianity, first published in a work of his own in 1916, was thus in itself the product of a long evolution that reached back more than two decades and was as much indebted to new methodological models introduced by the sciences as it was the result of personal engagement with the work of colleagues abroad.

Harnack's concentration on his second layer, his "palaeontologische Schicht" of the late second and third centuries, as the core of patristic study may appear as odd, especially considering that the patristic era is nowadays commonly taken to extend to Isidore of Seville (ob. 636) or even Bede (ob. 735) or, in the East, until the beginning of Iconoclasm

(726) or the Seventh Ecumenical Council at Nicaea (787). It is tempting to assume that for Harnack, as for so many other patristic scholars, the reign of Constantine represented a watershed between an early, pure Christianity that existed in obscurity and stood in opposition to the state, on the one hand, and a forceful religion that was shaped and indeed compromised by its new association with worldly power, on the other. But there seems to be no indication of such thinking in Harnack's work. It rather appears that this chronology was due to Harnack's particular interpretation of the forces that propelled history: the fathers and the church. The fathers were those influential individuals and powerful intellectuals who acted in the world as they were moved by the Spirit of God, while the church was the institution that represented the sublimated form of collective individual will and activity and ultimately became the vehicle that carried historical processes over long periods of time. For Harnack, institutions were the key to understanding historical developments. The history of institutions was evident and accessible in the evolution of dogma, in the formulation of church orders, in the establishment of the New Testament canon, and in the formulation of the Creed. The greatest contribution to the creation of institutions, according to Harnack, was made by thinking individuals, such as the fathers.[55] The history of Christian dogma was thus inextricably linked to, and indeed carried forward by, the history of Christian institutions. And the formative period for the development of both the fathers and the church was the late second and third centuries, when theological multiplicity gave way to church-regulated orthodoxy, when the hierarchy of ecclesiastical offices was firmly established, and when the meaning of church rituals such as baptism and the Eucharist was fixed — all of this as a result of the fusion of Christianity with the Greek intellectual tradition. This was the crucial step that gave the new religion the appeal, the language, and the drive to assert itself within the political, social, and intellectual context of the Roman Empire. One might say that, in Harnack's view, it was not the external political circumstances created by the Emperor Constantine that determined the triumph of Christianity but the religion's own inner forces that became manifest in the century before him.

Near the end of his life (Harnack died June 10, 1930), in conversation with one of his former pupils, Otto Dibelius, Harnack proclaimed his ambitions fulfilled: “The task of our generation was to re-gain recognition for theology among German scholars. You cannot imagine with how much derision theological scholarship was treated in the 1860s and 1870s. Our generation has accomplished this task.”[56] Already in 1892, Harnack’s cherished friend Edwin Hatch had announced confidently that the endeavor of history itself had been transformed by science and that it was possible to hear “the solemn tramp of the science of history marching slowly, but marching always to conquest. It is marching in our day, almost for the first time, into the domain of Christian history.”[57] If these footsteps have been heard loud and clear in the last decades of our times, in the anglophone world and beyond, this is not least thanks to the work of Philip Rousseau, to whom these musings are dedicated.

NOTES

1. Klebs, Dessau, and von Rohden, *Prosopographia imperii romani.* In 1901, Adolf Harnack invited colleagues throughout Germany to contribute to the continuation of this project for the period from Diocletian to the death of Justinian, 284 to 565— the nucleus for Jones, Martindale, and Morris, *Prosopography of the Later Roman Empire.* See Rebenich, “Mommsen, Harnack.” On the history of this and other large projects for the study of antiquity, see Rebenich, “Vom Nutzen und Nachteil.” I am most grateful to Stefan Rebenich for sharing his scholarship with me and for his valuable comments on a draft of this chapter. My greatest debt of gratitude is to Christoph Markschies, the current Projektleiter of the Griechischen Christlichen Schriftsteller at the Berlin-Brandenburgische Akademie der Wissenschaften. During my visit to Berlin in 2007, he encouraged and supported this project with his extensive knowledge of the history of patristic studies in Berlin, especially the role of Harnack, and enabled me to visit the Kirchenväterkommission and attend one of its editorial meetings.

2. For the most recent treatment of Mommsen’s indefatigable activities in the organization of scholarship relating to antiquity and late antiquity, see Rebenich, “Unser Werk.”

3. This was further augmented when, a result of the Austro-Prussian War, in 1866, the Kingdom of Hanover became part of the Kingdom of Prussia, including the university town of Göttingen with its distinguished tradition of scholars and intellectuals who took an active role in politics.

4. Wehler, *Deutsche Gesellschaftsgeschichte*, 1223.

5. Rebenich, “Wilhelm von Humboldt.”

6. The authoritative and most detailed biography is that by his daughter, herself a formidable scholar and advocate for women's rights, Agnes von Zahn-Harnack, *Adolf von Harnack*. Detailed information is available online at the Harnack-Forum: www.snts2005.uni-halle.de/ST/harnack. Short treatments of Harnack's life in English are Hirsch, "Scholar as Librarian," and Frend, "Church Historians." Frend, "Church Historians," 98, refers to Harnack's association with Hatch, which will concern us later, but without giving it full recognition.

7. Harnack to Rade, January 14, 1918, in Jantsch, *Briefwechsel*.

8. Adolf von Harnack, *Geschichte*. The Humboldt Universität was founded in 1810.

9. Bruch, "Adolf von Harnack."

10. A first bibliography of Harnack's writings had been compiled on the occasion of his sixtieth birthday, in 1911. It was updated and published on the occasion of his seventy-fifth birthday by Smend, *Adolf von Harnack: Verzeichnis seiner Schriften* [1927]. The posthumous addendum brought the number of titles up to 1,775 (which included writings dedicated to Harnack): Smend and von Harnack, *Adolf von Harnack, Verzeichnis seiner Schriften, 1927–1930* [1931]. See now Smend, *Adolf von Harnack: Verzeichnis seiner Schriften bis 1930* [1990]. A further update of Harnack's publication list was assembled by Picker, "Ergänzungen."

11. Axel von Harnack, "Bibliothek Adolf von Harnacks," 6.

12. Adolf von Harnack to Wilhelm Stintzing, 1868, quoted in Zahn-Harnack, *Adolf von Harnack*, 23.

13. Ibid., 75.

14. Ibid., 106, explains that Harnack's fame had spread to Harvard because of some American students he had taught in Giessen. Harnack was invited to consider a professorship at Harvard a second time, in 1892 or 1893 (157); see Hirsch, "Scholar as Librarian," 301.

15. Kress, *Theologische Fakultäten,* 46–47. On Bismarck's intervention, see Aland, "Adolf Harnack," 7.

16. "Die Kirchengeschichte als Wissenschaft beginnt an der Universität Berlin erst mit Harnack" (Aland, "Adolf Harnack," 8).

17. Aland, "Adolf Harnack," 13. For the date, see Irmscher, "Kommission," 97, with reference to Adolf von Harnack, *Geschichte,* 2:263. See also Rebenich, "Altertumswissenschaften," 210.

18. This is how the classical philologist Hermann Diels recounts the election, which resulted in his own appointment, in a letter to Theodor Mommsen; see Rebenich, *Theodor Mommsen,* 73 n. 75. See also Moeller, "Adolf von Harnack," 17.

19. On the role of Mommsen in supporting Harnack and thus securing a role for patristics within the work of the Akademie in Berlin, see Rebenich, "Theodor Mommsen."

20. Rebenich, *Theodor Mommsen,* 792.

21. For the original draft of Harnack's application, see Nowak, "Theologie, Philologie und Geschichte," 197.

22. Irmscher, "Kommission," 99 n. 1, with reference to Huber, *Geschichte der Gründung,* 123 ff. The first volume of that series, the writings of Sulpicius Severus, appeared two years later, in 1866.

23. Rebenich, "Alte Meergreis," 49.

24. Rebenich, " Orbis Romanus," 45–46.

25. Adolf von Harnack, *Protokollbuch,* 114. See also Irmscher, "Kommission," 103 n. 27.

26. "Auch solche spätere Kirchenschriftsteller in die Sammlung aufzunehmen, die wichtiges Material zur älteren christlichen Literatur enthalten" (Adolf von Harnack, "Ausgabe," 352).

27. Rebenich, "Alte Meergreis," 50. The website of the GCS also offers information about the history of the series: "Überblick," n.d., www.bbaw.de/bbaw/Forschung/Forschungsprojekte/gcs/de/Ueberblick.

28. Rebenich, however, in "Alte Meergreis," 49 n. 50, remarks that Harnack evokes the "paläontologische Schicht" for the first time in 1916.

29. Adolf von Harnack, "Ausgabe," 349 (emphasis in text): "Aber hinter dieser umfangreichen Literatur des 4. und 5. Jahrhunderts, die der Aufarbeitung noch harrt, liegt nun noch eine — vom Mittelalter aus betrachtet —*paläontologische* Schicht. Ihre gewaltige Bedeutung und ihr unerschöpflicher Reiz besteht darin, dass sie die Dokumente jenes Zeitalters enthält, *in welchem das religiöse Gefühlsleben der Griechen und Römer mündig geworden ist*."

30. Adolf von Harnack, "Bericht über die Ausgabe," xxvii.

31. Preisigke, *Gotteskraft*. See also the critical remarks about this aspect of Preisigke's work in the obituary by H.I. Bell.

32. Aland, *Glanz und Niedergang*, 2, 74.

33. Krumbacher, "Photographie." See now Müller, "Von Umkehrprismen."

34. Zahn-Harnack, *Adolf von Harnack*, 10.

35. Ibid., 56.

36. Ibid., 82.

37. Ibid., 192.

38. "Das Streben nach vollständiger Induction, das Hinaufgehen zu den echten u. reinen Quellen, die nicht von der Doctrin getrübt sind." Harnack to Mommsen, February 20, 1899, with reference to an article by Scherer on the working method of Jakob Grimm, in Rebenich, *Theodor Mommsen,* 773, letter 137.

39. Hübner, *Adolf von Harnacks Vorlesungen*, esp. 58–97.

40. "Der Biologe studirte [*sic*] vor Allem die niedersten Organismen; der Psychologe wurde zum Psychophysiker, der Sprachphilosoph zum Lautphysi-

ologen, der Historiker zum Wirthschaftsstatistiker [*sic*] oder Urkundenforscher" (Adolf von Harnack, "Königlich Preussische Akademie," 20).

41. "Wenn ich aus Auge und Ohr eines versteinerten Tieres schliesse, dass es damals Licht und Töne gegeben hat, die Sonne schien und der Wind brauste, so schliesse ich mit demselben Recht aus unserer Anlage auf Gott und das Ewige, dass es ein ein [*sic*] Wirkliches gibt, das ihr entspricht" (Zahn-Harnack, *Adolf von Harnack*, 444).

42. On the absorption of St. Mary's Hall into Oriel College, see Green, *History of Oxford University*, 157. But a letter from Hatch of 1878 seems to indicate that the two institutions are still separate; Josaitis, *Edwin Hatch,* 15.

43. Hatch to William Sanday, May 12, 1878, in Josaitis, *Edwin Hatch*, 12.

44. Hatch, *Organization,* translated into German as *Gesellschaftsverfassung der christlichen Kirchen,* a work of 259 pages (Smend no. 219). Five years later, Hatch's *Growth of Church Institutions* appeared in German in Harnack's authorized translation (*Die Grundlegung der Kirchenverfassung Westeuropas im frühen Mittelalter*).

45. Adolf von Harnack, *Mission und Ausbreitung*, 1:481 n. 1.

46. Hatch, *Organization*, 14. In Harnack's translation: "Der Paläontologe z. B. zieht seine Folgerungen, indem er sowohl alle Reste der Fauna und Flora einer bestimmten Schicht zusammenstellt, als auch andererseits jede Species von Thieren und Pflanzen in allen Schichten verfolgt, um so zu Schlüssen in Bezug auf die Ordnung und Folge des Lebens auf der Erde zu gelangen" (*Gesellschaftsverfassung der christlichen Kirchen,* 11).

47. See also Hatch, *Progress in Theology*, 6, 9–10, 23–24.

48. Hatch, *Influence of Greek Ideas,* translated into German as *Griechentum und Christentum*. Harnack's *Nachwort* is on 263–68.

49. Hatch, *Influence of Greek Ideas*, 7–8. "'Die Litteratur zeigt uns einzelne Phasen der Entwickelung des christlichen Denkens mit genügender Deutlichkeit, und von anderen bietet sie uns nur ein paar Fossile.' . . . Die richtige Fragestellung lautet nicht, warum ist diese oder jene altchristliche Schrift untergegangen, sondern warum ist sie erhalten" (Harnack, *Geschichte der altchristlichen Literatur*, 1.1:xxviii).

50. Adolf von Harnack's afterword to the German translation of Hatch's *Influence of Greek Ideas* (*Griechentum und Christentum*, 265).

51. Adolf von Harnack, review of Hatch's *Essays in Biblical Greek.*

52. Cheyne, "Late Dr. Edwin Hatch," as referred to by Josaitis, *Edwin Hatch,* 15–16.

53. See also the reference to the "Hatch-Harnack theory" regarding the nomenclature of Christian clergy in Allen, "Organization of the Early Church," 801.

54. "Uebrigens habe ich bei neuerlicher Lektüre von Hatch's 'Greek Ideas' den Eindruck bekommen, dass — neben Ihnen — dieser Frühverstorbene die

bedeutendste, freieste Persönlichkeit, die tiefst angelegte war, weitsichting u. so besonnen kühn" (Kinzig, *Harnack, Marcion,* 278).

55. It would be interesting to find out more about the relation of Harnack's thinking on individual and institution to Max Weber's theory of charisma and institution. The two met while vacationing in Italy in 1913. Weber had been Mommsen's star pupil until he turned to sociology.

56. Dibelius, "Adolf Harnack," 34.

57. Hatch, *Influence of Greek Ideas,* 23.

Chapter Fifteen

From East to West

Christianity, Asceticism, and Nineteenth-Century Protestant Professors in America

ELIZABETH A. CLARK

Among the notable characteristics of Philip Rousseau's scholarship is his skillful and sympathetic treatment of both Eastern and Western forms of early Christian asceticism. By his several books —*Ascetics, Authority, and the Church in the Age of Jerome and Cassian; Pachomius: The Making of a Community in Fourth-Century Egypt*; and *Basil of Caesarea*— and magisterial essays (such as "Monasticism," in *The Cambridge Ancient History*), more than one generation of scholars has been illumined.

Professors who created the study of early Christian history in nineteenth-century Protestant seminaries in the United States, by contrast, struggled to accord early Christian asceticism its due.[1] Echoing the German Protestant scholars whose books they mined, they imagined early Christian asceticism to be a "foreign" import that had corrupted Jesus' pure and simple teaching of "inward spirituality." Yet because most of these pioneers had also imbibed from their German mentors notions of the church's "organic development" through time, of God's providential oversight of seemingly "dark" eras, they struggled to find something "good" in early Christian asceticism.[2] They found it in the West, not the East.

How, the professors wondered, had the (to them) incongruous phenomenon of Christian asceticism developed? Searching for explanations, they posited that it must have been a reaction — indeed, an overreaction — to the moral turpitude of the Greco-Roman world. Perhaps this misguided practice had also been abetted by a mistaken and too-literal exegesis (for example, of Mt 19:12 and 1 Cor 7). Following German scholars, they agreed that hot, enervating, "Oriental" climates had contributed to asceticism's rise: no wonder that asceticism had found its more spectacular manifestations in steamy Egypt (or in India), rather than in rugged northern Europe or the temperate United States.[3] Besides, these church historians agreed, asceticism was not a special or essential characteristic of Christianity; "Mahometans" and Buddhists likewise sported ascetic practitioners — and the "self-tortures" of Indian fakirs could outdo anything Christianity might offer![4]

The professors conceded that some forms of asceticism — largely Western and coenobitic — had contributed a few positive elements to civilization. "West" for them meant western (especially northwestern) Europe, with an occasional allowance for ancient Greece; "East" meant not only eastern Asia but also the Middle East, which in their time signaled the Ottoman Empire, then torn by conflict with other powers. That the professors believed that "the West" in general stood superior to "the East" accorded with their larger understanding of world history and of God's providential design for Christianity's progress. Most of them argued that the United States — outpost of the far West — stood to inherit the benefits of northern and western European cultures.

First, some brief introductions to these professors, who taught (variously) at Princeton Theological Seminary, Union Theological Seminary, the Yale "Theological Department" (i.e., what became Yale Divinity School), and Harvard Divinity School.

THE PROFESSORS

Samuel Miller (1769–1850), the first of the professors I consider, was a rigorous "Old School" Presbyterian. He graduated from the University of Pennsylvania and in 1791–92 read theology privately with an established minister, as was then the custom. Miller did not study in Germany, as did the other five professors, and remained largely oblivious to German historiographical currents. He served as a Presbyterian minister in New York City from 1793 until 1813, when he became the first professor of ecclesiastical history and church government at the Presbyterian Seminary recently founded at Princeton. He occupied this post for thirty-six years.

Henry Boynton Smith (1815–77) was appointed as the first professor of church history at Union Theological Seminary in New York. A native of Maine, Smith attended Bowdoin College, Andover Theological Seminary, and Bangor Seminary. He studied in Paris, and then in Germany (at the universities of Halle and Berlin) in 1838–40. Returning to America, he served as a pastor before becoming professor of philosophy at Amherst College. Several commentators deemed him instrumental in introducing German philosophy and theology to Americans. His professorship in church history at Union lasted only from 1850 to 1854, when he transferred to the professorship of theology, an area to which he felt more intellectually drawn. He edited the *American Theological Review* from its founding in 1859 and served as moderator of the (New School) Presbyterian Church in 1863.

Roswell D. Hitchcock (1817–87), a native of Maine, became the next professor of church history at Union. Hitchcock graduated from Amherst College and Andover Theological Seminary before studying in Germany. After a term as a minister, he became professor of natural and revealed religion at Bowdoin College in 1852. In 1855, Hitchcock was appointed to the Washburn Professorship of Church History at Union, where he served as president from 1880 until his death in 1887.

Hitchcock, moreover, had traveled in the Middle East and was deemed the leader of Americans who followed new archaeological discoveries in Palestine. After his travels, he lectured in 1877 on discoveries (with "stereopticon views") at the New York Science and Art Association.[5] Hitchcock had a considerable intellectual and emotional investment in the Middle

East: his students were notable for their service as missionaries in Turkey, Syria, and Egypt, and points further east.[6] At his death, he left his complete set of the journal *Bibliotheca Sacra* to the Syrian College at Beirut.[7]

Philip Schaff (1819–93), the third professor of church history at Union, was a native of Switzerland and was educated at German universities. At the age of twenty-five, Schaff arrived in the United States to teach at the Seminary of the German Reformed Church in Mercersburg, Pennsylvania. In 1870, he joined the faculty of Union Seminary but did not assume the professorship of church history until Roswell Hitchcock's death in 1887. Schaff was founder of the American Society of Church History, founding member of the Society of Biblical Literature, editor of the Nicene and Post-Nicene Fathers series, and head of the American Committee for the Authorized Revision of the Bible, among other positions. He was a voluminous writer whose early works sparked considerable controversy. Adolf von Harnack remarked upon Schaff's death that he was the last great "generalist" of church history.[8]

In 1877, Schaff visited the "Bible lands," as he called them — a trip that took him to Egypt, across the Sinai Peninsula, through Palestine, and on to Lebanon, Syria, Istanbul, and Greece.[9] By early 1877, when Schaff embarked on his trip, a new war between Russia and Turkey seemed inevitable. Although Russia declared war on Turkey on April 24, 1877, Schaff was nevertheless determined to continue his adventurous travels.[10] News of the impending conflict dogged him through Egypt, Syria, Lebanon, Istanbul, and Greece and on his return home in early August.[11] By the time he had completed his book *Through Bible Lands* in the summer of 1878, Turkey had been defeated and the Congress of Berlin Treaty signed.[12] As we shall see, the travels of Hitchcock and Schaff encouraged their decidedly negative views of the Middle East and of contemporary Eastern Christianity.

George Park Fisher (1827–1909), the first professor of church history at Yale Divinity School, was a native of Massachusetts and a Congregationalist. Graduating from Brown in 1847 and Andover Theological Seminary in 1851, he studied in Germany during 1852–53. He was then called to Yale as professor of divinity in Yale College and as pastor of the College Church. He joined the "Theological Department" of Yale in 1861, serving as its dean from 1895 to 1900. Like Schaff before him and Ephraim Emerton after him, he was elected president of the American Society of Church History. He remained at Yale throughout his entire teaching career, retiring in 1900.

Ephraim Emerton (1851–1935), the first professor of church history at Harvard, was born in Massachusetts, graduated from Harvard College in 1871, and attended Harvard Law School. He received his PhD from the University of Leipzig in 1876, working with J.G. Droysen and other noted historians. Returning from Europe, he was appointed instructor of German and history in Harvard College. In 1882, he was plucked from his duties in the college by President Charles Eliot to be the Winn Professor of Ecclesiastical History at Harvard Divinity School, a post he held until his resignation in 1918.[13] Emerton was a founding member of the American Historical Association and a fellow of the American Academy of Arts and Sciences, and he served as president of the American Society of Church History in 1921.[14] Most of his books treat the later Middle Ages, not the early church. Emerton, the latest of the six to assume his position, was unusual in never having studied theology; moreover, as a Unitarian, he stood outside the evangelical Presbyterian-Congregationalist nexus represented by the other professors.

These six were the first to hold professorial rank for the teaching of church history at their respective institutions.

THE PROFESSORS AND WORLD HISTORY: FROM EAST TO WEST

From German scholars, the professors had absorbed notions of Caucasian superiority that celebrated the "Teutons" in the westward march of civilization — a march that extended as far as America.[15] "Teutons," whom these Anglo-Saxon professors deemed their own ancestors, served as a way station on the road from pagan immorality to a spiritualized (and Hegelianized) modern Protestantism.[16] The professors' valorization of the West's superiority decisively influenced their views on Eastern Christianity and especially early Eastern asceticism.

The professors viewed history as a hypostasized agent that had risen (like the sun) in the Orient, marched on to Greece and Rome, settled for a time in Germany and England, and last, moved to the "Northern portion of the New World." History's course also followed that of human ontogeny: adopting Herder's scheme, Schaff imagined that the Oriental world, under absolute power, was the world's childhood; Greece, celebrating freedom, represented youth; and Rome, "full of calculation and action," corresponded to manhood. The Christian era, the apex of seasoned maturity, surpassed all other stages in reason and virtue.[17] In Schaff's view, just as Europe was a great advance over Asia, so America would, in the future, be "a higher continuation of the consolidated life of Europe. The eyes of the East are instinctively turned to the West, and civilization follows the march of the sun."[18] Following the general path of history, Schaff claimed, Christianity had arisen in the East and had been guided by Providence to spread northward and westward. The "Anglo-Saxon race," of all ethnic groups, was in Schaff's view the most "deeply imbued with the spirit and power of Christianity."[19] "Christianity," George Fisher taught his Yale students, "an Asiatic religion by birth, finds its best home in Europe."[20]

The influence of the East, the professors thought, had been, and remained, generally debilitating. In their view of antiquity, "Greece" represented the East and "Rome" the West. Far from lauding the Greeks, as did many of their German contemporaries, the professors believed (taking a line from ancient historians) that the Greek East had led to the degeneration of Rome: the "oriental conquest" had demolished Roman virtue, and after the Second Punic War morals had declined precipitously.[21] Then, Greek views of women — deemed an ontologically lower order, prone to evil, and fitted to serve only as mothers or as "toys" for men — sullied Roman life. Hence pre-Christian Rome knew nothing of the "true domestic" condition, "of proper family life."[22] Greece here did *not* represent the idealized humanity imagined by nineteenth-century German philhellenes, but the corrupting "Orient."[23] Roswell Hitchcock pondered why the Eastern Roman Empire had not fallen when the Western Empire (allegedly) had — after all, he told his students, the East was "racially inferior."[24]

In modern times, countries further to the East — China and Japan, in particular — were described by the professors as burdened with a "stagnant heathen civilization." These two Asian cultures, Philip Schaff believed, were characterized by a "narrow-minded and narrow-hearted nationalism," totally unbefitting "enlightened" Christians.[25] Roswell Hitchcock, while reviewing (and often praising) volumes 1 and 2 of James Legge's translation of the *Chinese Classics* (1861), criticized the Chinese on several grounds: their "intensely materialistic and utilitarian" brains, the narrowness of Confucius's worldview, and the failings of their ethics (formal, cold, lacking in regard for womanhood). Yet Legge's translations, Hitchcock claimed, would alert readers to the difficulty of budging the Chinese from their deficient system to adopt Christianity.[26] In his last public address before his sudden death, Hitchcock urged the audience to consider that although the Chinese were "cold-blooded Mongols . . . they are human."[27]

Philip Schaff's views on the Far East were, if anything, more derogatory. Writing at a time that had seen a large immigration of Chinese workers to America's Pacific coast, he claimed that the Chinese had brought with them their "mechanical culture," avarice, and "'filthy habits," along with their industry and "quiet disposition."[28] (Schaff doubted that the Chinese — or the Africans — could be assimilated to the "American character.")[29] America had a great mission, he thought, to Christianize and civilize "the vast empires of China and Japan" — and would serve as Europe's "high-way . . . to the mysterious wealth of Asia."[30]

The professors agreed that history, in its march from East to West, had overlooked some peoples. Hottentots, Caffrarians, Negroes, and New Zealanders, in Schaff's reckoning, were not "historical" and had to date "played no part whatever in the grand drama of history."[31] Even old civilizations such as China (so Yale's George Fisher believed), so excessively venerating the past and resistant to change, were barely "historical." Caucasians, he claimed, had played the most important part in history and the creation of civilization.[32] Why were they "the best"? Adopting a similar line to Schaff (borrowed from Hegel and Herder), Fisher posited that despotic Oriental kingdoms allowed no individual freedom for development. Only in Europe, taking a cue from the Greeks, could true notions of liberty and a more ideal type of humanity arise.[33]

The evangelical professors hastened to add that all who believed in Providence surely held that God's plan "extends over all of mankind and embraces all the ages of man's existence on the earth"[34] — civilized and uncivilized, "white or brown or black."[35] No one was excluded, not "the inhabitants of the isles of the Sea; Chinese and Greenlanders, Turks and

Tatars, and even the poor, despised, and downtrodden Africans."[36] Henry Smith cited Jesus' words to confirm this view: "Many shall come from the *East* and *West*, and sit down with Abraham."[37]

AMERICA IN WORLD HISTORY

The patriotic Union and Yale professors believed that the northward and westward march of Providence had made America's world-historical role "exceptional": Christianity had followed the course of the sun all the way to North American shores.[38] History had foresightedly and providentially prepared old, weary Europe to send forth her people to the New World.[39] Bishop Berkeley had so presciently penned his lines:

> Westward the course of empire takes its way;
> the first four acts already past. A fifth
> shall close the drama with the day;
> Time's noblest offspring is the last.[40]

Philip Schaff in particular, for whom America was an adopted country, wrote exuberantly that America was "destined to be the main theatre of the future history of the world and the church."[41] Although America was "the grave of all European nationalities," it was a "Phenix [*sic*] grave, from which they shall rise to new life and new activity in a new and essentially Anglo-Germanic form."[42] America, he proclaimed, was "magnificent," "Immanuel's land for all time to come."[43]

Schaff's colleague Roswell Hitchcock likewise accorded America a unique place in the grand westward sweep of history. By Providence, he wrote, Americans were "in charge of the final theatre and the final problems of history."[44] Although geology taught that North America had been one of the first continents to be heaved up from the ocean bed, it was "the last to be used in history." Why did Providence wait so long? Hitchcock answers: "Plainly it was not meant for those Indian tribes that were found in possession of it. They were not such lords of the forest as romance has delighted to picture them, but worn out Asiatics, who were here by sufferance to fulfill a temporary purpose, and then to pass away.

Not by an eastward, but by a westward migration; not by Asia, but by Europe, was the continent to be taken and made a theatre for new experiments in history, to be accomplished by a new mixing of the human races."[45] In America, Hitchcock claimed, we had a "new, vast Continent to subdue and save": this was our gigantic task.[46]

THE MIDDLE EAST: ISLAM

Given these views, it was perhaps inevitable that both contemporary "Oriental" Christianities and Islam received the professors' stinging critique. While Roswell Hitchcock found some few words of praise for Islam (at mosques, he told his students, "men *really pray*"; "a religion which takes such a deep hold must have power"), Philip Schaff had almost none.[47] *Why* God had allowed "the fairest portions of the earth, the native lands of classical literature and the Christian religion" to fall under Muslim rule, Schaff considered "one of the great mysteries of Providence."[48] But now, Mohammedanism (as the professors usually called Islam) had played its allotted role in God's scheme, and there was nothing more for it to contribute: its day was over, its purpose served.[49] Islam should now retreat to Asia, Schaff thought, and gradually be undermined from within. Then, he concluded, Muslims would open their doors for "a purer Christianity" (i.e., Protestantism).[50] He hoped for "the peaceful conversion of the Moslems to a better religion and a higher civilization than the Koran can give."[51] Sometimes, however, he did not see Islam's retreat as occurring so "naturally" and peacefully: its speedy demise and replacement by a Protestant form of Christianity might require some external force. Russia and England should perhaps be summoned to give the needed jolt to bring down the Ottoman Empire.[52] The time would soon come, Schaff felt sure, when the Cross would replace the Crescent, and mosques would become churches.[53]

In spring 1854, while in Germany, Schaff surveyed the worsening political situation that had developed between Russia and Turkey. He wrote: "It seems as if the time for the fall of the false prophet has come. Into Constantinople he forced his way by the sword and with the sword by a nemesis of history, he will have to be driven forth. Constantinople must again become a hearthstone of Christianity and exert a regenerating influence upon the Oriental Churches and advance the cause of civilization throughout Europe."[54] Schaff's hopes, we know, were not realized.

EASTERN CHURCHES IN THE CONTEMPORARY WORLD

A particular view of "true religion" colored the professors' judgment of the Eastern churches. They (especially the Union Seminary professors) believed that Christianity was intended from its outset to be "inward," "spiritual," unencumbered by intricate doctrine, and relatively plain in ritual. An acknowledgment of human sinfulness and divine forgiving grace, unrelated to human merit, stood at the center of their Calvinist belief. The divisive arguments over dogma in late antiquity and the development of an ornate ritual were features of Eastern Christianity with which they had little sympathy. Given their barely concealed intolerance for "degenerate" forms of Christianity as well as for Islam, they found little to praise in Eastern Orthodoxy's development. The professors' views on the general debilitation of the East were reflected in their derogatory comments upon Eastern forms of Christianity.

Roswell Hitchcock of Union, for example, told his students that the world's churches could be ranked in descending order: highest stood (unsurprisingly) Protestantism; second, Western Roman Catholicism; third, the Roman Rite churches of the East; and last, at the bottom, the Greek churches.[55] In the Middle Ages, Hitchcock claimed, the Greek Church had simply gotten left behind;[56] now the Eastern churches were "decayed."[57] The Coptic churches in Egypt disgusted him with their "trumpery."[58] There was more "simple and virile worship" in mosques of the Middle East, Hitchcock claimed, than in Eastern churches: the latter were "tawdry," while mosques were, at least, "simple." A Protestant, he told his students, felt almost more at home in a mosque than in Eastern churches.[59]

Philip Schaff's opinions were similar: the word *stagnant,* he claimed, well characterized the churches and sects of the East — a sad comedown for the region that had been "the cradle of the human race and of our holy religion."[60] In 1857, he reported to an international meeting of the Evangelical Alliance that American Protestant missionaries, "messengers of the cross," were now reaching out to "the stagnant sects of the decaying Turkish empire, extending to the venerable seats of primitive Christianity and binding thus the extreme west to the ancient east by the gospel of love and peace."[61] (Whether these "stagnant sects" saw the Western reach as an expression of "love" seems less obvious.)

Both Monophysites and Nestorians received Schaff's critique. The Monophysite Coptic Church, he wrote, characterized by "stagnation, ignorance, and superstition," had been preserved by Providence to provide a door through which Protestants could missionize Arabs and Turks.[62] The Monophysite churches, he believed, remained as "curious petrifications from the Christological battlefields of the fifth and sixth centuries, coming to view amidst Mohammedan scenes. But Providence has preserved them, like the Jews, and doubtless not without design, through storms of war and persecution, unchanged until the present time." Monophysite Christians of the Middle East, compared to Christians in other regions, were "as a praying corpse to a living man."[63] Copts, however, were not the only object of Schaff's concern: he was pleased that American missionaries had had some success in both evangelizing and "civilizing" Nestorian Christians in the Middle East.[64] Christian missions in the East, with their schools, orphanages, and hospitals, represented for Schaff "the Orient of the future."[65]

EARLY EASTERN CHRISTIANITY

The professors, echoing the German church historians on whose works they were largely dependent, found many faults in early as well as in contemporary Eastern Christianity. Greek Christianity's early reliance (in the professors' view, overreliance) on philosophy had led to bad ends, allowing Platonism and the "disease" of "Oriental superstition" to exert undue influence.[66] Roswell Hitchcock charged that the East had overvalued doctrine and had become "sordid"—although he also claimed that Western Christianity had become "cruel."[67] He judged that Eastern Christianity had succumbed so soon to superstition and ignorance that "Mohammedanism" served as "a terrible punishment inflicted by God upon the degenerate Christian churches of the East, destroying them rather than imparting new life."[68]

Hitchcock carried his preference for Western Christianity back to the earliest days of the church. For a religion to be "world-wide," as Christianity was intended to be, it "must not be oriental," he argued; it must be "more than Palestinian, more than Jewish." In his view, Christianity's survival had depended on the "Oriental" elements fading and the movement's looking westward.[69]

Philip Schaff's opinion was at least as negative. Although he acknowledged that the ancient Greek Church had been "the mother of oecumenical orthodoxy," the later Monophysite Church had long ago fallen into "stagnation, ignorance, and superstition."[70] The condemnation of Origen's theology, he claimed, had dealt "a death blow to theological science in the Greek church, and left it to stiffen gradually into a mechanical traditionalism and formalism."[71] That after the Fourth Ecumenical Council at Chalcedon the Greek Church had lost her way illustrated "the universal law of history," that "Westward the star of empire takes its way."[72]

Schaff particularly criticized Cyril of Alexandria, faulting Cyril's "violent" and "arrogant" conduct during the Christological controversies and claiming that his Christology "went to the brink of the monophysite error." Schaff partially exonerated Cyril in the murder of Hypatia, but he charged Cyril with bribery (using church funds) and especially denigrated his "pathetic and turgid eulogy on Mary."[73]

One consistent criticism the professors leveled — again borrowed from German scholars — was that the Greek East had become mired in doctrinal speculation and definition, leading to its "petrification."[74] The doctrinal controversies had led to the formulation of useful creeds, the professors conceded, but they had consumed much energy and had stalled further "Christian conquests," the "missionary spirit" being sadly lacking;[75] the formulation of doctrine, doubtless necessary, had impeded the more vital task of spreading the Gospel.[76] In the centuries after Chalcedon, Schaff charged, the Greek Church had "degenerated theologically into scholastic formalism and idle refinements."[77]

Other alleged faults of the Eastern churches were their "superstitious" practices: Oriental Christians, Hitchcock claimed, adopted fixed times for prayer and extensive fasting to curb the "sensuality" that left them at the devil's mercy.[78] Last, there was the issue of the florid rhetoric in which the Greek fathers indulged, to the detriment of their audiences' clear understanding and ready application: to Schaff, Gregory of Nazianzen was one culprit,[79] while Chrysostom's "untruthful exaggerations and artificial antitheses" he considered "defects and degeneracies" to a "healthy and cultivated taste" (i.e., his own).[80] Such views of early Eastern Christianity fueled the professors' negative assessment of Christian asceticism in the East.

ASCETICISM: EASTERN CHRISTIANITY

The American professors followed their German models in charging Eastern asceticism with spreading spiritual "disease" and promoting fanaticism, superstition, and credulity; they stressed how often Eastern monks fell into heterodoxy and "complete madness."[81] Although all asceticism, to be sure, was in their view "unscriptural, unnatural, and morally dangerous," the Greek and other Eastern versions came in for special critique.[82]

Samuel Miller of Princeton Seminary blamed Athanasius's *Life of Antony* for inspiring ascetic renunciation. And when Antony's disciple Hilarion brought the ascetic life to Palestine and Syria, it was not long (Miller claimed, echoing the German author Johannes Mosheim) before "the whole East was filled with a lazy set of mortals," who by self-inflicted penalties sought to reach intimate communion with God and angels.[83] It was, Miller thought, characteristic of someone bred in Palestine and "educated at the feet of those Gamaliels"—he refers to the ancient church historian Sozomen—to spout "monkish miracles."[84] Here Miller indulged in the now-familiar association of Jewish "legalism" with Roman Catholic practice.

American and German Protestant scholars alike emphasized the more outré forms of ascetic devotion in the Christian East—stylites on their pillars and "senseless fanatics" living naked among the beasts, eating grass.[85] Standing on a pillar for years was, in German historian August Neander's view, a "frivolous" expenditure of energy that could have been more profitably used in Christian service. Simeon Stylites could have displayed "a genuine Christian piety" by crafting a life in harmony with nature, rather than by "such artistic displays of a conquest over nature."

Other ascetics, Neander added, became so dehumanized as to appear "mere brutes," wandering about like wild animals.[86]

The American professors took up this line of critique. Stylites served as Samuel Miller's exemplars of Eastern monastic "superstition" at its most extreme.[87] In characteristic fashion, Miller responded to his Princeton students' questions that were raised during one class period in the next. When one of them asked, "Did Simeon Stylites remain constantly on his pillar, and if so, how did he pass the time?" Miller replied in the next session by reading a long extract from Theodoret on Simeon, warning students against this author's credulity. Only a few brave souls, such as Vigilantius, Miller rued, staunchly opposed such monastic superstition.[88]

Roswell Hitchcock of Union told his classes that Eastern monasticism was "more barren and austere" than Western. He repeated Montalembert's judgment: Eastern monasticism had no history because it never did anything — while Western monasticism had a history because it was active.[89] Hitchcock likewise dwelt on the Stylites, whom he described as a "mostly Oriental" phenomenon. Their practice he deemed a "travesty of monasticism — but an incarnation of its sterility." He expressed amazement that so few stylites — only six or seven on record — could have made so much "noise in history."[90]

Philip Schaff, for his part, wrote that monasticism "not rarely" got carried to "the borders of fanaticism and brutish stupefaction." The more eccentric the ascetics, the more they were venerated by the people.[91] Schaff, too, singled out Simeon Stylites' "heroism of abstinence" for critique. Such a feat, he added, was possible only in "the torrid climate of the East," not in the West.[92] Simeon could be considered "a Christian Diogenes"— but his approach was not true Christianity.[93] Regarding the Pillar Saints, Schaff concluded, "One knows not whether to wonder at their unexampled self-denial, or to pity their ignorance of the gospel salvation."[94] Schaff cited examples from early Christian literature of excessive asceticism leading to "madness, despair, and suicide."[95]

Schaff went even further with a political critique of Eastern asceticism, claiming that it had hastened "the decline of Egypt, Syria, Palestine, and the whole Roman empire" and had lowered the general standard of morality for ordinary Christians.[96] He continued: "Many of these saints [desert fathers] were no more than low sluggards or gloomy misanthropes, who would rather company with wild beasts, with lions, wolves, and hyenas, than with immortal men, and above all shunned the face of a woman more carefully than they did the devil."[97] Given their "morbid aversion" to women and "rude contempt" for marriage, it was no wonder "that in Egypt and the whole East, the land of monasticism, women and domestic life never attained their proper dignity, and to this day remain at a low stage of culture."[98]

On one point only concerning asceticism did Schaff think that the early Greek Christian Church had done better than the Latin: it had allowed priests to marry. To be sure, he hastened to add, this was not because the Greek Church had any "higher standard of marriage" but only because it kept closer to earlier Christian practice and was "less consistent" in its application of ascetic principles. It was only in practice, not in theory, that the Greek Church was less "remote from the evangelical Protestant church" than the Latin.[99] The Western Church, in its demand for clerical celibacy from the fourth century onward, adopted "the perverted and almost Manichaean ascetic principle, that the married state is incompatible with clerical dignity and holiness."[100]

Ephraim Emerton of Harvard, despite his much calmer assessment of ascetic developments in early Christianity, did not refrain from accusing the Eastern monks of "fanaticism," with (now predictably) Simeon Stylites singled out as exemplar. Yet in keeping with his broader historiographical approach, Emerton added: "We must try to learn to judge men and institutions by the use they had in the day in which they belonged, not by the use they might have for us in these better times." Despite this caveat, he thought the monastic life could be dangerous: these monks often seemed "quite as much like madmen as saints."[101]

ASCETICISM: WESTERN CHRISTIANITY

The professors believed that the temperate West, lacking torrid climes, was spared most of these ascetic excesses[102]—so ascetic renunciation in the West fared better in the professors' estimation than did its counterpart in the East. It was, Samuel Miller told his Princeton Seminary students, less austere than in the East.[103] Yet the West had first been "infected" by the East: Miller blamed Athanasius's *Life of Antony* (a work displaying the "grossest superstition and credulity") for introducing Egyptian monasticism at Rome, where formerly it had been despised.[104]

German scholars led the way in pointing out some good in early *Western* monasticism. Johann Gieseler credited Western monks for abandoning the "mechanical labor" of Eastern ascetics in order to pursue a more productive life. With time, Benedictines proved socially useful in reclaiming wastelands, advancing education for children, writing chronicles, and later, copying manuscripts.[105]

August Neander emphasized even more strongly the positive contributions of early Christian asceticism in general. Indeed, no era of Christian history had been destitute of God's providence.[106] One manifestation: during the barbarian incursions, Western monasteries, especially those in southern France, offered protection to refugees. They became "spiritual seminaries" that sent forth bishops and missionaries to labor for others' salvation.[107] Moreover, the brotherly love of coenobitic life supported a belief in human equality that eventually led to a critique of slavery. Last, in the West, monastic cloisters became institutions of hospitality, providing for the needy and educating the young.[108] All in all, Neander advised his readers not to mistake the "degeneracy" of asceticism for the whole monastic way of life. Its worthy points deserved credit, even if evangelical Protestants opposed the overestimation of ascetic virtue and undervaluation of married life.[109] Neander's more positive evaluation influenced Philip Schaff in particular.

Following their German predecessors and mentors, especially Neander, the American evangelical professors found something to praise in early Christian renunciation, especially as practiced in the West. Monasticism had performed a good service in transferring Christianity from the decaying and "effete" culture of Rome to the new world of the early Middle Ages. Unlike the "fruitless" monasticism of the East, Hitchcock claimed, Western monasticism had benefited the wider society, at least up to the time of Charlemagne.[110] It had stimulated the economy by its exemplary agricultural practices that restored the land; it had fostered learning by preserving manuscripts and having them copied; and it had served as a tool through which barbarians were Christianized.[111] George Fisher of Yale added more: monks in their "self-denying devotion" provided hospitality, helped the poor, and befriended those in distress.[112] These actions could be lauded, even by staunch Protestants.

Philip Schaff argued that Eastern eremitic monasticism was "too eccentric and unpractical for the West"—and "entirely unsuited" to women.[113] Yet despite his many critiques, Schaff believed that asceticism in the early Christian *West* had brought some benefits: it had been used by Providence to prepare the barbarian tribes of the early Middle Ages for Christian civilization.[114] Schaff picturesquely described the monastery of Iona as a "lighthouse in the darkness of heathenism."[115]

Benedict's *Rule*, Schaff thought, showed "a true knowledge of human nature" and was adaptable to Western customs.[116] In its later stages, monasticism helped to diffuse Christian teaching and ancient learning, warn against the immorality of the clergy, mitigate slavery, and level the class structure of society.[117] Benedict, Cassiodorus, and, later, the Benedictines were to be praised for their preservation of learning and education of the laity.[118] Moreover, Schaff claimed, monasticism stood as a warning against "the worldliness, frivolity, and immorality of the great cities, and [it was] a mighty call to repentance and conversion. . . . It was to invalids a hospital for the cure of moral diseases, and at the same time, to healthy and vigorous enthusiasts an arena for the exercise of heroic virtue."[119] Here asceticism is not so much a "disease," as Schaff and the other professors sometimes stated, as a "cure."

As a "hospital for invalids," monasticism helped to prepare the world for a new Christian civilization among the Romanic and Germanic nations. Yet, Schaff argued, just as the Mosaic law was a *paidagogus* for Paul, so monasticism was to Protestantism: a disciplinary institution that should be cast aside when a new era was reached.[120] Mission accomplished, the church's "higher duty" was to go on to transform and sanctify all divinely appointed human relations, thus penetrating society like a leaven. This transformation resulted, centuries later, in "the Protestant evangelical system of morality," which fostered the "inmost spirit of the New Testament" and the westward march of Protestant Christianity.[121]

Although Ephraim Emerton of Harvard as a Unitarian was outside the network of the Presbyterian and Congregationalist professors, he too accorded Western monasticism more tolerant treatment than Eastern. The "practical character" of the provisions of the Benedictine Rule, he wrote, made the "western system so different from the extravagant and fanatical monasticism of the East."[122] Since humans were innately social, even solitary ascetics were prompted to gather into groups, and from there religious orders were formed. Besides, in the West, since "the climate did not tempt men to solitary life, and the example of older religions [that fostered asceticism] was wanting," monasticism developed later, only in the fifth century or shortly before.[123] The order of St. Benedict, in Emerton's view, represented a mean between the "brutality" of the masses and the "fanaticism" of Eastern monks. In the West, the type of "insane devotion" associated with the stylites was almost unknown, and when it was known was frowned upon.[124]

The above discussion makes evident that "the East" fared badly in the American professors' imagination. Whether they considered the Far East or the Middle East, Islam or the Eastern Christian churches, "the East" came up lacking in comparison with "the West"—of which America stood as the heroic outpost. In particular, the type of asceticism Eastern Christianity fostered was inimical to Protestant ideals of service, industry, and an "inward spirituality." Borrowing arguments from their German predecessors and mentors, the American professors found some utility in Western monasticism, which had promoted values that, in new guise, supported the claim that history's course led all the way to America.

In the scholarship of our contemporaries and in that of Philip Rousseau in particular, these invidious comparisons have mercifully been discarded. Although the nineteenth-century professors doubtless thought that their assessments were "even-handed" and "scientific," we can thank Rousseau and others for treating us to a more just understanding of Christianity's past.

NOTES

The archival materials cited (largely professors' and students' class notes) are housed at the following libraries: for Samuel Miller, Princeton Theological Seminary; for Henry B. Smith, and Roswell D. Hitchcock, Union Theological Seminary; for George P. Fisher, Yale Divinity School and Yale University (Beinecke Library); for Ephraim Emerton, Harvard Divinity School. The papers of Philip Schaff are divided between the Lancaster Theological Seminary Library (which has many of Schaff's papers from his time at Mercersburg Theological Seminary) and the Union Theological Seminary Library (UTS). Students' and professors' class notes are listed by the professor's last name, title of the course, and date and name of the student note taker, if known.

1. More on the following materials can be found in my book *Founding the Fathers*.

2. On the operation of Providence in "dark" eras, see Neander, *Lectures,* 1:12, 14; P. Schaff, *What Is Church History?,* 5, 39, 80–91. Also see Meyer, "Philip Schaff's Concept"; and Shriver, "Philip Schaff's Concept."

3. For German scholars expressing these views, see Mosheim, *Ecclesiastical History,* 1:192–97, 275; Neander, *General History*, 1:274; 2:270, 294, 296. For American scholars, see Hitchcock, "Church History: First Period," early 1880s, J.D. Burrell's notes (Hitchcock Papers, Box 1, Notebook 1, p. 242); Hitchcock, "Church History: First Period," 1883, E.C. Moore's notes (Hitchcock Papers, Box 2, Notebook 2, p. 281); Hitchcock, "Church History: First Period," 1872–73, S.M. Jackson's notes (Jackson Papers, Box 1, Notebook 1, p. 81). Jesus, Hitchcock reminded his students, came into "a semi-tropical civilization"—presumably to counsel fortitude; Hitchcock, "Life of Christ," early 1880s, J.D. Burrell's notes (Hitchcock Papers, Box 1, Notebook 1, p. 25). Similarly, Fisher, *History,* 111, 114; P. Schaff, "Rise and Progress," 391; Emerton, *Introduction to the Study,* 136, and *Unitarian Thought,* 241.

4. For German scholars expressing these views, see Mosheim, *Ecclesiastical History*, 1:275; Neander, *General History*, 2:263, 291, and *Memorials of Christian Life,* 196. For American scholars, see P. Schaff, *History,* 2:398; 3:149–51, 168 (Schaff reports incidents from "ancient and modern travellers," including Alexander von Humboldt's encounter with Hindus at Astracan), "Ascetic System," 601, and "Rise and Progress," 384–88, 399, 401–2; Emerton, *Introduction to the Study*, 135.

5. "Editorial Notes," *New York Evangelist*, February 1, 1877, 4.

6. Rev. Spencer S. Roche, "Roswell D. Hitchcock, D.D., LL.D.," paper read before the Brooklyn (Episcopal) Clerical Club, June 27, 1887, in J.D. Burrell's notebook (Hitchcock Papers, Box 1, Notebook 2, Memorial Notices).

7. "In Memoriam-President Hitchcock," *New York Evangelist,* December(?) 15, 1887, clipping in J.D. Burrell's notebook (Hitchcock Papers, Box 1, Notebook 2, Memorial Notices).

8. Memorial by Adolf von Harnack, cited in D. Schaff, *Life of Philip Schaff*, 458.

9. P. Schaff, *Through Bible Lands.*

10. See the detailed discussion of nineteenth-century relations between Turkey and Russia in the *Encyclopaedia Britannica* 22 (1973 ed.), 379–82; previous diplomacy efforts are treated in Mosely, *Russian Diplomacy.* For essays and sketches on the topic written by contemporary authors, see Palgrave, *Essays on Eastern Questions*, and Latimer, *Russia and Turkey,* esp. chs. 6, 7, 10.

11. See P. Schaff's diary entries for February through August 1877 (Schaff Papers, UTS, Box 4, Diaries).

12. On July 13, 1878. In addition to keeping a travel diary, Schaff supplied accounts for American newspapers as he proceeded on his trip. A year later, Schaff published *Through Bible Lands*. David Schaff's *Life* of his father fills in some details — and omits some disparaging remarks from his father's travel diary (D. Schaff, *Life of Philip Schaff*, esp. 301–16).

13. Gabriele Lingelbach claims that Emerton was the first professor in America to be appointed to a position in church history outside a divinity school (Lingelbach, *Klio macht Karriere,* 260).

14. Details on Emerton's life taken from clippings in the Emerton Correspondence in the Harvard Divinity School Archives. His address as president of the American Society of Church History was published as "A Definition of Church History."

15. H. Smith, "Sermon" (on Zech 4:6) (Smith Papers, Ser. 2, Box 3.8–9, 14–15). Similarly, Hitchcock, *Laws of Civilization*, 22; Hitchcock, "Lectures on Church History: Second Period, 325–800," 1883, E.C. Moore's notes (Hitchcock Papers, Box 2, Notebook 2, pp. 412–14— Luther and Hegel in embryo); Hitchcock, "Lectures in Church History: Second Period, 323–800," 1883–84, J.D. Burrell's notes (Hitchcock Papers, Box 1, Notebook 2, p. 39).

16. H. Smith, *History of the Church,* 20.

17. P. Schaff, *What Is Church History?,* 40, 73–74. Schaff did not highlight the negative features of "old age." The scheme is reminiscent of Hegel's *Philosophy of History*.

18. P. Schaff, *American Nationality*, 8.

19. P. Schaff, "Theology of Our Age," 15.

20. Fisher, "Church History," 1870–71, B. Perrin's notes (Beinecke Library, Yale University, Notebook, p. 30).

21. Hitchcock, "Historical Development," 41; Hitchcock, "Life of Christ," early 1880s, J.D. Burrell's notes (Hitchcock Papers, Box 1, Notebook 1, p. 27); Hitchcock, "Life of Christ," 1865, E.B. Wright's notes (Hitchcock Papers, Box 2, Notebook 1, n.p.); H. Smith, "Church History," 1850?, T.S. Hastings's notes (Smith Papers, Ser. 5, Box 1, Folder 3, Notebook, pp. 106–7). Rome defeated Carthage in 146 BCE.

22. Read Euripides, Plato, and Aristotle, Hitchcock exhorted his class! The Greek hatred of women ran so deep, he claimed, that men took to pederasty, and

he noted the sexual predilections of the viceroy of Egypt; see Hitchcock, "Church History: First Period," 1872–73, S.T. Jackson's notes (Jackson Papers, Box 1, Notebook 1, pp. 71, 76); Hitchcock, "Church History: First Period," 1883, E.C. Moore's notes (Hitchcock Papers, Box 2, Notebook 2, p. 288); Hitchcock, "Apostolic Church," 1882, E.C. Moore's notes (Hitchcock Papers, Box 2, Notebook 2, p. 110).

23. For an informative and lively account of one aspect of German philhellenism in this era, see Marchand, *Down from Olympus,* esp. ch. 3–6.

24. Hitchcock, "Church History: Second Period," 1883–84, E.C. Moore's notes (Hitchcock Papers, Box 2, Notebook 2, p. 408). Hitchcock suggests that the East's having a middle class arrested its fall (pp. 408–9).

25. P. Schaff, "American Nationality," 4.

26. Hitchcock, "Chinese Classics," 632, 634–38.

27. [Roswell D. Hitchcock], "His Last Words in Public," clipping in J.D. Burrell's notebook (Hitchcock Papers, Box 1, Memorial Notices).

28. P. Schaff, *America*, 45.

29. Ibid., 46.

30. P. Schaff, "American Nationality," 20. Here Schaff acknowledged that the English had excelled in developing "the highways of commerce to the extremities of the inhabitable globe" (8). It was not, he elsewhere added, any merit on the part of Americans that they had been called to this great purpose. P. Schaff, "Report," 218.

31. Schaff, *What Is Church History?,* 39. George Park Fisher of Yale agreed that "savages," lacking written records, were not truly "historical" but should be considered under the rubric of anthropology (*Brief History,* 1, 2, 42).

32. Fisher, *Brief History*, 18, 3.

33. Ibid., 58.

34. Ibid., 12.

35. H. Smith, "Sermon" (on 1 Tim 1:11), n.d. (Smith Papers, Ser. 2, Box 3, p. 27).

36. H. Smith, "Sermon" (on 2 Tim 2:10), n.d. (Smith Papers, Ser. 2, Box 3, p. 19). Even the vilest man could be saved: H. Smith, "Sermon" (on Is 45:22, "Look unto me and be saved, all the ends of the earth"), n.d. (Smith Papers, Ser. 2, Box 1, p. 28).

37. H. Smith, "Sermon" (on Lk 7:9), n.d. (Smith Papers, Ser. 2, Box 2, p. 19, emphasis added).

38. See Lingelbach, *Klio macht Karriere*, 86–87; Lingelbach sees this theme prominently displayed in the writings of historian George Bancroft (an admirer of Henry Smith). Also see P. Schaff, *What Is Church History?,* 111–14. For a helpful explanation of American exceptionalism, see Rodgers, "Exceptionalism," 21–40.

39. Schaf [*sic*], *Anglo-Germanism,* 5–6; Schaff thought that Germany would strongly influence the American educational system (15). See also P. Schaff, *America*, 20, 103, 191, 208, *What Is Church History?,* 111–14, and *History,* 3:28, 288.

40. Berkeley, "Prospect of Planting Arts," 186.

41. P. Schaff, *History,* 3:315.

42. Schaff, *America*, 51.

43. Schaff, "Theology of Our Age," 13.

44. Hitchcock, *Laws of Civilization*, 23; this would be so if our crimes and follies did not lead Providence to dash us to pieces (24).

45. Hitchcock, *Address on Colportage,* 4. Hitchcock rejected the term *Native Americans:* no continent except Asia [with the beginnings of the human race] had ever had any "natives" (4–5). Elsewhere, Hitchcock writes that the "Aborigines" of North America were now perishing, Christianity having arrived too late to save them (*Laws of Civilization*, 8); Asian civilizations, in any case, never raised themselves above thralldom to nature (18, 19).

46. Hitchcock, *Address on Colportage,* 6.

47. Hitchcock stated in "Church History: Second Period, 323–800," 1872–73, according to S.M. Jackson's notes (Jackson Papers, Box 1, Notebook, vol. 1, pp. 197–98), that "Mohammedanism rendered two conspicuous services": it gave an intellectual impetus to the Middle Ages (our culture had one of its roots in Arabic culture, especially in Spain); and it raised men from the idolatry and cannibalism and fetish worship of the African tribes. Ethnologists, he told his students, had concluded that Mohammedanism over the centuries increased the brain power of these tribes and improved their physique.

48. Schaff, *Through Bible Lands*, 391.

49. P. Schaff, "The Protestant Mission in the East," clipping in Schaff Scrapbook (Schaff Papers, UTS, Box 6, Scrapbook 1, p. 107).

50. Schaff, *Through Bible Lands*, 121, 109; Philip Schaff, "A Visit to the Great Pyramid," *New York Observer*, n.d. [1877] (written from Cairo, February 28, 1877), clipping in Schaff Scrapbook (Schaff Papers, UTS, Box 6, Scrapbook 1, p. 91).

51. Schaff, *Through Bible Lands*, 411–12.

52. Ibid., 258; likewise, Schaff, "Protestant Mission in the East" (Schaff Papers, UTS, Box 6, Scrapbook 1, p. 107). Russia might have selfish motives for conquest, Schaff conceded, but he nevertheless believed that she was an agent in the hands of providence to bring about a higher purpose, namely, the defeat of Turkey and Islam. Thus Schaff disagreed with those who argued that Turkey should be allowed to "die a natural death," without Russian intervention (P. Schaff, "Eastern Conflict").

53. Schaff, *Through Bible Lands*, 412, 258.

54. Schaff, diary excerpts for March–May 1854, cited in D. Schaff, *Life*, 181–82. Schaff believed that Islam had received a theological mission in the world, namely, to stand against "idolatry." In its stalwart and uncompromising monotheism, Islam had played a providential role in overcoming the "idolatry" of the pre-Islamic tribes of Arabia. As Schaff put it, Mohammad "had the providential mission to destroy the gross idolatry of the heathen nations" (*Through Bible Lands*, 392).

55. Hitchcock, "Church History: Middle Ages, 800–1294," n.d., J. D. Burrell's notes (Hitchcock Papers, Box 1, Notebook 2, p. 74).

56. Hitchcock, "Church History: Modern Age, 1517–1884," n.d., J. D. Burrell's notes (Hitchcock Papers, Box 1, Notebook 2, p. 121).

57. Hitchcock, "Life of Christ," 1865, E. B. Wright's notes (Hitchcock Papers, Box 2, Notebook 1, Section 3, n.p.).

58. Hitchcock, "Lectures on Church History: Second Period, 323–800," 1872–73, S. M. Jackson's notes (Jackson Papers, Box 1, Notebook 1, p. 197).

59. Hitchcock, "Lectures on Church History: Second Period, 323–800," 1883–84, J. D. Burrell's notes (Hitchcock Papers, Box 1, Notebook 2, p. 21).

60. Schaff, "American Nationality," 20.

61. P. Schaff, "Christianity in America."

62. Schaff, *History,* 3:772–73.

63. Ibid., 3:772.

64. Ibid., 3:733.

65. Schaff, *Through Bible Lands*, 5.

66. For German scholars expressing these views, see Mosheim, *Ecclesiastical History,* 1:193; Neander, *Memorials*, 72, 50–51; Neander, *General History,* 1:275, 43–45, 48–49, 58–60; cf. Neander, *Lectures,* 1:78, 83). As for American scholars, in Samuel Miller's view, Platonic philosophy had promoted "mischief" and heresy; see Miller, "Ecclesiastical History, No. 2. II and III Centuries," n.d. (Miller Papers, Box 2, Folder 14, pp. 1–3). In Smith's view, to adopt the tendencies of Neo-Platonism would mean that "history was wrecked" (H. Smith, *Introduction to Christian Theology*, 72–73). Hitchcock wrote that the Catholic faith had managed to "survive" Platonic speculation ("Ante-Nicene Trinitarianism," 54). Schaff downplayed the influence: doctrine did not arise from Neo-Platonism (P. Schaff, "Conflict of Trinitarianism and Unitarianism," 728, 726).

67. "Sordid": Hitchcock, "Church History: Second Period, 325–800," 1883–84, E. C. Moore's notes (Hitchcock Papers, Box 2, Notebook 2, p. 413). "Cruel": Hitchcock, "History of the Apostolic Church," early 1880s, J. D. Burrell's notes (Hitchcock Papers, Box 1, Notebook 1, p. 147).

68. Hitchcock, "Church History: First Period," 1872–73, S. M. Jackson's notes (Jackson Papers, Box 1, Notebook 1, p. 67). Yet early in Christian history, the East (so Hitchcock alleged) had exhibited greater spirituality and fervor than

the West, which had rather stressed the practical, the "external," and the organizational; Hitchcock, "Church History: Second Period, 323–800," 1883–84, J.D. Burrell's notes (Hitchcock Papers, Box 1, Notebook 2, p. 57). Hitchcock attributed (without elaboration) this difference to a "racial reason." On this one point, "the East" was deemed better than "the West."

69. It was better that the temple and the altar perished so that religion would be "driven out to seek new fields. [The] mother dies, [the] child lives": Hitchcock, "Lectures on the Life of Christ," early 1880s, J.D. Burrell's notes (Hitchcock Papers, Box 1, Notebook 1, p. 90).

70. P. Schaff, "Theology of Our Age," 10, and *History,* 3:772.

71. P. Schaff, *History*, 3:698.

72. Ibid., 3:288: Schaff slightly misquotes Bishop Berkeley's poem.

73. Ibid., 3:729 n. 1, 942–46. Schaff was apparently referring to Cyril's *In Ioannis Evangelium* 12 (on Jn 19:25–27) (PG 74.661, 664–65).

74. Hitchcock, "Lectures on Church History: Second Period, 325–800," 1883, E.C. Moore's notes (Hitchcock Papers, Box 2, Notebook 2, pp. 412–13); P. Schaff, *History* 3:772–73; Fisher, *History,* 173; Miller, "Ecclesiastical History, No. III. IV and V Centuries" (Miller Papers, Box 2, Folder 15, pp. 26–27); Miller, "Practical Results from a Course of Ecclesiastical History" (Miller Papers, Box 2, Folder 10, pp. 11, 7, 9, 18); Miller, "Notes on Mosheim, Century V," March 7, 1814 (Miller Papers, Box 5, Folder 13, p. 28); Miller, "Ecclesiastical History," O. Douglass's notes (Miller Papers, Box 26, Folder 4, p. 45). Miller told his students that many of their contemporaries thought that neither Nestorius's nor Eutyches' teachings were "materially erroneous, or dangerous to the orthodox faith"; the issue was one of language. Scholars even deemed Nestorius's Christology orthodox; similarly, Schaff, *History,* 3:729 n. 1. For an example of a German scholar on the Trinitarian and Christological controversies, see Gieseler, *Text-Book,* 1:348–51, 353, 292–93).

75. Hitchcock, "Lectures on Church History," 1872–73, S.M. Jackson's notes (Jackson Papers, Box 1, Notebook 1, pp. 215–16).

76. Hitchcock, "Church History: Second Period, 325–800," 1883, E.C. Moore's notes (Hitchcock Papers, Box 2, Notebook 2, p. 432).

77. P. Schaff, *History,* 3:603.

78. Hitchcock, "Church History: First Period," 1872–1873, S.M. Jackson's notes (Jackson Papers, Box 1, Notebook 1, p. 67).

79. P. Schaff, *History,* 3:921.

80. Ibid., 3:939. In general, however, Schaff thought Chrysostom superior to many other Eastern Christian fathers.

81. On fanaticism, see Mosheim, *Ecclesiastical History,* 2:117. (On the violent behavior of Egyptian hermits, see Hitchcock, *True Idea,* 41.) On the fostering of superstition and credulity, see Miller, "Lecture Notes on Mosheim:

Century IV, No. 2," February 21, 1814 (Miller Papers, Box 5, Folder 12, pp. 3, 9 [Jerome as source], 11). On the decline into "madness," see Gieseler, *Text-Book*, 1:405–6, 399–400; Neander, *General History,* 2:274.

82. P. Schaff, *History,* 3:247.

83. Miller, "Lecture Notes on Mosheim: Century IV, No. 2," February 21, 1814 (Miller Papers, Box 5, Folder 12, pp. 3, 9 [Jerome as source], 11).

84. Miller, "Lecture Notes on Mosheim: Cent. V, No. 1," March 7, 1814 (Miller Papers, Box 5, Folder 13, p. 17).

85. Mosheim, *Ecclesiastical History,* 2:47–50; Gieseler, *Text-Book*, 1:407. The stylite's mortifications were to be expected in men whose passions had been blocked from "natural" outlets, in whom spiritual pride triumphed and wild fanaticism raged (1:404). That women could not practice these wilder forms of asceticism showed that the practices were faulty (1:407).

86. Neander, *General History,* 2:292–93. Neander quotes Sozomen on the *boskoi* (*Historia ecclesiastica* 6.33).

87. Miller, "Ecclesiastical History, No. III, IV, and V Centuries" (Miller Papers, Box 2, Folder 15, p. 22).

88. Miller, "Lecture Notes on Mosheim, Cent. V, No. 1," March 7, 1814 (Miller Papers, Box 5, Folder 13, pp. 3–4 [extract on pp. 4–8], 20, 22).

89. Hitchcock, "Church History: Second Period, 323–800," 1872–73, S.M. Jackson's notes (Jackson Papers, Box 1, Notebook 1, pp. 255, 257). He refers to Montalembert's *Monks of the West.*

90. Hitchcock, "Church History: Second Period, 325–800," 1883–84, E.C. Moore's notes (Hitchcock Papers, Box 2, Notebook 2, p, 467); Hitchcock, "Church History: Second Period, 323–800," early 1880s, J.D. Burrell's notes (Hitchcock Papers, Box 1, Notebook 2, pp. 41–42).

91. P. Schaff, *History,* 3:5, 6.

92. Ibid., 3:166. Schaff further wrote of the stylites, "One knows not whether to wonder at their unexampled self-denial, or to pity their ignorance of the gospel salvation" (3:191–92).

93. Ibid., 3:165–66. Schaff advised readers to judge such aberrations leniently in light of the age, despite their foreignness to the morality of the Bible.

94. Ibid., 3:192 n.

95. Ibid., 3:171, citing *Life of Pachomius* 61 and Nilus, *Epistularum libri* 2.140.

96. Ibid., 3:177; Schaff, "Rise and Progress," 413–14.

97. P. Schaff, *History,* 3:167.

98. Ibid., 3:171.

99. Ibid., 3:243, 247.

100. Ibid., 3:247.

101. Emerton, *Introduction to the Study,* 149, 144–45.

102. Gieseler, *Text-Book*, 1:399–400, 510. Also see Neander, *General History,* 1:274; 2:270, 294, 296 (in hot climates, people did not eat much; the climates of Egypt, Palestine, and Syria favored asceticism).

103. Miller, "Ecclesiastical History, No. III, IV, and V Centuries" (Miller Papers, Box 2, Folder 15, p. 13).

104. Miller, "Lecture Notes on Mosheim: Century IV, No. 2," February 21, 1814 (Miller Papers, Box 5, Folder 12, pp. 3, 9 [Jerome as source], 11).

105. Gieseler, *Text-Book*, 1:411, 510.

106. Neander, *General History,* 1:249. Even the attempt of Julian "the Apostate" to reinstate paganism showed how little human schemes could effect if they stood against Providence, which guided and fashioned "the spirit of the times according to its own everlasting decrees": Augustus Neander, *Emperor Julian,* 18.

107. Neander, *Memorials*, 313; Neander, *General History,* 2:296.

108. Neander, *General History,* 2:284–88.

109. Ibid., 2:301–2.

110. Hitchcock, "Church History: Second Period, 323–800," 1872–73, S.M. Jackson's notes (Jackson Papers, Box 1, Notebook 1, p. 257). Hitchcock touches on Columba's founding a "religious fraternity" at Iona in 563; of this "missionary band," only a minority were celibate (p. 226).

111. Hitchcock, "Church History: Second Period, 323–800," early 1880s, J.D. Burrell's notes (Hitchcock Papers, Box 1, Notebook 2, pp. 42–43); Hitchcock, "Church History: Second Period, 323–800," 1872–73, S.M. Jackson's notes (Jackson Papers, Box 1, Notebook 1, p. 257); Hitchcock, "Church History: Second Period, 325–800," 1883, E.C. Moore's notes (Hitchcock Papers, Box 2, Notebook 2, pp. 469–70).

112. Fisher, *History,* 115–16.

113. Schaff, *History,* 3:156.

114. Schaff, "Ascetic System," 612. Monasticism became "the means of converting the Heathen and advancing all the interests of civilization"; Schaff, "Church History, 311–590," Mercersburg Theological Seminary, 1855, C.C. Russell's notes (P. Schaff Papers, LTS, Ms. Collection 163, Box 4, ff. 03, Notebook, p. 62).

115. Philip Schaff, "Staffa and Iona," unidentified newspaper clipping, from July 25, 1877 (*New-York Evangelist*?) (Schaff Papers, UTS, Box 6, Scrapbook 1, p. 94). Schaff writes from Oban, Scotland.

116. Schaff, *History,* 3:220.

117. Schaff, "Rise and Progress," 394, 412, 411; Schaff, *History,* 3:176, 200–201.

118. Schaff, *History,* 3:217, 220, 225, 176–77 (Schaff added that the education of the people was not part of the intention of the original monastic found-

ers but that "in seeking first the kingdom of heaven, these other things were added to them").

119. Schaff, *History,* 3:175.

120. Schaff, "Rise and Progress," 411, 394.

121. Schaff, "Ascetic System," 612–13.

122. Emerton, *Introduction to the Study*, 138.

123. Ibid., 136; similarly, Emerton, *Unitarian Thought*, 241.

124. Emerton, *Introduction to the Study*, 149, 144–45.

Select Publications of Philip Rousseau

BOOKS

Ascetics, Authority and the Church in the Age of Jerome and Cassian. Oxford Historical Monographs. Oxford: Oxford University Press, 1978. 2nd ed., Notre Dame: University of Notre Dame Press, 2010.

Pachomius: The Making of a Community in Fourth-Century Egypt. TCH 6. Berkeley: University of California Press, 1985. Paperback ed., with a new preface, 1999.

Basil of Caesarea. TCH 20. Berkeley: University of California Press, 1994. Paperback ed., 1998.

Ed. with Tomas Hägg. *Greek Biography and Panegyric in Late Antiquity*. Berkeley: University of California Press, 2000.

The Early Christian Centuries. London: Longman, 2002.

Ed. *A Companion to Late Antiquity*. Chichester: Wiley-Blackwell, 2009.

Ed. with Manolis Papoutsakis. *Transformations of Late Antiquity: Essays for Peter Brown*. Farnham: Ashgate, 2009.

ARTICLES

"The Spiritual Authority of the 'Monk-Bishop': Eastern Elements in Some Western Hagiography of the Fourth and Fifth Centuries." *JTS* 22 (1971): 380–419.

"Blood-Relationships among Early Eastern Ascetics." *JTS* 23 (1972): 135–44.

"The Formation of Early Ascetic Communities: Some Further Reflections." *JTS* 25 (1974): 113–17.

"Rule of St Augustine of Hippo" and "St Macarius of Egypt." In *The Oxford Dictionary of the Christian Church*, 2nd ed., edited by F. L. Cross and E. A. Livingstone. London: Oxford University Press, 1974.

"Cassian, Contemplation, and the Coenobitic Life." *Journal of Ecclesiastical History* 26 (1975): 113–26.
"Structure and Event in Anthropology and History." *New Zealand Journal of History* 9 (1975): 22–40.
"In Search of Sidonius the Bishop." *Historia* 25 (1976): 356–77.
"Augustine and Ambrose: The Loyalty and Single-Mindedness of a Disciple." *Augustiniana* 27 (1977): 151–65.
"The Death of Boethius: The Charge of Maleficium." *Studi Medievali*, 3rd ser., 20 (1979): 871–89.
"Jerome: His Failures and Their Importance." In *The Heritage of Christian Thought,* edited by Gordon Harper and James Veitch, 35–58. Wellington: Victoria University Press, 1979.
"The Exegete as Historian: Hilary of Poitiers' Commentary on Matthew." In *History and Historians in Late Antiquity*, edited by Brian Croke and Alanna M. Emmett, 107–15. Sydney: Pergamon Press, 1983.
"The Desert Fathers: Antony and Pachomius." In *The Study of Spirituality,* edited by Cheslyn Jones, Geoffrey Wainwright, and Edward Yarnold, 119–30. London: Society for Promoting Christian Knowledge, 1986.
"Saint Augustine: Ascetical Theology." *Canadian Catholic Review* 5 (1987): 136–40.
"Ascetics in Their Place." Review article. *Heythrop Journal* 28 (1987): 194–97.
"Basil of Caesarea, Contra Eunomium: The Main Preoccupations." In *The Idea of Salvation*, edited by D. W. Dockrill and R. G. Tanner, 77–94. Auckland: University of Auckland, 1988.
"Basil of Caesarea: Choosing a Past." In *Reading the Past in Late Antiquity*, edited by Graeme Clarke, 37–58. Canberra: Australian National University Press, 1990.
"Christian Asceticism and the Early Monks." In *Early Christianity: Origins and Evolution to AD 600: Essays in Honour of W. H. C. Frend*, edited by Ian Hazlett, 112–22. London: Society for Promoting Christian Knowledge, 1990.
"The Development of Christianity in the Roman World: Elaine Pagels and Peter Brown." *Prudentia* 22 (1990): 49–70.
"Visigothic Migration and Settlement, 376–418: Some Excluded Hypotheses." *Historia* 41 (1992): 345–61.
"'Learned Women' and the Formation of a Christian Culture in Late Antiquity." *Symbolae Osloenses* 70 (1995): 116–47.
"Ambrose and the Christian Empire: Some Misgivings." In *Religion in the Ancient World: New Themes and Approaches*, edited by Matthew Dillon, 477–78. Amsterdam: Hakkert, 1996.
"Ambrose." "Asceticism." "Basil of Caesarea." "Cassian." "Christianity." "Conversion." "Gregory of Nazianzus." "Gregory of Nyssa." "Hilary of Arles."

"Paganism." "Palladius." In *The Oxford Classical Dictionary*, 3rd ed., edited by Simon Hornblower and Antony Spawforth. Oxford: Oxford University Press, 1996.

"Cassian: Monastery and World." In *The Certainty of Doubt: Tributes to Peter Munz*, edited by Miles Fairburn and W. H. Oliver, 68–89. Wellington: University of Victoria Press, 1996.

"Inheriting the Fifth Century: Who Bequeathed What?" In *The Sixth Century: End or Beginning?,* edited by Pauline Allen and Elizabeth Jeffreys, 1–19. Byzantina Australiensia 10. Brisbane: Australian Association for Byzantine Studies, 1996.

Contribution to "Peter Brown: The World of Late Antiquity Revisited." *Symbolae Osloenses* 72 (1997): 5–90 (52–55).

"Eccentrics and Cenobites in the Late Roman East." *Byzantinische Forschungun* 24 (1997): 35–50.

"Orthodoxy and the Coenobite." *SP* 30 (1997): 241–58.

"The Identity of the Ascetic Master in the *Historia Religiosa* of Theodoret of Cyrrhus: A New Paideia?" *Mediterranean Archaeology* 11 (1998): 229–44.

"Jerome's Search for Self-Identity." in *Prayer and Spirituality in the Early Church*, vol. 1, edited by Pauline Allen, Raymond Canning, and Lawrence Cross, with B. Janelle Caiger, 125–42. Everton Park, Queensland: Centre for Early Christian Studies, Australian Catholic University, 1998.

"'The Preacher's Audience': A More Optimistic View." In *Ancient History in a Modern University*, vol. 2, *Early Christianity, Late Antiquity and Beyond*, edited by T.W. Hillard, R.A. Kearsley, C.E.V. Nixon, and A.M. Nobbs, 391–400. Grand Rapids, MI: Eerdmans, 1998.

"Procopius's Buildings and Justinian's Pride." *Byzantion* 68 (1998): 121–30.

"Ascetics as Mediators and as Teachers." In *The Cult of Saints in Late Antiquity and the Early Middle Ages: Essays on the Contribution of Peter Brown*, edited by James Howard-Johnston and Paul Antony Hayward, 45–59. Oxford: Oxford University Press, 1999. Paperback ed., 2002.

"Baptism." "Basil of Caesarea." "Bishops." "Gregory of Nyssa." "Monks." "Nitria." "Pachomius." "Scetis." In *Late Antiquity: A Guide to the Postclassical World*, edited by G. W. Bowersock, Peter Brown, and Oleg Grabar. Cambridge, MA: Harvard University Press, 1999.

"Christian Culture and the Swine's Husks: Jerome, Augustine, and Paulinus." In *The Limits of Ancient Christianity: Essays on Late Antique Thought and Culture in Honor of R.A. Markus*, edited by William E. Klingshirn and Mark Vessey, 172–87. Ann Arbor: University of Michigan Press, 1999.

"Introduction: Biography and Panegyric." With Tomas Hägg. In *Greek Biography and Panegyric in Late Antiquity,* edited by Tomas Hägg and Philip Rousseau, 1–28. Berkeley: University of California Press, 2000.

"Antony as Teacher in the Greek Life." In *Greek Biography and Panegyric in Late Antiquity*, edited by P. Rousseau and T. Hägg, 89–109. Berkeley: University of California Press, 2000.

"Monasticism." In Vol. 15 of *The Cambridge Ancient History*, edited by Averil Cameron, Bryan Ward-Perkins, and Michael Whitby, 745–80. New ed. Cambridge: Cambridge University Press, 2000.

"Sidonius and Majorian: The Censure in Carmen V." *Historia* 49 (2000): 251–57.

"The Historiography of Asceticism: Current Achievements and Future Opportunities." In *The Past before Us: The Challenge of Historiographies of Late Antiquity*, edited by Carole Straw and Richard Lim, 89–101. Turnhout: Brepols, 2004.

"Moses, Monks, and Mountains in Theodoret's *Historia religiosa*." In *Il monachesimo tra eredità e aperture,* edited by Maciej Bielawski and Daniël Hombergen, 323–46. Rome: Centro Studi S. Anselmo, 2004.

"Cassian's Apophthegmata." *Jahrbuch für Antike und Christentum* 48/49 (2005–6): 19–34.

"Knowing Theodoret: Text and Self." In *The Cultural Turn in Late Ancient Studies: Gender, Asceticism, and Historiography,* edited by Dale B. Martin and Patricia Cox Miller, 278–97. Durham: Duke University Press, 2005.

"The Pious Household and the Virgin Chorus: Reflections on Gregory of Nyssa's *Life of Macrina*." *JECS* 13 (2005): 165–86.

"Ancient Ascetics and Modern Virtue: The Case of Anger." In *Prayer and Spirituality in the Early Church*, vol. 4, *The Spiritual Life*, edited by Wendy Mayer, Pauline Allen, and Lawrence Cross, 213–31. Strathfield, NSW: St Paul's Publications, for the Centre for Early Christian Studies, Australian Catholic University, 2006.

"Retrospect: Images, Reflections, and the 'Essential' Gregory." In *Gregory of Nazianzus: Images and Reflections*, edited by Jostein Børtnes and Tomas Hägg, 283–95. Copenhagen: Museum Tusculanum Press, 2006.

"The Desert Fathers and Their Broader Audience." In *Foundations of Power and Conflicts of Authority in Late-Antique Monasticism*, edited by Alberto Camplani and Giovanni Filoramo, 89–107. Louvain: Peeters, 2007.

"Introduction: From Binding to Burning." In *The Early Christian Book*, edited by William E. Klingshirn and Linda Safran, 1–9. CUA Studies in Early Christianity 1. Washington, DC: Catholic University of America Press, 2007.

"The Successors of Pachomius and the Nag Hammadi Library: Exegetical Themes and Literary Interpretations." In *The World of Early Egyptian Christianity: Language, Literature, and Social Context*, edited by James E. Goehring and Janet A. Timbie, 140–57. CUA Studies in Early Christianity 2. Washington, DC: Catholic University of America Press, 2007.

"Late Roman Christianities." In *The Cambridge History of Christianity*, 3: *Early Medieval Christianities, c.600–c.1100*, edited by Thomas F.X. Noble and Julia M.H. Smith, 21–45. Cambridge: Cambridge University Press, 2008.

"Human Nature and Its Material Setting in Basil of Caesarea's Sermons on the Creation." *Heythrop Journal* 49 (2008): 222–39.

"Jerome on Jeremiah: Exegesis and Recovery." In *Jerome of Stridon: His Life, Writings and Legacy,* edited by Andrew Cain and Josef Lössl, 73–83. Farnham: Ashgate, 2009.

"Language, Morality and Cult: Augustine and Varro." In *Transformations of Late Antiquity: Essays for Peter Brown*, edited by Philip Rousseau and Manolis Papoutsakis, 159–75. Farnham: Ashgate, 2009.

"Eusebius of Caesarea." "Jerome." In *The Oxford Encyclopedia of Ancient Greece and Rome*, edited by Michael Gagarin and Elaine Fantham, 3.141–4, 4.110–12. New York: Oxford University Press, 2010.

"Homily and Asceticism in the North Italian Episcopate." In *Chromatius of Aquileia and His Age*, edited by Pier Franco Beatrice and Alessio Peršic, 145–61. Turnhout: Brepols, 2011.

General Bibliography

PRIMARY SOURCES

Aelian. *Aelian: On the Characteristics of Animals*. Edited and translated by A.F. Scholfield. 3 vols. LCL. Cambridge, MA: Harvard University Press, 1959.

Ambrose of Milan. *Saint Ambrose: Hexameron, Paradise, and Cain and Abel*. Translated by John J. Savage. FC 42. New York: Fathers of the Church, Inc., 1961.

Amélineau, É., ed. *Monuments pour servir à l'histoire de l'Égypte chrétienne au IVe siècle: Histoire de saint Pakhôme et de ses communautés; Documents coptes et arabe inédits, publiés et traduits*. Annales du Musée Guimet 17. Paris: Leroux, 1889.

——, ed. *Monuments pour servir à l'histoire de l'Égypte chrétienne au IVe, Ve, VIe, VIIIe siècles*. 2 vols in 1. Memoire publiés par les membres de la Mission archéologique française au Caire 4.1–2. Paris: Leroux, 1895.

——, ed. *Monuments pour servir à l'histoire de l'Égypte chrétienne: Histoire des monastères de la Basse-Égypte, vies des saints Paul, Antoine, Macaire, Maxime et Domèce Jean le Nain*. Annales du Musée Guimet 25. Paris: Leroux, 1894.

Ammon. *The Letter of Ammon and Pachomian Monasticism*. Edited by J.E. Goehring. Berlin: De Gruyter, 1986.

Ammonas. *Ammonas, successeur de saint Antoine: Textes grecs et syriaques édités et traduits*. Edited by F. Nau. PO 11.4. Paris: Firmin-Didot, 1915.

——. *Ammonii Erimitae epistolae*. Edited by M. Kmosko. PO 10.6. Paris: Firmin-Didot, 1915.

Athanasius. *Die Apologien*. Edited by H.-G. Opitz. AW 2. Berlin: Akademie der Wissenschaften, 1940.

——. *Contra gentes and De incarnatione*. Edited by Robert W. Thomson. Oxford: Oxford University Press, 1971.

———. *The Coptic Life of Antony*. Translated by T. Vivian. San Francisco: International Scholars Publications, 1995.

———. *De virginitate: Eine echte Schrift des Athanasius.* Edited by E. von der Goltz. Texte und Untersuchungen 29.2. Leipzig: J.C. Hinrichs, 1905.

———. *The Letters of Saint Athanasius Concerning the Holy Spirit*. Translated by C. R. B. Shapland. New York: Philosophical Library, 1951.

———. *Lettres festales et pastorales en copte*. Edited by L.-Th. Lefort. CSCO 150. Louvain: Durbecq, 1955.

———. *The Life of Antony and the Letter to Marcellinus*. Translated by Robert C. Gregg. Classics of Western Spirituality. New York: Paulist Press, 1980.

———. *The Life of Antony: The Greek Life of Antony and the Coptic Life of Antony, and an Encomium on Saint Antony by John of Shmûn, and a Letter to the Disciples of Antony by Serapion of Thmuis*. Translated by T. Vivian and A.N. Athanassakis. Kalamazoo, MI: Cistercian Publications, 2003.

———. *The Life of Saint Antony*. Translated by Robert T. Meyer. ACW 10. New York: Newman Press, 1950.

———. *S. Antonii vitae, versio sahidica*. Edited by G. Garitte. Louvain: Secrétariat du CSCO, 1949.

———. *Select Writings and Letters of Athanasius, Bishop of Alexandria*. Edited and translated by Archibald Robertson. NPNF, 2nd ser., vol. 4. 1957. Reprint, Grand Rapids, MI: Eerdmans, 1978.

———. *Vie d'Antoine*. Edited by G.J.M. Bartelink. SC 400. 1994. Reprint, Paris: Éditions du Cerf, 2004.

———. *La vie primitive de S. Antoine conservée en syriaque.* Edited by R. Draguet. CSCO 417–18. Leuven: Peeters, 1980.

Augustine. *De civitate Dei*. Edited by Bernhard Dombart. Vol. 14 of *Sancti Augustini opera.* CCSL 47. Turnhout: Brepols, 1955.

———. *De opere monachorum*. Edited by J. Zycha. CSEL 41. Vienna: Tempsky, 1900.

Bagnall, Roger S., ed. *The Kellis Agricultural Account Book (P. Kell. IV Gr. 96).* DOPM 7. Oxford: Oxbow Books, 1997.

Bandt, Cordula, ed. and trans. *Der Traktat "Vom Mysterium der Buchstaben": Kritischer Text mit Einführung, Übersetzung und Anmerkungen*. Texte und Untersuchungen zur Geschichte der altchristlichen Literatur 162. Berlin: De Gruyter, 2007.

Bang, W., and A. von Gabain, eds. "Türkische Turfan-Texte, II: Manichaica." *Sitzungsberichte der Preussischen Akademie der Wissenschaften, Phil.-hist. Klasse* (1929): 411–30.

Basil of Caesarea. *Basile de Césarée: Homélies sur L'Hexaéméron*. Edited and translated by Stanislas Giet. 2nd ed. SC 26. Paris: Éditions du Cerf, 1968.

——. *Basile de Césarée: Sur l'origine de l'homme (Hom. X et XI de l'Hexaéméron)*. Edited and translated by Alexis Smets and Michel van Esbroeck. SC 160. Paris: Éditions du Cerf, 1970.

——. "Epistula 8." Edited by J. Gribomont. In *Basilio di Cesarea: Le lettere*, vol. 1, edited by M. Forlin-Patrucco, 84–113. Turin: Società Editrice Internationale, 1983.

——. *Saint Basil: Exegetic Homilies*. Translated by Sister Agnes Clare Way, C. D. P. FC 46. Washington, DC: Catholic University of America Press, 1963.

Bell, D. N., trans. *Besa: The Life of Shenoute*. Kalamazoo, MI: Cistercian Publications, 1983.

Berkeley, George. "Prospect of Planting Arts and Learning in America." In *A Miscellany, containing several tracts on various subjects*. Edited by G. Berkeley. Dublin: Faulkner, 1752.

Besa. *Letters and Sermons of Besa*. Edited by K. H. Kuhn. CSCO 157–58. Louvain: Peeters, 1956.

Betz, Hans Dieter, ed. *The Greek Magical Papyri in Translation, Including the Demotic Spells*. Vol. 1. *Texts.* 2nd ed. Chicago: University of Chicago Press, 1992.

Blaising, Craig A., and Carmen S. Harding, eds. *Psalms 1–50.* Ancient Christian Commentary on Scripture: Old Testament 7. Downers Grove, IL: InterVarsity Press, 2008.

Boon, Amand, ed. *Pachomiana Latina: Règle et épitres de S. Pachome, épitre de S. Théodore et "Liber" de S. Orsiesius; Texte latin de S. Jérôme*. Bibliothèque de la Revue d'histoire ecclésiastique 7. Louvain: Bureaux de la Revue, 1932.

Boud'hors, Anne, and Chantal Heurtel. *Les ostraca coptes de la TT 29: Autour du moine Frangé*. Brussels: CReA-Patrimoine, 2010.

Brottier, Laurence. *L'appel des "demi-chrétiens" à la "vie angélique": Jean Chrysostome prédicateur entre idéal monastique et réalité mondaine*. Paris: Éditions du Cerf, 2005.

Ciasca, A., ed. *Sacrorum bibliorum fragmenta Copto-Sahidica*. 3 vols. Rome: S. Congregationis, 1889.

Cicero. *Rhetorica ad Herennium.* Ed. and trans. Harry Caplan. LCL 403. Cambridge, MA: Harvard University Press, 1954.

Clement. *Stromata: Buch I–VI*. Edited by O. Stählin, L. Früchtel, and U. Treu 3 vols. Die Griechische Christliche Schriftsteller. Berlin: Akademie-Verlag, 1960.

Cranenburgh, H. van, ed. *La vie latine de saint Pachôme: Traduite du grec par Denys le Petit*. Brussels: Société des Bollandistes, 1969.

Crum, W. E., and H. I. Bell, eds. *Wadi Sarga: Coptic and Greek Texts*. Copenhagen: Gyldendalske Boghandel-Nordisk, 1922.

Dorotheus of Gaza. *Dorothée de Gaza: Oeuvres spirituelles.* Edited by L. Regnault and J. de Préville. SC 92. Paris: Éditions du Cerf, 1963.

Epiphanius of Salamis. *Epiphanius Werke.* Edited by K. Holl and J. Dummer. 3 vols. GCS 25, 31, 37. Berlin: Akademie-Verlag, 1915–33.

Eusebius of Caesarea. *Historia ecclesiastica.* Edited by Edouard Schwartz. Eusebius Werke II.1–3. GCS 9.1–3. Leipzig: Hinrichs, 1903–9.

———. *Letter to Carpanius.* Translated by Mark DelCogliano. 2004. http://tertullian.org/fathers/eusebius_letter_to_carpianus.htm.

Evagrius of Pontus. *Antirrhetikos.* In *Euagrios Ponticus*, edited by W. Frankenberg, 472–545. Abhandlungen der königlichen Gesellschaft der Wissenschaften zu Göttingen, Philol.-hist. Klasse, Neue Folge, 13.2. Berlin, 1912.

———. *Chapitres des disciples d'Evagre.* Edited and translated by Paul Géhin. SC 514. Paris: Éditions du Cerf, 2007.

———. *Evagrius of Pontus: The Greek Ascetic Corpus.* Translated by Robert E. Sinkewicz. Oxford: Oxford University Press, 2003.

———. *Le gnostique, ou À celui qui est devenu digne de la science.* Edited and translated by Antoine Guillaumont and Claire Guillaumont. SC 356. Paris: Éditions du Cerf, 1989.

———. *Sur les pensées.* Edited and translated by Paul Géhin, Claire Guillaumont, and Antoine Guillaumont. SC 438. Paris: Éditions du Cerf, 1998.

———. *Talking Back/Antirrhêtikos: A Monastic Handbook for Combating Demons.* Translated by David Brakke. Collegeville, MN: Liturgical Press, 2009.

———. *To the Monks: The Mind's Long Journey to the Holy Trinity: The Ad Monachos of Evagrius Ponticus.* Translated by Jeremy Driscoll. Collegeville, MN: Liturgical Press, 1993.

Evetts, B., ed. *History of the Patriarchs of the Coptic Church of Alexandria.* Vol. 2. *Peter I to Benjamin I (661).* PO 1.4. Paris: Didot, 1948.

———, ed. *Vie de Théodore de Sykéôn.* Subsidia Hagiographica 48. Brussels: Société des Bollandistes, 1970.

Gardner, Iain, ed. *Kellis Literary Texts.* DOPM 4. Oxford: Oxbow Books, 1996.

Gardner, Iain, et al., eds. *Coptic Documentary Texts from Kellis.* Vol. 1. DOPM 9. Oxford: Oxbow Books, 1999.

Gregory of Nazianzus. *Grégoire de Nazianze: Discours 24–26.* Edited and translated by J. Mossay. SC 284. Paris: Éditions du Cerf, 1981.

———. *Grégoire de Nazianze: Discours 32–37.* Edited and translated by Claudio Moreschini and P. Gallay. SC 318. Paris: Éditions du Cerf, 1985.

Gregory of Nyssa. *Ascetical Works.* Translated by Virginia Woods Callahan. FC. Washington, DC: Catholic University of America Press, 1967.

———. *Grégoire de Nyssa: Vie de sainte Macrine.* Edited by Pierre Maraval. SC 178. Paris: Éditions du Cerf, 1971.

———. *Gregory of Nyssa's Treatise on the Inscription of the Psalms*. Introduction, translation, and notes by Ronald E. Heine. Oxford: Clarendon Press, 1995.

———. *Saint Gregory of Nyssa: Commentary on the Inscriptions of the Psalms*. Translated by Casimir McCambley. Archbishop Iakovos Library of Ecclesiastical and Historical Sources, no. 17. Brookline, MA: Hellenic College Press, n.d.

Guy, J.-C., ed. *Les apophtegmes des Pères: Collection systématique*. SC 387, 474, 498. Paris: Éditions du Cerf, 1993–2005.

Haelst, J. van, ed. *Catalogue des papyrus littéraires juifs et chrétiens*. Paris: Publications de la Sorbonne, 1976.

Halkin, F., ed. *S. Pachomii vitae Graecae*. Brussels: Société des Bollandistes, 1932.

Hebbelynck, Adolphe, ed. and trans. *Les mystères des lettres grecques*. Louvain: Istas, 1902. Compiled from five articles published in *Le Muséon*: 19 (1900): 5–36, 105–36, 269–300; and 20 (1901): 5–33, 369–414.

Historia monachorum in Aegypto. Ed. A.-J. Festugière. Brussels: Société des Bollandistes, 1961.

Horner, George, ed. *The Coptic Version of the New Testament in the Northern Dialect, Otherwise Called Memphitic and Bohairi*. 4 vols. Oxford: Clarendon Press, 1898–1905.

———, ed. *The Coptic Version of the New Testament in the Southern Dialect*. 7 vols. Oxford: Clarendon Press, 1911–24.

Iamblichus. *De mysteriis*. In *Les mystères d'Égypte*, edited by Édouard des Places. Paris: Belles Lettres, 1966.

———. *De vita Pythagorica*. In *Jamblich. Pythagoras. Legende—Lehre—Lebensgestaltung*, edited by Michael von Albrecht. Darmstadt: Wissenschaftliche Buchgesellschaft, 2002.

Isaiah of Scetis. *Abba Isaiah of Scetis: Ascetic Discourses*. Translated by J. Chryssavgis and P. Penkett. CS 150. Kalamazoo, MI: Cistercian Publications, 2002.

John Cassian. *Jean Cassien: Conférences*. Edited by E. Pichery. 3 vols. SC 42, 54, 64. Paris: Éditions du Cerf, 1955–59.

———. *Jean Cassien: Institutions Cénobitiques*. Edited by Jean-Claude Guy. SC 109. Paris: Éditions du Cerf, 2001.

———. *John Cassian: The Conferences*. Translated by Boniface Ramsay. ACW 57. New York: Newman, 1997.

———. *John Cassian: The Institutes*. Translated by Boniface Ramsay. ACW 58. New York: Newman, 2000.

John Chrysostom. *A Comparison between a King and a Monk; Against the Opponents of the Monastic Life: Two Treatises by John Chrysostom*. Translated by David G. Hunter. Lewiston, NY: Edwin Mellen Press, 1988.

———. *The Cult of the Saints*. Translated by Wendy Mayer. Crestwood, NJ: St. Vladimir's Seminary Press, 2006.

———. *Discourses against Judaizing Christians.* Translated by Paul W. Harkins. FC 68. Washington, DC: Catholic University of America Press, 1979.

———. *John Chrysostom: On Wealth and Poverty*. Translated by Catharine P. Roth. Crestwood, NJ: St. Vladimir's Seminary Press, 1984.

———. *Saint John Chrysostom: Commentaries on the Sages*. Translated by Robert Charles Hill. 2 vols. Brookline, MA: Holy Cross Orthodox Press, 2006.

———. *Saint John Chrysostom: Commentary on the Psalms*. Translated by Robert C. Hill. Brookline, MA: Holy Cross Orthodox Press, 1998.

———. *Saint John Chrysostom: Homilies on Genesis 1–17*. Translated by Robert C. Hill. FC 74. Washington, DC: Catholic University of America Press, 1986.

———. *Saint John Chrysostom: Old Testament Homilies*. 3 vols. Brookline, MA: Holy Cross Orthodox Press, 2003.

———. *Saint John Chrysostom: On Repentance and Almsgiving*. Translated by Gus Christo. Washington, DC: Catholic University of America Press, 1998.

John Climacus. *John Climacus: The Ladder of Divine Ascent*. Translated by C. Luibheid and N. Russell. Mahwah, NJ: Paulist Press, 1982.

John of Ephesus. *Lives of the Eastern Saints*. Edited and translated by E. W. Brooks. PO 17. Paris: Firmin-Dodot, 1907.

Johnson, D.W., ed. and trans. *A Panegyric on Macarius, Bishop of Tkôw, Attributed to Dioscorus of Alexandria*. CSCO 415–16, Scriptores Coptici 41–42. Louvain: Secrétariat du CSCO, 1980.

Kahle, P.E., ed. *Bala'izah: Coptic Texts from Deir el-Bala'izah in Upper Egypt*. 2 vols. London: Oxford University Press, 1954.

Kenyon, Frederic G., ed. *The Codex Alexandrinus (Royal Ms. 1 D. V–VIII) in Reduced Photographic Facsimile. Part 4, Old Testament: I Esdras–Ecclesiasticus*. 5 vols. London: Trustees of the British Museum, 1957.

Kuhn, K.H., ed. and trans. *A Panegyric on Apollo Archimandrite of the Monastery of Isaac, by Stephen Bishop of Heracleopolis Magna*. CSCO 394–95, Scriptores Coptici 39–40. Louvain: Secrétariat du CSCO, 1978.

Lefebvre, G., ed. *Recueil des inscriptions grecques chrétiennes d'Égypte*. Cairo: Institut français d'archéologie orientale, 1907.

Lefort, L.-Th., ed. and trans. *Oeuvres de S. Pachôme et de ses disciples*. CSCO 159. Louvain: Durbecq, 1956.

———, ed. *S. Pachomii vita Bohairice scripta*. CSCO 89. Paris: E Typographeo Reipublicae, 1925. Reprint, Leuven: Peeters, 1965.

———, ed. *S. Pachomii vitae Sahidice scriptae*. 2 vols. CSCO 99–100. Paris: E Typographeo Reipublicae, 1933.

——, ed. *Les Vies coptes de Saint Pachôme et de ses premiers successeurs.* Louvain: Bureaux du Muséon, 1943.

Leipoldt, Johannes, ed. *Sinuthii Archimandritae vita et opera omnia.* Vols. 1, 3, and 4. CSCO 41, 42, and 73. Paris: Imprimerie nationale, 1908, 1913.

——, ed. *Sinuthii vita Bohairice: Coptic Text.* CSCO 16. Louvain: L. Durbecq, 1951.

Lucian. *Philopseudès et De morte Peregrini.* Edited by Jacques Schwartz. Strasbourg: Belles Lettres, 1951.

Nestle, E., and K. Aland, eds. *Novum Testamentum Graece.* 26th ed. Stuttgart: Deutsche Bibelgesellschaft, 1979.

Orlandi, Tito, ed. *Storia della Chiesa di Alessandria.* 2 vols. Testi e documenti per lo studio dell'antichità 31. Milan: Instituto Editoriale Cisalpino, 1968–70.

——, ed. *Testi Copti: 1, Encomio di Atanasio; 2, Vita di Atanasio.* Testi e documenti per lo studio dell'antichità 21; Studi Copti 3. Milan: Istituto Editoriale Cisalpino, 1961.

Pachomius. *Die Briefe Pachoms: Griechischer Text der Handschrift W. 145 der Chester Beatty Library.* Edited by Hans Quecke. Textus patristici et liturgici 11. Regensburg: Friedrich Pustet, 1975.

Paphnutis. *Histories of the Monks of Upper Egypt and the Life of Onnophrius.* Translated by Tim Vivian. CS 140. Kalamazoo, MI: Cistercian Publcations, 1993.

Philostratus. *Philostratus: The Life of Apollonius of Tyana.* Edited by Christopher P. Jones. 2 vols. LCL 16–17. Cambridge, MA: Harvard University Press, 2005.

Physiologus: A Medieval Book of Nature Lore. Translated by Michael J. Curley. Austin: University of Texas Press, 1979.

Physiologus latinus versio y. Edited by Francis J. Carmody. University of California Publications in Classical Philology 12.7. Berkeley: University of California Press, 1941.

Porphyry. "Life of Pythagorus." Translated by Moses Hadas in *Heroes and Gods: Spiritual Biographies in Antiquity*, by Moses Hadas and Morton Smith. Routledge: London, 1965.

——. *Porphyry, On the Cave of the Nymphs.* Translated by Robert Lamberton. Barrytown, NY: Station Hill Press, 1983.

——. *Vie de Pythagore, Lettre à Marcella.* Edited by Edouard des Places. Paris: Société d'édition Belles Lettres, 1982.

——. *Vita Plotini.* Edited by A. H. Armstrong. LCL. Cambridge, MA: Harvard University Press, 1968.

Preisendanz, Karl, and Albert Henrichs, eds. *Papyri Graecae magicae: Die griechischen Zauberpapyri.* 2 vols. Stuttgart: Teubner, 1973–74.

Russell, Norman, trans. *The Lives of the Desert Fathers*. Cistercian Studies 34. Kalamazoo, MI: Cistercian Publications, 1980.

Schüssler, Karlheinz, ed. *Biblia Coptica*. 4 vols. Wiesbaden: Harrassowitz, 1995–2004.

Sefer Yesira: Edition, Translation and Text-Critical Commentary. Edited and translated by A. Peter Hayman. Tübingen: Mohr Siebeck, 2004.

Shenoute. *Oeuvres de Schenoudi*. Edited by E. Amélineau. 2 vols. Paris: Leroux, 1907–14.

———. *Shenute contra Origenistas: Testo con introduzione e traduzione*. Edited and translated by T. Orlandi. Rome: C.I.M., 1985.

Socrates Scholasticus. *Historia ecclesiastica*. Edited by G. C. Hansen. GCS n.f. 1. Berlin: de Gruyter, 1995.

Theodoret of Cyr. *A History of the Monks of Syria*. Translated by R.M. Price. CS 88. Kalamazoo, MI: Cistercian Publications, 1985.

———. *Théodoret de Cyr: Histoire des moines de Syrie*. Edited by P. Canivet and A. Leroy-Molinghen. 2 vols. SC 234, 257. Paris: Éditions du Cerf, 1977–79.

Thompson, Herbert, ed. *The Coptic (Sahidic) Version of Certain Books of the Old Testament*. London: Oxford University Press, 1908.

Usener, H., ed. *Der Heilige Theodosios*. Leipzig: Teubner, 1890.

Veilleux, ed. and trans. *Pachomian Koinonia.* 3 vols. CS 45–47. Kalamazoo, MI: Cistercian Publications, 1980–82.

Vivian, Tim, trans., with the assistance of Rowan Greer. *Four Desert Fathers: Pambo, Evagrius, Macarius of Egypt and Macarius of Alexandria*. Crestwood, NY: St. Vladimir's Seminary Press, 2004.

Vööbus, A., ed. *Syriac and Arabic Documents Regarding Legislation Relative to Syrian Asceticism*. Stockholm: Estonian Theological Society in Exile, 1960.

Winlock, H.E., W.E. Crum, and H.G. Evelyn-White, eds. *The Monastery of Epiphanius at Thebes*. 2 vols. New York: Metropolitan Museum of Art, 1926.

Zachariah of Mitylene. *The Life of Severus.* In *Sévère, patriarche d'Antioche, 512–518: Textes syriaques publiés, traduits et annotés,* edited by M.-A. Kugener. Paris: Firmin-Didot, 1907.

SECONDARY SOURCES

Abramowski, L. "Vertritt die syrische Fassung die ursprüngliche Gestalt der *Vita Antonii*?" In *Mélanges Antoine Guillaumont: Contributions à l'étude des christianismes orientaux*, edited by R.-G. Coquin, 47–56. Geneva: Cramer, 1988.

Aland, K. "Adolf Harnack als wissenschaftlicher Organisator." In *Adolf Harnack in memoriam: Reden zum 100. Geburtstag am 7. Mai 1951.* Berlin: Evangelische Verlagsanstalt, 1951.

——. *Glanz und Niedergang der deutschen Universität: 50 Jahre deutscher Wissenschaftsgeschichte in Briefen an und von Hans Lietzmann (1892–1942).* Berlin: De Gruyter, 1979.

Allen, A.V.G. "The Organization of the Early Church." *American Journal of Theology* 8 (1904): 799–804.

Anatolios, Khaled. *Athanasius: The Coherence of His Thought.* London: Routledge, 1998.

Aravecchia, Nicola. "Hermitages and Spatial Analysis: Use of Space at the Kellia." In *Shaping Community: The Art and Archaeology of Monasticism*, edited by Sheila McNally, 29–38. Oxford: British Archaeological Reports, 2001.

Atiya, Aziz Suryal, ed. *Coptic Encyclopedia*. 8 vols. New York: Macmillan, 1991.

Baarda, Tjitze. "ΔΙΑΦΩΝΙΑ—ΣΥΜΦΩΝΙΑ: Factors in the Harmonization of the Gospels, Especially in the *Diatessaron* of Tatian." In *Gospel Traditions in the Second Century: Origins, Recensions, Text and Transmission*, edited by William L. Petersen, 133–54. Notre Dame: University of Notre Dame Press, 1989.

Bacht, H. "Antonius und Pachomius: Von der Anachorese zum Cönobitentum." In *Antonius Magnus Eremita*, edited by Basilius Steidle, 66–107. Rome: Orbis Catholicus, 1956.

Badger, Carlton Mills, Jr. "The New Man Created in God: Christology, Congregation and Asceticism in Athanasius of Alexandria." PhD diss, Duke University, 1990.

Bagnall, R. S. *Egypt in Late Antiquity*. Princeton: Princeton University Press, 1993.

Barnard, L.W. "Athanasius and the Pachomians." *SP* 32 (1997): 3–11.

——. "The Date of S. Athanasius' *Vita Antonii*." *VC* 27 (1974): 169–75.

——. "Did Athanasius Know Antony?" *Ancient Society* 24 (1993): 139–49.

Barnes, T.D. "Angel of Light or Mystic Initiate? The Problem of the *Life of Antony*." *JTS*, n.s., 37 (1986): 353–68.

——. *Athanasius and Constantius: Theology and Politics in the Constantinian Empire*. Cambridge, MA: Harvard University Press, 1993.

——. *Early Christian Hagiography and Roman History*. Tübingen: Mohr Siebeck, 2010.

——. "Scholarship or Propaganda? Porphyry *Against the Christians* and Its Historical Setting." *Bulletin of the Institute of Classical Studies* 39 (1994): 53–65.

Barrett-Lennard, R. J. S. *Christian Healing after the New Testament*. Lanham: University Press of America, 1994.

Bartelink, G. J. M. "Die literarische Gattung der *Vita Antonii*: Struktur und Motive." *VC* 36 (1982): 38–62.

Bataille, Georges. *Theory of Religion*. Translated by Robert Hurley. New York: Zone Books, 1989.

Beavis, Ian. *Insects and Other Invertebrates in Classical Antiquity*. Exeter: University of Exeter Press, 1988.

Beck, E. "Eine Beitrag zur Terminologie des ältesten syrischen Mönchtums." *Studia Anselmiana* 38 (1956): 260–67.

Behlmer, Heike. "'Do Not Believe Every Word Like the Fool . . . !' Rhetorical Strategies in Shenoute, *Canon* 6." In *Christianity and Monasticism in Upper Egypt*, edited by G. Gabra and H. Takla, 1–12. Cairo: American University in Cairo Press, 2008.

———. "Historical Evidence from Shenoute's *De extremo iudicio*." In *Sesto Congresso Internazionale di Egittologia: Atti*, 2 vols., edited by G.M. Zaccone et al., 1:11–19. Turin: International Association of Egyptologists, 1993.

Bell, H. Idris. *Jews and Christians in Egypt: The Jewish Troubles in Alexandria and the Athanasian Controversies*. 1924. Reprint, Westport, CT: Greenwood Press, 1972.

———. Obituary for Friedrich Preisigke. *Journal of Egyptian Archaeology* 10, no. 2 (1924): 172–73.

Bellet, P. "Nou Testimoni de les lletres de sant Antoni (Cambridge, University Lib. Add. 1876.2)." *SM* 31 (1989): 251–57.

Bergmann, Bettina. "Exploring the Grove: Pastoral Space on Roman Walls." In *The Pastoral Landscape*, edited by John Dixon Hunt, 21–46. Washington, DC: National Gallery of Art, 1992.

———. "Staging the Supernatural: Interior Gardens of Pompeian Houses." In *Pompeii and the Roman Villa: Art and Culture around the Bay of Naples*, edited by Carol C. Mattusch. New York: Thames and Hudson, 2008.

Bertalanffy, Ludwig von. "The History and Status of General Systems Theory." *Academy of Management Journal* 15 (1972): 407–26.

———. "An Outline of General System Theory." *British Journal for the Philosophy of Science* 1 (1950): 134–65.

Bitton-Ashkelony, B. "Counseling through Enigmas: Monastic Leadership and Linguistic Techniques in Sixth-Century Gaza." In *The Poetics of Grammar and the Metaphysics of Sound and Sign*, edited by S. La Porta and D. Shulman, 177–99. Leiden: Brill, 2007.

———. *Encountering the Sacred: The Debate on Christian Pilgrimage in Late Antiquity*. Berkeley: University of California Press, 2005.

———. "Penitence in Late Antique Monastic Literature." In *Transformations of the Inner Self in Ancient Religions*, edited by J. Assmann and G. Stroumsa, 179–94. Studies in the History of Religions 83. Leiden: Brill, 1999.

Bolman, E. *Monastic Visions: Wall Paintings from the Monastery of St. Antony at the Red Sea*. New Haven: Yale University Press, 2002.

Borthwick, E.K. "A Grasshopper's Diet: Notes on an Epigram of Meleager and a Fragment of Eubulus." *Classical Quarterly*, n.s., 16, no. 1 (1966): 103–12.

Bostock, Gerald. "Origen and the Pythagoreanism of Alexandria." In *Origeniana Octava: Origen and the Alexandrian Tradition. Papers of the 8th International Origen Congress, Pisa, 27–31 August 2001*, edited by L. Perrone, 465–78. Leuven: Peeters, 2003.

Bousset, W. *Apophthegmata: Studien zur Geschichte des ältesten Mönchtums*. Tübingen: Mohr, 1923.

Boyarin, Daniel. *Carnal Israel: Reading Sex in Talmudic Culture*. Berkeley: University of California Press, 1993.

———. *Unheroic Conduct: The Rise of Heterosexuality and the Invention of the Jewish Man*. Contraversions: Critical Studies in Jewish Literature, Culture, and Society. Berkeley: University of California Press, 1997.

Bradley, Keith R. *Discovering the Roman Family: Studies in Roman Social History*. New York: Oxford University Press, 1991.

Brakke, David. *Athanasius and the Politics of Asceticism*. Oxford: Oxford University Press, 1995.

———. "The Authenticity of the Ascetic Athanasiana." *Orientalia* 63 (1994): 17–56.

———. *Demons and the Making of the Monk: Spiritual Combat in Early Christianity*. Cambridge, MA: Harvard University Press, 2006.

———. "The Greek and Syriac Versions of the *Life of Antony*." *Le Muséon* 107 (1994): 29–53.

———. "Making Public the Monastic Life: Reading the Self in Evagrius Ponticus's *Talking Back*." In *Religion and the Self in Antiquity*, 222–33. Bloomington: Indiana University Press, 2005.

———. Review of *The Life of Antony: The Greek Life of Antony and the Coptic Life of Antony*, translated by T. Vivian and A. N. Athanassakis. *Spiritus* 4 (2004): 247–50.

Brakke, David, Michael L. Satlow, and Steven Weitzman, eds. *Religion and the Self in Antiquity*. Bloomington: Indiana University Press, 2005.

Brennan, B. R. "Dating Athanasius' *Vita Antonii*." *VC* 30 (1976): 52–54.

Brottier, Laurence. "Antoine l'ermite à travers les sources anciennes: Des regards divers sur un modèle unique." *Revue des études augustiniennes* 43 (1997): 15–39.

Brown, Peter. *The Body and Society: Men, Women, and Sexual Renunciation in Early Christianity*. Lectures on the History of Religions, n.s., 13. New York: Columbia University Press, 1988.

———. *The Cult of the Saints: Its Rise and Function in Latin Christianity*. Chicago: University of Chicago Press, 1981.

———. *Power and Persuasion in Late Antiquity: Towards a Christian Empire*. Madison: University of Wisconsin Press, 1992.

———. "The Rise and Function of the Holy Man in Late Antiquity." *Journal of Roman Studies* 61 (1971): 80–101.

Brown, T. S. "Euhemerus and the Historians." *HTR* 39, no. 4 (1946): 259–74.
Browne, G. M. "Coptico-Graeca: The Sahidic Version of St Athanasius' Vita Antonii." *Journal of Greek, Byzantine and Roman Studies* 12 (1971): 59–64.
Bruch, R. vom. "Adolf von Harnack und Wilhelm II." In *Adolf von Harnack: Theologe, Historiker, Wissenschaftspolitiker*, edited by K. Nowak and O. G. Oexle, 82–94. Veröffentlichungen des Max-Planck-Instituts für Geschichte 161. Göttingen: Vandenhoeck und Ruprecht, 2001.
Buffière, Félix. *Les mythes d'Homère et la pensée grecque*. Paris: Belles Lettres, 1956.
Bumaznov, D. F. "The Evil Angels in the 'Vita' and the 'Letters' of St. Antony the Great: Some Observations Concerning the Problem of the Authenticity of the 'Letters.'" *Zeitschrift für antikes Christentum* 11 (2007): 500–516.
Bunge, Gabriel. *Briefe aus der Wüste.* Trier: Paulinus-Verlag, 1986.
———. "Evagre le Pontique et les deux Macaires." *Irénikon* 56 (1983): 215–27.
Burns, Paul. "Augustine's Distinctive Use of the Psalms in the *Confessions*: The Role of Music and Recitation" [1993]. In *Forms of Devotion: Conversion, Worship, Spirituality, and Asceticism,* edited by Everett Ferguson, 157–70. New York: Garland.
Burrus, Virginia. *"Begotten, Not Made": Conceiving Manhood in Late Antiquity.* Stanford: Stanford University Press, 2000.
———. "Macrina's Tattoo." In *The Cultural Turn in Late Ancient Studies: Gender, Asceticism, and Historiography*, edited by Dale B. Martin and Patricia Cox Miller, 103–17. Durham: Duke University Press, 2005.
———. *Saving Shame: Martyrs, Saints, and Other Abject Subjects*. Philadelphia: University of Pennsylvania Press, 2008.
———. *The Sex Lives of Saints: An Erotics of Ancient Hagiography*. Divinations: Rereading Late Ancient Religion. Philadelphia: University of Pennsylvania Press, 2004.
Bushnell, Horace. "The Age of Homespun." In *Work and Play*, 374–408. Literary Varieties I, Centenary Edition. New York: Charles Scribner's Sons, 1910.
Butler, C. *The Lausiac History of Palladius*. 2 vols. Cambridge: Cambridge University Press, 1898–1904.
Cadell, H., and R. Rémondon. "Sens et emplois de τὸ ὄϱος dans les documents papyrologiques." *REG* 80 (1967): 343–49.
Callanan, Christopher K. "A Rediscovered Text of Porphyry on Mystic Formulae." *Classical Quarterly* 45 (1995): 215–30.
Cameron, Alan. "The Authenticity of the Letters of St Nilus of Ancyra." *Journal of Greek, Byzantine and Roman Studies* 17 (1976): 118–19.
Cameron, Averil. *Christianity and the Rhetoric of Empire: The Development of Christian Discourse*. Sather Classical Lectures 55. Berkeley: University of California Press, 1991.

Cameron, Averil, Bryan Ward-Perkins, and Michael Whitby, eds. *The Cambridge Ancient History*. Vol. 14. *Late Antiquity: Empire and Successors, A.D. 425–600*. Cambridge: Cambridge University Press, 2000.

Campenhausen, Hans von. "The Ascetic Idea of Exile in Ancient and Early Medieval Monasticism." In *Tradition and Life in the Church*, translated by A.V. Littledale, 231–51. Philadelphia: Fortress Press, 1968.

Camplani, A. *Le Lettere festali di Atanasio di Alessandria: Studio storico-critico*. Rome: C.I.M., 1989.

Caner, D. "Nilus of Ancyra and the Promotion of a Monastic Elite." *Arethusa* 33 (2000): 401–10.

———. *Wandering, Begging Monks: Spiritual Authority and the Promotion of Monasticism in Late Antiquity*. TCH 33. Berkeley: University of California Press, 2002.

Carruthers, Mary J. *The Book of Memory: A Study of Memory in Medieval Culture*. Cambridge Studies in Medieval Culture 10. Cambridge: Cambridge University Press, 1990.

———. *The Craft of Thought: Meditation, Rhetoric, and the Making of Images, 400–1200*. Cambridge Studies in Medieval Literature 34. New York: Cambridge University Press, 1998.

———. "Mechanisms for the Transmission of Culture: The Role of 'Place' in the Arts of Memory." In *Translatio, or, The Transmission of Culture in the Middle Ages,* edited by Laura Hollengreen, 1–26. Turnhout: Brepols, 2008.

Carruthers, Mary, and J.M. Ziolkowski. General introduction to *The Medieval Craft of Memory,* edited by Mary Carruthers and J. M. Ziolkowski, 1–31. Philadelphia: University of Pennsylvania Press, 2002.

Casiday, Augustine M.C. *Tradition and Theology in St John Cassian*. Oxford: Oxford University Press, 2007.

Cauwenbergh, Paul van. *Étude sur les moines d'Égypte depuis le Concile de Chalcédoine (451) jusqu'a l'invasion arabe (640)*. 1914. Reprint, Milan: Cisalpino-Goliardica, 1973.

Cavallin, Samuel. *Literarhistorische und textkritische Studien zur Vita S. Caesarii Arelatensis*. Lund: Lunds Universitets Årsskrift, 1934.

Chadwick, Owen. *John Cassian*. 2nd ed. Cambridge: Cambridge University Press, 1968.

Cheyne, T.K. "The Late Dr. Edwin Hatch." *Oxford Magazine: A Weekly Newspaper and Review*, November 20, 1889, 90–91.

Chitty, D. *The Desert a City: An Introduction to the Study of Egyptian and Palestinian Monasticism under the Christian Empire*. Oxford: Basil Blackwell, 1966.

Choat, M. "The Development and Use of Terms for 'Monk' in Late Antique Egypt." *Jahrbuch für Antike und Christentum* 45 (2002): 5–23.

——. "Epistolary Formulae in Early Coptic Letters." In *Actes du congres du Paris, 28 juin–3 juillet 2004*, edited by N. Bosson and A. Boud'hors, 667–77. Louvain: Peeters, 2007.

Chryssavgis, J. *John Climacus: From the Egyptian Desert to the Sinaite Mountain*. Aldershot: Ashgate, 2004.

Clark, Andy. *Being There*. Cambridge, MA: MIT Press, 1998.

Clark, Andy, and David Chalmers. "The Extended Mind." *Analysis* 58 (1998): 7–19.

Clark, Elizabeth A. "Foucault, the Fathers, and Sex." *Journal of the American Academy of Religion* 56 (1988): 619–41.

——. *Founding the Fathers: Early Church History and Protestant Professors in Nineteenth-Century America.* Philadelphia: University of Pennsylvania Press, 2011.

——. *History, Theory, Text: Historians and the Linguistic Turn*. Cambridge, MA: Harvard University Press, 2004.

——. "Ideology, History, and the Construction of 'Woman' in Late Ancient Christianity." *JECS* 2 (1994): 155–84.

——. "New Perspectives on the Origenist Controversy: Human Embodiment and Ascetic Strategies." *CH* 59 (1990): 145–62.

——. *The Origenist Controversy*. Princeton: Princeton University Press, 1992.

Clark, Gillian. "The Fathers and the Animals: The Rule of Reason?" In *Animals on the Agenda: Questions about Animals for Theology and Ethics*, edited by Andrew Linzey and Dorothy Yamamoto, 67–78. Urbana: University of Illinois Press, 1998.

Clédat, J. *Le monastère et la nécropole de Baouit*. Cairo: Institut français d'archéologie orientale, 1999.

Cohn-Sherbok, Dan. "The Alphabet in Mandaean and Jewish Gnosticism." *Religion* 11 (1981): 227–34.

Connolly, Joy. "The New World Order: Greek Rhetoric in Rome." In *A Companion to Greek Rhetoric,* edited by Ian Worthington, 139–65. Oxford: Blackwell, 2007.

Constantinides, Constas N., and Robert Browning. *Dated Greek Manuscripts from Cyprus to the Year 1570*. Dumbarton Oaks Studies 30. Washington, DC: Dumbarton Oaks, 1993.

Coquin, R.-G., ed. "Le catalogue de la bibliothèque du couvent de saint Elie du Rocher." *Bulletin de l'Institut français d'archéologie orientale* 75 (1975): 207–39.

Coquin, R.-G., and Maurice Martin. "Dayr Anba Shinudah." In *The Coptic Encyclopedia*, edited by Aziz Suryal Atiya, 3:761–70. New York: Macmillan, 1991.

Coquin, R.-G., et al. "Dayr Anba Antuniyus." In *The Coptic Encyclopedia*, edited by Aziz Suryal Atiya, 3:719–29. New York: Macmillan, 1991.

Corrigan, Kevin. *Evagrius and Gregory: Mind, Soul and Body in the Fourth Century*. Surrey: Ashgate, 2009.

Cribiore, Raffaella. *Gymnastics of the Mind: Greek Education in Hellenistic and Roman Egypt*. Princeton: Princeton University Press, 2001.

——. "Higher Education in Early Byzantine Egypt: Rhetoric, Latin, and the Law." In *Egypt in the Byzantine World, 300–700,* edited by Roger Bagnall, 47–65. Cambridge: Cambridge University Press, 2007.

Crum, W. E. "Inscriptions from Shenoute's Monastery." *JTS* 5 (1904): 552–69.

Curtius, E. R. *European Literature and the Latin Middle Ages*. Translated by W. Trask. Reprinted with epilogue by P. Goodman. Princeton: Princeton University Press, 1990.

Dagron, G. "L'empire romain d'Orient au IVe siècle et les traditions politiques de l'hellénisme: Le témoignage de Thémistios." *Travaux et mémoires* 3 (1968): 1–242.

Daley, Brian, S.J. "Finding the Right Key: The Aims and Strategies of Early Christian Interpretation of the Psalms." In *Psalms in Community: Jewish and Christian Textual, Liturgical, and Artistic Traditions*, edited by Harold W. Attridge and Margot E. Fassler, 189–205. Atlanta, GA: Society of Biblical Literature, 2003.

Davies, Malcolm, and Jeyaraney Kathirithamby. *Greek Insects*. New York: Oxford University Press, 1986.

Depuydt, L. *Catalogue of Coptic Manuscripts in the Pierpont Morgan Library*. Leuven: Peeters, 1993.

——. "In Sinuthiam Graecum." *Orientalia* 59 (1990): 67–71.

Dibelius, Otto. "Adolf Harnack als akademischer Lehrer." In *Adolf Harnack in memoriam: Reden zum 100. Geburtstag am 7. Mai 1951 gehalten bei der Gedenkfeier der Theologischen Fakultät der Humboldt-Universität Berlin*. Berlin: Evangelische Verlagsanstalt, 1951.

Dickerman, Sherwood Owen. "Some Stock Illustrations of Animal Intelligence in Greek Psychology." *Transactions and Proceedings of the American Philological Association* 42 (1911): 123–30.

Dieleman, Jacco. *Priests, Tongues, and Rites: The London–Leiden Magical Manuscripts and Translation in Egyptian Ritual (100–300 CE)*. Leiden: Brill, 2005.

Dihle, Albrecht. "The Poem on the Cicada." *Harvard Studies in Classical Philology* 71 (1967): 107–13.

Dörries, Hermann. *Die Vita Antonii als Geschichtsquelle.* Göttingen: Akademie der Wissenschaften, 1949.

Dornseiff, Franz. *Das Alphabet in Mystik und Magie*. Leipzig: Teubner, 1925.

Driver, Steven D. *John Cassian and the Reading of Egyptian Monastic Culture.* New York: Routledge, 2002.

Dubois, Jean-Daniel. "Y a-t-il eu des moines manichéens dans le site de Kellis?" In *Monachismes d'orient: Images, échanges, influences. Homages à Antoine Guillaumont*, ed. Florence Jullien et Marie-Joseph Pierre, 327–37. Bibliothèque de l'École des Hautes Études, Sciences religieuses 148. Turnhout: Brepols, 2011.

Duffy, J. "Embellishing the Steps: Elements of Presentation and Style in *The Heavenly Ladder* of John Climacus." *Dumbarton Oaks Papers* 53 (1999): 1–17.

Dysinger, Luke. *Psalmody and Prayer in the Writings of Evagrius Ponticus*. Oxford Theological Monographs. Oxford: Oxford University Press, 2005.

Elliott, Alison Goddard. *Roads to Paradise: Reading the Lives of the Early Saints*. Hanover, NH: University Press of New England, 1987.

Elm, Susanna. "The Dog That Did Not Bark: Doctrine and Patriarchal Authority in the Conflict between Theophilus of Alexandria and John Chrysostom of Constantinople." In *Christian Origins: Theology, Rhetoric and Community*, edited by L. Ayres and G. Jones, 68–93. London: Routledge, 1998.

———. "Gregory of Nazianzus's Life of Julian Revisited (Or. 4 and 5): The Art of Governance by Invective." In *From the Tetrarchs to the Theodosians*, edited by S. McGill, C. Sogno, and E. Watts, 171–82. Cambridge: Cambridge University Press, 2010.

———. "A Programmatic Life: Gregory of Nazianzus' Orations 42 and 43 and the Constantinopolitan Elites." *Arethusa* 33 (200): 411–27.

———. *Sons of Hellenism, Fathers of the Church: Emperor Julian, Gregory of Nazianzus, and the Vision of Rome*. TCH 49. Berkeley: University of California Press, 2012.

———. "Translating Culture: Gregory of Nazianzus, *Hellenism*, and the Claim to *Romanitas*." In *Intermedien: Zur kulturellen und artistischen Dynamik*, edited by A. Kleihues, B. Naumann, and E. Pankow, 17–26. Zurich: Chronos, 2010.

———. *'Virgins of God': The Making of Asceticism in Late Antiquity*. Oxford Classical Monographs. Oxford: Clarendon Press, 1994.

Elm, Susanna, and Naomi Janowitz, eds. "The 'Holy Man' Revisited (1971–1997): Charisma, Texts, and Communities in Late Antiquity." Special issue, *JECS* 6, no. 3 (1988).

Emerton, Ephraim. "A Definition of Church History." In *Papers of the American Society of Church History*, edited by Frederick William Loetscher, 2nd ser., 7:55–68. New York: Putnam's Sons, 1923.

———. *An Introduction to the Study of the Middle Ages, 375–814*. Boston: Ginn, 1896.

———. *Unitarian Thought*. New York: Macmillan, 1911.

Emmel, Stephen. "From the Other Side of the Nile: Shenute and Panopolis." In *Perspectives on Panopolis: An Egyptian Town from Alexander the Great to the Arab Conquest*, edited by A. Egberts, Brian Muhs, and Jacques van der Vliet, 95–111. Leiden: Brill, 2002.

———. "The Historical Circumstances of Shenute's Sermon *God Is Blessed*." In *ΘΕΜΕΛΙΑ: Spätantike und koptologische Studien Peter Grossmann zum 65. Geburtstag*, edited by Martin Krause and Sofia Schaten, 81–96. Wiesbaden: Ludwig Reichert, 1998.

———. "The Library of the Monastery of the Archangel Michael at Phantoou (al-Hamuli)." In *Christianity and Monasticism in the Fayoum Oasis*, edited by G. Gabra, 63–70. Cairo: American University in Cairo Press, 2005.

———. "Shenoute of Atripe and the Christian Destruction of Temples in Egypt: Rhetoric and Reality." In *From Temple to Church: Destruction and Renewal of Local Cultic Topography in Late Antiquity*, edited by Johannes Hahn, Stephen Emmel, and Ulrich Gotter, 161–201. Religions in the Greco-Roman World 162. Leiden: Brill, 2008.

———. "Shenoute's Literary Corpus." PhD diss, Yale University, 1993.

———. *Shenoute's Literary Corpus*. 2 vols. CSCO 599–600. Leuven: Peeters, 2004.

———. "Shenoute the Monk: The Early Monastic Career of Shenoute of Atripe." In *Il monachesimo tra eredità e aperture*, edited by M. Bielawski and D. Hombergen, 151–74. Studia Anselmiana 140. Rome: Centro Studi Sant'Anselmo, 2004.

Emmett, Alanna. "Female Ascetics in the Greek Papyri." In *Akten des XVI Internationaler Byzantinistenkongress Wien, 4–9. Oktober 1981* (= *Jahrbuch der österreichischen Byzantinistik* 23.2), edited by Wolfram Hörander et al., 507–15. Vienna: Der österreichischen Akademie der Wissenschaften, 1982.

Erman, A. "Schenute und Aristophanes." *Zeitschrift für Ägyptische Sprache und Altertumskunde* 32 (1894): 134–35.

Ernest, James D. "Athanasius of Alexandria: The Scope of Scripture in Polemical and Pastoral Context." *VC* 47 (1993): 341–62.

———. *The Bible in Athanasius of Alexandria.* Leiden: Brill, 2004.

Errington, R. M. "Christian Accounts of the Religious Legislation of Theodosius I." *Klio* 79 (1997): 398–443.

———. "Church and State in the First Years of Theodosius I." *Chiron* 27 (1997): 21–72.

Escribano Paño, M. "Ley religiosa y propaganda política bajo Teodosios I." In *Religión y propaganda política en el mundo romano*, edited by M. F. Simón, F. Pina Polo, and R. J. Rodriguez, 143–58. Barcelona: Publicacions Universitat de Barcelona, 2002.

Evans, Rhiannon. *Utopia Antiqua: Readings of the Golden Age and Decline at Rome*. London: Routledge, 2008.

Fanar, Emma Maayan. *Byzantine Illuminated Initial Letters*. Forthcoming.

Ferguson, Everett. "Athanasius, Epistola ad Marcellinum in interpretationem Psalmorum." *SP* 16, no. 2 (1985): 295–308.

——, ed. *Encyclopedia of Early Christianity*. 2nd ed. New York: Garland, 1999.

Festugière, André. "Sur une nouvelle edition du *De vita pythagorica* de Jamblique." *REG* 50 (1937): 470–94.

Finley, M.I. "Utopianism Ancient and Modern." In *The Critical Spirit*, edited by K. Wolff and D. Moore Jr. Boston: Beacon Press, 1967.

Fisher, George Park. *A Brief History of the Nations and of Their Progress in Civilization*. New York: American Book Company, 1896.

——. *History of the Christian Church.* New York: Charles Scribner's Sons, 1887.

Fitschen, K. *Serapion von Thmuis: Echte und unechte Schriften sowie die Zeugnisse des Athanasius und anderer*. Berlin: De Gruyter, 1992.

Förster, Niclas. *Marcus Magus: Kult, Lehre und Gemeindeleben einer valentinianischen Gnostikergruppe; Sammlung der Quellen und Kommentar.* Tübingen: Mohr Siebeck, 1999.

Foucault, Michel. "About the Beginning of the Hermeneutics of the Self." In *Religion and Culture: Michel Foucault*, edited by Jeremy R. Carrette, 158–81. New York: Routledge, 1999.

——. *The Care of the Self.* Vol. 3 of *The History of Sexuality.* Translated by Robert Hurley. New York: Random House, 1986. Originally published as *Le souci de soi* (Paris: Gallimard, 1984).

——. *The Use of Pleasure.* Vol. 2 of *The History of Sexuality.* Translated by Robert Hurley. New York: Random House, 1985. Originally published as *L'usage des plaisirs* (Paris: Gallimard, 1984).

Frake, Charles O. "Cognitive Maps of Time and Tide among Medieval Seafarers." *Man* 20 (1985): 254–70.

Francis, J. A. *Subversive Virtue: Asceticism and Authority in the Second-Century Pagan World.* University Park: Pennsylvania State University Press, 1995.

Frank, Georgia. "Loca Sancta Souvenirs and the Art of Memory." In *Pèlerinages et lieux saints dans l'antiquité et le Moyen Âge: Mélanges offerts à Pierre Maraval,* edited by Béatrice Caseau, Jean-Claude Cheynet, and Vincent Déroche, 193–201. Travaux et mémoires. Paris: Association des amis du Centre d'histoire et civilisation de Byzance, 2006.

——. "Macrina's Scar: Homeric Allusion and Heroic Identity in Gregory of Nyssa's *Life of Macrina*." *JECS* 8 (2000): 511–30.

——. *The Memory of the Eyes: Pilgrims to Living Saints in Christian Late Antiquity*. TCH 30. Berkeley: University of California Press, 2000.

Frank, P. Suso. *Angelikos Bios: Begriffsanalytische und begriffsgeschichtliche Untersuchung zum "Engelgelichen Leben" im frühen Mönchtum*. Beiträge zur Geschichte des alten Mönchtums und des Benediktinerordens 26. Münster: Aschendorffs, 1964.

French, Roger. *Ancient Natural History: Histories of Nature*. London: Routledge, 1994.

Frend, W. H. C. "Church Historians of the Early Twentieth Century: Adolf von Harnack (1851–1930)." *Journal of Ecclesiastical History* 52, no. 1 (2001): 83–102.

Gardner, I. M. F. "The Manichaean Community at Kellis: Directions and Possibilities for Research." Paper presented at the Dahkleh Oasis Project Conference, University of Durham, 1994.

Gardner, I. M. F., and S. N. E. Lieu. "From Narmouthis (Medinet Madi) to Kellis (Ismant el-Kharab): Manichaean Documents from Roman Egypt." *Journal of Roman Studies* 86 (1996): 146–69.

Garitte, G. "À propos des lettres de saint Antoine l'eremite." *Le Muséon* 52 (1939): 11–31.

———. "Panégyrique de saint Antoine par Jean, évêque d'Hermopolis." *Orientalia Christiana periodica* 9 (1943): 100–134, 330–65.

———. "Le texte grec et les versions anciennes de la vie de saint Antoine." In *Antonius Magnus Eremita, 356–1956: Studia ad antiquum monachismum spectantia*, edited by B. Steidle, 1–12. Rome: Editrice Anselminana, 1956.

Gautier, F. *Le retraite et le sacerdoce chez Grégoire de Nazianze*. Brepols: Turnhout, 2002.

Gemeinhardt, Peter. "*Vita Antonii* oder *Passio Antonii?* Biographische Genre und martyrologische Topik in der ersten Asketenvita." In *Christian Martyrdom in Late Antiquity (300–450 AD): History and Discourse, Tradition and Religious Identity,* edited by Peter Gemeinhardt and Johan Leemans, 79–114. Berlin: de Gruyter, 2012.

Giere, Ronald N. "The Role of Agency in Distributed Cognitive Systems." *Philosophy of Science* 73 (2006): 710–19.

Giere, Ronald N., and Barton Moffatt. "Distributed Cognition: Where the Cognitive and the Social Merge." *Social Studies of Science* 33 (2003): 301–10.

Gieryn, Thomas F. "What Buildings Do." *Theory and Society* 31 (2002): 35–74.

Gieseler, J. C. L. *Text-Book of Church History*. Translated by S. Davidson and Henry B. Smith from the 4th German ed. 5 vols. New York: Harper and Brothers, 1857–60.

Gilhus, Ingvild Sælid. *Animals, Gods and Humans: Changing Attitudes to Animals in Greek, Roman and Early Christian Ideas*. London: Routledge, 2006.

Goehring, James E. "The Dark Side of Landscape: Ideology and Power in the Christian Myth of the Desert." In "Rereading Late Ancient Christianity," edited Dale B. Martin and Patricia Cox Miller, special issue, *Journal of Medieval and Early Modern Studies* 33, no. 3 (2003): 437–51.

——. "The Encroaching Desert: Literary Production and Ascetic Space in Early Christian Egypt." In *Ascetics, Society, and the Desert: Studies in Early Egyptian Monasticism*, 73–88. Harrisburg, PA: Trinity Press International, 1999. Originally published in *JECS* 1 (1993): 281–96.

——. "Hieracas of Leontopolis: The Making of a Desert Ascetic." In *Ascetics, Society, and the Desert: Studies in Early Egyptian Monasticism*, 110–33. Harrisburg, PA: Trinity Press International, 1999.

——. "Melitian Monastic Organization: A Challenge to Pachomian Originality." In *Ascetics, Society, and the Desert,* 187–95. Harrisburg, PA: Trinity Press International, 1999. Originally published in *Papers Presented at the Eleventh International Conference on Patristic Studies Held in Oxford 1991: Biblica et Apocrypha, Orientalia, Ascetica* (special issue *SP* 25 [1993]), edited by Elizabeth A. Livingstone, 388–95 (Leuven: Peeters Press, 1993).

——. "Monastic Diversity and Ideological Boundaries in Fourth-Century Christian Egypt." In *Ascetics, Society, and the Desert*, 208–9. Harrisburg, PA: Trinity Press International, 1999. Originally published in *JECS* 5 (1997): 61–84.

——. "Through a Glass Darkly: Diverse Images of the Ἀποτακτικοί(αί) in Early Egyptian Monasticism." In *Ascetics, Society, and the Desert: Studies in Early Egyptian Monasticism*, 53–72. Harrisburg, PA: Trinity Press International 1999. Originally published in *Discursive Formations, Ascetic Piety and the Interpretation of Early Christian Literature* (special issue *Semeia* 58 [1992]: 25–45), edited by Vincent L. Wimbush (Atlanta: Scholars Press, 1992).

——. "Withdrawing from the Desert: Pachomius and the Development of Village Monasticism in Upper Egypt." In *Ascetics, Society, and the Desert: Studies in Early Egyptian Monasticism*, 89–109. Harrisburg, PA: Trinity Press International, 1999. Originally published in *HTR* 89 (1996): 267–85.

——. "The World Engaged: The Social and Economic World of Early Egyptian Monasticism." In *Ascetics, Society and the Desert: Studies in Early Egyptian Monasticism*, 39–52. Harrisburg, PA: Trinity Press International, 1999. Originally published in *Gnosticism and the Early Christian World: In Honor of James M. Robinson,* edited by James E. Goehring, 134–44 (Sonoma, CA: Polebridge Press, 1990).

Gómez Villegas, N. *Gregorio de Nazianzo en Constantinopla: Ortodoxia, heterodoxia y régimen teodosiano en una capital cristiana*. Madrid: Consejo Superior de Investigaciones Científicas, 2000.

Goodrich, Richard J. *Contextualizing Cassian: Aristocrats, Asceticism, and Reformation in Fifth-Century Gaul.* Oxford: Oxford University Press, 2007.

Gould, Graham. *The Desert Fathers on Monastic Community*. Oxford: Oxford University Press, 1993.

Green, Vivian Hubert Howard. *A History of Oxford University*. London: Batsford, 1974.

Gregg, Robert C., and Denis E. Groh. *Early Arianism: A View of Salvation.* Philadelphia: Fortress Press, 1981.

Gribomont, Jean. *Histoire du texte des Ascétiques de S. Basile*. Bibliothèque du Muséon 32. Louvain: Publications universitaires / Institut orientaliste, 1953.

Grossmann, J.K. "Some Observations on the Arabic Life of Pachomios (MS Göttingen University Library 116) Compared to the Coptic and Greek Lives." *Bulletin de la société d'archéologie copte* 45 (2006): 43–58.

Guillaumont, Antoine. "Le dépaysement comme forme d'ascèse dans le monachisme ancien." *École pratique des hautes études, Ve section: Sciences religieuses annuaire, 1968–1969* 76 (1968): 31–58.

———. "Le gnostique chez Clément d'Alexandrie et chez Evagre le Pontique." In *Alexandrina: Hellénisme, judaïsme et christianisme à Alexandrie. Mélanges offerts a Claude Mondesert, S.J.,* 195–201. Paris: Éditions Cerf, 1987.

———. *Un philosophe au désert: Evagre le Pontique*. Paris: Vrin, 2004.

———. "Le problème de deux Macaires." *Irénikon* 48 (1975): 42–59.

Guillou, A. "Le monde carceral en Italie du sud et en Sicile au VIe–VIIe siècle." *Jahrbuch der österreichischen Byzantinistik* 33 (1983): 79–86.

Gutzwiller, Kathryn J. "The Herdsman in Greek Thought." In *Brill's Companion to Greek and Latin Pastoral*, edited by Marco Fantuzzi and Theodore Papanghelis, 1–23. Leiden: Brill, 2006.

———. *Theocritus' Pastoral Analogies: The Formation of a Genre*. Madison: University of Wisconsin Press, 1991.

Guy, Jean-Claude. "Educational Innovation in the Desert Fathers." *Eastern Churches Review* 6 (1974): 44–51.

———. *Jean Cassien: Vie et doctrine spirituelle*. Paris: Lethielleux, 1961.

Haas, Christopher. *Alexandria in Late Antiquity: Topography and Social Conflict.* Baltimore: Johns Hopkins University Press, 1997.

Hägg, Tomas. "The Life of St. Antony between Biography and Hagiography." In *The Ashgate Research Companion to Byzantine Hagiography,* vol. 1, *Periods and Places*, edited by Stephanos Efthymiadis, 17–34. Farnham: Ashgate, 2011.

Halperin, David M. "Why Is Diotima a Woman? Platonic Erōs and the Figuration of Gender." In *Before Sexuality: The Construction of Erotic Experience in the Ancient Greek World*, edited by David Halperin, Jack Winkler, and Froma Zeitlin, 257–308. Princeton: Princeton University Press, 1990.

Harnack, Adolf von. "Die Ausgabe der griechischen Kirchenväter der drei ersten Jahrhunderte: Bericht über die Tätigkeit der Kommission, 1891–1915."

Sitzungsberichte der Königlich Preussischen Akademie der Wissenschaften (1916): 104–12. Reprinted in *Aus der Friedens- und Kriegsarbeit* (Giessen: Töpelmann, 1916) as well as in *Kleine Schriften zur Alten Kirche: Berliner Akademieschriften, 1908–1930,* edited by J. Dummer (Leipzig: Zentralantiquariat der Deutschen Demokratischen Republik, 1980).

———. "Bericht über die Ausgabe der griechischen Kirchenväter der ersten drei Jahrhunderte (1916–1926)." *Sitzungsberichte der Königlich Preussischen Akademie der Wissenschaften* (1927): xxvi–xxx. Reprinted in *Kleine Schriften zur Alten Kirche: Berliner Akademieschriften, 1908–1930,* edited by J. Dummer (Leipzig: Zentralantiquariat der Deutschen Demokratischen Republik, 1980).

———. *Geschichte der altchristlichen Literatur bis Eusebius*. 2 vols in 4. 2nd ed. 1893–1904. Reprint, Leipzig: Hinrichs, 1958.

———. *Geschichte der Königlich Preussischen Akademie der Wissenschaften zu Berlin*. 3 vols in 4. Berlin: Reichsdruckerei, 1900.

———. "Die Königlich Preussische Akademie der Wissenschaften: Rede zur Zweihundertjahrfeier, 20. March 1900." Akademiebibliothek Berlin, Ha 66090-1-24.

———. *Die Mission und Ausbreitung des Christentums in den ersten drei Jahrhunderten.* 2 vols. 4th ed. Leipzig: Hinrichs, 1923–24.

———. *Protokollbuch der Kirchenväter-Kommission der Preussischen Akademie der Wissenschaften, 1897–1928.* Edited by S. Rebenich and C. Markschies. Berlin: De Gruyter, 2000.

———. Review of *Essays in Biblical Greek,* by E. Hatch. *Theologische Literaturzeitung* 12 (1890): col. 298.

Harnack, Axel von. "Die Bibliothek Adolf von Harnacks." *Zentralblatt für Bibliothekswesen* 49 (1932): 1–12.

Harrill, J. Albert. "Paul and the Slave Self." In *Religion and the Self in Antiquity,* edited by David Brakke, Michael L. Satlow, and Steven Weitzman, 51–69. Bloomington: Indiana University Press, 2005.

Hartog, François. *The Mirror of Herodotus: The Representation of the Other in the Writings of History*. Translated by Janet Lloyd. Berkeley: University of California Press, 1988.

Harvey, Susan Ashbrook. *Asceticism and Society in Crisis: John of Ephesus and the Lives of the Eastern Saints*. TCH 18. Berkeley: University of California Press, 1990.

———. "Sacred Bonding: Mothers and Daughters in Early Syriac Hagiography." *JECS* 4, no. 1 (1996): 27–56.

———. "The Sense of a Stylite: Perpectives on Simeon the Elder." *VC* 42 (1988): 376–94.

———. "The Stylite's Liturgy: Ritual and Religious Identity in Late Antiquity." *JECS* 6 (1998): 523–39.

Hatch, Edwin. *The Growth of Church Institutions*. London: Hodder and Stoughton, 1887. Translated into German by Adolf von Harnack as *Die Grundlegung der Kirchenverfassung Westeuropas im frühen Mittelalter* (Giessen: Ricker, 1888).

———. *The Influence of Greek Ideas and Usages upon the Christian Church*. London: Williams and Norgate, 1890. Translated into German by Erwin Preuschen, with an afterword by Adolf von Harnack, as *Griechentum und Christentum: Zwölf Hibbertvorlesungen über den Einfluss griechischer Ideen und Gebräuche auf die christliche Kirche* (Freiburg: Mohr, 1892).

———. *The Organization of the Early Christian Churches: Eight Lectures Delivered before the University of Oxford, in the Year 1880*. London: Rivingtons, 1881. Translated into German by Adolf von Harnack as *Die Gesellschaftsverfassung der christlichen Kirchen im Alterthum: Acht Vorlesungen gehalten an der Universität Oxford im Jahre 1880* (Giessen: Ricker, 1883).

———. *Progress in Theology: An Address Delivered to the Edinburgh University Theological Society, on Friday, November 14, 1884*. Edinburgh: Macniven and Wallace, 1885. Oxford, Bodleian Library, Mansfield 56 (15).

Hausherr, I. *Penthos: La doctrine de componction dans l'Orient chrétien*. Orientalia Christiana Analecta 132. Rome, 1944. Translated into English by A. Hufstader as *Penthos: The Doctrine of Compunction in Eastern Christianity*, CS 53 (Kalamazoo, MI: Cistercian Publications, 1982).

Hayles, N. Katherine. *How We Became Posthuman: Virtual Bodies in Cybernetics, Literature, and Informatics*. Chicago: University of Chicago Press, 1999.

Heath, Malcolm. "Invention." In *Handbook of Classical Rhetoric in the Hellenistic Period, 330 B.C.–A.D. 400*, edited by Stanley E. Porter, 89–119. 1997. Reprint, Leiden: Brill, 2001.

Hedstrom, Darlene Brooks. "'Your Cell Will Teach You All Things': The Relationship between Monastic Practice and the Architectural Design of the Cell in Coptic Monasticism, 400–1000." PhD diss., Miami University, 2001.

Henze, M. *The Madness of King Nebuchadnezzar: The Ancient Near Eastern Origins and Early History of Interpretation of Daniel 4*. Supplements to the Journal for the Study of Judaism 61. Leiden: Brill, 1999.

Heussi, K. *Der Ursprung des Mönchtums*. Tübingen: Mohr, 1936.

Hillner, J. "Monastic Imprisonment in Justinian's Novels." *JECS* 15 (2007): 204–37.

Hinds, Stephen. "Landscape with Figures: Aesthetics of Place in the Metamorphoses and Its Tradition." In *Cambridge Companion to Ovid*, edited by Philip Hardie. Cambridge: Cambridge University Press, 2006.

Hirsch, F. E. "The Scholar as Librarian: To the Memory of Adolf von Harnack." *Library Quarterly* 9, no. 3 (1939): 299–320.

Hitchcock, Roswell D. *An Address on Colportage before the American Tract Society, at Their Forty-first Anniversary in Boston, May 30, 1855*. Boston: American Tract Society, 1855.

———. "The Ante-Nicene Trinitarianism." *American Theological Review* 4, no. 13 (January 1862): 54.

———. "The Chinese Classics." *American Presbyterian and Theological Review* 1, no. 4 (October 1863): 631–38.

———. "His Last Words in Public: Roswell D. Hitchcock's Address at the Dedication of the Dunfee High School at Fall River, Massachusetts, June 16, 1887." *New York Evangelist,* June 30, 1887.

———. "Historical Development of Christianity." *American Theological Review* 2, no. 5 (February 1860): 28–54.

———. *The Laws of Civilization: The Substance of an Address Delivered on Several Occasions during the Summer of 1860.* New York: John A. Gray, 1860.

———. *The True Idea and Uses of Church History.* Inaugural Address, May 6, 1856, Madison Square Presbyterian Church. New York: John Trow, 1856.

Holl, Karl. "Der schriftstellerische Form des griechischen Heiligenlebens." *Neue Jahrbücher für das klassische Altertum* 29 (1912): 406–27.

Hope, C. A. "The Find Context of the Kellis Agricultural Account Book." In *The Kellis Agricultural Account Book (P. Kell. IV Gr. 96),* edited by Roger S. Bagnall, 5–16. DOPM 7. Oxford: Oxbow Books, 1997.

Horden, Peregrine, and Nicholas Purcell. *The Corrupting Sea: A Study of Mediterranean History*. Oxford: Blackwell, 2000.

Howard-Johnston, James, and Paul Antony Hayward, eds. *The Cult of Saints in Late Antiquity and the Middle Ages: Essays on the Contribution of Peter Brown*. Oxford: Oxford University Press, 1999.

Huber, A. *Geschichte der Gründung und der Wirksamkeit der Kaiserlichen Akademie der Wissenschaften während der ersten fünfzig Jahre ihres Bestandes*. Vienna: C. Gerold's Sohn, 1897.

Hübner, Thomas. *Adolf von Harnacks Vorlesungen über das Wesen des Christentums unter besonderer Berücksichtigung der Methodenfragen als sachgemässer Zugang zu ihrer Christologie und Wirkungsgeschichte*. Europäische Hochschulschriften, ser. 23, Theologie, vol. 493. Frankfurt: Lang, 1994.

Humfress, C. "Roman Law, Forensic Argument and the Formation of Christian Orthodoxy (III–IV Centuries)." In *Orthodoxie, Christianisme, histoire*, edited by S. Elm, E. Rebillard, and A. Romano, 125–47. Rome: École française de Rome, 2000.

Hunt, John Dixon, ed. *The Pastoral Landscape.* Studies in the History of Art 36. Washington, DC: National Gallery of Art, 1992.

Hunter, Richard. "Virgil's Ecl. 1 and the Origins of Pastoral." In *Brill's Companion to Greek and Latin Pastoral*, edited by Marco Fantuzzi and Theodore Papanghelis. Leiden: Brill, 2006.

Hutchins, Edwin. *Cognition in the Wild*. Cambridge, MA: MIT Press, 1995.

Ilan, Tal. "Learned Jewish Women in Antiquity." In *Religiöses Lernen in der Biblischen, Frühjüdischen und Frühchristlichen Überlieferung*, edited by Beate Ego and Helmut Merkel, 175–90. Tübingen: Mohr Siebeck, 2005.

Irmscher, J. "Die Kommission für spätantike Religionsgeschichte der Deutschen Akademie der Wissenschaften zu Berlin." *Nuovo Didaskaleion* 13 (1963): 97–116.

Jager, Eric. *The Book of the Heart*. Chicago: University of Chicago Press, 2000.

Jantsch, J., ed. *Der Briefwechsel zwischen Adolf von Harnack und Martin Rade. Theologie auf dem öffentlichen Markt*. Berlin: De Gruyter, 1996.

Jashemski, Wilhelmina Mary Feemster. *The Gardens of Pompeii: Herculaneum and the Villas Destroyed by Vesuvius*. New Rochelle, NY: Caratzas Brothers, 1979.

Jeffreys, Elizabeth. "Rhetoric." In *Oxford Handbook of Byzantine Studies,* edited by Elizabeth Jeffreys, John Haldon, and Robin Cormack, 827–37. Oxford: Oxford University Press, 2008.

Jerphanion, Guillaume de. "Ibora — Gazioura? Étude de géographie pontique." *Mélanges de la Faculté orientale, Université Saint-Joseph, Beyrouth* 5 (1911): 333–54.

Joest, Christoph. "Das Anliegen des Pachomius nach seinem Brief Nr. 3." *Zeitschrift für Kirchengeschichte* 103 (1992): 1–32.

———. "Das Buchstabenquadrat im Pachomianischen Briefcorpus." *Le Muséon* 115 (2002): 241–60.

———. "Die Geheimschrift Pachoms — Versuch einer Entschlüsselung: Mit Übersetzung und Deutung der Pachom-Briefe 9a und 9b." *Ostkirchliche Studien* 45 (1996): 268–89.

———. "Die Pachom-Briefe 1 und 2: Auflösung der Geheimbuchstaben und Entdeckungen zu den Briefüberschriften." *Journal of Coptic Studies* 4 (2002): 25–98.

———. "Die Pachomianische Geheimschrift im Spiegel der Hieronymus-Übersetzung: Mit dem deutschen Text von Brief 11b des Pachomianischen Schriftencorpus und dem Versuch einer Übertragung." *Le Muséon* 112 (1999): 21–46.

Johnsén, H.R. *Reading John Climacus: Rhetorical Argumentation, Literary Convention and the Tradition of Monastic Formation*. Lund: Lund University Press, 2007.

Jones, A.H.M., J.R. Martindale, and J. Morris, eds. *The Prosopography of the Later Roman Empire*. 4 vols. Cambridge: Cambridge University Press, 1971–92.

Josaitis, Norman F. *Edwin Hatch and Early Church Order*. Recherches et syntheses, section d'histoire 3. Gembloux: Duculot, 1971.

Jungck, C. *Gregor von Nazianz: De vita sua*. Heidelberg: Carl Winter, 1974.

Kannengiesser, Charles. "The Athanasian Understanding of Scripture." In *The Early Church in Its Context: Essays in Honor of Everett Ferguson,* edited by Abraham J. Malherbe, Frederick W. Norris, and James W. Thompson, 221–29. Leiden: Brill, 1998.

——, ed. *Early Christian Spirituality*. Translated by Pamela Bright. Philadelphia: Fortress Press, 1986.

Keil, Volkmar. "Zur Form der Regel des Schenute." *Göttinger Miszellen* 30 (1978): 39–44.

Kennedy, George Alexander. *Greek Rhetoric under Christian Emperors*. Princeton: Princeton University Press, 1983.

——. *Progymnasmata: Greek Textbooks of Prose Composition and Rhetoric*. Writings from the Greco-Roman World 10. Atlanta, GA: Society of Biblical Literature, 2003.

Kessler, Herbert L. "Diptych with Old and New Testament Scenes." In *Age of Spirituality: Late Antique and Early Christian Art, Third to Seventh Century*, edited by Kurt Weitzmann, 449–512. New York: Metropolitan Museum of Art; Princeton: Princeton University Press, 1979.

Kinzig, W. *Harnack, Marcion und das Judentum: Nebst einer kommentierten Edition des Briefwechsels Adolf von Harnacks mit Houston Stewart Chamberlain*. Arbeiten zur Kirchen- und Theologiegeschichte 13. Leipzig: Evangelische Verlagsanstalt, 2004.

Klebs, E., P. von Rohden, and H. Dessau, eds. *Prosopographia imperii Romani saec. I. II. III.* Berlin: Reaimerus, 1897–98.

Klingshirn, William E., and Linda Safran, eds. *The Early Christian Book*. CUA Studies in Early Christianity 1. Washington, DC: Catholic University of America Press, 2007.

Koenen, Ludwig. "Manichäische Mission und Klöster in Ägypten." In *Das römisch-byzantinische Ägypten: Akten des internationalen Symposions 26.–30. September 1978 in Trier,* edited by Günter Grimm et al., 93–108. Aegyptiaca Treverensia: Trier Studien zum griechisch-römischen Ägypten 2. Mainz: Philipp von Zabern, 1983.

Kogan-Zehani, E. "The Tomb and Memorial of a Chain-Wearing Anchorite." *Aliquot* 35 (1998): 135–49.

Kolbet, Paul. "Athanasius, the Psalms, and the Reformation of the Self." *HTR* 99 (2006): 85–101.

Kolenkow, A. B. "Sharing the Pain: Saint and Sinner in Late Antique Egypt." In *Acts of the Fifth International Congress of Coptic Studies, Washington, D.C., 12–15 August, 1992*, edited by D. W. Johnson, 247–61. Rome: C.I.M., 1993.

Konowitz, Ellen. "The Program of the Carrand Diptych." *Art Bulletin* 66 (1984): 484–88.

Konstantinovsky, Julia S. *Evagrius Ponticus: The Making of a Gnostic*. Farnham: Ashgate, 2009.

Kotsifou, C. "Books and Book Production in the Monastic Communities of Byzantine Egypt." In *The Early Christian Book*, edited by William E. Klingshirn and Linda Safran, 48–66. CUA Studies in Early Christianity 1. Washington, DC: Catholic University of America Press, 2007.

Kramer, Bärbel, and John C. Shelton. *Das Archiv des Nepheros und verwandte Texte*. Aegyptiaca Treverensia 4. Mainz: Philipp von Zabern, 1987.

Krause, Martin. "Das Apa-Apollon-Kloster zu Bawit: Untersuchungen unveröffentlichter Urkunden als Beitrag zur Geschichte des ägyptischen Mönchtums." PhD diss, Karl-Marx-Universität, 1958.

Krawiec, Rebecca. "'Garments of Salvation': Representations of Monastic Clothing in Late Antiquity." *JECS* 17 (2009): 125–50.

———. *Shenoute and the Women of the White Monastery*. Oxford: Oxford University Press, 2002.

Kress, H., ed. *Theologische Fakultäten an staatlichen Universitäten in der Perspektive von Ernst Troelsch, Adolf von Harnack und Hans von Schubert*. Waltrop: Spenner, 2004.

Krevans, Nita. "Is There an Urban Pastoral? The Case of Theocritus' *Id*. 15." In *Brill's Companion to Greek and Latin Pastoral*, edited by Marco Fantuzzi and Theodore Papanghelis. Leiden: Brill, 2006.

Krueger, Derek. "Homoerotic Spectacle and the Monastic Body in Symeon the New Theologian." In *Toward a Theology of Eros: Transfiguring Passion at the Limits of Discipline*, edited by Virginia Burrus and Catherine Keller, 99–118. New York: Fordham University Press, 2006.

———. "The Old Testament and Monasticism." In *The Old Testament in Byzantium*, edited by Paul Magdalino and Robert Nelson, 199–222. Washington, DC: Dumbarton Oaks, 2010.

———. "Romanos the Melodist and the Christian Self in Early Byzantium." In *Proceedings of the 21st International Congress of Byzantine Studies: London, 21–26 August, 2006,* edited by Elizabeth Jeffreys, Fiona K. Haarer, and Judith Gilliland, 3 vols., 1:255–74. Aldershot: Ashgate, 2006.

———. *Writing and Holiness: The Practice of Authorship in the Early Christian East*. Philadelphia: University of Pennsylvania Press, 2004.

———. "Writing and the Liturgy of Memory in Gregory of Nyssa's Life of Macrina." *JECS* 8 (2000): 483–510.

Krumbacher, K. "Die Photographie im Dienste der Geisteswissenschaften." *Neue Jahrbücher für das klassische Altertum* 17 (Leipzig, 1906).

Kugel, James L. *How to Read the Bible: A Guide to Scripture Then and Now*. New York: Free Press, 2007.

Kuhn, K.H. "Besa." In *The Coptic Encyclopedia*, edited by Aziz Suryal Atiya, 2:378–79. New York: Macmillan, 1991.

———. "A Fifth Century Egyptian Abbot." *JTS* 5 (1954): 36–48, 174–87; 6 (1955): 35–48.

Kumar, K. *Utopianism*. Milton Keynes: Open University Press, 1991.

Ladeuze, P. *Étude sur le cénobitisme pakhomien pendant le IVe siècle et la première moitié du Ve.* Louvain: Linthout and Fontemoing, 1898.

Ladner, Gerhart B. "Homo Viator: Mediaeval Ideas on Alienation and Order." *Speculum* 42, no. 2 (1967): 233–59.

Lagarde, P. *Der Pentateuch koptisch.* Leipzig: Teubner, 1867.

Lamberton, Robert. *Homer the Theologian: Neoplatonist Allegorical Reading and the Growth of the Epic Tradition*. Berkeley: University of California Press, 1989.

———. "The Neoplatonists and the Spiritualization of Homer." In *Homer's Ancient Readers: The Hermeneutics of Greek Epic's Earliest Exegetes*, edited by Robert Lamberton and John J. Keaney, 115–33. Princeton: Princeton University Press, 1992.

Latimer, Elizabeth Wormeley. *Russia and Turkey in the Nineteenth Century*. Chicago: McClurg, 1894.

Layton, Bentley. "The Ancient Rules of Shenoute's Monastic Federation." In *Christianity and Monasticism in Upper Egypt*, edited by Gawdat Gabra and Hany N. Takla, 73–81. Cairo: American University in Cairo Press, 2008.

———. *A Coptic Grammar.* 2nd ed. Wiesbaden: Harrassowitz, 2004.

———. "Rules, Patterns, and the Exercise of Power in Shenoute's Monastery: The Problem of World Replacement and Identity Maintenance." *JECS* 15 (2007): 45–73.

———. "Social Structure and Food Consumption in an Early Christian Monastery: The Evidence of Shenoute's *Canons* and the White Monastery Federation, A. D. 385–465." *Le Muséon* 115 (2002): 25–55.

Layton, Richard. *Didymus the Blind and His Circle in Late-Antique Alexandria: Virtue and Narrative in Biblical Scholarship*. Urbana: University of Illinois Press, 2004.

Leach, Eleanor. *The Rhetoric of Space: Literary and Artistic Representations*. Princeton: Princeton University Press, 1988.

Lefort, L.-T. "Athanase, Ambroise et Chenoute '*sur la virginite*.'" *Le Museon* 48 (1935): 55–73.

Leipoldt, J. *Shenute von Atripe und die Entstehung des national ägyptischen Christentums.* Leipzig: Hinrichs, 1903.

Leroy, J. "Le cénobitisme chez Cassien." *Revue d'ascétique et de mystique* 43 (1967): 121–58.

Levitas, Ruth. *The Concept of Utopia*. New York: Philip Allen, 1990.

Leyerle, Blake. "John Chrysostom on Almsgiving and the Use of Money." *HTR* 87, no. 1 (1994): 34–37.

———. "Monks and Other Animals." In *The Cultural Turn in Late Ancient Studies: Gender, Asceticism, and Historiography*, edited by Dale B. Martin and Patricia Cox Miller, 150–71. Durham: Duke University Press, 2005.

———. "Refuse, Filth, and Excrement in the Homilies of John Chrysostom." *Journal of Late Antiquity* 2 (2009): 337–56.

Leyser, Conrad. *Authority and Asceticism from Augustine to Gregory the Great*. Oxford: Oxford University Press, 2000.

Lewis, Helen Block. "Introduction: Shame — The 'Sleeper' in Psychopathology." In *The Role of Shame in Symptom Formation*, edited by Helen Block Lewis, 1–28. Hillsdale, NJ: Lawrence Erlbaum, 1987.

Liebeschuetz, J. H. W. G. *Ambrose and John Chrysostom: Clerics between Desert and Empire*. Oxford: Oxford University Press, 2011.

Lim, Richard. "The Politics of Interpretation in Basil of Caesarea's *Hexaemeron*." *VC* 44 (1990): 351–70.

Lingelbach, Gabriele. *Klio macht Karriere: Die Institutionalisierung der Geschichtswissenschaft in Frankreich und den U.S.A. in der Zweiten Hälfte des 19. Jahrhunderts*. Veröffentlichungen des Max-Planck-Instituts für Geschichte181. Göttingen: Vandenhoeck und Ruprecht, 2003.

List, Johann. *Das Antoniusleben des Hl. Athanasius des Grossen: Eine literarhistorische Studie zu den Anfängen der byzantinischen Hagiographie*. Athens: Sakellarios, 1930.

Loraux, Nicole. "Ponos: Sur quelques difficultés de la peine comme nom du travail." *Annali del Seminario di studi del mondo classico, sezione di archeologia e storia antica* 4 (1982): 171–92.

Lorenz, R. "Die griechische *Vita Antonii* des Athanasius und ihre syrische Fassung: Bemerkungen zu einer These von R. Draguet." *Zeitschrift für Kirchengeschichte* 100 (1989): 77–84.

———. *Der zehnte Osterfestbrief des Athanasius von Alexandrien*. Berlin: De Gruyter, 1986.

Louth, A. "St. Athanasius and the Greek *Life of Antony*." *JTS*, n.s., 39 (1988): 504–9.

Lubomierski, Nina. "The Coptic Life of Shenoute." In *Christianity and Monasticism in Upper Egypt*, edited by Gawdat Gabre and Hany N. Takla, 91–98. Cairo: American University in Cairo Press, 2008.

———. *Die Vita Sinuthii: Form- und Überlieferungsgeschichte der hagiographischen Texte über Schenute den Archimandriten*. Tübingen: Mohr Siebeck, 2007.

Lucchesi, E. "Chenoute a-t-il écrit en grec?" In *Mélanges Antoine Guillaumont: Contributions à l'étude des christianismes orientaux,* edited by R.-G. Coquin, 201–10. Geneva: Cramer, 1988.

MacCoull, Leslie. "The Prophecy of Charour." *Oriens Christianus* 91 (2007): 44–55.

MacDonald, Dennis R. *Christianizing Homer: The Odyssey, Plato and the Acts of Andrew*. Oxford: Oxford University Press, 1994.

———. *Does the New Testament Imitate Homer? Four Cases from the Acts of the Apostles*. New Haven: Yale University Press, 2007.

Maguire, Henry. "Adam and the Animals: Allegory and the Literal Sense in Early Christian Art." *Dumbarton Oaks Papers* 41 (1987): 363–73.

Marchand, Suzanne L. *Down from Olympus: Archaeology and Philhellenism in Germany, 1750–1970*. Princeton: Princeton University Press, 1996.

Markus, Robert A. *The End of Ancient Christianity*. Cambridge: Cambridge University Press, 1990.

Marrou, H.I. *A History of Education in Antiquity*. Translated by George Lamb. New York: Sheed and Ward, 1956.

Marsili, Salvatore. *Giovanni Cassiano ed Evagrio Pontico: Dottrina sulla carità e contemplazione*. Rome: Anselmiana, 1936.

Martin, A. *Athanase d'Alexandrie et l'église d'Égypte au IVe siècle (328–373)*. Rome: École française de Rome, 1996.

Martin, Dale B., and Patricia Cox Miller, eds. *The Cultural Turn in Late Ancient Studies: Gender, Asceticism, and Historiography*. Durham: Duke University Press, 2005.

Mauser, Ulrich W. *Christ in the Wilderness: The Wilderness Theme in the Second Gospel and Its Basis in the Biblical Tradition*. Studies in Biblical Theology. Naperville, IL: Allenson, 1963.

Maxwell, Jaclyn L. *Christianization and Communication in Late Antiquity: John Chrysostom and His Congregation in Antioch*. Cambridge: Cambridge University Press, 2006.

Mayer, Wendy. *The Homilies of St John Chrysostom: Provenance; Reshaping the Foundations*. Rome: Pontifico Istituto Orientale, 2005.

Mayer, Wendy, and Pauline Allen. *John Chrysostom*. London: Routledge, 2000.

McGill, S., C. Sogno, and E. Watts, eds. *From the Tetrarchs to the Theodosians: Later Roman History and Culture, 284–450 CE*. Cambridge: Cambridge University Press, 2010.

McGing, Brian C. "Melitian Monks at Labla." *Tyche* 5 (1990): 65–73.

McGuckin, John. "Aliens and Citizens of Elsewhere: *Xeniteia* in East Christian Monastic Literature." In *Strangers to Themselves: The Byzantine Outsider*, edited by Dion Smythe, 23–38. Aldershot: Ashgate, 2000.

———. *Saint Gregory of Nazianzus: An Intellectual Biography*. Crestwood, NY: St. Vladimir's Seminary Press, 2001.

McKendrick, Scot. "The Codex Alexandrinus, or the Dangers of Being a Named Manuscript." In *The Bible as Book: The Transmission of the Greek Text*, edited by Scot McKendrick and Orlaith A. O'Sullivan, 1–16. London: British Library, 2003.

McLynn, N. *Ambrose of Milan: Church and Court in a Christian Capital*. TCH 22. Berkeley: University of California Press, 1994.

———. "'Genere Hispanus': Theodosius, Spain, and Nicene Orthodoxy." In *Hispania in Late Antiquity*, edited by K. Bowes and M. Kulikowski, 77–120. Leiden: Brill, 2005.

———. "Moments of Truth: Gregory of Nazianzus and Theodosius I." In *From the Tetrarchs to the Theodosians*, edited by S. McGill, C. Sogno, and E. Watts, 215–39. Cambridge: Cambridge University Press, 2010.

Meinardus, O. *Monks and Monasteries of the Egyptian Deserts*. Rev. ed. Cairo: American University in Cairo Press, 1989.

Meredith, Anthony. "Porphyry and Julian against the Christians." *Aufstieg und Niedergang der römischen Welt,* ser. 2, 23, no. 2 (1980): 1120–49.

Mertel, Hans. *Die biographischen Formen der griechischen Heiligenlegenden*. Munich: Wolf, 1909.

Metzger, Bruce. *Manuscripts of the Greek Bible: An Introduction to Greek Palaeography*. New York: Oxford University Press, 1981.

Meyer, John Charles. "Philip Schaff's Concept of Organic Historiography as Related to the Development of Doctrine: A Catholic Appraisal." PhD diss, Catholic University of America, 1968.

Miller, Patricia Cox. "'Adam Ate from the Animal Tree.'" *Dionysius* 5 (1981): 165–80. Reprinted in *The Poetry of Thought in Late Antiquity: Essays in Imagination and Religion* (Aldershot: Ashgate, 2001).

———. *Biography in Late Antiquity: A Quest for the Holy Man*. Berkeley: University of California Press, 1983.

———. "Desert Asceticism and 'The Body from Nowhere.'" *JECS* 2 (1994): 137–53. Reprinted in *The Poetry of Thought in Late Antiquity: Essays in Imagination and Religion* (Aldershot: Ashgate, 2001).

———. *Dreams in Late Antiquity: Studies in the Imagination of a Culture.* Princeton: Princeton University Press, 1994.

———. "In Praise of Nonsense." In *Classical Mediterranean Spirituality: Egyptian, Greek, Roman*, edited by A.H. Armstrong, 481–505. London: Routledge and Kegan Paul, 1986.

———. "Jerome's Centaur: A Hyper-icon of the Desert." *JECS* 4 (1996): 209–33.

———. "Origen on the Bestial Soul: A Poetics of Nature." *VC* 36 (1982): 115–40. Reprinted in *The Poetry of Thought in Late Antiquity: Essays in Imagination and Religion* (Aldershot: Ashgate, 2001).

———. "The *Physiologus:* A Poiesis of Nature." *CH* 52 (1983): 433–43. Reprinted in *The Poetry of Thought in Late Antiquity: Essays in Imagination and Religion* (Aldershot: Ashgate, 2001).

———. *The Poetry of Thought in Late Antiquity: Essays in Imagination and Religion*. Aldershot: Ashgate, 2001.

Miller, Timothy S. *The Birth of the Hospital in the Byzantine Empire*. Baltimore: Johns Hopkins University Press, 1985.

Mitchell, W.J.T. *What Do Pictures Want? The Lives and Loves of Images*. Chicago: University of Chicago Press, 2005.

Moeller, B. "Adolf von Harnack — der Aussenseiter als Zentralfigur." In *Adolf von Harnack: Theologe, Historiker, Wissenschaftspolitiker*, edited by K. Nowak and O.G. Oexle, 9–22. Veröffentlichungen des Max-Planck-Instituts für Geschichte 161. Göttingen: Vandenhoeck und Ruprecht, 2001.

Montalembert, Count Charles de. *The Monks of the West from St. Benedict to St. Bernard*. 6 vols. London: John C. Nimmo, 1861–79.

Morgan, Teresa. *Literate Education in the Hellenistic and Roman Worlds*. Cambridge: Cambridge University Press, 1998.

Morris, Christine. "Animals into Art in the Ancient World." In *A Cultural History of Animals*, vol. 1, *A Cultural History of Animals in Antiquity*, edited by Linda Kalof, 175–98. Oxford: Berg, 2007.

Mosely, Philip E. *Russian Diplomacy and the Opening of the Eastern Question in 1838 and 1839*. Harvard Historical Monographs 4. Cambridge, MA: Harvard University Press, 1934.

Mosheim, John Laurence. *An Ecclesiastical History, Ancient and Modern, from the Birth of Christ to the Beginning of the Eighteenth Century*. Translated from the Latin by Archibald Maclaine. 2nd ed. 2 vols. London: Haddon, 1810.

Mossay, J. "Note sur Héron-Maximine écrivain ecclésiastique." *Analecta Bollandiana* 100 (1982): 229–36.

Muehlberger, Ellen. "Ambivalence about the Angelic Life: The Promise and Perils of an Early Christian Discourse of Asceticism." *JECS* 16 (2008): 447–78.

Müller, Andreas E. *Das Konzept des geistlichen Gehorsams bei Johannes Sinaites: Zur Entwicklungsgeschichte eines Elements orthodoxer Konfessionskultur*. Studien und Texte zu Antike und Christentum 37. Tübingen: Mohr Siebeck, 2006.

———. "Von Umkehrprismen, Lumièreplatten und dem Photometer: Karl Krumbacher und die Photographie." In *Byzantina Mediterranea: Festschrift für Johannes Koder zum 65. Geburtstag*, edited by K. Belke et al., 459–66. Vienna: Böhlau, 2007.

Muir, John. *The Mountains of California*. 1984. Reprint, New York: Modern Library, 2001.

Nagel, Peter. *Die Motivierung der Askese in der alten Kirche und der Ursprung des Mönchtums*. Berlin: Academie-Verlag, 1966.

Neander, Augustus. *The Emperor Julian and His Generation: A Historical Picture*. Translated by G.V. Cox. 1812. Reprint, Oxford: Riker, 1850.

———. *General History of the Christian Religion and Church.* Vol. 1. *Comprising the First Great Division of the History.* Vol. 2. *Comprising the Second Great Division of the History*. Translated by Joseph Torrey. 11th American ed., rev., enl. Boston: Crocker and Brewster, 1872.

———. *Lectures on the History of Christian Dogmas*. Edited by J.L. Jacobi. Translated by J.E. Ryland. 2 vols. London: Bohn, 1858.

———. *Memorials of Christian Life in the Early and Middle Ages*. Translated by J.E. Ryland. London: Bohn, 1852.

Newmyer, Stephen. "Animals in Ancient Philosophy." In *A Cultural History of Animals in Antiquity*, edited by Linda Kalof, 151–74. Oxford: Berg, 2007.

———. "Paws to Reflect: Ancients and Moderns on the Religious Sensibilities of Animals." *Quaderni urbinati di cultura classica*, n.s., 75 (2003): 111–29.

Nordberg, H. "On the Bible Text of St Athanasius." *Arctos: Acta Philologica Fennica*, n.s., 3 (1962): 119–41.

Nowak, N. "Theologie, Philologie und Geschichte: Adolf von Harnack als Kirchenhistoriker." In *Adolf von Harnack: Theologe, Historiker, Wissenschaftspolitiker*, edited by K. Nowak and O.G. Oexle, 189–238. Veröffentlichungen des Max-Planck-Instituts für Geschichte 161. Göttingen: Vandenhoeck und Ruprecht, 2001.

Oates, J. F., et al. *Checklist of Greek, Latin, Demotic and Coptic Papyri, Ostraca and Tablets*. January 13. http://scriptorium.lib.duke.edu/papyrus/texts/clist.html.

O'Laughlin, Michael W. "Closing the Gap between Antony and Evagrius." In *Origeniana Septima: Origenes in den Auseinandersetzungen des 4. Jahrhunderts*, edited by W.A. Bienert and U. Kühneweg, 345–54. Leuven: University Press, 1999.

———. "Evagrius Ponticus, *Antirrheticus* (selections)." In *Ascetic Behavior in Greco-Roman Antiquity: A Sourcebook*, edited by Vincent L. Wimbush, 243–62. Studies in Antiquity and Christianity. Minneapolis: Fortress Press, 1990.

Opelt, Ilona. "Lingua ab angelo tradita: Dekodierungsversuch der Pachomiusbriefe." In *Mémorial Jean Gribomont (1920–1986)*, 453–61. Studia ephemeridis Augustinianum 27. Rome: Institutum Patristicum Augustinianum, 1988.

Orlandi, Tito. "John of Shmun." In *The Coptic Encyclopedia,* edited by Aziz Suryal Atiya, 5:1369. New York: Macmillan, 1991.

———. "The Library of the Monastery of Saint Shenute at Atripe." In *Perspectives on Panopolis: An Egyptian Town from Alexander the Great to the Arab Conquest*, edited by A. Egberts, B.P. Muhs, and J. van der Vliet, 211–31. Leiden: Brill, 2002.

———. "Les papyrus coptes du Musee Egyptien de Turin." *Le Museon* 87 (1974): 115–27.

Ostriker, Alicia Suskin. *For the Love of God: The Bible as an Open Book*. New Brunswick: Rutgers University Press, 2007.

Otranto, R. *Antiche liste di libri su papiro*. Rome: Edizioni di Storia e Letteratura, 2000.

Palgrave, William Gifford. *Essays on Eastern Questions*. London: Macmillan, 1872.

Palmer, A. *Monk and Mason on the Tigris Frontier*. Cambridge: Cambridge University Press, 1990.

Parpulov, Georgi. "Toward a History of Byzantine Psalters." PhD diss., University of Chicago, 2004.

Paxson, James J. *The Poetics of Personification*. Cambridge: Cambridge University Press, 1994.

Peeters, P. "À propos de la Vie sahidique de s. Pacôme." *Analecta Bollandiana* 52 (1934): 286–320.

Peña, I., P. Castellana, and R. Fernandez. *Les reclus Syriens: Recherches sur les anciennes formes de vie solitaire en Syrie*. Studium Biblicum Franciscanum 23. Jerusalem: Franciscan Press, 1975.

Pépin, Jean. *Mythe et allégorie: Origines grecques et contestations judéo-chrétiennes*. Paris: Études augustiniennes, 1958.

———. "The Platonic and Christian Ulysses." In *Neoplatonism and Christian Thought*, vol. 2, edited by Hans Blumenthal and Robert Markus. Albany: SUNY Press, 1982.

Perkins, D. N. "Person-Plus: A Distributed View of Thinking and Learning." In *Distributed Cognitions: Psychological and Educational Considerations*, edited by Gavriel Salomon, 88–110. Cambridge: Cambridge University Press, 1996.

Peters, E. M. "Prison before Prisons." In *The Oxford History of the Prison: The Practice of Punishment in Western Society*, edited by N. Morris and D. J. Rothman, 27–30. New York: Oxford University Press, 1995.

Petersen, William L. "Diatessaron." In *The Anchor Bible Dictionary,* edited by David Noel Freedman, 2:189–90. New York: Doubleday, 1992.

Picker, H.-C. "Ergänzungen zur Personalbibliographie Harnacks." In *Adolf von Harnack als Zeitgenosse: Reden und Schriften aus den Jahren des Kaiserreichs und der Weimarer Republik*, edited by K. Nowack, 2:1655–83. Berlin: De Gruyter, 1996.

Pinto, John. "Pastoral Landscape and Antiquity: Hadrian's Villa." In *The Pastoral Landscape*, edited by John Dixon Hunt, 179–95. Washington, DC: National Gallery of Art, 1992.

Plagnieux, J. *Saint Grégoire de Nazianze théologien*. Paris: Éditiones franciscaines, 1951.

Poggioli, Renato. *The Oaten Flute: Essays on Pastoral Poetry and the Pastoral Ideal.* Cambridge, MA: Harvard University Press, 1975.

Preisigke, F. *Die Gotteskraft der frühchristlichen Zeit*. Papyrusinstitut Heidelberg, Schrift 6. Berlin: De Gruyter, 1922.

Priessnig, Anton. *Die biographischen Formen der griechischen Heiligenlegenden in ihrer geschichtlichen Entwicklung*. Munich: Ludwig-Maximilians-Universität, 1924.

Purcell, Nicholas. "Town in Country and Country in Town." In *Ancient Roman Villa Gardens*, edited by Elisabeth MacDougall. Washington, DC: Dumbarton Oaks, 1987.

Rahner, Hugo. "Odysseus at the Mast." In *Greek Myths and Christian Mystery*, 328–86. Translated by B. Battershaw. London: Burnes and Oates, 1964.

Rapp, Claudia. "Desert, City, and Countryside in the Early Christian Imagination." In *The Encroaching Desert: Egyptian Hagiography and the Medieval West*, edited by Jitse Dijkstra and Mathilde van Dijk, 93–112. Leiden: Brill, 2006.

———. *Holy Bishops in Late Antiquity: The Nature of Christian Leadership in an Age of Transition*. TCH 37. Berkeley: University of California Press, 2005.

———. "Holy Texts, Holy Men, and Holy Scribes: Aspects of Scriptural Holiness in Late Antiquity." In *The Early Christian Book,* edited by William E. Klingshirn and Linda Safran, 194–222. Washington, DC: Catholic University of America Press, 2007.

———. "Spiritual Guarantors at Penance, Baptism, and Ordination in the Late Antique East." In *A New History of Penance*, edited by A. Firey, 121–48. Leiden: Brill, 2008.

———. "Storytelling as Spiritual Communication in Early Greek Hagiography: The Use of Diegesis." *JECS* 6 (1998): 431–48.

Rebenich, S. "Der alte Meergreis, die Rose von Jericho und ein höchst vortrefflicher Schwiegersohn: Mommsen, Harnack, und Wilamowitz." In *Adolf von Harnack: Theologe, Historiker, Wissenschaftspolitiker*, edited by K. Nowak and O.G. Oexle, 39–70. Veröffentlichungen des Max-Planck-Instituts für Geschichte 161. Göttingen: Vandenhoeck und Ruprecht, 2001.

———. "Die Altertumswissenschaften und die Kirchenväterkommission an der Akademie." In *Die Königlich Preussische Akademie der Wissenschaften zu Berlin im Kaiserreich*, edited by J. Kocka, 199–233. Berlin: Akademie Verlag, 1999.

———. "Mommsen, Harnack und die Prosopographie der Spätantike." In *Studia Patristica 29: Papers Presented at the Twelfth International Conference on Patristic Studies Held in Oxford 1995*, 109–18. Leuven: Peeters, 1997.

———. "Orbis Romanus: Deutungen der römischen Geschichte im Zeitalter des Historismus." In *Adolf von Harnack: Christentum, Wissenschaft und Gesellschaft: Wissenschaftliches Symposion aus Anlass des 150. Geburtstages*, edited by K. Nowak et al., 29–50. Veröffentlichungen des Max-Planck-Instituts für Geschichte 204. Göttingen: Vandenhoeck und Ruprecht, 2003.

——. *Theodor Mommsen und Adolf Harnack: Wissenschaft und Politik im Berlin des ausgehenden 19. Jahrhunderts. Mit einem Anhang: Edition und Kommentierung des Briefwechsels.* Berlin: De Gruyter, 1997.

——. "Theodor Mommsen und das Verhältnis von alter Geschichte und Patristik." In *Patristique et antiquité tardive en Allemagne et en France de 1870 à 1930: Influences et échanges: Actes du colloque franco-allemand de Chantilly, 25–27 octobre 1991,* edited by J. Fontaine, R. Herzog, and K. Pollmann, 131–54. Paris: Institut d'études augustiniennes, 1991.

——. "'Unser Werk lobt keinen Meister.' Theodor Mommsen und die Wissenschaft vom Altertum." In *Theodor Mommsen: Gelehrter, Politiker und Literat,* edited by J. Wiesehöfer, 185–206. Stuttgart: Steiner, 2005.

——. "Vom Nutzen und Nachteil der Grosswissenschaft: Altertumswissenschaftliche Unternehmungen an der Berliner Akademie und Universität im 19. Jahrhundert." In *Die modernen Väter der Antike: Die Entwicklung der Altertumswissenschaften an Akademie und Universität im Berlin des 19. Jahrhunderts*, edited by A. M. Baertschi and C. G. King, 397–421. Berlin: De Gruyter, 2009.

——. "Wilhelm von Humboldt oder: Die Entstehung des Bürgertums aus dem Geist der Antike." In *Applied Classics: Comparisons, Constructs, Controversies*, edited by A. Chaniotis, A. Kuhn, and C. Kuhn, 98–118. Stuttgart: Steiner, 2009.

Reitzenstein, Richard. *Des Athanasius Werk über das Leben des Antonius: Ein philologischer Beitrag zur Geschichte des Mönchtums*. Sitzungsberichte der Heidelberger Akademie der Wissenschaften, Philosophisch-historische Klasse 8. Heidelberg: Carl Winters Universitätsbuchhandlung, 1914.

Renehan, Robert. "The Greek Anthropocentric View of Man." *Harvard Studies in Classical Philology* 85 (1981): 239–59.

Ritter, A.-M. *Das Konzil von Constantinopel und sein Symbol*. Göttingen: Vandenhoeck und Ruprecht, 1961.

Rodgers, Daniel T. "Exceptionalism." In *Imagined Histories: American Historians Interpret the Past*, edited by Anthony Molho and Gordon S. Wood, 21–40. Princeton: Princeton University Press, 1998.

Roldanus, Johannes. *Le Christ et l'homme dans la théologie d'Athanase d'Alexandrie*. Leiden: Brill, 1968.

——. "Die *Vita Antonii* als Spiegel der Theologie des Athanasius und ihr Weiterwirken bis ins 5. Jahrhundert." *TP* 58 (1983): 194–216.

Romm, James S. *The Edges of the Earth in Ancient Thought*. Princeton: Princeton University Press, 1992.

Rondeau, Marie-Josèphe. *Les commentaires patristiques du psautier (IIIe–Ve siècles).* 2 vols. Orientalia Christiana Analecta 219, 220. Rome: Pontificium Institutum Studiorum Orientalium, 1982–85.

——. "L'Epître à Marcellinus sur les psaumes." *VC* 22 (1968): 176–97.

Rosand, David. "Pastoral Topoi: On the Construction of Meaning in Landscape." In *The Pastoral Landscape*, edited by John Dixon Hunt, 161–77. Washington, DC: National Gallery of Art, 1992.

Rousseau, Philip. "Antony as Teacher in the Greek Life." In *Greek Biography and Panegyric in Late Antiquity*, edited by P. Rousseau and T. Hägg, 89–105. Berkeley: University of California Press, 2000.

———. *Ascetics, Authority and the Church in the Age of Jerome and Cassian*. 2nd ed. 1978. Notre Dame: University of Notre Dame Press, 2010.

———. *Basil of Caesarea*. TCH 20. Berkeley: University of California Press, 1994.

———. "Cassian, Contemplation, and the Coenobitic Life." *Journal of Ecclesiastical History* 26 (1975): 113–26.

———. "Eccentrics and Cenobites in the Late Roman East." *Byzantinische Forschungun* 24 (1997): 35–50.

———. "Knowing Theodoret: Text and Self." In *The Cultural Turn in Late Ancient Studies: Gender, Asceticism, and Historiography*, edited by Dale B. Martin and Patricia Cox Miller, 278–97. Durham: Duke University Press, 2005.

———. "'Learned Women' and the Development of a Christian Culture in Late Antiquity." *Symbolae Osloenses* 70 (1995): 116–47.

———. "Monasticism." In *The Cambridge Ancient History*, edited by Averil Cameron, Bryan Ward-Perkins, and Michael Whitby, new ed., 15:745–80. Cambridge: Cambridge University Press, 2000.

———. *Pachomius: The Making of a Community in Fourth-Century Egypt*. 2nd ed. TCH 6. Berkeley: University of California Press, 1985.

———. "The Pious Household and the Virgin Chorus: Reflections on Gregory of Nyssa's *Life of Macrina*." *JECS* 13 (2005): 165–86.

———. "The Successors of Pachomius and the Nag Hammadi Codices." In *The World of Egyptian Christianity: Language, Literature, and Social Context; Essays in Honor of David W. Johnson,* edited by James E. Goehring and Janet A. Timbie, 140–47. CUA Studies in Early Christianity 2. Washington, DC: Catholic University of America Press, 2007.

Rubenson, S. "Anthony and Pythagoras: A Reappraisal of the Appropriation of Classical Biography in Athanasius' *Vita Antonii*." In *Beyond Reception: Mutual Influences between Antique Religion, Judaism, and Early Christianity*, edited by D. Brakke, A.-C. Jacobsen, and J. Ulrich, 191–208. Frankfurt: Peter Lang, 2006.

———. "Christian Asceticism and the Emergence of the Monastic Tradition." In *Asceticism*, edited by Vincent L. Wimbush and Richard Valantasis, 49–57. Oxford: Oxford University Press, 1995.

———. "Evagrios Pontikos und die Theologie der Wüste." In *Logos: Festschrift für Louise Abramowski zum 8. Juli 1993*, edited by H.C. Brennecke, E.L. Grasmück, and C. Markschies, 384–401. Berlin: De Gruyter, 1993.

———. *The Letters of St. Antony: Monasticism and the Making of a Saint.* Minneapolis: Fortress Press, 1995.

———. "Monasticism and the Philosophical Heritage." In *Oxford Handbook of Late Antiquity,* edited by Scott Fitzgerald Johnson, 487–512. Oxford: Oxford University Press, 2012.

Runia, David. "Why Does Clement of Alexandria Call Philo 'The Pythagorean'?" *VC* 49 (1995): 1–22.

Salomon, Gavriel, ed. *Distributed Cognitions.* Cambridge: Cambridge University Press, 1993.

———. "No Distribution without Individuals' Cognition: A Dynamic Interactional View." In *Distributed Cognitions*, edited by Gavriel Salomon, 111–38. Cambridge: Cambridge University Press, 1993.

Sandnes, Karl Olav. *The Challenge of Homer: School, Pagan Poets and Early Christianity*. London: T and T Clark, 2009.

Sayce, A.H. "Deux contrats grecs du Fayoum." *REG* 3 (1890): 131–44.

Schaf [*sic*], Philip. *Anglo-Germanism, or the Significance of the German Nationality in the United States.* Address before the Schiller Society of Marshall College, March 10, 1846. Translated by J.S. Ermentrout. Chambersburg, PA: Publication Office of the German Reformed Church, 1846.

Schaff, David S. *The Life of Philip Schaff*. New York: Charles Scribner's Sons, 1897.

Schaff, Philip. *America: A Sketch of Its Political, Social, and Religious Character*. 1855. Edited by Perry Miller. Cambridge, MA: Harvard University Press, 1961.

———. *American Nationality: An Address Delivered before the Irving Society of the College of St. James, Md., June 11th, 1856.* Chambersburg, PA: Irving Society, 1856.

———. *Ante-Nicene Christianity, A.D. 100–325.* Vol. 2 of *History of the Christian Church,* 4th ed. New York: Charles Scribner's Sons, 1887.

———. "The Ascetic System." *Mercersburg Review* 10 (October 1858): 600–613.

———. "Christianity in America: A Report Prepared for the Meeting of the Evangelical Alliance Held at Berlin in September 1857." *Mercersburg Review* 9 (October 1857): 536–37.

———. "The Conflict of Trinitarianism and Unitarianism in the Ante-Nicene Age." *Bibliotheca Sacra* 15, no. 60 (October 1858).

———. "The Eastern Conflict." *New York Observer*, June 14, 1877. Written from Istanbul, May 11, 1877. Clipping in Schaff Scrapbook (Schaff Papers, UTS, Box 6, Scrapbook 1, p. 97).

———. *History of the Apostolic Church with a General Introduction to Church History.* Vol. 2. Edinburgh: T. and T. Clark, 1854. Excerpted in *Reformed and Catholic: Selected Historical and Theological Writings of Philip Schaff,* edited by Charles Yrigoyen Jr. and George M. Bricker. Pittsburgh Original Texts and Translations, ser. 4. Pittsburgh, PA: Pickwick Press, 1979.

———. *Nicene and Post-Nicene Christianity.* Vol. 3 of *History of the Christian Church,* 5th ed. New York: Charles Scribner's Sons, 1906.

———. "The Protestant Mission in the East." *Christian at Work*, July 5, 1877. Written from Corfu, 22 May 1877.

———. "Report to the German Evangelical Church Diet at Frankfort on the Maine." Translated by Thomas C. Porter for the *New York Observer*. In *America: A Sketch of Its Political, Social, and Religious Character,* by Philip Schaff, edited by Perry Miller, 218. 1855. Reprint, Cambridge, MA: Harvard University Press, 1961.

———. "The Rise and Progress of Monasticism." *Bibliotheca Sacra* 21, no. 82 (April 1964): 384–424.

———. "The Theology of Our Age and Country." In *Christ and Christianity: Studies on Christology, Creed and Confessions, Protestantism and Romanism, Reformation Principles, Sunday Observance, Religious Freedom, and Christian Union*. New York: Charles Scribner's Sons, 1885.

———. *Through Bible Lands: Notes of Travel in Egypt, the Desert, and Palestine*. New ed., rev. and enl. London: Nisbet, 1878.

———. *What Is Church History?* Philadelphia: Lippincott, 1846.

Schama, Simon. *Landscape and Memory*. New York: Knopf, 1995.

Scholten, C. "Die Nag-Hammadi-Texte als Buchbesitz der Pachomianer." *Jahrbuch für Antike und Christentum* 31 (1988): 144–72.

Schouler, Bernard. "L' Éthopée chez Libanios ou l'évasion esthétique." In *Ethopoiia: La représentation de caractères entre fiction scolaire et réalité vivante à l'époque impériale et tardive*, edited by Eugenio Amato and Jacques Schamp. Salerno: Helios, 2005.

Schroeder, Caroline T. *Monastic Bodies: Discipline and Salvation in Shenoute of Atripe*. Philadelphia: University of Pennsylvania Press, 2007.

Scott, Alan. "The Date of the *Physiologus*." *VC* 52 (1998): 430–41.

———. "Zoological Marvel and Exegetical Method in Origen and the *Physiologus*." In *Reading in Christian Communities: Essays on Interpretation in the Early Church*, edited by Charles A. Bobertz and David Brakke, 80–89. Notre Dame: University of Notre Dame Press, 2002.

Scullard, H.H. *The Elephant in the Greek and Roman World*. Ithaca: Cornell University Press, 1974.

Sellin, T. "Dom Jean Mabillon: A Prison Reformer of the Seventeenth Century." *Journal of the American Institute of Criminal Law and Criminology* 17 (1927): 581–602.

Sellew, Philip. "Achilles or Christ? Porphyry and Didymus in Debate over Allegorical Interpretation." *HTR* 82 (1989): 79–100.

Shaw, B. "Judicial Nightmares and Christian Memory." *JECS* 11 (2003): 533–63.

Sheridan, Mark. "The Controversy over *Apatheia*: Cassian's Sources and His Use of Them." *SM* 40 (1998): 287–310.

Shisha-Halevy, Ariel. "Bohairic." In *Coptic Encyclopedia,* 8.53–60. New York: Macmillan, 1991.

Shriver, George H., Jr. "Philip Schaff's Concept of Organic Historiography Interpreted in Relation to the Realization of an 'Evangelical Catholicism' within the Christian Community." PhD diss., Duke University, 1960.

Shuger, Debora. "The 'I' of the Beholder: Renaissance Mirrors and the Reflexive Mind." In *Renaissance Culture and the Everyday,* edited by Patricia Fumeron and Simon Hunt, 21–41. Philadelphia: University of Pennsylvania Press, 1999.

Sieben, Hermann-Josef, S.J. "Athanasius über den Psalter: Analyse seines Briefes an Marcellinus." *TP* 48 (1973): 157–73.

———. "Der Psalter und die Bekehrung der *voces* und *affectus* zu Augustinus, *Confessiones* IX, 4.6 und X, 33." *TP* 52 (1977): 481–97.

Silvas, Anna M. *The Asketikon of St. Basil the Great*. Oxford: University Press, 2005.

Small, Jocelyn Penny. *Wax Tablets of the Mind: Cognitive Studies of Memory and Literacy in Classical Antiquity*. London: Routledge, 1997.

Smend, F. *Adolf von Harnack: Verzeichnis seiner Schriften*. Leipzig: Hinrichs, 1927.

———. *Adolf von Harnack: Verzeichnis seiner Schriften bis 1930. Mit einem Geleitwort und bibliographischen Nachträgen bis 1985 von Jürgen Dummer*. Leipzig: Zentralantiquariat der DDR, 1990.

Smend, F., and Axel von Harnack. *Adolf von Harnack: Verzeichnis seiner Schriften, 1927–1930, und Verzeichnis der ihm gewidmeten Schriften.* Leipzig: Hinrichs, 1931.

Smith, Gregory A. "How Thin Is a Demon?" *JECS* 16 (2008): 479–512.

Smith, Henry B. *History of the Church of Christ, in Chronological Tables*. Rev ed. New York: Charles Scribner, 1861.

———. *Introduction to Christian Theology*. New York: Armstrong and Son, 1883.

Snee, E.R. "Gregory Nazianzen's Constantinopolitan Career." PhD diss., University of Washington, 1981.

Sorabji, Richard. *Animal Minds and Human Morals: The Origins of the Western Debate*. Ithaca: Cornell University Press, 1993.

———. *Emotion and Peace of Mind: From Stoic Agitation to Christian Temptation*. Oxford: Oxford University Press, 2000.

Stead, G. Christopher. "Rhetorical Method in Athanasius." *VC* 30 (1976): 121–37.

———. "St Athanasius on the Psalms." *VC* 39 (1985): 65–78.

Stewart, Columba. *Cassian the Monk*. New York: Oxford University Press, 1998.

———. "Radical Honesty about the Self: The Practice of the Desert Fathers." *Sobornost* 12 (1990): 25–39.

———. "The Use of Biblical Texts in Prayer and the Formation of Early Monastic Culture." *American Benedictine Review* 62 (2011): 188–201.

Stowers, Stanley K. *A Rereading of Romans: Justice, Jews, and Gentiles*. New Haven: Yale University Press, 1994.

Strothmann, Werner. "Erste Homilie des Makarius." *Göttinger Orientalischen Forschungen* 24 (1983): 99–108.

Takeda, F. "Monastic Theology of the Syriac Version of the Life of Antony." *SP* 35 (2001): 148–57.

———. "The Syriac Version of the Life of Antony: A Meeting Point of Egyptian Monasticism with Native Syriac Asceticism." In *Symposium Syriacum VII*, edited by R. Lavenant, 185–94. Rome: Pontificio Istituto Orientale, 1998.

Takla, Hany. "The Library of the Monastery of St. Shenouda the Archimandrite." *Coptica* 4 (2005): 43–51.

Tetz, M. "Athanasius und die *Vita Antonii:* Literarische und theologische Relationen." *Zeitschrift für neutestamentliche Wissenschaft* 73 (1982): 1–30.

Thissen, Heinz-Josef. "Zur Begegnung von Christentum und 'Heidentum': Shenoute und Gesios." *Enchoria* 19–20 (1992–93): 155–64.

Timbie, Janet. "Non-canonical Scriptural Citation in Shenoute." In *Actes du huitième Congrès internationale d'études coptes*, edited by N. Bosson and A. Boud'hors, 2 vols., 2:625–34. Orientalia Lovaniensia Analecta 163. Leuven: Peeters, 2007.

Toynbee, J.M.C. *Animals in Roman Life and Art*. Ithaca: Cornell University Press, 1973.

Treu, U. "Aristophanes bei Shenoute." *Philologia* 101 (1957): 325–28.

Tribble, Evelyn. "Distributing Cognition in the Globe." *Shakespeare Quarterly* 56 (2005): 135–55.

Ulrich, Laurel Thatcher. *The Age of Homespun: Objects and Stories in the Creation of an American Myth*. New York: Knopf, 2001.

Urbano, Arthur. "'Read It Also to the Gentiles': The Displacement and Recasting of the Philosopher in the *Vita Antonii*." *CH* 77 (2008): 877–914.

Vaage, Leif E., and Vincent L. Wimbush, eds. *Asceticism and the New Testament*. New York: Routledge, 1999.

Valantasis, Richard. *Spiritual Guides of the Third Century: A Semiotic Study of the Guide-Disciple Relationship in Christianity, Neoplatonism, Hermetism, and Gnosticism*. Harvard Dissertations in Religion. Minneapolis: Fortress Press, 1991.

———. "A Theory of the Social Function of Asceticism." In *Asceticism*, edited by Vincent L. Wimbush and Richard Valantasis, 544–52. New York: Oxford University Press, 1995.

Veilleux, A. *La liturgie dans le cénobitisme pachômien au quatrième siècle*. Rome: Herder, 1968.

Veyne, Paul. "The Roman Empire." In *A History of Private Life,* vol. 1, *From Pagan Rome to Byzantium*, edited by Paul Veyne, 5–234. Cambridge, MA: Harvard University Press, 1987.

Vivian, Tim. "Monks, Middle Egypt, and Metanoia: The Life of Phib by Papohe the Steward (Translation and Introduction)." *JECS* 7 (1999): 547–71.

———. *St. Peter of Alexandria: Bishop and Martyr*. Studies in Antiquity and Christianity. Philadelphia: Fortress Press, 1988.

Vööbus, A. *A History of Asceticism in the Syrian Orient*. Vol. 2. CSCO 197, subs. 17. Louvain: Secrétariat du CSCO, 1960.

Vogüé, Adalbert de. "Deux réminiscences scripturaires non encore remarquées dan les règles de saint Pachôme et de saint Benoît." *SM* 25 (1983): 7–8.

———. "Les sources des quatre premiers livres des Institutions de Jean Cassien: Introduction aux recherches sur les anciennes règles monastiques latines." *SM* 27 (1985): 241–311.

Watkins, O.D. *A History of Penance: Being a Study of the Authorities*. 2 vols. New York: Burt Franklin, 1961.

Watts, Edward. *City and School in Late Antique Athens and Alexandria.* Berkeley: University of California Press, 2006.

Weaver, Rebecca Harding. *Divine Grace and Human Agency: A Study of the Semi-Pelagian Controversy*. Macon: Mercer University Press, 1996.

Webb, Ruth. "*Ekphrasis* Ancient and Modern: The Invention of a Genre." *Word and Image* 15 (1999): 7–18.

———. *Ekphrasis, Imagination, and Persuasion in Ancient Rhetorical Theory and Practice*. Farnham: Ashgate, 2009.

———. "The Progymnasmata as Practice." In *Education in Greek and Roman Antiquity,* edited by Yun Lee Too, 289–316. Leiden: Brill, 2001.

Wehler, H.-U. *Deutsche Gesellschaftsgeschichte*. Vol. 3. *Von der "Deutschen Doppelrevolution" bis zum Beginn des Ersten Weltkrieges, 1849–1914*. Munich: Beck, 1995.

Wilken, Robert. *The Christians as the Romans Saw Them.* New Haven: Yale University Press, 1984.

Williams, Craig A. *Roman Homosexuality: Ideologies of Masculinity in Classical Antiquity*. New York: Oxford University Press, 1999.

Williams, Michael. "The Life of Antony and the Domestication of Charismatic Wisdom." In *Charisma and Sacred Biography* (special issue *Journal of the American Academy of Religion Studies* 48 [1982]), edited by Michael Williams, 23–45. Chambersburg, PA: American Academy of Religion, 1982.

Williams, Stephen, and Gerard Friell. *Theodosius: The Empire at Bay*. London: Routledge, 1994.

Wimbush, Vincent L. *Ascetic Behavior in Greco-Roman Antiquity: A Sourcebook*. Minneapolis: Fortress Press, 1990.

Wimbush, Vincent L., and Richard Valantasis, eds. *Asceticism*. New York: Oxford University Press, 1995.

Wipszycka, Ewa. "Le monachisme égyptien et les villes." *Travaux et mémoires* 12 (1994): 1–44. Reprinted in *Études sur le christianisme dans l'Égypte de l'antiquité tardive*, 282–336, Studia ephemeridis Augustinianum 52 (Rome: Institutum Patristicum Augustinianum, 1996).

Wisse, Frederik. "Language Mysticism in the Nag Hammadi Texts and in Early Coptic Monasticism I: Cryptography." *Enchoria* 8 (1979): 101–20.

Young, Robin Darling. "Evagrius the Iconographer: Monastic Pedagogy in the *Gnostikos*." *JECS* 9 (2001): 45–71.

Zahn-Harnack, Agnes von. *Adolf von Harnack*. 2nd ed. Berlin: De Gruyer, 1951.

Zanetti, U. *Les manuscrits de Dair Abû Maqâr: Inventaire*. Geneva: Cramer, 1986.

Contributors

VIRGINIA BURRUS is Professor of Early Church History and Chair of the Graduate Division of Religion at Drew University. Her most recent books are *Saving Shame: Martyrs, Saints and Other Abject Subjects* (University of Pennsylvania Press, 2007) and *Seducing Augustine: Bodies, Desires, Confessions* (Fordham University Press, 2010), coauthored with Mark Jordan and Karmen MacKendrick. *The Life of Saint Helia: Critical Edition, Translation, Introduction, and Commentary*, coauthored with Marco Conti, is forthcoming.

DANIEL F. CANER is Associate Professor in the Departments of History and Classics at the University of Connecticut, Storrs. He is the author of *Wandering, Begging Monks: Spiritual Authority and the Promotion of Monasticism in Late Antiquity* (University of California Press, 2002) and *History and Hagiography from the Late Antique Sinai* (Liverpool University Press, 2010). He is currently writing a book entitled *The Rich and the Pure: Christian Gifts, Wealth and Religious Society in Early Byzantium*.

CATHERINE M. CHIN is Associate Professor and Chair of the Department of Religious Studies, University of California, Davis. Her book *Grammar and Christianity in the Late Roman World* was published by the University of Pennsylvania Press in 2008. Her next book is tentatively entitled *The Momentum of the Word: Rufinus of Aquileia and the Birth of Christian Literature*.

MALCOLM CHOAT is Senior Lecturer in the Department of Ancient History at Macquarie University, Sydney. Most recently, he has published *Belief and Cult in Fourth-Century Papyri* (Brepols, 2006). His next book, *A Coptic Handbook of Ritual Power*, coedited with Iain Gardner, is forthcoming from Brepols.

ELIZABETH A. CLARK is the John Carlisle Kilgo Professor of Religion and History at Duke University. She has recently published *Founding the Fathers: Early Church History and Protestant Professors in Nineteenth-Century America* (University of Pennsylvania Press, 2011), the first volume in a projected two-volume set.

SUSANNA ELM is Professor of History and Classics at the University of California, Berkeley. In 2012, she published *Sons of Hellenism, Fathers of the Church: Emperor Julian, Gregory of Nazianzus, and the Vision of Rome* (University of California Press).

GEORGIA FRANK is Professor of Religion at Colgate University. She has written *The Memory of the Eyes: Pilgrims to Living Saints in Christian Late Antiquity* (University of California Press, 2000).

JAMES E. GOEHRING is Professor of Religion at the University of Mary Washington. He has recently published *Politics, Monasticism, and Miracles in Sixth Century Upper Egypt: A Critical Edition and Translation of the Coptic Texts on Abraham of Farshut* (Mohr Siebeck, 2012).

JOEL KALVESMAKI is Editor in Byzantine Studies at Dumbarton Oaks. His book *The Early Christian Theology of Arithmetic: Number Symbolism in Platonism and Early Christianity* was published in 2013 by the Center for Hellenic Studies, Washington, D.C. With Robin Darling Young, he is editing *Evagrius and His Legacy*.

BLAKE LEYERLE is Associate Professor of Theology and Classics at the University of Notre Dame. She is the author of *Theatrical Shows and Ascetic Lives: John Chrysostom's Attack on Spiritual Marriage* (University of California Press, 2001). She is currently completing a book on early Christian pilgrimage.

PATRICIA COX MILLER is the W. Earl Ledden Professor Emerita of Religion at Syracuse University. Her most recent book is *The Corporeal Imagination: Signifying the Holy in Late Ancient Christianity* (University of Pennsylvania Press, 2009). Her next book is tentatively entitled *In the Eye of the Animal: Zoological Imagination in Early Christianity.*

CLAUDIA RAPP is Professor in the Department of Byzantine and Modern Greek Studies at the University of Vienna and Director of the Division of Byzantine Research in the Institute for Medieval Studies of the Austrian Academy of Sciences. She has written *Holy Bishops in Late Antiquity: The Nature of Christian Leadership in a Time of Transition* (University of California Press, 2005).

SAMUEL RUBENSON is Professor of Church History at Lund University, Sweden. He is the author of *The Letters of St. Antony: Monasticism and the Making of a Saint* (Trinity Press International, 1998).

JANET A. TIMBIE is Adjunct Associate Professor in the Department of Semitic and Egyptian Languages and Literature at the Catholic University of America. In 2007, she coedited *The World of Early Egyptian Christianity* with James Goehring (Catholic University of America Press).

ROBIN DARLING YOUNG is Associate Professor in the Department of Theology at the University of Notre Dame. She has published *In Procession before the World: Martyrs' Sacrifices as Public Liturgy in Early Christianity* (Marquette University Press, 2001). She is currently preparing a translation of and commentary on the *Letters of Evagrius of Pontus*.

Index

www.ingramcontent.com/pod-product-compliance
Lightning Source LLC
Chambersburg PA
CBHW020945310726
48980CB00001B/63

* 9 7 8 0 2 6 8 0 3 3 8 8 0 *